WE CALLED HIM JEB

ᴥ THE LOCHLAINN SEABROOK COLLECTION ᴥ

AMERICAN CIVIL WAR
Abraham Lincoln Was a Liberal, Jefferson Davis Was a Conservative: The Missing Key to Understanding the American Civil War
Confederacy 101: Amazing Facts You Never Knew About America's Oldest Political Tradition
Confederate Blood and Treasure: An Interview With Lochlainn Seabrook
Everything You Were Taught About African-Americans and the Civil War is Wrong, Ask a Southerner!
Everything You Were Taught About the Civil War is Wrong, Ask a Southerner!
Give This Book to a Yankee! A Southern Guide to the Civil War For Northerners
Heroes of the Southern Confederacy: The Illustrated Book of Confederate Officials, Soldiers, and Civilians
Lincoln's War: The Real Cause, the Real Winner, the Real Loser
Seabrook's Complete Battle Book: War Between the States, 1861-1865
The Great Yankee Coverup: What the North Doesn't Want You to Know About Lincoln's War!
The Hampton Roads Conference: The Southern View
The Ultimate Civil War Quiz Book: How Much Do You Really Know About America's Most Misunderstood Conflict?
Women in Gray: A Tribute to the Ladies Who Supported the Southern Confederacy

CONFEDERATE MONUMENTS
Confederate Monuments: Why Every American Should Honor Confederate Soldiers and Their Memorials

CONFEDERATE FLAG
Confederate Flag Facts: What Every American Should Know About Dixie's Southern Cross
What the Confederate Flag Means to Me: Americans Speak Out in Defense of Southern Honor, Heritage, and History

SECESSION
All We Ask Is To Be Let Alone: The Southern Secession Fact Book

RECONSTRUCTION
Twelve Years in Hell: Victorian Southerners Debunk the Myth of Reconstruction, 1865-1877

SLAVERY
Everything You Were Taught About American Slavery is Wrong, Ask a Southerner!
Slavery 101: Amazing Facts You Never Knew About America's "Peculiar Institution"
The Bittersweet Bond: Race Relations in the Old South as Described by White and Black Southerners

NATHAN BEDFORD FORREST
A Rebel Born: A Defense of Nathan Bedford Forrest - Confederate General, American Legend (winner of the 2011 Jefferson Davis Historical Gold Medal)
A Rebel Born: The Screenplay (film about N. B. Forrest)
Forrest! 99 Reasons to Love Nathan Bedford Forrest
Give 'Em Hell Boys! The Complete Military Correspondence of Nathan Bedford Forrest
I Rode With Forrest! Confederate Soldiers Who Served With the World's Greatest Cavalry Leader
Nathan Bedford Forrest and African-Americans: Yankee Myth, Confederate Fact
Nathan Bedford Forrest and the Battle of Fort Pillow: Yankee Myth, Confederate Fact
Nathan Bedford Forrest and the Ku Klux Klan: Yankee Myth, Confederate Fact
Nathan Bedford Forrest: Southern Hero, American Patriot - Honoring a Confederate Icon and the Old South
Saddle, Sword, and Gun: A Biography of Nathan Bedford Forrest For Teens
The God of War: Nathan Bedford Forrest As He Was Seen By His Contemporaries
The Quotable Nathan Bedford Forrest: Selections From the Writings and Speeches of the Confederacy's Most Brilliant Cavalryman

QUOTABLE SERIES
The Alexander H. Stephens Reader: Excerpts From the Works of a Confederate Founding Father
The Quotable Alexander H. Stephens: Selections From the Writings and Speeches of the Confederacy's First Vice President
The Quotable Jefferson Davis: Selections From the Writings and Speeches of the Confederacy's First President
The Quotable Nathan Bedford Forrest: Selections From the Writings and Speeches of the Confederacy's Most Brilliant Cavalryman
The Quotable Robert E. Lee: Selections From the Writings and Speeches of the South's Most Beloved Civil War General
The Quotable Stonewall Jackson: Selections From the Writings and Speeches of the South's Most Famous General
The Unquotable Abraham Lincoln: The President's Quotes They Don't Want You To Know!

CIVIL WAR BATTLES
Encyclopedia of the Battle of Franklin - A Comprehensive Guide to the Conflict that Changed the Civil War
Nathan Bedford Forrest and the Battle of Fort Pillow: Yankee Myth, Confederate Fact
Seabrook's Complete Battle Book: War Between the States, 1861-1865
The Battle of Franklin: Recollections of Confederate and Union Soldiers
The Battle of Nashville: Recollections of Confederate and Union Soldiers
The Battle of Spring Hill: Recollections of Confederate and Union Soldiers

CONSTITUTIONAL HISTORY
America's Three Constitutions: Complete Texts of the Articles of Confederation, Constitution of the United States of America, and Constitution of the Confederate States of America
The Articles of Confederation Explained: A Clause-by-Clause Study of America's First Constitution
The Constitution of the Confederate States of America Explained: A Clause-by-Clause Study of the South's Magna Carta

CHILDREN
Honest Jeff and Dishonest Abe: A Southern Children's Guide to the Civil War
Saddle, Sword, and Gun: A Biography of Nathan Bedford Forrest For Teens

VICTORIAN CONFEDERATE LITERATURE
I, Confederate: Why Dixie Seceded and Fought in the Words of Southern Soldiers
Rise Up and Call Them Blessed: Victorian Tributes to the Confederate Soldier, 1861-1901
Support Your Local Confederate: Wit and Humor in the Southern Confederacy
The Bittersweet Bond: Race Relations in the Old South as Described by White and Black Southerners
The God of War: Nathan Bedford Forrest As He Was Seen By His Contemporaries
The Old Rebel: Robert E. Lee As He Was Seen By His Contemporaries
Victorian Confederate Poetry: The Southern Cause in Verse, 1861-1901
We Called Him Jeb: James Ewell Brown Stuart As He Was Seen By His Contemporaries

ABRAHAM LINCOLN
Abraham Lincoln: The Southern View - Demythologizing America's Sixteenth President
Lincolnology: The Real Abraham Lincoln Revealed in His Own Words - A Study of Lincoln's Suppressed, Misinterpreted, and Forgotten Writings and Speeches
Lincoln's War: The Real Cause, the Real Winner, the Real Loser
The Great Impersonator! 99 Reasons to Dislike Abraham Lincoln
The Unholy Crusade: Lincoln's Legacy of Destruction in the American South
The Unquotable Abraham Lincoln: The President's Quotes They Don't Want You To Know!

NATURAL HISTORY
North America's Amazing Mammals: An Encyclopedia for the Whole Family
The Concise Book of Owls: A Guide to Nature's Most Mysterious Birds
The Concise Book of Tigers: A Guide to Nature's Most Remarkable Cats

FAMILY HISTORIES
The Blakeneys: An Etymological, Ethnological, and Genealogical Study - Uncovering the Mysterious Origins of the Blakeney Family and Name
The Caudills: An Etymological, Ethnological, and Genealogical Study - Exploring the Name and National Origins of a European-American Family
The McGavocks of Carnton Plantation: A Southern History - Celebrating One of Dixie's Most Noble Confederate Families and Their Tennessee Home

MIND, BODY, SPIRIT
Authentic Victorian Ghost Stories: Genuine Early Reports of Apparitions, Wraiths, Poltergeists, and Haunted Houses
Autobiography of a Non-Yogi: A Scientist's Journey From Hinduism to Christianity (Dr. Amitava Dasgupta, with Lochlainn Seabrook)
Britannia Rules: Goddess-Worship in Ancient Anglo-Celtic Society—An Academic Look at the United Kingdom's Matricentric Spiritual Past
Carnton Plantation Ghost Stories: True Tales of the Unexplained from Tennessee's Most Haunted Civil War House!
Christ Is All and In All: Rediscovering Your Divine Nature and the Kingdom Within
Christmas Before Christianity: How the Birthday of the "Sun" Became the Birthday of the "Son"
Jesus and the Gospel of Q: Christ's Pre-Christian Teachings As Recorded in the New Testament
Jesus and the Law of Attraction: The Bible-Based Guide to Creating Perfect Health, Wealth, and Happiness Following Christ's Simple Formula
Mysterious Invaders: Twelve Famous 20th-Century Scientists Confront the UFO Phenomenon
Seabrook's Bible Dictionary of Traditional and Mystical Christian Doctrines
Sea Raven Press Blank Page Journal: For Reflections, Notes, and Sketches
Secrets of Celebrity Surnames: An Onomastic Dictionary of Famous People
The Bible and the Law of Attraction: 99 Teachings of Jesus, the Apostles, and the Prophets
The Book of Kelle: An Introduction to Goddess-Worship and the Great Celtic Mother-Goddess Kelle, Original Blessed Lady of Ireland
The Goddess Dictionary of Words and Phrases: Introducing a New Core Vocabulary for the Women's Spirituality Movement
The Greatest Jesus Mystery of All Time: Where Was Christ Between the Ages of 12 and 30?
The Martian Anomalies: A Photographic Search for Intelligent Life on Mars
UFOs and Aliens: The Complete Guidebook
Victorian Hernia Cures: Nonsurgical Self-Treatment of Inguinal Hernia
Vintage Southern Cookbook: 2,000 Delicious Dishes From Dixie
Your Soul Lives Forever: Documented Victorian Case Studies Proving Consciousness Survives Death

WOMEN
Aphrodite's Trade: The Hidden History of Prostitution Unveiled
Princess Diana: Modern Day Moon-Goddess - A Psychoanalytical and Mythological Look at Diana Spencer's Life, Marriage, and Death (with Dr. Jane Goldberg)
Women in Gray: A Tribute to the Ladies Who Supported the Southern Confederacy

REPRINTS
A Short History of the Confederate States of America (author Jefferson Davis; editor Lochlainn Seabrook)
Prison Life of Jefferson Davis (author John J. Craven; editor Lochlainn Seabrook)
Life of Beethoven (author Ludwig Nohl; editor Lochlainn Seabrook)
The New Revelation (author Arthur Conan Doyle; editor Lochlainn Seabrook)
The Rise and Fall of the Confederate Government (author Jefferson Davis; editor Lochlainn Seabrook)

Lochlainn Seabrook does not author books for fame and glory, but for the love of writing and sharing his knowledge.

SeaRavenPress.com

WE CALLED HIM JEB

James Ewell Brown Stuart
As He Was Seen By His Contemporaries

CONCEIVED, COLLECTED, EDITED, ARRANGED, & DESIGNED, WITH AN INTRODUCTION BY
"THE VOICE OF THE TRADITIONAL SOUTH," HISTORIAN COLONEL

LOCHLAINN SEABROOK

SCV MEMBER AND JEFFERSON DAVIS HISTORICAL GOLD MEDAL WINNER

**Diligently Researched and Generously Illustrated
by the Author for the Elucidation of the Reader**

"THOUGH MEN DESERVE, THEY MAY NOT WIN, SUCCESS; THE BRAVE WILL HONOR THE BRAVE, VANQUISHED NONE THE LESS."

2024

Sea Raven Press, Park County, Wyoming, USA

WE CALLED HIM JEB

Published by
Sea Raven Press, Cassidy Ravensdale, President
Park County, Wyoming, USA
SeaRavenPress.com

Copyright © all text and illustrations Lochlainn Seabrook 2024
in accordance with U.S. and international copyright laws and regulations, as stated and protected under the Berne Union for the Protection of Literary and Artistic Property (Berne Convention), and the Universal Copyright Convention (the UCC). All rights reserved under the Pan-American and International Copyright Conventions.

PRINTING HISTORY
1st SRP paperback edition, 1st printing, April 2024 • ISBN: 978-1-955351-42-3
1st SRP hardcover edition, 1st printing, April 2024 • ISBN: 978-1-955351-43-0

ISBN: 978-1-955351-42-3 (paperback)
Library of Congress Catalog Number: 2024937123

This work is the copyrighted intellectual property of Lochlainn Seabrook and has been registered with the Copyright Office at the Library of Congress in Washington, D.C., USA. No part of this work (including text, covers, drawings, photos, illustrations, maps, images, diagrams, etc.), in whole or in part, may be used, reproduced, stored in a retrieval system, or transmitted, in any form or by any means now known or hereafter invented, without written permission from the publisher. The sale, duplication, hire, lending, copying, digitalization, or reproduction of this material, in any manner or form whatsoever, is also prohibited, and is a violation of federal, civil, and digital copyright law, which provides severe civil and criminal penalties for any violations.

We Called Him Jeb: James Ewell Brown Stuart As He Was Seen By His Contemporaries, by Lochlainn Seabrook. Includes an introduction, illustrations, index, endnotes, appendices, and bibliography.

ARTWORK
Front and back cover design and art, book design, layout, font selection, and interior art by Lochlainn Seabrook.
All images, image captions, graphic design, and graphic art copyright © Lochlainn Seabrook.
All images selected, placed, manipulated, cleaned, colored, tinted, and/or created by Lochlainn Seabrook.
Cover image: Confederate Maj. Gen. J. E. B. Stuart, Commander Cavalry Corps, A.N.V.; photo circa 1862

All persons who approve of the authority and principles of Colonel Lochlainn Seabrook's literary work, and realize its benefits as a means of reeducating the world about facts left out of mainstream books, are hereby requested to avidly recommend his titles to others and to vigorously cooperate in extending their reach, scope, and influence around the globe.

The views documented in this book concerning the War for the Constitution, 1861-1865, are those of the publisher.

WRITTEN, DESIGNED, PUBLISHED   IN THE UNITED STATES OF AMERICA

Dedication

To the Memory of my Cousin James Ewell Brown Stuart,
who fell Fighting for Liberty, Right and Justice.

Epigraph

"The two ablest cavalry officers which were developed by the war were Gen. J. E. B. Stuart, of Virginia, and Gen. Joseph Wheeler, of the Army of Tennessee."
  Confederate General Robert E. Lee

"Jeb Stuart was the greatest cavalryman America ever saw."
  Confederate General James Longstreet

"Gen. Stuart was the finest cavalry general that this world did ever see."
  Black Confederate, Uncle Isaac, C.S.A., 1899

CONTENTS

Notes to the Reader, by Lochlainn Seabrook ❧ page 11
The Life of Jeb Stuart: A Time Line ❧ page 21
Introduction, by Lochlainn Seabrook ❧ page 23

SECTION ONE
BIOGRAPHICAL PORTRAITS & SCHOLARLY COMMENTARY

CHAPTER 1 ❧ page 31
CHAPTER 2 ❧ page 51
CHAPTER 3 ❧ page 63
CHAPTER 4 ❧ page 85

SECTION TWO
MILITARY RECOLLECTIONS & PERSONAL OBSERVATIONS

CHAPTER 5 ❧ page 107
CHAPTER 6 ❧ page 127
CHAPTER 7 ❧ page 147
CHAPTER 8 ❧ page 169
CHAPTER 9 ❧ page 191
CHAPTER 10 ❧ page 211
CHAPTER 11 ❧ page 231
CHAPTER 12 ❧ page 253

Appendix A: Stuart's Report on the Battle of Dranesville ❧ page 283
Appendix B: Four Years of the War in Brief ❧ page 287
Notes ❧ page 291
Bibliography ❧ page 301
Index ❧ page 313
Meet the Author-Editor ❧ page 335
Learn More ❧ page 337

NOTES TO THE READER

"NOTHING IN THE PAST IS DEAD TO THE MAN WHO WOULD
LEARN HOW THE PRESENT CAME TO BE WHAT IT IS."
WILLIAM STUBBS, VICTORIAN ENGLISH HISTORIAN

THE TWO MAIN POLITICAL PARTIES IN 1860
☛ In any study of America's antebellum, bellum, and postbellum periods, it is vitally important to understand that in 1860 the two major political parties—the Democrats and the newly formed Republicans—were the opposite of what they are today. In other words, the Democrats of the mid 19th Century (founded by what we now call "right-wingers" or "traditionalists")[1] were Conservatives, akin to the Republican Party of today, while the Republicans of the mid 19th Century (founded by what we now call "left-wingers" or "progressives")[2] were Liberals, akin to the Democratic Party of today.[3]

Thus the Confederacy's Democratic president, Jefferson Davis, was a Conservative (with libertarian leanings); the Union's Republican president, Abraham Lincoln, was a Liberal (with socialistic leanings).[4] This is why, in the mid 1800s, the conservative wing of the Democratic Party was known as "the States' Rights Party,"[5] as opposed to the Republican Party, which was widely known to have been created in 1854 by "progressive elements."[6] Indeed, the party's first candidate was radical (that is, socialist), and later Union general, John C. Frémont. As socialist Eugene V. Debs asserted: "Lincoln would not join today's Republican Party any more than Thomas Jefferson would become a member of today's Democratic Party";[7] correctly adding: "The Republican Party was once Red."[8]

The author's cousin, Confederate Vice President and Democrat Alexander H. Stephens: a Southern Conservative.

Hence, the Democrats of the Civil War period referred to themselves as "conservatives," "confederates," "anti-centralists," or "constitutionalists" (the latter because they favored strict adherence to the original Constitution—which tacitly guaranteed states' rights—as created by the Founding Fathers). The Civil War Republicans, on the other hand, called themselves "liberals," "nationalists," "centralists," or "consolidationists" (the latter three because their goal was to nationalize the central government and consolidate political power in Washington, D.C.).[9]

The War for Southern Independence pitted Northern Liberals (then the Republican Party) against Southern Conservatives (then the Democratic Party).

More evidence comes from a common phrase used at the time, "states' rights Democrats," a term that could have only applied to Conservatives, since then, as today, Liberals are squarely against states' rights (unless, in hypocritical fashion, they find that states' rights benefit their agenda in some way).[10] This is in perfect keeping with what *Confederate Veteran* once referred to as "the Mussolini-like procedure of the Federal authorities,"[11] that is, the fascist dictatorial views and actions of the then Left-wing Republican Party.

In 1889 Right-wing Democrat President Davis himself, who referred to the 1860 Democrats as "the conservative power of the country,"[12] described the political situation at the time in the following manner:

> . . . the names adopted by political parties in the United States have not always been strictly significant of their principles. In general terms it may be said that the old Federal party [Liberal] inclined to nationalism [then a term for big government], or consolidation [that is, consolidation of power in the Federal government], and that the Whig party [liberalistic], which succeeded it, although not identical with it, was favorable, in the main, to a strong Central Government [liberalism, socialism, communism]. On the other hand, its opponent, the Republican [Conservative], afterward known as the Democratic party, was dominated by the idea of the sovereignty of the States and the federal or confederate character of the Union [Americanism, traditionalism, conservatism]. Although other elements have entered into its organization at different periods, this has been its vital, cardinal, and abiding principle.[13]

We will note here that, while Davis would not live to witness the transition, a mere six years after he penned these words, during the 1896 U.S. presidential election, the two major parties would reverse positions, the Democratic Party adopting a Left-wing platform, the Republican Party adopting a Right-wing platform—the status they hold to this day.

Since this idea is new to most of my readers, let us further demystify it by viewing it from the perspective of the American Revolutionary War. If Davis and his Conservative Southern constituents (the Democrats of 1861) had been alive in 1775, they would have sided with George Washington and his followers, the independence-loving American colonists (known as "patriots" or "rebels")—who sought to secede from the tyrannical government of Great Britain; if Lincoln and his Liberal Northern constituents (the Republicans of 1861) had been alive at that time, they would have sided with King George III and the English monarchy, who sought to maintain the American colonies as possessions of the British Empire. It is due to this very comparison that we Southerners often refer to our secession from the U.S. as the Second Declaration of Independence, and the "Civil War" as the Second American Revolutionary War.

Without a basic understanding of these facts, the American "Civil War" will forever remain incomprehensible. For a full discussion of this all-important topic see my book, *Abraham Lincoln Was a Liberal, Jefferson Davis Was a Conservative: The Missing Key to Understanding the American Civil War*.

THE TERM "CIVIL WAR"

☞ As I heartily dislike the phrase "Civil War," its use throughout this book (as well as in my other works) is worthy of explanation.

Our entire modern literary system refers to the conflict of 1861 using the Northern term the "Civil War," whether we in the South like it or not. Of course, this is purposeful, for America's book industry, which determines everything from how books are categorized and designed to how they are marketed and sold, is almost solely controlled by Liberals, socialists, globalists, collectivists, and communists, individuals who will do anything to prevent the truth about Lincoln's War

The American "Civil War" was not a true civil war as Webster defines it: "A conflict between opposing groups of citizens of the *same* country." It was a fight between two individual countries; or to be more specific, two separate and constitutionally formed confederacies: the C.S.A. and the U.S.A.

from coming out. An important aspect of this wholesale revisionism of American history is the use of the phrase "Civil War," which Yankee Liberals thrust into the public forum even as big government Left-winger Lincoln was diabolically tricking the Conservative South into firing the first shot at the First Battle of Fort Sumter in April 1861.[14]

The progressives' blatant American "Civil War" coverup continues to this day, one of the more overt results which pertains to how books are coded, indexed, and identified.[15] Thus, as all book searches by readers, libraries, and retail outlets are now performed online, and as all bookstores categorize works from or about this period under the heading "Civil War," honest book publishers and authors who deal with this particular topic have little choice but to use this deceptive term. If I were to refuse to use it, as some of my Southern colleagues have suggested, few people would ever find or read my books.

Add to this the fact that scarcely any non-Southerners have ever heard of the names we in the South use for the conflict, such as "the War for Southern Independence," "the War Against Northern Aggression," "Lincoln's War," or my personal preference, because it is the most accurate: "the War for the Constitution." It only makes sense then to use the term "Civil War" in most commercial situations, historically inaccurate though it is.

Confederate General Nathan Bedford Forrest, just one of many Southern officials who referred to the conflict of 1861 as the "Civil War."

We should also bear in mind that while today educated persons, particularly educated Southerners, all share an abhorrence for the phrase "Civil War," it was not always so. Confederates who lived through and even fought in the conflict regularly used the term throughout the 1860s, and even long after. Among them were Confederate generals such as Nathan Bedford Forrest, Richard Taylor, and Joseph E. Johnston, not to mention the Confederacy's vice president, Alexander H. Stephens.

In 1895 Confederate General James Longstreet wrote about his military experiences in a work subtitled, *Memoirs of the Civil War in America*, while in 1903 Confederate General John Brown Gordon, the first commander-in-chief of the United Confederate Veterans, entitled his autobiography, *Reminiscences of the Civil War*. Even the

Confederacy's highest leader, President Jefferson Davis, used the term "Civil War,"[16] and in one case at least, as late as 1881—the year he wrote his brilliant exposition, *The Rise and Fall of the Confederate Government* (see the Sea Raven Press reprint of this book, of which I am the editor, collector, technician, and designer).[17]

Authors writing for *Confederate Veteran* magazine sometimes used the phrase well into the early 1900s,[18] and in 1898, at the Eighth Annual Meeting and Reunion of the United Confederate Veterans (the forerunner of today's Sons of Confederate Veterans), the following resolution was proposed: that from then on the Great War of 1861 was to be designated "the Civil War Between the States."[19]

A WORD ON EARLY AMERICAN MATERIAL

☛ In order to preserve the authentic historicity of the antebellum, bellum, and postbellum periods, I have retained the original spellings, formatting, and punctuation of the early Americans I quote. These include such items as British-English spellings, long-running paragraphs, obsolete words, and various literary devices peculiar to the time. However, I have corrected misspelled names to prevent confusion, and also *where possible*, inaccurate dates and locations (the inevitable result of aging and faulty memories). Bracketed words are *always* my additions and clarifications (added mainly for my new, foreign, and young readers), while italicized words are (where indicated) my emphasis.

Union General August von Willich: Typically labeled a "radical" in mainstream history books, Willich was actually a card-carrying communist who led a revolutionary workers' party, studiously followed the teachings of Karl Marx, and participated in the failed European socialist revolution of 1848—all before joining Lincoln's army in 1861.

19TH-CENTURY CODE WORDS

☛ An early American *Southern* abolitionist was someone who simply desired the end of slavery. *Northern* abolitionists, however, were something quite different altogether: they identified themselves with socialism and communism[20]—the modern forms which were developed in the 1840s by German revolutionary Karl Marx.[21] Also, as noted above, our modern political party names have different meanings than those of the mid 1800s. Hence, one must bear the following in mind when reading 19th-Century literature:

1. "Abolitionist" (Northern): A 19th-Century Left-wing euphemism for a socialist or communist—still used in this false sense today.
2. "Radical" (Northern): Also a 19th-Century Left-wing euphemism for a socialist or communist—still used in this false sense today.
3. "Republican": Between 1854 and 1896 the Republicans were the major Left-wing or Liberal party of that era.
4. "Democrat": Between 1828 and 1896, the Democrats were the major Right-wing or Conservative party of that era.

For more information on items 1 and 2 above, see my introduction in my book *The Bittersweet Bond: Race Relations in the Old South As Described by White and Black Southerners*.

For more information on items 3 and 4 above, see my books *Abraham Lincoln Was a Liberal, Jefferson Davis Was a Conservative: The Missing Key to Understanding the American Civil War*, and *Lincoln's War: The Real Cause, the Real Winner, the Real Loser*.

REPETITION

☞ As with all works of this kind, there is inevitably some repetition, as those familiar with Stuart repeat many of the more common beliefs, opinions, and stories related to him. I have retained these recapitulations, however, as they are told from different perspectives by different people, thereby contributing additional historical value and personal interest to my subject.

AMERICANISM

☞ Throughout this book I refer to the Confederate or Southern Cause as "Americanism." To ensure that the meaning behind this word is clear I will define it here: Americanism is an ardent allegiance to the traditions, interests, ideals, practices, and political principles of the U.S.A.

In other words, *Americanism* is simply another way of saying *American conservatism*, a belief system that has been permanently set down in our many all-American documents, such as the Declaration of Independence, the Kentucky and Virginia Resolutions, and our three American constitutions.[22]

Thus conservatism includes the following concepts and doctrines: traditionalism, constitutionalism, patriotism, small restricted government, states' rights, capitalism, equality, independent thinking, individualism, meritocracism, morality, an unwavering love of liberty, and above all, republicanism—not in the political sense (as in the Republican Party), but more specifically I am speaking of a type of government, one known as a "republic." Here supreme power lies with its citizens, who in turn elect governmental officials to represent them (a political system also known as popular sovereignty).

The Southern Confederacy, a product of the then right-wing Democrat Party, fought for no more and no less. The effort to maintain the Americanistic doctrines (set down by our Founding Fathers) in the face of evil continues to this day.

PRESENTISM

☞ As a historian I view *presentism* (judging the past according to present day mores and customs) as the enemy of authentic history. And this is precisely why the Left employs it in its ongoing war against traditional American, conservative, and Christian values. By looking at history through the lens of modern day beliefs—and, just as heinous, fabricating obviously fake history based on emotion, opinion, and political ideology—they are able to distort, revise, and reshape the past into a false narrative that fits their ideological agenda: the liberalization *and* Northernization of America, the enlargement and further centralization of the national government, and total control of American political, economic, educational, and social power, the same plan that Lincoln championed.[23]

Judging our ancestors by our own standards is dishonest, unfair, unjust, misleading, and unethical.

This book rejects presentism and replaces it with what I call *historicalism*: judging our ancestors based on the values of their own time.

To get the most from this work the reader is invited to reject presentism as well. In this way—along with casting aside preconceived notions and the fake history churned out by our Left-wing education system—the truth in this work will be most readily ascertained and absorbed; truth that has been rigorously researched and forensically uncovered by myself using the scientific method. In 1901 Confederate Colonel Bennett H. Young noted:

> History is valuable only as it is true. Opinions concerning acts are not history; acts themselves alone are historic.[24]

CONTINUE YOUR SOUTHERN HISTORY EDUCATION

☛ Lincoln's War on the Constitution and the American people can never be fully understood without a thorough knowledge of the South's perspective. As this book only briefly touches on these topics, one cannot hope to learn the complete story here. For those who are interested in additional material from Dixie's viewpoint, please see my comprehensive histories listed on pages 2 and 3.

You are either for or against the Truth. There is not and can never be true neutrality on this subject, which is why there is no such thing as a purely "neutral" book on the War Between the States—despite the claims of many pro-North partisans. Thus in the year 1900, former Confederate General John Brown Gordon wrote:

> Neutrality has no place in masterful minds nor in heroic hearts. Neutrality has never yet developed a great character nor characterized a great people nor written one sparkling page in human history.[25]

FINAL THOUGHTS: HOW TO HONOR BOTH OUR SOUTHERN & OUR AMERICAN HERITAGE

☛ To all Americans, and interested foreigners: It is time to resurrect the South's true history. It is time to allow the authentic chronicle of past events to be told accurately and honestly. It is time to disseminate this knowledge far and wide, guilelessly and decisively. It is time to shine the Light of Truth into the dark corners of ignorance, malice, divisiveness, and deceit fomented by the gaslighting enemies of both the South and historical reality.[26] Then and only then do we truly honor our gallant Confederate ancestors, do justice to their names, military service, and memories, and confer upon them the respect and reverence so they richly deserve as American patriots.

DEO VINDICE, LOCHLAINN SEABROOK

Loyalty to the truth of Confederate history.

U.D.C. MOTTO, 1921

SEA RAVEN PRESS

was founded for the express purpose of publishing and circulating such books as are calculated to store the mind with useful knowledge. We therefore publish only books of a high moral tone and tendency—such works as will be welcomed in every home and at every fireside as valuable family treasures.

L. SEABROOK

THE LIFE OF JEB STUART
A Time Line

- Born in Patrick County, Virginia, February 6, 1833.
- Graduated from West Point, 1854.
- U.S. Second Lieutenant, October 31, 1854.
- Married Miss Flora Cooke, November 14, 1855.
- U.S. First Lieutenant, December 20, 1855.
- Served as a U.S. soldier in Kansas in 1856.
- First child, a daughter, Flora Stuart, born September 15, 1857.
- Served as a U.S. soldier against the Indians in 1857.
- Served as a U.S. soldier in the West till 1860.
- Volunteered as a U.S. soldier under then U.S. Col. Robert E. Lee in the John Brown Raid, 1859.
- Second child, a son, Philip St. George Cooke Stuart—named after his father-in-law—born June 26, 1860; later renamed James E. B. Stuart, II, when his father-in-law sided with the Union.
- C.S. Colonel, Confederate Army, July 16, 1861.
- C.S. Brigadier-General, September 24, 1861.
- C.S. Major-General, July 25, 1862.
- Served with the Army of Northern Virginia throughout the War.
- Commanded Stonewall Jackson's corps after Jackson's death at the Battle of Chancellorsville.
- Returned to cavalry command, May 1863.
- Third child, a daughter, Virginia Pelham Stuart, born October 9, 1863.
- Fatally wounded at the Battle of Yellow Tavern, May 11, 1864.
- Died, May 12, 1864, age 31.

Confederate Navy Yard, Pensacola, Florida.

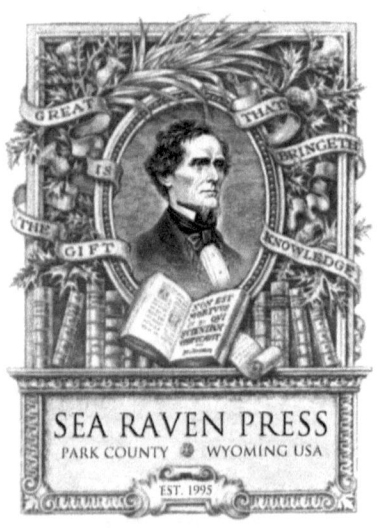

"Books invite all; they constrain none."
Hartley Burr Alexander (1873-1939)

INTRODUCTION

JAMES EWELL BROWN STUART—more affectionately known by his acronymic initials, "Jeb"—was a man of varied and even contrasting characteristics. We can gain a better understanding of him through the articulate voices of the Victorians who shared his time and place, which is the purpose of my book.

It was said, for example, that Stuart, who operated under "the luster of fame"[27] as well as the mantle of "chivalrous manhood,"[28] was "bold,"[29] "daring,"[30] "fiery,"[31] "knightly,"[32] "dashing,"[33] "peerless,"[34] "adventurous,"[35] "brave,"[36] "joyous,"[37] "distinguished,"[38] "skillful,"[39] "genial,"[40] "princely,"[41] a "beloved commander,"[42] a "grand man,"[43] a "genius,"[44] "indefatigable,"[45] "intrepid,"[46] "illustrious,"[47] "noble,"[48] "magnetic,"[49] "glorious,"[50] "beautiful,"[51] "exceptional,"[52] "of high spirits and perpetually cheerful,"[53] "chivalric,"[54] "self-reliant," "merry," "quick-witted," "fun-loving,"[55] "lovable,"[56] "eccentric,"[57] "provoking,"[58] "impulsive,"[59] "incomparable,"[60] "enterprising,"[61] a "gay cavalier,"[62] a Southern "martyr,"[63] and "a loyal servant of Christ."[64] According to many, his "grand and noble soul" proved his "knighthood," which was always "in flower."[65] A "premier intelligence officer,"[66] to all true Southerners at the time, he was "the Plumed Knight,"[67] "the Knight of the Black Plume";[68] a "cavalry leader of renown,"[69] "the immortal Stuart,"[70] "our warrior Stuart, our bonnie Stuart."[71]

"Crowned with a glorious immortality,"[72] and "magnificent heroism,"[73] Stuart, "whose equal as a cavalry leader is not to be found in the armies of any nation,"[74] was the "Chevalier of the Southern Cause,"[75] a "brilliant leader,"[76] an "extraordinary military genius,"[77] "bold as the Lion Heart, dauntless and brave,"[78] and "our Chevalier Bayard [French knight, Pierre Terrail] of the South"[79]—a "hero to us that the world can never match."[80] "Every inch a soldier," he was possessed of a "cool bravery, dashing heroism, manly beauty, and all that went into make up our ideal of a military chieftain."[81] Indeed, such was Stuart's expertise in the saddle that it was held that as "the eyes" of the Southern army, it was he "who discovered the possibility of the most dramatic, tragic, and effective flank movement of the Civil War."[82]

Confederate Gen. Jeb Stuart in his prime.

Said to be a descendant of Robert the Bruce (whether true or not), his Victorian admirers asserted that Stuart, "that true knight,"[83] having "certainly inherited the kingly talent for leading men and making war,"[84] always executed "masterful raids" on the enemy.[85] A "master in the art of war,"[86] the popular Scottish-American Confederate was also seen as "the great cavalry man,"[87] a "cavalier hero,"[88] "superb in every movement,"[89] "the personification of grace and gallantry combined,"[90] "the Prince Rupert [noted German military officer] of Southern cavaliers,"[91] "our Harry of Navarre" (that is, King Henry IV of France),[92] "the brilliant *sabreur*,"[93] "the [Michel] Ney of the Confederacy,"[94] "the flower of the cavaliers,"[95] "the gay [i.e., optimistic] and gifted cavalryman,"[96] "the [Prince] Rupert of sable plume,"[97] "the great cavalry chieftain,"[98] and the "Sir Galahad of the Confederacy,"[99] among many other monikers.

A member of "the flower of West Point,"[100] the "handsome, blue-eyed" Stuart,[101] who was "fond of singing"[102] and had a "passion for banjo music,"[103] was well-known for his "gaiety and exuberance of spirits";[104] even more significant, to many he was one of "the invincible heroes who glorified arms and gave posterity an unchallenged record of daring and deeds";[105] a Southern master of horsemanship possessing "daring and skill,"[106] whose name, when mentioned, "makes the pulse beat faster and the blood flow with a quicker throb."[107] And while it was said that Robert E. Lee was the brain of the Confederate army and Stonewall Jackson its arm, Stuart was considered its "soul."[108] He was one, along with a host of other Southern icons, "whose name will be cherished by the sons and daughters of the South throughout time."[109]

Victorian Southern women in particular were impressed by "the purity of Stuart's personal life," by the "great power he had over his men," and by his "light-heartedness" while on the march, which contrasted so strongly with his "resolution and fierceness when in action." "Of all our knights," the U.D.C., wrote, "he was the flower."[110] The Berkeley [West Virginia] U.D.C. Chapter kept a lock of Stuart's hair—donated by Miss Estelle Blaudell—as a "prized memento" of the great Confederate hero.[111]

The women of Dixie were also enamored by Stuart's courage on the battlefield, referring to him as one of the "many who fell in the strife," an "immortal leader whose name will go sounding down the ages as the exponents of all that is loved and honored by the true of heart and enlightened of mind through all ages."[112] Women also adored Stuart's "devotion to home and parents," his love for "the society of pure women," his "charm of conversation," his "love of music," and, above all, his "cavalier manner"—all which made him "the idol of the hour with the fair sex, most of whom adore the military and are hero worshipers."[113]

"Always ready for any venture and sanguine of success,"[114] under "the magic influence of his bold manipulation" of his forces[115]—known to be "the finest lot of cavalrymen that ever fought on American soil"[116]—after May 10, 1863, Stuart courageously led his men onto each field of action with the watchword "remember Jackson,"[117] flashing his saber or waving his cherished Le Mat revolvers in the air.[118] His May 1862 "ride around Union General McClellan" is still celebrated as "one of the most brilliant affairs of the war, bold in conception, most brilliant in execution."[119]

Clearly, Stuart had a "fighting spirit,"[120] an energy that placed him among those "whose names are destined to be immortal," one of the "stars" in the "brilliant galaxy that gathered together in answer to call of the Southern Confederacy."[121] Those who rode with the man who was "as famous for his gallantry toward women as for his reckless courage,"[122] were said to "follow the plume of Stuart,"[123] otherwise known—as he liked to think of himself—as "the Knight of the Golden Spurs."[124] These special men, who "galloped over many a contested field in many campaigns with . . . Stuart," won "by their unsurpassed valor . . . undying fame." These were the same men who "followed Robert E. Lee in a series of campaigns in which were displayed a courage, skill, fortitude, energy, and devotion unsurpassed in the history of the world."[125]

Mounted on his superlative warhorse "Maryland,"[126] and sometimes carrying two bird dogs on his saddle with him,[127] Stuart led his 12,000-man cavalry[128] into one battle after another, always intentionally seeking out the "hottest part of the fray."[129] Preferring "the white arm" (that is, the "knightly sabre") over pistols,[130] this resplendent equine unit—like other cavalry, often referred to by military horsemen as a "critter company"—was known as both a "brotherhood"[131] and "the magnificent cavalry organization which startled the world with its heroism."[132] It was said that

> "the marvelous endurance of the men who followed Stuart [as well as Confederate cavalrymen like Nathan Bedford Forrest, John Hunt Morgan, Fitzhugh Lee, Joseph Wheeler, Wade Hampton, Joseph Orville Shelby, Thomas Green, Ben McCulloch, John Sappington Marmaduke, and Sterling Price] has never been equaled. Storms and floods had no terror for them. No enemy was safe from their avenging hand, and no vigilance could defy their enterprise. There were no alarms in any work for these brave and tireless riders. Single riders and even small troops of cavalry had made marches of a hundred miles in a day; but it remained for generals like . . . Stuart to demonstrate the potency and tremendous value of cavalry in war and lengthen the possibility of a day's march."[133] It was common knowledge in Dixie that the Union had "no cavalry to compare to the horsemen of Jeb Stuart."[134]

Stuart, who predicted his own premature death,[135] was "a man born to lead," one whose "his conduct inspired every man under him with the same daring spirit."[136] Not surprisingly, Stuart was numbered among the "gallery of heroes,"[137] those twelve great Southern wartime celebrities, with the other eleven being Jefferson Davis, Robert Edward Lee, Thomas Jonathan "Stonewall" Jackson, Joseph Eggleston Johnston, Albert Sidney Johnston, Pierre Gustave Toutant Beauregard, James Byron Gordon, Ambrose Powell Hill, Nathan Bedford Forrest, Wade Hampton, and John Hunt Morgan.[138]

Monuments to Stuart, the chestnut-bearded cavalry leader who won the complete confidence of both Robert E. Lee and Stonewall Jackson, were proposed within 30 years after the War, at least as early as 1893, when *Confederate Veteran* magazine begin to fill up with requests and articles on the subject.[139] The periodical itself put Stuart on its September 1903 cover (Vol. 11, No. 9). Countless Confederate veterans camps and bivouacs have been named after Stuart,[140] along with several U.D.C. chapters.[141] Numerous poems have been written about him and many honors have been dedicated to him.[142] So beloved was the Southern icon that 19th-Century Southern parents even named their children—both boys and girls—"Stuart," after the lionized Confederate chieftain.[143]

While Stuart, the ever-cheerful jokester and lover of humorous banjo music, certainly had an uplifting effect on his war-worn troops, he also had a serious side, one that was not to be trifled with. For instance, in September 1863 he brought charges against one of his cavalry leaders, Col. William E. Jones, for "using disrespectful language to his superior officer." Jones was subsequently court-martialed, removed from his command, and transferred to duty in Southwest Virginia.[144]

According to some Southern soldiers, Stuart also had his faults, the "greatest" being an inordinate love of "military foppery and display," that sometimes cost his troops precious time and energy that could have been spent on more important military matters.[145] This near obsession with ostentatious fashion prompted Stuart to purchase a brand new, stiff, modern uniform for an embarrassed and old-fashioned Stonewall Jackson (his troopers loved the suit, however), who was fatally wounded in the military apparel not long after.[146] Stuart certainly had his critics, both Union and Confederate; but his Victorian admirers far outnumbered them—and among today's enlightened and educated, they still do.

Who was this extraordinary individual who had musical compositions (like the *Southern Troopers Song*) dedicated to him, and who has had schools, highways, and even British military tanks named after him?

Read on now and thrill to the detailed personal descriptions of this legendary Virginian by his contemporaries, in which they describe his childhood, his educational background, his extraordinary rise to fame, his gallant exploits during the War for the Constitution, and his catastrophic death at the youthful age of 31. You will come away with a renewed admiration not only for the glorious Stuart himself, but also the Great Southern Cause for which he made the ultimate sacrifice.

Lochlainn Seabrook
Park County, Wyoming USA
April 2024
In Nobis Regnat Christus

Why the South fought . . .

SECTION ONE

Biographical Portraits
& Scholarly Commentary

CHAPTER 1

THE EARLY YEARS

☛ James Ewell Brown Stuart, commonly known as "Jeb" Stuart from the first three initials of his name, was born in Patrick County, Virginia, February 6, 1833. On each side of his family, he could point to a line of ancestors who had served their country well in war and peace and from whom he inherited his high ideals of duty, patriotism, and religion.

He was of Scotch descent and his ancestors belonged to a clan of note in the history of Scotland. From Scotland a member of this clan went to Ireland.

Stuart on the cover of the September 1903 issue of *Confederate Veteran* magazine.

About the year 1726, Jeb Stuart's great-great-grandfather, Archibald Stuart, fled from Londonderry, Ireland, to the wilds of Pennsylvania, in order to escape religious persecution. Eleven years later, he removed from Pennsylvania to Augusta County, Virginia, where he became a large land-holder. At Tinkling Spring Church, the graves of the immigrant and his wife may still be seen.

Archibald Stuart's second son, Alexander, joined the Continental army and fought with signal bravery during the whole of the War of the Revolution. After the war, he practiced law. He showed his interest in education by becoming one of the founders of Liberty Hall, at Lexington, Virginia, a school which afterwards became Washington College and has now grown into Washington and Lee University.

His youngest son who bore his name, was also a lawyer; he held positions of trust in his native State, Virginia, as well as in Illinois and Missouri where he held the responsible and honored position of a United States judge.

Our general's father, Archibald Stuart, the son of Judge Stuart, after a brief military career in the War of 1812, became a successful lawyer. His wit and eloquence soon won him distinction, and his district sent him as representative to the Congress of the United States where he served four years.

There is an interesting story told about General Stuart's mother's grandfather, William Letcher. He had enraged the Loyalists, or Tories, on the North Carolina border, by a defeat that he and a little company of volunteers had inflicted on them in the War of the Revolution. One day in June, 1780, as Mrs. Letcher was alone at home with her baby girl, only six weeks old, a stranger, dressed as a hunter and carrying a gun in his hand, appeared at the door and asked for Letcher. While his wife was explaining that he would be at home in a short time, he [Letcher] entered and asked the man to be seated.

Ruins of Liberty Hall Academy, at Lexington, VA.

The latter, however, raised his gun, saying: "I demand you in the name of the king."

When Letcher tried to seize the gun, the Tory fired and the patriot fell mortally wounded, in the presence of his young wife and babe.

Bethenia Letcher, the tiny fatherless babe, grew to womanhood and married David Pannill; and her daughter, Elizabeth Letcher Pannill, married Archibald Stuart, the father of our hero.

Mrs. Archibald Stuart inherited from her grandfather, William Letcher, a large estate in Patrick County. The place, commanding fine views of the Blue Ridge mountains, was called Laurel Hill, and here in a comfortable old mansion set amid a grove of oak trees, Jeb Stuart was born and spent the earlier years of his boyhood.

Mrs. Stuart was a great lover of flowers and surrounding the house was a beautiful old-fashioned flower garden, where Jeb, who loved flowers as much as his mother did, spent many happy days. He always loved this boyhood home and often thought of it during the hard and stirring years of war. Once near the close of the war, he told his brother that he would like nothing better, when the long struggle was at an end, than to go back to the old home and live a quiet, peaceful life.

When Jeb was fourteen years old, he was sent to school in Wytheville, and in 1848 he entered Emory and Henry College. Here, under the influence of a religious revival, he joined the Methodist church, but about ten years later he became a member of the Episcopal church of which his wife was a member.

Emory and Henry College, about 1850.

Though always gay and high-spirited, Stuart even as a boy possessed a deep religious sentiment which grew in strength as he grew in years and kept his heart pure and his hands clean through the many temptations that beset him in the freedom and conviviality of army life. A promise that he made his mother never to taste strong drink was kept faithfully to his death, and none of his soldiers ever heard him use an oath even in the heat of battle. His gallantry, boldness, and continual gaiety and good nature, coupled with his high Christian virtues, caused all who came in contact with him not only to love but to respect and admire him.

He left Emory and Henry College in 1850 and entered the United States Military Academy at West Point where he had received an appointment.

At this time, Colonel Robert E. Lee was superintendent at West Point. Young Stuart spent many pleasant hours at the home of the superintendent where he was a great favorite with the ladies of the family. [George Washington] Custis Lee, the eldest son of Colonel Lee, was Stuart's best friend while he was a student at the Academy.

An interesting incident is told about Stuart while he was on a vacation from West Point. Mr. Benjamin B. Minor of Richmond, had a case to be tried at Williamsburg, and when he arrived at the hotel it was so crowded that he was put in an "omnibus" room, so called because it contained three double beds.

Late in the afternoon when the stage drove up, he saw three young cadets step from it and he soon found that they were to share with him the "omnibus" room.

He went to bed early, but put a lamp on the table by the head of his bed and got out his papers to go over his case. After a while the three cadets came in laughing and singing, and soon they were all three piled into one bed where they continued to laugh and joke in uproarious spirits.

Finally one of them said, "See here, fellows, we have had our fun long enough and we are disturbing that gentleman over there; let us hush up and go to sleep."

"No need for that, boys," said Mr. Minor, "I have just finished."

Then as he tells us he 'pitched in' and had a good time with them.

The cadet who had shown such thoughtfulness and courtesy was young Jeb Stuart who as Mr. Minor discovered was one of his wife's cousins. He was very much pleased with the boy and invited him to come to Richmond. Stuart accepted the invitation and called several times at the Minor home.

He explained to Mr. Minor his plan for an invention which was to be called "Stuart's lightning horse-hitcher" and to be used in Indian raids. He excited Mr. Minor's admiration because he had such gallant and genial courtesy and professional pride. He wanted even then to accomplish something useful and important to his country and himself.

General Fitzhugh Lee, who was at West Point with Stuart, and who later served under General Stuart as a trusted commander, tells us that as a cadet he was remarkable for

> "strict attendance to military duties, and erect, soldierly bearing, an immediate and almost thankful acceptance of a challenge to fight any cadet who might in any way feel himself aggrieved, and a clear, metallic, ringing voice."

Although the boys called him a "Bible class man" and "Beauty Stuart," it was in good-natured boyish teasing; where he felt it to be intended differently or where his high standards of conduct seemed to be sneered at, he was well able with his quick temper and superb physical strength to teach the offender a lesson.

As 'Fitz' Lee tells us, Stuart was always ready to accept a challenge, but he did not fight without good cause, and his father, a fair-minded and intelligent man, approved of his son's course in these fisticuff encounters. Between his father and himself there was the best kind of comradeship and sympathy, and young Stuart was always ready to consult his father before taking any important step in life. The decision as to what he should do when he left West Point, however, was left to him, and just after his graduation he wrote home that he had decided to enter the regular army instead of becoming a lawyer.

"Each profession has its labors and rewards," he wrote, "and in making the selection I shall rely upon Him whose judgment cannot err, for it is not with the man that walketh to direct his steps."

Meanwhile, by his daring and skill in horsemanship, his diligence in his studies, and his ability to command, he had risen rapidly from the position of corporal to that of captain, and then to the rank of cavalry sergeant which is the highest rank in that arm of the service at West Point. He graduated thirteenth in a class of forty-six, and started his brief but brilliant military career well equipped with youth, courage, skill, and a firm reliance on the love and wisdom of God.[147] — MRS. MARY LYNN WILLIAMSON, NEW MARKET, VIRGINIA

ANCESTRY, BOYHOOD & YOUTH

☛ James Ewell Brown Stuart was born in Patrick County, Virginia, on the 6th of February, 1833.

His ancestry is traced on his father's side to Archibald Stuart, a native of Londonderry, Ireland, but of Scotch-Presbyterian parentage, who, about the year 1726, was compelled by religious persecution to fly from his native country. He found refuge in western Pennsylvania, where he remained in seclusion for seven years. At the expiration of this period the passage of an act of amnesty rendered it safe for him to disclose his hiding-place, and his wife and children joined him in his new home. About the year 1738 he removed from Pennsylvania to Augusta County, Va., where he acquired large landed estates, which, either during his lifetime or by will, he divided among his four children.

His second son and third child, Major Alexander Stuart, was early in the Revolutionary War commissioned as major in Colonel Samuel McDowell's regiment, in which he served throughout the war. During Colonel McDowell's illness he commanded the regiment at the battle of Guilford Court House. Two horses were killed under him in this action, and he himself, dangerously wounded, was left upon the field and fell into the hands of the enemy. He was subsequently exchanged, and his sword was returned to him. This valued relic is now in the possession of his grandson, the Hon. Alexander H. H. Stuart, of Virginia. Major

Stuart was a warm friend of education, and aided liberally in the endowment of the school which afterwards expanded into Washington College, and is now known as Washington and Lee University. He was a man of large stature and uncommon intelligence. He died at the advanced age of ninety years.

Londonderry, County Derry, Ireland.

Judge Alexander Stuart, the youngest son of Major Alexander Stuart, was a lawyer by profession. He resided for some years in Cumberland County, Va., but having been elected a member of the Executive Council of the State, removed thence to Richmond. He subsequently resided in Illinois, where he held the office of United States Judge; and in Missouri, where he held office as United States Judge, Judge of the Circuit Court of the State, and Speaker of the Missouri Legislature. He died in Staunton, Va., in 1832, and was there buried.

The Hon. Archibald Stuart, of Patrick County, Va., the eldest son of Judge Alexander Stuart and the father of General J. E. B. Stuart, was an officer in the United States Army in the War of 1812. He embraced the profession of law. Throughout his long and eventful life he was actively engaged in the practice of his profession and in political life. He represented, first, the county of Campbell in the Virginia Legislature, and was repeatedly elected to both branches of that body from the county of Patrick. He was a member of the Constitutional Convention of 1829-30, and of the Convention of 1850. In this latter body, he and the Hon. Henry A. Wise were two of the four members residing east of the Blue Ridge who advocated a "white basis" of representation for the State. He represented the Patrick district in the Federal Congress during the Nullification agitation, and was a strong supporter of Mr. [John C.] Calhoun in that crisis. He is represented as a man of splendid talents and wonderful versatility.

"A powerful orator and advocate, he charmed the multitude on the hustings, and convinced juries and courts. In addition to these gifts, he was one of the most charming social companions the State ever produced. Possessing wonderful wit and humor, combined with rare gift for song, he at once became the centre of attraction at every social gathering. Among the people of the counties where he practised his name is held in great respect, and his memory is cherished with an affection rarely equalled in the history of any public man."

He married Elizabeth Letcher Pannill, of Pittsylvania County, Va., by whom he had four sons and six daughters. Among these, James E. B. Stuart was the seventh child and youngest son.

On his mother's side the ancestry of General Stuart is not less distinguished.

Giles Letcher was descended from ancient Welsh families the Hughses, Gileses, and Leches. He was born in Ireland, to which country one of his ancestors had removed from Wales during the reign of Charles the Second. He emigrated to the New World before the Revolutionary War, and was married in Richmond, Va., to Miss Hannah Hughes, a lady of fortune and of Welsh extraction. He settled in Goochland County, Va. He had four sons and one daughter. His eldest son, Stephen Letcher, was the father of Robert P. Letcher, of Kentucky. Letcher, married the daughter of the Hon. Sam Houston, of Texas, and was the father of Governor John Letcher, of Virginia. His second son, William Letcher, removed to Pittsylvania County, Va., where he married Elizabeth Perkins, daughter of Nicholas Perkins, who owned a considerable estate upon the Dan River. He finally settled in Patrick County, on the Ararat, a small stream which rises in the Blue Ridge and empties into the Yadkin River in North Carolina.

The settlers in that part of Virginia were greatly annoyed by the Tories, who were numerous in North Carolina, and many encounters had taken place between them and the Whigs in that border land. William Letcher had served in a volunteer company from his county that had defeated the Tories at the battle of the

Shallow Ford, on the Yadkin, a place which is still considered historic in that locality. This victory had inspired the Whigs with new courage; and William Letcher, prominent among them, had openly expressed his determination to resist the robberies and depredations of the Tories, and to hunt them down to the death.

In the latter part of June, 1780, while Mrs. Letcher was in her house alone with her infant daughter, then only six weeks old, a stranger appeared at the door and inquired for Mr. Letcher. There was nothing unusual in his manner, and Mrs. Letcher replied that her husband would soon be at home. While she was speaking, Mr. Letcher entered and invited the stranger to be seated. To this courtesy the stranger (he was a Tory named Nichols) replied by presenting his gun and saying: "I demand you in his Majesty's name." Letcher seized the gun to get possession of it; the Tory fired, and Letcher fell mortally wounded. He survived a few moments, but never spoke. Nichols fled. The terror-stricken wife despatched messengers to her relatives on the Dan River, who came to her as soon as possible, and attended to the burial of her husband. Nichols committed other murders and many robberies, but was finally overtaken in the southern part of North Carolina, and expiated his crimes on the gallows.

Washington and Lee University, Lexington, VA.

William Letcher was a man of fine appearance, and was greatly beloved and esteemed. His widow returned to her paternal home, with her little daughter Bethenia, and there remained until her second marriage with Colonel George Hairston, of Henry County, Va. In after years Bethenia Letcher married David Pannill, of Pittsylvania County, Va. Her daughter, Elizabeth Letcher Pannill, married Archibald Stuart.

She inherited from her grandfather, William Letcher, a beautiful and fertile farm in the southwestern part of Patrick County, which was named "Laurel Hill." Here her children were born. The large and comfortable house was surrounded by native oaks and was beautified with a flower garden, which was one of the childish delights of her son James, to whom she had transmitted her own passionate love of flowers. The site commanded a fine view of the Blue Ridge Mountains, and near at hand was the monument erected to the memory of William Letcher by his daughter Bethenia.

Amid these surroundings James Stuart passed a happy boyhood. He loved the old homestead with all the enthusiasm of his nature; and one of the fondest dreams of his manhood was that he might own the place of his birth, and there end his days in quiet retirement. He writes thus to his mother from Fort Leavenworth, in 1857:

> "I wish to devote one hundred dollars to the purchase of a comfortable log church near your place, because in all my observation I believe one is more needed in that neighborhood than any other that I know of; and besides, 'charity begins at home.' Seventy-five of this one hundred dollars I have in trust for that purpose, and the remainder is my own contribution. If you will join me with twenty-five dollars, a contribution of a like amount from two or three others interested will build a very respectable free church. . . . What will you take for the south half of your plantation? I want to buy it."

A near relative writes:

> "I well remember his speaking thus to his brother in 1863: 'I would give anything to make a pilgrimage to the old place, and when the war is over quietly to spend the rest of my days there.'"

At the age of fourteen years James Stuart was placed 1832 at school in Wytheville; and in August, 1848, he entered Emory and Henry College. During a revival of religion among the students he professed conversion, and joined the Methodist Church. Throughout his afterlife he maintained a consistent Christian character. Ten years later, in 1859, he was confirmed in the Protestant Episcopal Church by Bishop Hawkes, in St. Louis. The reasons for this change in his church connections were simple and natural. His mother was an Episcopalian, and had early instilled into him a love for her own church. His wife was a member of the same communion. He found, also, that a majority of the chaplains in the United States Army at that time were Episcopalian divines, and he considered that his opportunities for Christian fellowship and church privileges would be increased by the change. His spirit toward all denominations of Christians was as far removed as possible from narrow sectarianism.

Painting of West Point by Andrew Melrose, circa 1887.

In April, 1850, James Stuart left Emory and Henry College, having obtained an appointment as cadet in the United States Military Academy at West Point, on the recommendation of the Hon. T. H. [Thomas Hamlet] Averett, of the Third District of Virginia. During his career as cadet, Stuart applied himself assiduously to study, and graduated thirteenth in a class of forty-six members. He appears to have been more ambitious of soldierly than of scholarly distinction, and held in succession the cadet offices of corporal, sergeant, orderly sergeant, captain of the second company, and cavalry sergeant; the last being the highest office in that arm of the service at the Academy. General Fitzhugh Lee speaks thus of this period:

> "I recall his distinguishing characteristics, which were a strict attention to his military duties, an erect, soldierly bearing, an immediate and almost thankful acceptance of a challenge to fight from any cadet who might in any way feel himself aggrieved, and a clear, metallic, ringing voice."

The reader must not suppose from this description that Stuart was an advocate of the duel. The difficulties referred to were of such a character as are always liable to occur between boys at school, especially where, under a military organization, boys bear authority over boys. Another fellow-cadet gives the testimony that Stuart was known as a "Bible-class man," but was always ready to defend his own rights or his honor; and that the singular feature of his encounters with his fellow-students was, that his antagonists were physically far superior to him, and that although generally worsted in the encounter, Stuart always gained ground in the estimation of his fellows by his manly pluck and endurance. What his conduct was under these circumstances may be inferred from the following extracts from letters written by his father, who was a man of prudence and of honor. Under date of June 15, 1853, Archibald Stuart thus writes to his son:

> "I am proud to say that your conduct has given me entire satisfaction. I heard, it is true (but no thanks to you for the information), of the little scrape in which you involved yourself; but I confess, from what I understand of the transaction, I did not consider you so much to blame. An insult should be resented under all circumstances. If a man in your circumstances gains credit by submitting to insult as a strict observer of discipline, he loses more in proportion in his standing as a gentleman and a man of courage."

Again on January 5, 1854, he [Archibald] writes:

> "I have received your letter, and much regret that you have been involved in another fighting scrape. My dear son, I can excuse more readily a fault of the sort you have committed, in which you maintained your character as a man of honor and courage, than almost any other. But I hope you will hereafter, as far as possible, avoid getting into difficulties in which such maintenance may be demanded at your hands."

The relations existing between the father and son, as revealed by their correspondence during Stuart's cadetship, were of the most admirable character. Mutual affection was founded on mutual respect. As the time of graduation approached, the minds of both were greatly exercised over the important question of a choice of profession; and while the father seems to have preferred that his son should adopt the profession of arms, he throws the responsibility of the decision on his son, as the one most interested in, and the one most capable of making, a wise decision. The religious element in Stuart's character seems to have had a decided influence at this crisis of his life, and he was doubtless led to his decision by that Providence in which he trusted, and which was even then preparing him for his after life. During his last year at West Point he writes thus to his father:

> "I have not as yet any fixed course determined upon after graduation; still I can't help but regard it as the important crisis of my life. Two courses will be left for my adoption, the profession of arms and that of law; the one securing an ample support, with a life of hardship and

uncertainty,—laurels, if any, dearly bought, and leaving an empty title as a bequeathment; the other an overcrowded thoroughfare, which may or may not yield a support,— may possibly secure honors, but of doubtful worth. Each has its labors and its rewards. In making the selection I will rely upon the guidance of Him whose judgment cannot err, for 'it is not with man that walketh to direct his steps.'"

After Stuart had fairly embarked on his military career his father writes thus:

"Before I conclude I must express the deep solicitude I feel on your account. Just embarking in military life (a life which tests, perhaps more than any other, a young man's prudence and steadiness), at an immense distance from your friends, great responsibility rests upon your shoulders. It is true that you have, to start with, good morals fortified by religion, a good temper, and a good constitution, which if preserved will carry you through the trial safely. But the temptations of a camp to a young man of sanguine temperament, like yourself, are not to be trifled with or despised. I conjure you to be constantly on your guard, repelling and avoiding the slightest approach towards vice or immorality. You have to go through a fiery ordeal, but it is one through which many great and pious men have gone unscathed. But the greater portion have not escaped unscorched, and many have perished. Your military training at West Point will strengthen you greatly in the struggle. By it you have been taught the necessity of strict subordination to superiors, and of kind and conciliatory manners toward equals; and I trust that you will carry those lessons into practice now that you have exchanged the Academy for the camp."

Words of wisdom are these; words which the young man laid close to his heart. No stain of vice or immorality was ever found upon him.[148] — CONFEDERATE CHIEF OF STAFF, CAVALRY, A.N.V., HENRY BRAINERD MCCLELLAN

THE BRAVE YOUNG LIFE OF J. E. B. STUART

☞ It is to be deplored that so little is ever known of the boyhood of great men. It is only when they become conspicuous in noble, or perchance ignoble, deeds that the world stops to ask, Were they born in hovel or hall, of virtuous or wicked parents?

From all conditions, from every phase of life, the inborn soul of the poet, the painter, the soldier, the statesman will sometime claim its own and give out to humanity the latent spark of divine fire burning within. Many claim that heredity and environment have nothing to do with the building of a great character. "Act well your part; there all the honor lies." Be that as it may, the boy of whom we write was exceptionally fortunate in birth and home training. His very name suggests feudal castles, baronial halls, and princely palaces; but his progenitor in America cared far less for the emblazoned arms of lordly houses than for liberty of religious thought, and, like [Virginia] Governor [Robert] Dinwiddie, preferred to exchange his proud crest for the American eagle and adopt as his motto, "Where liberty is, there is my country." And so we find, in the year 1716, one Archibald Stuart, who first had taken refuge in Ireland from persecution, sailing the seas and finding his home in the wilds of Western Pennsylvania. Later he moved with his family to Virginia, and as the years rolled on brave men and virtuous women descended from him.

Afar back in the annals of history there lived a Sir Archibald Stuart, of Blackhall, Scotland. It is recorded that "he was a man of consummate ability, a member of the Privy Council both of Charles I and Charles II." Several centuries later, during the stirring period of nullification, another Archibald Stuart, a Virginian and descendant of the emigrant, served his country with "consummate ability" in the halls of Congress of the great United States of America.

Loch Katrine in the Scottish Highlands.

To this Hon. Archibald Stuart and Elizabeth Letcher Pannill, his wife, was born on February 6, 1833, a son—this tiny scion of a noble Scottish tree, who found in the old county of Patrick, Va., a most congenial clime and soil. The boy grew and waxed strong amid surroundings scarcely less romantic than those of his plaided ancestors.

The bonnie braes of [Scotland's River] Doon or [River] Dee could never surpass in loveliness the flowery banks of [Virginia's] Dan [River] when carpeted with the blue-eyed Myosotis; the dark crags of Glencoe [Scotland] were no more picturesque than the jagged pinnacles of that river when silhouetted against a gloomy or a golden sky. The broad sweep of the [River] Clyde, bearing on its bosom the innumerable sails of merchant ships, brought to the hearts of Scotland's lads no prouder thrills than to those of Virginia boys who, as Daniel said, heard the horn of the old packet boat reechoing along the banks of the James [River], or saw that river catch in her arms the sparkling waves of the Elizabeth and together broaden out into the majestic and historical bay of Hampton Roads.

To all men, we are told, the memories of childhood are dear; but to this one, through his brief and glorious manhood, they were peculiarly cherished—the old-fashioned farmhouse to which his eyes first opened, to the light of day, the mountains and meadows, streams and forests surrounding it, his horses and dogs, the quarters with their dusky inmates, and, above all, the flower garden in which he had walked hand in hand with his mother and learned of her the names and fragrance of rose, pink, and lily with which she decorated the pier tables and tall mantels of the old mansion. In after years, no matter where he was, to catch the odor of these flowers upon the breeze was to transport him, a boy again, to the old garden with his mother and sisters.

Victorian Southerners viewed Stuart as a 19th-Century medieval knight, and for good reason.

Many of his finer qualities were transmitted to him from his mother. She was a matron of the highest type, "looking well to the ways of her household and eating not the bread of idleness." She inculcated in her sons, as did their father, the fundamental principles of true knighthood, a reverence for womanhood and a strict and chivalrous sense of duty. These characteristics were exemplified in this son to such a marked degree that he has been called the Sir Galahad of the Confederacy, "whose strength was as the strength of ten, because his heart was pure." The sons of this home were also taught the dangers of the wine cup, and we have it from indisputable authority (from Mrs. J. E. B. Stuart herself) that this one, standing a little fellow by his sister's side as she read to him of some good and great man who never touched spirituous liquors, declared that he would be like him, and never from that hour did a drop of spirits pass his lips (save the wine of holy communion) until at the earnest request of his physician, and in his longing to live to look once again on the faces of his wife and children hurrying to his bed, he took a little brandy.

And yet there was never a merrier, happier lad than he. He inherited his father's rare gift of song and went singing on his way through the weary march and through the distant roar of cannon the same songs he had sung at the country churches, or with the banjo pickers on the moonlit sward, or when running with bridle in hand to capture and mount the wild and untamed colts on the laurel hills of his native heath.

Here is a letter written as a little [teenage] boy and signed with his name, now immortalized, which, in its analysis, shows many of the characteristics which dominated his loving, dauntless spirit:

"To Mrs. Elizabeth L. Stuart. Mount Ivory, Va. Politeness of Uncle Jack. Cobblers Spring, Va., December 6, 1846.

"My Dear Mother: I took it upon myself to borrow a horse and come up here to-day (being Sunday), and here I find Uncle Jack, who expects to start for home to-morrow, and I thought I would take advantage of this opportunity to write to you, though I must confess that my conscience is in opposition with my pen, for I can't see why you don't write to me, for you have no idea how acceptable a letter from home is to any son, but especially to one away off at a boarding school where I never hear from home or anywhere else. I have no doubt that you all have experienced this, and for that reason it appears still more astounding why you do not have mercy upon a poor, little, insignificant whelp away from his mammy. I hope you will not defer writing any longer, but write, write, write.

"I saw Brother Alec [his brother William Alexander] in town to-day; he was well.

"I know by this time you are impatient to hear something about Mr. Painter. All I have to say is simply this: It is a first-rate place, but I had rather go to Mr. Buckingham's.

"Tell Vic [his sister Victoria] that I have got an arithmetic for her, and it is a pretty one, and if I had had any idea of Uncle Jack being here, I would have brought it up. Kiss her for me, also Dave. I would also tell you to kiss Black and Dallas, but I know you wouldn't do that. Give my love to papa, sisters, M. and C., and Vic. Give my best respects to Mr. Ayers when you see him. I wrote a long letter yesterday.

"I ever remain your affectionate son, J. E. B. Stuart.

"P. S.—I deemed it unnecessary to say in this I am well, as you know I am never anything else. J. E. B. S."

A few short years, and the little homesick schoolboy is a youth at Emory and Henry [College]. Here his record is fair, and here he hearkened to the still small voice, "Son, give me thine heart," and stayed his faith on the joys of a better world, a faith which never faltered and which, through roar of cannon and hail of musketry, inspired him with the spirit of the noble Roman known to every schoolboy through [Thomas Babington] Macaulay's poem:

> "Then out spake brave Horatius,
>   The captain of the gate:
> To every one upon this earth
>   Death cometh soon or late;
> And how can man die better
>   Than facing fearful odds
> For the ashes of his fathers
>   And the temples of his gods?"

After a year at Emory he was appointed to West Point, which he entered in June, 1850, and soon became noted as "the most skillful and daring horseman among his fellows." Having finished his cadetship, he was commissioned a lieutenant in the United States army. He served faithfully and fearlessly in Indian warfare in Southern Texas and was then sent to the Far West to quell mutterings of trouble between Southern and Northern factions. It was there that he met the one woman of his choice, Miss Flora Cooke, daughter of Gen. P. St. George Cooke, of the United States army [and sister of Gen. John Rogers Cooke, C.S.A.].

When in Kansas he saw for the first time the fanatical insurrectionist [and socialist], John Brown, and smilingly recognized him as "Old Osawatomie Brown" in demanding his surrender at the barricaded door of the house in which he and his sons had taken refuge at Harpers Ferry, Va., October, 1859.

This tragedy widened the breach already broadening between the North and the South, and in less than a year was ushered in the saddest era in American history—an era in which the words of the beloved apostle seem to be verified, ushered in the saddest era in American history, an era in which the sons of the Revolution who had stood shoulder to shoulder, and whose unity was their strength, exchanged their blue coats for gray and rushed madly toward a yawning chasm waiting to engulf them in the land of their forefathers.

[Southern poet Henry] Timrod, the sweetest singer of the South at that time, caught in his sensitive ear the jarring sounds of discord. With almost prophetic pen he pictured the opening of spring on Virginia plains:

"O, standing on this desecrated mold,
Methinks that I behold,
Lifting her bloody daisies up to God,
Spring kneeling on the sod."

Alas, how true! The white petals of the daisies had just begun to sprinkle the green fields of Manassas when whiter tents were stretched upon them, and a marshaled host in gray awaited an invading foe. Then it was that a body of troopers came riding from the mountains, the valleys, and the sun-kissed plantations of the South, a brilliant pageant in those early sixties and as brave as any of the knights of old who e'er broke lance for the love of land or lady. Their silken banners, proudly flaunting defiance in the face of the foe, were yet unsullied by the grime of battle, brilliant in the red and white and blue of the stars and bars; their gray coats, heavily trimmed with gold braid and brass buttons, their lances gleaming and flashing, their good swords in burnished scabbards buckled to their sturdy sides, their war chargers scarcely less richly caparisoned than that of their leader, whom they followed eager to be nearest his confidence and his peril that, if need be, their own bodies might be his shield and buckler. And this knightly leader, this flower of all their chivalry, with his sweeping plume and erect form, his lips ever ready to break into smiles, reining in his plunging charger more with the power of his indomitable will than with the strength of his strong arm—who by virtue of his intrepidity of soul and his military training could so inspire men to do and die as J. E. B. Stuart?

Harpers Ferry, 1861.

Alas, those heroic hearts that followed him! Poets, historians, and orators have written and spoken in burning words of their great, heroic deeds. Of [Wade] Hampton at the head of his legions, of [John Singleton] Mosby's dare-devil guerrillas, of the thunder of [John] Pelham's guns, of their charges and onslaughts, their unflagging marches, their cruel sufferings, uncomplainingly borne in field and in prison, inspired by one of the brightest stars in the galaxy of Southern stars.

    Those who rode closest to him and lived to see that star set on the plains of Yellow Tavern (John Esten Cooke, [Henry Brainerd] McClellan, his chief of staff, and Judge Theodore [S.] Garnett, who delivered a most eloquent address at the unveiling of the equestrian statue of Stuart, May 30, 1907) were far better fitted than I to tell of his military achievements, nor is it my purpose to attempt it. I could not add one leaf to the laurel wreath of his fame. But, as a daughter of the Southern Confederacy for which he gave his life, I would fain call the attention of the conquered and the conqueror to the spirit of the boy and the soldier that led him on in the path of duty and inspired within his breast that high sense of honor attainable to all who reach out, as he did, to high ideals. The turn came in the tide of his affairs, the crucial moment when he must halt between two opinions, and, having chosen he did his part faithfully and honorably to the end.

    Little he knew the glorious destiny awaiting him when he penned the boyish letter, given now for the first time to public notice; but in it we see something of the brave, self-reliant, merry, and fun-loving heart of the dashing cavalryman of the Confederacy.

    Analyze the first sentence in it, "I took it upon myself to borrow a horse." History tells us he often took it upon himself to make reconnoitering expeditions, keeping their extent and purpose entirely to himself. He rode under the black mantle of night, his men following blindly, even to the sound of the enemy's encampment. His song and laughter cheered his weary men, but doubtless it was often stilled and the smiling lips grew stern as he thought he might, perchance, be leading his men to their doom. Sometimes he recklessly rode alone, and once, coming unexpectedly upon forty-six Union soldiers resting in a field on the border line, his quick wit and daring instantly prompted the order: "Throw down your arms." The men, seeing Stuart and thinking his troopers were just behind him, obeyed with alacrity, and he marched the whole squadron into camp.

    He professes in his letter that his conscience was in opposition to his writing home when his people were so chary in their letters to him, but history tells us he could write in kindly terms and with Christian moderation and restraint to one who had made aspersions against him. Quick as a boy to resent any insinuations of shortcomings or unkind thought of him by others, yet he learned as a man and soldier the art of self-control. There is a tenderness in the sentence that brings a tear to the eye when he asks how they can be so neglectful of "an insignificant little whelp so far away from his mammy," and a smile such as must have spread over his own face when he said that he would have his stately mother kiss his little brute playmates, Black and Dallas. His sense of duty kept him from complaining of the school to which his parents thought fit to send him, though he greatly preferred another; and we know of only one instance in which the great heart beating within his breast prompted him to shirk responsibility or duty, and that was to send a boy deserter to his superior officer, saying to the guard: "Take him to General Lee and tell him the circumstances." He loathed disloyalty, but he loved truth, and he saw the stamp of it perhaps on the brow of the pale stripling as he told, in defense of his own act, the story which had doomed him to be hanged on a near-by tree.

Gen. Wade Hampton, C.S.A.

His letter shows devotion to home, parents, and a special fondness for a certain sister. He loved the society of pure women. His charm of conversation, his love of music, his dash and daring, and, above all, his cavalier manner, made him the idol of the hour with the fair sex, most of whom adore the military and are hero worshipers.

But enshrined in the inmost core of his being was the vision of one woman, afar from the roar of guns, in her cottage home, bending over his children with a mother's love and, with uplifted heart, praying to the God of battles for the safe return of her hero. But God decreed otherwise; he spared him to turn the tide of many conflicts, and he was spared the Gethsemane of Appomattox; but there came a day in the spring of 1864 when all his prowess was called upon to stay the enemy from his beloved capital city of Richmond. The rushing by of a few blue-coated cavalrymen, the pointing of a pistol, a fatal shot, and Spring, kneeling on the plains of Yellow Tavern, fell prostrate among her bloody daisies, gathering the knightliest flower in all Virginia's fields to her bosom. Ah! then she cried with the voice of all her rills, her mountains, and desolated land for resignation to God's will. The voice of mourning was heard near and far; only the stricken warrior murmured not.

As his comrades tenderly lifted him he called out to some of his panic stricken followers dashing past: "Go back, my men, go back and do your duty as I have done mine, and our country will yet be free." And once again, a few hours later, with dying lips: "If God and my countrymen think I have done my duty, I am ready to go." These parting words to the world he was fast leaving were a keynote to the greatness of the man and the passport of the warrior's soul to immortality.[149] — MRS. W. B. ROBERTSON, PLASTERCO, VA.

Confederate monument, Woodlawn Cemetery, Terre Haute, IN.

CHAPTER 2

FROM WEST POINT TO WAR

☛ Gen. James Ewell Brown Stuart, born in Patrick County, Va., February 6, 1833, was the fourth son of Hon. Archibald Stuart and Elizabeth Letcher Pannill. The grandfather was Alexander Stuart, Chief Justice of Missouri and otherwise a man of distinction, having fought in the Revolutionary War and being conspicuously heroic in the battle of Guilford Court House.

J. E. B. Stuart went to West Point in 1850, leaving Emory and Henry College (Virginia) to accept the appointment from Hon. Mr. [Thomas Salem] Bocock, his representative in Congress. He graduated after four years of faithful service and study, and was made second lieutenant in the regiment of Mounted Rifles, which regiment was then stationed in Texas. In 1855 he was transferred to the First Cavalry, which was then being organized at Fort Leavenworth, Kan., under Col. Edwin Sumner, in which he served until the War between the States. During this time he was in active service against the frontier Indians, and also in Kansas during the difficulties originating there with [socialist and murderer] John Brown and other such leaders.

Stuart before the War. It is said that he later grew a beard due to criticism of his "weak chin."

While on leave of absence from his regiment in 1859, and being in Washington City, he acted as aid to Col. R. E. Lee, who was sent to Harper's Ferry to disarm and disband the party of abolitionists [that is, socialists and communists] gathered there. It was J. E. B. Stuart who demanded the surrender of the party then holding "the armory," and who resisted. He led a body of United States Marines against the [far-left] outlaws, their weapon of attack being a very heavy iron-shod ladder. [Socialist leader] John Brown, of Kansas, was then recognized and captured. The informed world knows the results—as well as the awful struggle from 1861 to 1865.

John Esten Cooke wrote of him: "Young, gay, gallant: wearing a uniform brilliant with gold braid, golden spurs, and a hat looped up with a golden star and decorated with a black plume; going on marches at the head of his cavalry column, with his banjo player [Joe Sweeney][150] gayly thrumming behind him; leading his troops to battle with a camp song on his lips; here to-day and away to-morrow raiding, fighting, laughing, dancing, and as famous for his gallantry toward women as for his reckless courage. Stuart was in every particular a singular and striking human being, drawing to himself the strongest public interest both as a man and a soldier. Of his military ability as a cavalry leader, [Union] Gen. [John] Sedgwick probably summed up the general opinion when he said: 'Stuart is the best cavalryman ever foaled in North America.' Of his courage, devotion, and many lovable traits, Gen. Lee bore testimony on his death, when he retired to his tent with the words: 'I can scarcely think of him without weeping.' Stuart thus made a very strong impression both on the people at large and on the eminent soldiers with whom he was associated. The writer enjoyed his personal friendship, and observed him during a large part of his career. From the first his cavalry operations were full of fire and vigor, and Gen. J. E. Johnston, under whom he served in the Valley, called him 'the indefatigable Stuart.'

Stuart played a role in the capture and arrest of South-hating, psychopath-socialist John Brown at Harpers Ferry in October 1859.

"In May, 1863, at Chancellorsville, when Jackson was disabled and Stuart assumed command and sent to ascertain Jackson's views and wishes as to the attack on the next morning, the wounded commander replied: "Go back and tell Gen. Stuart to act on his own judgment, and do what he thinks best. I have implicit confidence in him.'

"Stuart's attack with Jackson's Corps on the next morning fully justified this confidence. His employment of artillery in mass on the Federal left went far to decide this critical action. At the battle of Fredericksburg, in the preceding December, the same masterly handling of his guns had protected Jackson's right toward the Massaponnax, which was the real key to the battle; and in these two great actions, as on the left at Sharpsburg, Stuart exhibited a genius for the management of artillery which would have delighted Napoleon [III].

"When the Confederate forces advanced northward in the Summer of 1862, Stuart's cavalry accompanied the column, and took part in all the important operations of that year on the Rapidan, the Rappahannock, the Second Manassas, Sharpsburg, and Fredericksburg. In these bustling scenes Stuart acted with immense energy and enthusiasm, laying broad and deep his reputation as a cavalry officer. By incessant fighting and an ardor and activity which seemed to pass all bounds, he had by this time won the full confidence of Gen. Lee.

Rappahannock River, Fredericksburg, VA.

"When [Union] Gen. [Ulysses S.] Grant moved toward Spotsylvania Court House, it was Stuart who, according to Northern historians, so obstructed the roads as to enable Gen. Lee to interpose his army at this important point. Had this not been effected, Richmond, it would seem, must have fallen—Stuart thus having the melancholy glory of prolonging for an additional year the contest, ending only in April, 1865. His death speedily followed.

[Union] Gen. [Philip Henry] Sheridan turned against him his own system, organized on the Chickahominy in June, 1862. The

Federal horse pushed past Lee's army to surprise Richmond. Stuart followed in haste with such force of cavalry as he could collect on the instant. The collision took place at Yellow Tavern, near Richmond; and in the engagement Stuart was mortally wounded, and two or three days afterwards expired. He fell defending the capital in a desperate struggle, and came to his death by reckless exposure of himself—his only thought having been to accomplish his end. And as his life had been one of earnest devotion to the cause in which he believed, so his last hours were tranquil, his confidence in the mercy of Heaven unfailing. When he was asked how he felt, he said: 'Easy, but willing to die if God and my country think I have done my duty.' His last words were: 'I am going fast now; I am resigned. God's will be done.'

"Although his utter carelessness as to the impression he produced subjected him to many calumnies, it is here placed on record, by one who knew his private life thoroughly and was with him day and night for years, that he was in morals among the purest of men: a faithful husband, absolutely without vices of any description, and, if not demonstrative in his religious views, an earnest and exemplary Christian. His love for his wife was deep and devoted, and on the death of his little daughter Flora he said to me, with tears in his eyes: 'I shall never get over it.'

"When one day some person in my presence indulged in sneers at the expense of 'preachers,' supposing that the roystering young commander would echo them, Stuart said coldly: "I regard the Christian ministry as the noblest work in which any human being can engage.' He never touched spirits in any form during his whole life, having promised his mother [Elizabeth], he told me, that he would not; did not use tobacco even.

[As for peculiar personal characteristics,] he had none of the mock dignity of small men in command, and spoke and acted with entire naturalness. Often his utterances were full of rough humor. Having reported to him on one occasion that a force of Federal cavalry had crossed the Rappahannock below Fleetwood, and were drawn up on the southern bank, I received from him the order: 'Well, tell Col. [Richard Lee Turberville] Beale to lick into 'em, and jam 'em right into the river.'

"At Fredericksburg, in the evening, when one of the officers sent a courier to ask how the battle was going, his answer was: 'Tell him Jackson has not advanced, but I have, and that I am going on, crowding 'em with artillery.'

"While conversing with him one day in regard to his hazardous expedition around [Union] Gen. [George Brinton] McClellan's

Stuart had a deep appreciation for the banjo, and kept his banjo player Joe Sweeney nearby, often even in the heat of battle.

army on the Chickahominy, I said that if attacked while crossing below he would certainly have been obliged to surrender, when his reply was: 'No; one other course was left—to die game.' In these straightforward and unceremonious utterances Stuart expressed his character, as he worded it on another occasion, to 'Go through or die trying.'

"In camp he was both a lovable and a provoking person; lovable from the genuine warmth of his character, and provoking from the entire disregard of the feelings of those around him, or, at least, from his proneness to amuse himself at any and everybody's expense. When the humor seized him, he laughed at nearly everybody. Gen. Lee he invariably spoke of, as he treated him, with profound respect, but he even made merry with so great a man as Jackson, or 'Old Stonewall,' as he affectionately styled him. The two distinguished men seemed to have a sincere friendship for each other, which always impressed me as a very singular circumstance indeed, but so it was. They were strongly contrasted in character and temperament, for Stuart was the most impulsive and Jackson the most reserved and reticent of men. But it was plain that a strong bond of mutual admiration and confidence united them. Jackson would visit Stuart and hold long confidential conversations with him, listening to his views with evident attention, and Stuart exhibited, on the intelligence of this great man's death, the strongest emotion.

"Stuart's delight was to have his banjo player, Sweeney, in his tent: and even while busily engaged in his official correspondence he loved to hear the gay rattle of the instrument and the voice of Sweeney singing, 'Jine the Cavalry,' 'Sweet Evelina,' or some other favorite ditty. From time to time he would lay down his pen, throw one knee over the arm of his chair, and call his two dogs, two handsome young setters, which he had brought across the

Rappahannock, or, falling back, would utter some jest at the expense of his staff. Frequently he would join in the song, or volunteer one of his own, his favorites being 'The Bugles Sang Truce,' 'The Dew Is on the Blossom,' and some comic ballads, of which the one beginning 'My Wife's in Castle Thunder' was a fair specimen. These he roared out with immense glee, rising and gesticulating, slapping his officers on the back, throwing back his head while he sang, and generally ending in a burst of laughter.

"The foregoing are extracts from a long and interesting sketch by the beloved author, John Esten Cooke, while the concluding testimony is from one who knew him most intimately: "His sense of duty and implicit trust in his God was the mainspring of his life—a life as pure and true as a child's. He never expected to survive the war, and to his wife he often spoke of this, but always with the confidence of one ready for the call whenever it should come. His last hours were marked with the beautiful resignation of an earnest Christian. The one trial was not having his wife and two little children with him. He had married in 1855 [Flora Cooke,] a daughter of Gen. P. [Philip] St. George Cooke, of the Second United States Dragoons."[151]— *CONFEDERATE VETERAN*

JEB STUAR—FIGHTING MAN

☞ Through forest paths, through country lanes, through sunny Virginia valleys, men hummed that lilting ditty as they galloped along after young James Ewell Brown Stuart, with his rollicking voice booming out on the chorus, and long-legged, laconic Joe Sweeney's gifted fingers thumping out the accompaniment on the strings of his captured Yankee banjo.

Major General young Stuart was, and serving under the immortal [Stonewall] Jackson, but to the men in gray who followed where he led he was romance incarnate. No march too long, no force of enemy too overwhelming for them if Jeb Stuart rode at their head, with his ostrich feather floating in the wind and the tassels of his yellow sash beating against the high tops of his polished boots—and his merry blue eyes challenging them to follow.

All the Launcelots and Galahads are gone. Not even the bravest would dare to wear a sash and a plumed hat these days, and wars are fought by men dressed as much alike as possible, and battles led by generals miles in the rear. Cavalry is practically obsolete, and the world has become stodgy and commonplace since that gay feather fell in the dust of Yellow Tavern.

But while it yet adorned a broad-brimmed felt, men knew that the world was still a good place in which to live, and that nothing was important save honor and courage and a good stiff fight, a gallant death, and a blanket shroud.

A short life in the saddle, Lord, not long life by the fire! It might have been their motto those men who rode in Stuart's cavalry, for only a handful of them lived to see that black April at Appomattox Court House when Lee rode by them with hat in hand, that gray head of his proud even in defeat, and the pitiful remnant of his army gazing at his beloved face with sorrowing eyes that were striving to impress his likeness on loyal hearts that would never forget that day.

They carried back to their firesides memories that could soften the blow of defeat. Through dark days that tried their souls, their hearts still rode through Virginia in that long line with Jeb Stuart at their head.

They knew him. And some of those who had been with him put down on paper his deeds, his words, the way he laughed, the teasing light in his blue eyes, so that posterity of theirs might know that a man had lived.

"The last meeting of Lee and Jackson at Chancellorsville."

Prosaic histories give accounts of his military campaigns. The eyes and the ears of Lee's army, they call him, but not even their weighty words can quite conceal the glamor of the man himself.

He was so young. Men don't become generals these days at twenty-eight, even men who finish at West Point as he did, but at that age Stuart was a seasoned soldier and had smelled the smoke of battle and been wounded in an Indian skirmish. Already he had shown the resource and courage he possessed, so that when he offered his sword in defense of his native State, it was a great day for the Confederacy.

They sent him to serve under Jackson in the Shenandoah, and in the space of five months he was promoted from lieutenant colonel to brigadier general, and Union soldiers slept uneasily in their camps and dreamed that that laughing, fighting devil of a Stuart was after them.

He became a nightmare to Union generals aspiring to fame and glory—and promotion. They saw their high hopes vanish; they saw their lines falter and fall back before a mere handful of Rebels inspired to superhuman courage by a madman who charged at their head with flashing sword and laughter on his lips, and in his eyes the joy of martial combat.

Useless to explain to the newspapers, useless to try to make "Old Abe" understand that they couldn't stop a man like that! Wars aren't won by excuses, and when superior numbers can't conquer, something must be wrong with the general. Jackson and Stuart, advancing, retreating, in that beautiful Valley of the Shenandoah, keeping two armies at bay while the world looked on in amazement, and writing military history that excites the admiration of men even today, was something the North hadn't planned for.

But it was sport for young Stuart. War was an amusing game that he played to the best of his ability, and he was willing to pay for it when fate should demand an accounting. He had martial blood in his veins—and he had Irish blood. It was inevitable with a heritage such as that that he should love the smell of powder; inevitable that he should play the role of cavalier to the end. There is a potency, a color, about Irish blood that lends a glamor to the history of the world. It has helped to dye the soil of so many battle fields; will fertilize the grass roots of many more.

Hot Irish blood that loves a merry song and a good fight, and yet has its deep undercurrent of faith in God and love of fellow-man—Stuart was all that.

His men said that they had never heard him use an oath, and though many women admired him, theirs, too, was the tribute that womankind always pay to a fighting man.

No scandal ever touched his name. One woman he loved [Flora Cooke], and that one he had married. She was his darling wife, and so he addressed her in letters from many a camp fire, and, when life for him was over, with May sunshine outside his window and the guns just beyond Richmond booming in his ears, he sighed that he must go out to join his beloved old Stonewall without one last sight of her cherished face.

He was made of wire and steel, and sleep didn't figure in his plans. While his soldiers slept the sleep of exhaustion from long wearying rides over incredible distances, Stuart, accompanied by Sweeney with his banjo under his arm, would set out for some home in the neighborhood.

The news would spread, and some old darky who knew how to make a fiddle talk would come up from the quarters to play with

Camp life with Stuart at the helm was never dull.

Sweeney, and soon a dance would be in full swing, just as if Yankee troops weren't encamped a few rods away, just as if the old plantation life with its balls, its white-columned old homes, its grinning Negro servants, its easy hospitality, hadn't come to an end. Just as if the Bonnie Blue Flag would wave forever over the capitol at Richmond.

Stuart and Sweeney were always welcome. Sweeney's supply of ballads was almost inexhaustible, and sometimes the young General would join in—"Sweet Evelina," "Faded Old Letters," "Bonnie Blue Flag," and ending up with "Jine the Cavalry!" Sweeney, minstrel to a knight errant, the airs he plunked from his banjo made long miles drop away as if by magic under the horses' feet.

Like the great leader he was, Stuart taught his men to trust him. Had they been afraid of his judgment, the story of his career would not have been so breath-taking. But they were with him to a man. They followed his feather, as they said. Around McClellan's army they went after that gay plume, almost constantly in sight of the enemy, exposed to great danger, but safe through their own daring.

When they hesitated to ride by a gunboat lying in the James, he led them in an attack on it, and his battery soon forced the ship to up-anchor and drift down the river, since its own guns could do no damage to the attackers at such short range.

With light hearts they followed him on his raid into Pennsylvania, confident that somehow their Jeb would get them back onto Dixie soil safely again. Miles into the enemy country they went, with Washington [D.C.] shaking in its boots and the order out to stop that fellow Stuart at any cost, guard every ford of the Potomac and not let him back across it.

But with the boldness characteristic of him, he outguessed them and crossed at a ford miles below where he was expected and nearest the greatest number of enemy! He brought with him a large party of horses conscripted from the Pennsylvania countryside, and he left behind him people who praised the gentlemanly conduct of his men.

There had been no plundering, and for the horses and clothing seized, Stuart had commanded that receipts be given so that redress might be asked of the United States Government.

In a day that prided itself on its gentlemen, young Stuart was admittedly the pride of Virginia chivalry. A great friend of his said that the young general's head was one that a helmet should have graced, and men much older than he envied him the brain under that feathered hat of his.

He outwitted the enemy on more than one occasion, and, at such times, that brain of Stuart's made up for superior forces before him. It served him in good stead at Fredericksburg, when the day went against his small band and defeat seemed certain. Confronted by troops almost four times as many as his own, he stationed men with banners in the rear so that it seemed he had several regiments in reserve. Then, leading the charge himself, he swept them on to victory.

But in spite of his military genius, and no one who reads the accounts of his maneuvers can doubt it for a moment, the man himself was very human, and it was that picture of him his men remembered and smiled mistily over for long years afterward.

He was their comrade. He slept with them, ate with them, joked with them, and grieved with them. They idolized him and knew in their hearts that they couldn't be beaten as long as they had him with them.

He had pet names for some of them, and the slang they quote him as using smacks of a much later date than the sixties. Men growing old remembered, long after that deep voice behind the heavy auburn beard was silent forever, how he would lean back in his saddle and roar at a joke. He really meant it when he sang that if you wanted to have a good time you should join the cavalry. For Stuart had a grand time. Old enough to realize the seriousness of the war, but young enough to take it as it came and not quarrel with fate over the decision, his smiling face under the quizzical eyebrows never betrayed to his men any anxiety he might feel.

When the joke was on him, he laughed just as loudly. The enemy came so near to capturing him one morning when he imprudently slept on the porch of an old, abandoned house near Verdiersville without a picket, that he escaped only by leaving his hat and coat behind and leaping a fence.

But the Northern general didn't laugh long over the possession of Stuart's hat and coat, for, some nights later, the young Rebel led a night attack on the general's camp while that worthy man was sound asleep. The poor [Union] general [John Pope] escaped in his night clothes, and Stuart, in great glee, took back with him the general's whole uniform! A store in Richmond displayed it in its shop window while the whole Confederacy chuckled.

And even Lincoln had to laugh at his imprudence when Stuart, after capturing a telegraph station and intercepting messages of the gravest importance, had his operator send in a complaint about the poor grade of mules being furnished the Union army. "They caused me great hindrance in removing my captured wagons," Stuart said.

He was a dozen men rolled into one, for they could never be sure just where he'd show up next, and so they were never easy. To the men in blue he was a devil who never slept. Hard to convince them that he was just a boy with a bushy beard that he was very proud of—riding half across the State of Virginia with a couple of bird pups on his saddle that some one had given him.

But at last they molded the bullet with his name on it. He had been sure that they would some day, but, like Jackson, he had been fatalistic about it. He believed that he had a destiny to fulfil and that he would be spared to complete it.

Battle after battle the shells flew thick and fast about his gallant head, and men he loved fell all around him, but he remained untouched. Through three hard years he gave of his best,

The Battle of Brandy Station, with Stuart—singing at the top of his lungs—leading the charge.

and men fought under his blood-red battle flag and died with the picture of his smiling face in their hearts.

Three years exactly that day in May the bullet found him. The star of the Confederacy was setting. Stuart had twice saved Richmond; she would need him sorely again, but his destiny had run its course. Lee, with his best generals dead and his army ragged and starving, couldn't holdout much longer. A kind fate meant that Stuart should be spared that.

His men wavered when they saw that he had fallen in the charge. They responded to his rallying cry as he was carried from the field, but hope died within them that day at Yellow Tavern. "I have done my best for my country! See that you do yours!" said their invincible leader to them for the last time. "I had rather die than be whipped!"

And so they took him into Richmond to die in that city where he had known gaiety and laughter and love.

Only thirty-one he was as he lay there with the sands of his life running low, and though the guns sounded in the distance, the flag he had fought for, shed his precious blood for—the beautiful folds of the Bonnie Blue Flag still floated over his beloved Richmond when he closed his eyes for the last time.

And there in a public place stands today his bronze likeness looking out across a city that still speaks of his gallantry and courage, after sixty-eight years.

Time tarnishes the brightest name, but it will be long before the nation—a united North and South—forgets Jeb Stuart. For the whole world loves a fighting man—one who plays the game squarely, one who fights for what he thinks is right, gives his life's blood gladly, and dies with laughter on his lips. For such a one there are no lost causes.[152] — THELMAR WYCHE COX, SHREVEPORT, LA.

Stuart's men regrouping after battle.

CHAPTER 3

BIOGRAPHICAL SKETCH BY A NORTHERN BIOGRAPHER
☛ Stuart was a fighter by nature. When he was at West Point in the early fifties, his distinguishing characteristics, as chronicled by Fitzhugh Lee, were

> "a strict attendance to his military duties, an erect, soldierly bearing, an immediate and almost thankful acceptance of a challenge from any cadet to fight, who might in anyway feel himself aggrieved."

The tendency, if not inherited, did not lack paternal encouragement; for the elder Stuart [Archibald] writes to his son, in regard to one of these combats: "I did not consider you so much to blame. An insult should be resented under all circumstances." The young cadet also showed himself to be a fearless and an exceptionally skillful horseman.

These qualities served him well in the Indian warfare to which he was immediately transferred from West Point. His recklessness in taking chances was equaled only by his ingenuity in pulling through. One of his superiors writes:

> "Lieutenant Stuart was brave and gallant, always prompt in execution of orders and reckless of danger and exposure. I considered him at that time one of the most promising young officers in the United States Army."

Later Stuart took a prominent part in the capture of [socialist] John Brown [with then U.S. Colonel Robert E. Lee]. He himself wrote an account of the matter at the time for the newspapers, simply to explain and justify Lee's conduct. He also wrote a letter to his mother, with a characteristic description of his own doings:

> "I approached the door in the presence of perhaps two thousand spectators, and told Mr. Smith that I had a communication for him from Colonel Lee. He opened the door about four inches, and placed his body against the crack, with a cocked carbine in his hand; hence his remark after his capture that he could have wiped me out like a mosquito. . . . When Smith first came to the door I recognized old

Osawatomie Brown, who had given us so much trouble in Kansas. No one present but myself could have performed that service. I got his Bowie-knife from his person, and have it yet."

From the very beginning of the war Stuart maintained this fighting reputation. He would attack anything anywhere, and the men who served under him had to do the same; what is more, and marks the born leader, he made them wish to do the same. "How can I eat, sleep, or rest in peace without you upon the outpost?" wrote Joseph Johnston; and a noble enemy, who had been a friend, [Union] Gen. [John] Sedgwick, is reported to have said that Stuart was "the greatest cavalry officer ever foaled in America."

Danger he met with more than stolid indifference, a sort of furious bravado, thrusting himself into it with manifest pleasure, and holding back, when he did hold back, with a sigh. And some men's luck! Johnston was wounded a dozen times, was always getting wounded. Yet Stuart, probably far more exposed, was wounded only once in his life, among the Indians; in the war not at all. His clothes were pierced again and again. According to [Heros] Von Borcke, the general had half of his moustache cut off by a bullet "as neatly as it could have been done by the hand of an experienced barber." Yet nothing ever drew blood till the shot which was mortal. Such an immunity naturally encouraged the sort of fatalism not unusual with great soldiers, and Stuart once said of the proximity of his enemies, "You might have shot a marble at them—but I am not afraid of any ball aimed at me."

Gen. Joseph E. Johnston, C.S.A.

In this spirit he got into scores of difficult places—and got out again. Sometimes it was by quick action and a mad rush, as when he left his hat and a few officers behind him. Sometimes it was by stealth and secrecy, as when he hid his whole command all night within a few hundred yards of the marching enemy. [Wrote one his soldiers:]

"And nothing now remained but to watch and wait and keep quiet. Quiet? Yes, the men kept very quiet, for they realized that even Stuart never before had them in so tight a place. But many a time did we fear that we were betrayed by the weary, hungry, headstrong mules of the ordnance train. Men were stationed at the head of every team; but in spite of all precautions, a discordant bray would every now and then fill the air. Never was the voice of a mule so harsh!"

The men who had watched and tried and tested him on such occasions as these knew what he was and gave him their trust. He asked nothing of them that he would not do himself. Therefore they did what he asked of them. [J.] Scheibert says that

"he won their confidence and inspired them by his whole bearing and personality, by his kindling speech, his flashing eye, and his cheerfulness which no reverse could overcome."

Stuart himself describes his followers' enthusiastic loyalty with a naïveté as winning as it is characteristic.

"There was something of the sublime in the implicit confidence and unquestioning trust of the rank and file in a leader guiding them straight, apparently, into the very jaws of the enemy, every step appearing to them to diminish the very faintest hope of extrication."

Yet he asked this trust and they gave it simply on the strength of his word.

"You are about to engage in an enterprise which, to ensure success, imperatively demands at your hands, coolness, decision, and the strictest order and sobriety on the march and in the bivouac. The destination and extent of this expedition had better be kept to myself than known to you."

The men loved him also because, when the strain was removed, he put on no airs, pretense, or remoteness of superiority, but treated them as man to man.

"He was the most approachable of major-generals, and jested with the private soldiers of his command as jovially as though he had been one of themselves. The men were perfectly unconstrained in his presence, and treated him more like the chief huntsman of a hunting party than as a major general."

His officers also loved him, and not only trusted him for war, but enjoyed his company in peace. He was constantly on the watch to do them kindnesses, and would frolic with them—marbles, snowballs, quoits, what not?—like a boy with boys.

And Stuart loved his men as they loved him, did not regard them as mere food for cannon, to be used, and abused, and forgotten. There is something almost pathetic in his neglect of self in praising them.

> "The horseman who, at his officer's bidding, without question, leaps into unexplored darkness, knowing nothing except that there is danger ahead, possesses the highest attribute of the patriot soldier. It is a great source of pride to me to command a division of such men."

Careless of his own danger always, he was far more thoughtful of those about him. In the last battle he was peculiarly reckless, and [Confederate] Major [Henry Brainerd] McClellan noticed that the general kept sending him with messages to [Confederate] General [George Thomas] Anderson.

> "At last the thought occurred to me that he was endeavoring to shield me from danger. I said to him: 'General, my horse is weary. You are exposing yourself, and you are alone. Please let me remain with you.' He smiled at me kindly, but bade me go to General Anderson with another message."

Any reflection on his command arouses him at once to its defense.

> "There seems to be a growing tendency to abuse and underrate the services of that arm of the service [cavalry] by a few officers of infantry, among whom I regret to find [Confederate] General [Isaac Ridgeway] Trimble. Troops should be taught to take pride in other branches of the service than their own."

It is very rare that Stuart has any occasion to address himself directly to the authorities at Richmond. Fighting, not writing, was his business. But when he feels that his men and horses are being starved unnecessarily, he bestirs himself, and sends [Confederate Secretary of War James Alexander] Seddon a letter which is as interesting for nervous and vigorous expression as for the character of the writer.

> "I beg to urge that in no case should persons not connected with the army, and who are amply compensated for all that is taken, be allowed more subsistence per day than the noble veterans who are periling their lives in the cause and at every sacrifice are enduring hardship and exposure in the ranks."

Jefferson Davis, celebrated American statesman and President of the Confederate States of America.

And the general's care and enthusiasm for his officers was as great as for the privates. It is charming to see how earnestly and how specifically he commends them in every report. Particularly, he is anxious to impress upon Lee that no family considerations should prevent the merited advancement of Lee's own son and nephew. Even on his deathbed one of his last wishes was that his faithful followers should have his horses, and he allotted them thoughtfully according to each officer's needs.

The general did not allow his feelings to interfere with subordination, however. His discipline "was as firm as could be with such men as composed the cavalry of General Lee's army," writes Judge [Theodore Stanford] Garnett. "He never tolerated nor overlooked disobedience of orders."

Even his favorites, Mosby and Fitz Lee, come in for reproof when needed. Of the latter's failure to arrive at Raccoon Ford when expected he writes:

> "By this failure to comply with instructions not only the movement of the cavalry across the Rapidan was postponed a day, but a fine opportunity was lost to overhaul a body of the enemy's cavalry on a predatory excursion far beyond their lines."

His tendency to severity in regard to a certain subordinate calls forth one of Lee's gently tactful cautions:

> "I am perfectly willing to transfer him to [Confederate Gen. Elisha Franklin] Paxton's brigade, if he desires it; but if he does not, I know of no act of his to justify my doing so. Do not let your judgment be warped."

There were officers with whom Stuart could not get along; for instance, [Confederate Gen. William Edmundson] "Grumble Jones," who perhaps could get along with no one. Yet, after Stuart's death, Jones said of him:

> "By God, Martin! You know I had little love for Stuart, and he had just as little for me; but that is the greatest loss that army has ever

sustained except the death of Jackson."

From these various considerations it will be surmised that Stuart was no mere reckless sworder, no Rupert, good with sabre, furious in onset, beyond that signifying nothing. He knew the spirit of the antique maxim, "Be bold, and evermore be bold; be not too bold." He had learned the hardest lesson and the essential corrective for such a temperament, self-control. To me there is an immense pathos in his quiet, almost plaintive explanation to Lee, on one occasion:

> "The commanding general will, I am sure, appreciate how hard it was to desist from the undertaking, but to any one on the spot there could be but one opinion—its impossibility. I gave it up."

On the other hand, no one knew better that in some cases perfect prudence and splendid boldness are one and the same thing. To use again his own language:

> "Although the expedition was prosecuted further than was contemplated in your instructions, I feel assured that the considerations which actuated me will convince you that I did not depart from their spirit and that the bold development in the subsequent direction of the march was the quintessence of prudence."

Lee always found the right words. In one of his reports he says of Stuart:

> "I take occasion to express to the Department my sense of the boldness, judgment, and prudence he displayed in its execution."

But one may have self-control without commanding intelligence. [British army Gen. Arthur Lyon] Fremantle's description of Stuart's movements does not suggest much of the latter quality.

> "He seems to roam over the country at his own discretion, and always gives a good account of himself, turning up at the right moment, and hitherto he has not got himself into any serious trouble."

Later, more studious observers do not take quite the same view. One should read the whole of the Prussian colonel Scheibert's account of Stuart's thorough planning, his careful calculation, his exact methods of procedure.

"Before Stuart undertook any movement, he spared nothing in the way of preparation which might make it succeed. He informed himself as exactly as possible by scouts and spies, himself reconnoitered with his staff, often far beyond the outposts, had his engineer officers constantly fill out and improve the rather inadequate maps and ascertain the practicability of roads, fords, etc. In short, he omitted no precaution and spared no pains or effort to secure the best possible results for such undertakings as he planned; therefore he was in the saddle almost as long again as his men."

Similar testimony can be gathered incidentally everywhere in Stuart's letters and reports, proving that he was no chance roamer, but went where he planned to go and came back when he intended. For instance, he writes of the Peninsular operations:

"It is proper to remark here that the commanding general had, on the occasion of my late expedition to the Pamunkey, imparted to me his design of bringing Jackson down upon the enemy's right flank and rear, and directed that I should examine the country with reference to its practicability for such a movement. I therefore had studied the features of the country very thoroughly and knew exactly how to conform my movements to Jackson's route."

On the strength of these larger military qualities it has sometimes been contended that Stuart should have had an even more responsible command than fell to him and that Lee should have retained him at the head of Jackson's corps after Jackson's death. Certainly Lee can have expressed no higher opinion of any one: "A more zealous, ardent, brave and devoted soldier than Stuart the Confederacy cannot have." Johnston called him

"calm, firm, acute, active, and enterprising. I know of no one more competent than he to estimate occurrences at their true value."

[James] Longstreet, hitting Jackson as well as praising Stuart, said:

"His death was possibly a greater loss to the Confederate army than that of the swift-moving General Stonewall Jackson."

Among foreign authorities Scheibert writes that

"General [Karl] von Schmidt, the regenerator of our [Prussian] cavalry tactics, has told me that Stuart was the model cavalry leader of this century and has questioned me very often about his mode of fighting."

And Captain Battine thinks that he should have had Jackson's place. Finally, [Edward Porter] Alexander, sanest of Confederate writers, expresses the same view strongly and definitely:

> "I always thought it an injustice to Stuart and a loss to the army that he was not from that moment continued in command of Jackson's corps. He had won the right to it. I believe he had all of Jackson's genius and dash and originality, without that eccentricity of character which sometimes led to disappointment. Jackson's spirit and inspiration were uneven. Stuart, however, possessed the rare quality of being always equal to himself at his very best."

This is magnificent praise, coming from such a source. Nevertheless, I find it hard to question Lee's judgment. There was nothing in the world to prevent his giving Stuart the position, if he thought him qualified. It is not absolutely certain how Stuart would have carried independent command. I can hardly imagine [Jefferson] Davis, even early in the war, writing of Jackson as he did of Stuart:

> "The letter of General Hill painfully impresses me with that which has before been indicated—a want of vigilance and intelligent observation on the part of General Stuart."

Major Bigelow, who knows the battle of Chancellorsville as well as any one living, does not judge Stuart's action so favorably as Alexander. And [John Esten] Cooke, who adored Stuart and served constantly under him, says:

> "At Chancellorsville, when he succeeded Jackson, the troops, although quite enthusiastic about him, complained that he led them too recklessly against artillery; and it is hard for those who knew the man to believe that, as an army commander, he would have consented to a strictly defensive campaign. Fighting was a necessity of his blood, and the slow movements of infantry did not suit his genius."

May it not be also that Lee thought Stuart indispensable where he was and believed it would be as difficult to replace him as Jackson? Most of Stuart's correspondence has perished and we are obliged to gather its tenor from letters written to him, which is much like listening to a one-sided conversation over the telephone. From one of Lee's letters, however, it is fairly evident that neither he nor Stuart himself had seriously considered the latter's taking Jackson's place. Lee writes:

> "I am obliged to you for your views as to the successor of the great and good Jackson. Unless God in his mercy will raise us up one, I do not know what we shall do. I agree with you on the subject, and have so

expressed myself."

In any event, what his countrymen will always remember of Stuart is the fighting figure, the glory of battle, the sudden and tumultuous fury of charge and onset. And what above all distinguishes him in this is his splendid joy in it. Others fought with clenched fist and set teeth, rejoicing, perhaps, but with deadly determination of lip and brow. He laughed and sang. His blue eyes sparkled and his white teeth gleamed. To others it was the valley of the shadow of death. To him it was a picnic and a pleasure party. He views everything by its picturesque side, catches the theatrical detail which turns terror and death into a scenic surprise.

> "My arrival could not have been more fortunately timed, for, arriving after dark, the ponderous march, with the rolling artillery, must have impressed the enemy's cavalry, watching their rear, with the idea of an immense army about to cut off their retreat."

Confederate Gen. James Longstreet at the Battle of Gettysburg, July 2, 1863.

He rushed gayly into battle, singing, "Old Joe Hooker, won't you come out of the Wilderness?" or his favorite of favorites, "If you want to have a good time, jine the cavalry." When he is riding off, as it were into the mouth of hell, his adjutant asks, "How long?" and he answers, as Touchstone might, with a bit of old ballad, "It may be for years and it may be for ever."

His clear laughter, in the sternest crises, echoes through dusty war books, like a silver bell. As he sped back from his Peninsular raid, the Union troops were close upon him and the swollen Chickahominy in front, impassable, it seemed. Stuart thought a moment, pulling at his beard. Then he found the remains of an old bridge and set his men to rebuild it.

> "While the men were at work upon it, Stuart was lying down on the bank of the stream, in the gayest humor I ever saw, laughing at the prank he had played on McClellan."

It is needless to enlarge on the effect of such a temper, such exuberant confidence and cheerfulness in danger, on subordinates. It lightened labor, banished fatigue, warmed chill limbs and fainting courage. "My men and horses are tired, hungry, jaded, but all right," was the last despatch he ever wrote. So long as he was with them, they were all right. His very voice was like music, says Fitz Lee, "like the silver trumpet of the Archangel." It sounded oblivion of everything but glory. His gaiety, his laughter, were infectious and turned a raid into a revel. [Writes Mosby of the McClellan expedition:]

> "That summer night was a carnival of fun I can never forget. Nobody thought of danger or sleep, when champagne bottles were bursting and wine was flowing in copious streams. All had perfect confidence in their leader. . . . The discipline of the soldiers for a while gave way to the wild revelry of Comus."

And this spirit of adventure, of romance, of buoyant optimism and energy, was not merely reserved for occasions of excitement, was not the triumphant outcome of glory and success. It was constant and unfailing. To begin with, Stuart had a magnificent physique. "Nothing seemed strong enough to break down his powerful organization of mind and body," says his biographer; and Mosby: "Although he had been in the saddle two days and nights without sleep, he was as gay as a lark." When exhaustion finally fell upon him, he would drop off his horse by the roadside, anywhere, sleep for an hour, and arise as active as ever. Universal testimony proves that he was overcome and disheartened by no disaster. He would be thoughtful for a moment, pulling at his beard, then seize upon the best decision that presented itself and push on. Dreariness sometimes crushes those who can well resist actual misfortune. Not Stuart.

Confederate Col. John S. Mosby.

> "In the midst of rainstorms, when everybody was riding along glum and cowering beneath the flood pouring down, he would trot on, head up, and singing gayly."

The list of his personal adventures and achievements is endless.

He braved capture and death with entire indifference, trusting in his admirable horsemanship, which often saved him, trusting in Providence, trusting in nothing at all but his quick wit and strong arm, curious mainly, perhaps, to see what would happen. On one occasion he is said to have captured forty-four Union soldiers. He was riding absolutely alone and ran into them taking their ease in a field. Instantly he chose his course. "Throw down your arms or you are all dead men." They were green troops and threw down their arms, and Stuart marched the whole squad into camp. When duty forbids a choice adventure, he sighs, as might Don Quixote:

> "A scouting party of one hundred and fifty lancers had just passed toward Gettysburg. I regretted exceedingly that my march did not admit of the delay necessary to catch them."

"Three Heroes." From left to right: Stonewall Jackson, Robert E. Lee, and Jeb Stuart, on the morning of the Battle of Fredericksburg.

I have sometimes asked myself how much of this spirit of romantic adventure, of knight-errantry, as it were, in Stuart was conscious. Did he, like [John Graham of] Claverhouse, read Homer and [Jean] Froissart, and try to realize in modern Virginia the heroic deeds, still more, the heroic spirit, of antique chivalry? In common with all Southerners, he probably knew the prose and poetry of [Walter] Scott and dreamed of the plume of Marmion and the lance of Ivanhoe. He must have felt the weight of his name, also, and believed that "James Stuart" might be aptly fitted with valorous adventure, and knightly deeds, and sudden glory. It is extremely interesting to find him writing to Jackson: "Did you receive the volume of Napoleon and his Maxims I sent you?" I should like to own that volume. And in his newspaper account of [John] Brown's raid he quotes Horace, horribly, but still Horace: *Erant fortes ante*

Agamemnona ("Brave men lived before Agamemnon").

Yet I do not gather that he was much of a student. He preferred to live poems rather than read them. The spirit of romance, the instinct of the picturesque, was born in him and would out anywhere and everywhere. Life was a perpetual play, with ever shifting scenes, and gay limelight, and hurrying incident, and passionate climax. Again and again he reminds me of a boy playing soldiers. His ambition, his love of glory, was of this order, not a bit the ardent, devouring, frowning, far-sighted passion of Jackson, but a jovial sense of pleasant things that can be touched and heard and tasted here, to-day. He had a childlike, simple vanity which all his biographers smile at, liked parade, display, and pomp and gorgeousness, utterly differing in this from Jackson, who was too proud, or Lee, who was too lofty. Stuart rode fine horses, never was seen on an inferior animal. He wore fine clothes, all that his position justified, perhaps a little more. Here is Fitz Lee's picture of him:

> "His strong figure, his big brown beard, his piercing, laughing blue eyes, the drooping hat and black feather, the 'fighting jacket' as he termed it, the tall cavalry boots, forming one of the most jubilant and striking figures in the war."

And Cooke is even more particular:

> "His fighting jacket shone with dazzling buttons and was covered with gold braid; his hat was looped up with a golden star, and decorated with a black ostrich plume; his fine buff gauntlets reached to the elbow; around his waist was tied a splendid yellow sash, and his spurs were of pure gold."

After this, we appreciate the biographer's assertion that Stuart was as fond of colors as a boy or girl, and elsewhere we read that he never moved without his gorgeous red battle-flag which often drew the fire of the enemy.

As to the spurs, they were presented to the general by the ladies of Baltimore and he took great pride in them, signing himself sometimes in his private letters, K.G.S., Knight of the Golden Spurs.

This last touch is perfectly characteristic and the Stuart of the pen is precisely the same as the Stuart of the sword. He could express himself as simply as Napoleon:

> "Tell General Lee that all is right. Jackson has not advanced, but I have; and I am going to crowd them with artillery."

But usually he did not. Indeed, the severe taste of Lee recoiled from his subordinate's fashions of speech:

> "The general deals in the flowery style, as you will perceive, if you ever see his reports in detail."

But I love them, they ring and resound so with the temper of the man, gorgeous scraps of tawdry rhetoric, made charming by their riotous sincerity, as with [Walter] Scott and [Alexandre] Dumas.

> "Their brave men behaved with coolness and intrepidity in danger, unswerving resolution before difficulties, and stood unappalled before the rushing torrent of the Chickahominy, with the probability of an enemy at their heels armed with the fury of a tigress robbed of her whelps."

Could anything be worse from Lee's point of view? But it does put some life into an official report.

Or take this Homeric picture of a charge, which rushes like a half dozen stanzas of "Chevy Chase":

> "Lieutenant Robbins [or Robins], handling it in the most skillful manner, managed to clear the way for the march with little delay, and infused by a sudden dash at a picket such a wholesome terror that it never paused to take a second look. . . . On, on dashed Robbins, here skirting a field, there leaping a fence or ditch, and clearing the woods beyond."

When I read these things, I cannot but remember Madame de Sévigné's fascinating comment on the historical novels of her day.

> "The style of La Calprenède is detestable in a thousand ways: long-winded, romantic phrases, ill-chosen words, I admit it all. I agree that it is detestable; yet it holds me like glue. The beauty of the sentiments, the violence of the passions, the grandeur of the events, and the miraculous success of the hero's redoubtable sword—it sweeps me away as if I were a child."

And Stuart's was a real sword!

Then, too, as in Shakespearean tragedy or modern melodrama, the tension, in Stuart's case, is constantly relieved by hearty, wholesome, cheery laughter, which shook his broad shoulders and sparkled in his blue eyes. See what a strange comedy his report makes of this lurid night scene, in which another might have found only shadow and death:

> "It so far succeeded as to get possession of his [Union General Joseph Jackson Bartlett's] headquarters at one o'clock at night, the general having saved himself by precipitate flight in his nether garments. The headquarters flag was brought away. No prisoners were attempted to be taken, the party shooting down every one within reach. Some horses breaking loose near headquarters ran through an adjacent regimental camp, causing the greatest commotion, mid firing and yelling and cries of 'Halt!' 'Rally!' mingling in wild disorder, and ludicrous stampede which beggars description."

Can't you hear him laugh?

It must not be concluded from this that Stuart was cruel in his jesting. Where gentleness and sympathy were really called for, all the evidence shows that no man could give more. But he believed that the rough places are made smooth and the hard places soft and the barren places green and smiling by genial laughter. Who shall say that he was wrong? Therefore he would have his jest, with inferior and superior, with friend and enemy. Even the sombre Jackson was not spared. Once he had floundered into winter-quarters oddly decorated. Stuart suggested

> "that a drawing of the apartment should be made, with the race-horses, gamecocks, and terrier in bold relief, the picture to be labelled: 'View of the winter quarters of General Jackson, affording an insight into the tastes and character of the individual.'"

And Jackson enjoyed it.

When it came to his adversaries, Stuart's fun was unlimited. Everybody knows his telegraphed complaint to the United States Commissary Department that the mules he had been getting lately were most unsatisfactory and he wished they would provide a better quality. Even more amusing is the correspondence that occurred at Lewinsville. One of Stuart's old comrades [Union Gen. Orlando Metcalfe Poe] wrote, addressing him by his West Point nickname.

> "My dear Beauty, I am sorry that circumstances are such that I can't have the pleasure of seeing you, although so near you. [Union Gen. Charles] Griffin says he would like to have you dine with him at Willard's at 5 o'clock on Saturday next. Keep your Black Horse [Cavalry] off me, if you please. Yours, etc., Orlando M. Poe."

On the back of this was penciled in Stuart's writing:

"I have the honor to report that 'circumstances' were such that they could have seen me if they had stopped to look behind, and I answered both at the cannon's mouth. Judging from his speed, Griffin surely left for Washington to hurry up that dinner."

U.S. Col. (later Gen.) Orlando Metcalfe Poe (left) and U.S. Col. Orville E. Babcock (right) at Fort Sanders, Knoxville, TN, circa 1863. Poe and Stuart engaged in playful but deadly correspondence during the War.

I had an old friend who adored the most violent melodrama. When the curtain and his tears had fallen together, he would sigh and murmur, "Now let's have a little of that snare-drum music." Such was Stuart. "It might almost be said that music was his passion," writes his biographer.

I doubt, however, whether he dealt largely in the fugues of Bach. His favorites, in the serious order, are said to have been "The Dew is on the Blossom," and "Sweet Evelina." But his joy was the uproarious "If You Get There Before I Do"; or his precious "If You Want to Have a Good Time, Jine the Cavalry." He liked to live in the blare of trumpets and the crash of cymbals, liked to have his nerves tingle and his blood leap to a merry hunts-up or a riotous chorus, liked to have the high strain of war's melodrama broken by the sudden crackle of the snare-drum. His banjo-player, [Joe] Sweeney, was as near to him as an aide-de-camp, followed him everywhere.

"Stuart wrote his most important correspondence with the rattle of the gay instrument stunning everybody, and would turn round from his work, burst into a laugh, and join uproariously in Sweeney's chorus."

Stuart enjoyed both song and dance, especially when it included "pretty girls."

And dance was as keen a spice to peril as song and laughter. To fight all day and dance all night was a good day's work to this creature of perfect physique and inexhaustible energy. If his staff officers could not keep pace with him and preferred a little sleep, the general did not like it at all. What? Here is—or was—a gay town, and pretty girls. Just because we are here to-day and gone to-morrow, shall we not fleet the time carelessly, as they did in the golden world? And the girls are got together, and a ball is organized, and the fun grows swifter and swifter. Perhaps a fortunate officer picks the prettiest and is about to stand up with her. Stuart whispers in his ear that a hurried message must be carried, laughs his gay laugh, and slips into the vacant place. Then an orderly hurries in, covered with dust. The enemy are upon us.

> "The officers rushed to their weapons and called for their horses, panic-stricken fathers and mothers endeavored to collect around them their bewildered children, while the young ladies ran to and fro in most admired despair. General Stuart maintained his accustomed coolness and composure. Our horses were immediately saddled, and in less than five minutes we were in rapid gallop to the front."

Oh, what a life!

You divine that with such a temperament Stuart would love women. So he did. Not that he let them interfere with duty. He would have heartily accepted the profound doctrine of Enobarbus in regard to the fair:

> "It were pity to cast them away for nothing; yet between them and a great cause they should be esteemed as nothing."

Stuart arrested [that is, captivated] hundreds of ladies, says his biographer, and remained inexorable to their petitions. Cooke's charming account of one of these arrests should be read in full: how the fair captives first raved, and then listened, and then laughed, and then were charmed by the mellifluous Sweeney and the persuasive general, and at last departed with kissed hands and kindly hearts, leaving Stuart to explain to his puzzled aide, who inquired why he took so much pains:

> "Don't you understand? When those ladies arrived they were mad enough with me to bite my head off, and I determined to put them in good humor before they left me."

But Cooke dresses his viands. I prefer the following taste of Stuart and girls and duty, as we get it unspiced from the rough-spoken common soldier:

> "General Lee would come up and spend hours studying the situation with his splendid [field] glasses; and the glorious Stuart would dash up, always with a lady, and a pretty one, too. I wonder if the girl is yet alive who rode the general's fine horse and raced with him to charge our station. When they had reached the level platform, and Stuart had left her in care of one of us and took the other off to one side and questioned the very sweat out of him about the enemy's position, he was General Stuart then, but when he got back and lifted the beauty into the saddle and rode off humming a breezy air . . . he was Stuart the beau."

And the women liked Stuart. It was a grand thing to be the first officer in the Confederate cavalry, with a blue eye and a fair beard, and all gold, like Horace's Lydia, from hat to spurs. When he rode singing and laughing into a little town, "by river or seashore," they flocked to meet him, young and old, and touched his garments, and begged his buttons and kissed his gloved hands, until he suggested that his cheeks were available, and then they kissed those, young and old alike.

They showered him with flowers also, buried him under nosegays and garlands, till he rode like old god Bacchus or the queen of May. What an odd fashion of making war! And the best I have met with is, that one day Stuart described one of these occurrences to his great chieftain.

"I had to wear her garland, till I was out of sight," apologized the young cavalier.

"Why aren't you wearing it now?" retorted Lee.

Isn't that admirable? I verily believe that if any young woman had had the unimaginable audacity to throw a garland over Lee, he would have worn it through the streets of Richmond itself.

You say, then, this Stuart was dissipated, perhaps, a scapegrace, a rioter, imitating Rupert and Murat in other things than great

Stuart took his responsibilities to his country, the C.S.A., seriously—even placing them over his own family.

cavalry charges. That is the curious point. The man was nothing of the sort. With all his instinct of revelry, he had no vices, a very Puritan of laughter. He liked pretty girls everywhere; but when he was charged with libertinism, he answered, in the boldness of innocence, "That person does not live who can say that I ever did anything improper of that description"; and he liked his wife [Flora] better than any other pretty girl. He married her when he was twenty-two years old and his last wish was that she might reach him before he died. His few letters to her that have been printed are charming in their playful affection. He adored his children also; in short, was a pattern of domesticity. He did, indeed, love his country more, and telegraphed to his wife, when she called him to his dying daughter's [also named Flora] bedside, "My duty to the country must be performed before I can give way to the feelings of a father"; but the child's death was a cruel blow to him. With his intimates he constantly referred to her, and when he himself was dying, he whispered, "I shall soon be with my little Flora again."

"I never saw him touch a card," writes one who was very near him," and he never dreamed of uttering an oath [an expletive] under any provocation, nor would he permit it at his headquarters." We are assured by many that he never drank and an explicit statement of his own on the subject is reported:

> "I promised my mother in my childhood never to touch ardent spirits and a drop has never passed my lips, except the wine of the communion."

As the last words show, he had religion as well as morals. He joined the Methodist church when he was fifteen; later the Episcopal. When he was twenty-four, he sent money home to his mother to aid in the building of a church. He carried his Bible with him always. In his reports religion is not obtrusive. When it does occur, it is evidently sincere. [Wrote Stuart:]

> "The Lord of Hosts was plainly fighting on our side, and the solid walls of Federal infantry melted away before the straggling, but nevertheless

determined, onset of our infantry columns. . . . Believing that the hand of God was clearly manifested in the signal deliverance of my command from danger, and the crowning success attending it, I ascribe to Him the praise, the honor, and the glory."

He inclined to strictness in the observance of Sunday. Captain Colston writes me that when twelve struck of a Saturday night Stuart held up his hand relentlessly and stopped song and dance in their full tide, though youth and beauty begged for just one more. He was equally scrupulous in the field, though, in his feeling of injury because the enemy were not, I seem to detect his habitual touch of humor:

> "The next morning being the Sabbath, I recognized my obligation to do no duty other than what was absolutely necessary, and determined, so far as possible, to devote it to rest. Not so the enemy, whose guns about 8 A.M. showed that he would not observe it."

I have no doubt that Stuart's religion was inward as well as outward and remoulded his heart. But, after all, he was but little over thirty when he died, and I love to trace in him the occasional working of the old Adam which had such lively play in the bosom of many an officer who was unjustly blamed or missed some well-deserved promotion. Stuart's own letters are too few to afford much insight of this kind. But here again we get that one-sided correspondence with Lee which is so teasingly suggestive. On one occasion Lee writes:

> "The expression 'appropriated by the Stuart Horse Artillery' was not taken from a report of Colonel Baldwin, nor intended in any objectionable sense, but used for want of a better phrase, without any intention on my part of wounding."

And again, after Chancellorsville:

> "As regards the closing remarks of your note, I am at a loss to understand their reference or to know what has given rise to them. In the management of the difficult operations at Chancellorsville, which you so promptly undertook and creditably performed, I saw no errors to correct, nor has there been a fit opportunity to commend your conduct. I prefer your acts to speak for themselves, nor does your character or reputation require bolstering up by out-of-place expressions of my opinion."

But by far the most interesting human revelation of this kind is one letter of Stuart's own, written to justify himself against some aspersions of [Confederate] General [Isaac Ridgeway] Trimble. With the right or wrong of the case we are not concerned; simply with the fascinating study of Stuart's state of mind. He begins evidently with firm restraint and a Christian moderation: "Human memory is frail I know." But the exposure of his wrongs heats his blood, as he goes on, and spurs him, though he still endeavors to check himself:

> "It is true I am not in the habit of giving orders, particularly to my seniors in years, in a dictatorial and authoritative manner, and my manner very likely on this occasion was more restive than imperative; indeed, I may have been content to satisfy myself that the dispositions which he himself proposed accorded with my own ideas, without any blustering show of orders to do this or that. . . .
>
> General Trimble says I did not reach the place until seven or eight o'clock. I was in plain view all the time, and rode through, around, and all about the place soon after its capture. General Trimble is mistaken."

Nay, in his stammering eagerness to right himself, his phrases, usually so crisp and clear, stumble and fall over each other:

> "In the face of General Trimble's positive denial of sending me such a message, 'that he would prefer waiting until daylight,' or anything like it, while my recollection is clear that I did receive such a message, and received it as coming from General Trimble.
>
> "Yet, as he is so positive to not having sent such a message or anything like it, I feel bound to believe that either the message was misrepresented or made up by the messenger, or that it was a message received from General [Beverly Holcombe] Robertson, whose sharpshooters had been previously deployed."

Gen. Beverly H. Robertson, C.S.A.

Photo of a Virginia church, circa 1864. Stuart was able to combine intense religiosity with a casual sense of playfulness and cheerfulness, much to the delight of his soldiers.

A real man, you see, like the rest of us; but a noble one, and lovable. Fortunate, also, in his death as in his life. For he was not shot down in the early days, like Jackson and Sidney Johnston, when it seemed as if his great aid might have changed destiny. He had done all a man in his position could do. When he went, hope too was going. He was spared the long, weary days of Petersburg, spared the bitter cup of Appomattox, spared the cruel domination of the conqueror, spared what was perhaps worst of all, the harsh words and reproaches which flew too hotly where there should have been nothing but love and silence. He slept untroubled in his glory, while his countrymen mourned and Lee "yearned for him." His best epitaph has been written by a magnanimous opponent [Union Gen. Theophilus Francis Rodenbough]:

> "Deep in the hearts of all true cavalrymen, North and South, will ever burn a sentiment of admiration mingled with regret for this knightly soldier and generous man."[153] — GAMALIEL BRADFORD, AMERICAN BIOGRAPHER FROM BOSTON, MA.

Soldiers' prayer meeting, with Gen. Lee standing left of center (with right hand on hip). Religion was an important part of Confederate camp life. Despite being passionate Christians, Southern leaders like Stuart, Lee, and Jackson were not religiously biased. Instead, they accepted and welcomed all Christian denominations, and even Judaism, into their armies.

CHAPTER 4

THE LIFE OF JEB STUART

☞ Perhaps the best-remembered figure of the war in Virginia from its uniqueness and brilliancy was that of Stuart and his brave troopers scouring the country, making magnificent surprises of the enemy, always startling the public with sudden apparitions, and bounding the most distant parts of the chief theatre of war with a luminous track of romance and adventure. Nearly everybody in Northern Virginia had at some time or other seen the commander, and obtained the impression of a face and figure not easily forgotten. The drooping hat, caught up with a star and decorated with an ebon plume; the tall cavalry boots decked with golden spurs; the "fighting jacket"; the magnificent charger, mud-splashed from head to foot, were all familiar objects—the popular marks of the famous cavalier.

The badge of West Point graduates in the mid 1800s, bearing the arms of the U.S. Academy with a gold bar containing the date of the graduate's class.

He had a face to be remembered. Beneath a lofty forehead were brilliant blue eyes, which, when lighted up, were piercing and full of deep expression. A heavy beard covered the lower part of his face; a huge moustache gave some fierceness to the expression, but curled at the least provocation with contagious laughter; a ruddy complexion and dancing eyes told of high health and the exuberant vitality of the man. He had a gay careless manner which greeted with indifference "the thunder or the sunshine."

Full of ready jest; always in for a frolic; fond of practical jokes; attended in camp by the thrum of the banjo; often waking up the little country towns on his march for impromptu balls and merry-makings; as ready for an opossum-hunt as for a battle; with all sorts of odds and ends in his train, including a French cook, [Joe]

Sweeney, Jr., of the banjo, and a Prussian adjutant; the idol of the country belles who "followed his feather," and among whom he distributed complimentary commissions as his "lieutenants," there was an appearance of lightness in the young man, not yet turned his thirtieth year; and in the midst of so much of what we must call downright frivolity, one would have scarcely recognized the cavalry commander who filled the whole country with the fame of his sword and was the eyes and ears of Gen. Lee's army. It is a unique figure and character, in which we introduce one of the most brilliant and exceptional men of the war.

Before the War for the Constitution (1861-1865), as a U.S. soldier Stuart was at one time engaged in "active service against the frontier Indians" while stationed in the Western states.

James E. B. Stuart was born in Patrick County, Virginia; graduated at West Point in 1854; and saw his first active [U.S.] military service in the wilds of New Mexico, where he had abundant opportunity of indulging his inclination in riding and fighting; and no doubt got much of the roving, dashing, adventurous habit apparent in his future career. In the John Brown affair at Harper's Ferry, he was acting as [Robert E.] Lee's aide, and it was his sword that brought the outlaw to the ground. On accepting the service of the Confederate States, in the war of which [socialist] John Brown was messenger and prophet, Stuart was sent with the rank of lieutenant-colonel to command a small body of cavalry in the valley of Virginia, then within the department of Gen. J. E. Johnston. In this campaign, in which Johnston foiled [Union Gen. Francis Engle] Patterson and succeeded in transferring his army to Manassas, Stuart did most important service, watching the enemy with lynx-eyed vigilance, moving to and fro on his front, picketing the Potomac from the Blue Ridge to the Alleghenies, and hanging on his march as he advanced towards Winchester.

On one occasion he surprised a whole company of Patterson's green soldiers in rather amusing circumstances. With a handful of horsemen he came upon a company of skirmishers gathered in about a farm-house, the tired volunteers having stacked their arms in the fence corners, and betaken themselves to drinking milk and other pleasant and nonchalant occupations. Stuart rode boldly up to the house, exciting such little suspicion, that a civil soldier, having no idea of an enemy in the vicinity, and supposing that he was obliging a Federal officer, jumped forward and let down the bars that admitted the horsemen into the yard. The next moment there was a yell, a flourish of drawn pistols, and the astonished milk-drinking skirmishers found themselves prisoners of war, and were carried off in sight of the main army.

At another time a [Union] Capt. Perkins, of Patterson's army, commanding a battery of light artillery, was riding carelessly about half a mile in advance of his battery. He was suddenly accosted by three officers, one of whom exclaimed in a familiar voice and manner: "Hallo, Perk, I'm glad to see you; what are you doing here?" The captain, recognizing in the speaker his old West Point chum, J. E. B. Stuart, returned the salute heartily, recalling his college sobriquet: "Why, Beauty, how are you? I didn't know you were with us." "Nor did I know you were on our side," replied Stuart. "What command have yon?"

"There's my command coming over the hill," replied Perkins, pointing complacently to the well-equipped battery that was approaching with Federal colours displayed. "Oh, the devil!" exclaimed Stuart, wheeling suddenly and plunging into the forest. "Good-bye, Perk."

The adventurous Confederate might have taken another prisoner here, as there were two aides with him, and Perkins was alone; but it had been a mutual mistake, and Stuart, in his generous and high humour, forbore to take advantage of an old comrade's inadvertency.

After the battle of Manassas, in which he was mentioned by [Confederate] Gen. Beauregard for "enterprise and ability," Stuart was made a Brigadier-General, and did hard work on the Fairfax line. He continued in Northern Virginia under Gen. Johnston, who had remarked him in the Valley campaign, and then designated him as "the indefatigable Stuart." Such, indeed, was the confidence he secured that when, at a much later period of the war, Gen. Johnston was transferred from Virginia to the Department of the West, the distinguished commander was induced to exclaim: "How can I eat, or sleep, or rest in peace, without Stuart on the outpost!" But by this time Stuart, ascending in reputation, had obtained a division, then a corps, and was indispensable in the great campaigns of Lee, whose right-hand man he became.

In December, 1861, while on the lines of the Potomac, Stuart met with a serious disaster in an affair called by exaggeration the battle of Dranesville, where the Federals gained their first success since Rich Mountain. He had set out with a large foraging force of about 2,500 men, escorting nearly 300 wagons. He was successful in securing forage, and about midday of the 20th December, arrived near Dranesville. On the same day, a foraging force of the enemy had marched to the same neighbourhood. It consisted of [Union] Gen. [Edward Otho Cresap] Ord's brigade—four full regiments of "Bucktail rifles," and some artillery—in all, at least 3,500 men. A rocket shot up by the enemy gave to the Confederates the first intimation of their presence. They were deployed in heavy clouds of skirmishers in the woods.

A young Stonewall Jackson.

To give his wagon-train time to retreat in safety, Gen. Stuart instantly prepared for battle. He was taken at disadvantage; the enemy, in superior force, occupied a strong position, and was sheltered by the woods; the Confederate artillery could gain no position except by advancing right up the road. The consequence was that Stuart's command was thrown into disorder; and after an irregular fight, he ordered a retreat, having, however, saved his wagon-train, and the enemy making no attempt to pursue him. His loss in killed and wounded was about 200 men.

The adventure which gave Stuart his first instalment of brilliant reputation was his famous "ride around McClellan," on the Richmond lines. He had already done excellent service in the preceding campaigns, operating in front of the enemy towards Arlington Heights, and covering the rear of Johnston's army when it fell back from Centreville. He had now become the chief cavalry leader of the war. On the 13th, 14th, and 15th June, 1861, with portions of the First, Fourth, and Ninth Virginia cavalry, a part of the Jeff Davis Legion, with whom were the Boykin Rangers and a section of the Stuart horse artillery, the daring commander made a reconnoissance between the Pamunkey and Chickahominy Rivers, and succeeded in passing around the rear of the whole of the Federal army, routing the enemy in a series of skirmishes, taking a number of prisoners, and destroying and capturing stores to a large amount. He lost but one man on the perilous circuit.

On his return he came upon the Chickahominy below all the bridges, and where deepwater flowed. He found it impossible to cross his command. It was a desperate suspense. The enemy had blocked up all the main roads, and had thousands scouring the country, eager to entrap the daring cavalier. He was but two miles from McClellan's headquarters. In the darkness of night cavalryman after cavalryman essayed to swim the river. Not more than fifty succeeded in getting over, and as they stood on the opposite bank, a strange but friendly voice whispered in the dark: "The old bridge is a few yards higher up; it can be mended."

The men on the other side caught at the new hope, and soon found the wrecked bridge. It was severe work; tree after tree was felled; earth, and twigs, and branches were carried and piled up on the main props; old logs were rolled and patched across the stream; and after long and weary labour the bridge was built, and the silent procession of cavalry, artillery, prisoners, and spoils, safely and quietly passed on the frail, impromptu support, scarcely any sounds being heard but the rush of waters beneath.

Once across, and as the rising sun crimsoned the tree tops, the command, seeking the shade of the woods, plunged through the last lines of the enemy, dashed into the open ground, and, speeding along the Charles City road, were soon in sight of the Confederate pickets.

The audacity of this enterprise delighted the people of Richmond, and they were especially pleased with the annoyance it caused the enemy. It was said that McClellan had got "his rear well spanked," and that the castigation was a proper prelude to his more severe punishment in the coming battle. There is no doubt the expedition was designed by Gen. Lee to discover all the positions of McClellan preparatory to the decisive battle, and that the information it obtained was more important than the *éclat* reckoned by the popular applause.

In referring some time afterwards to the perils of the expedition, especially when it confronted the swollen waters of the Chickahominy, fifteen feet deep, with an aroused enemy in the rear, one of Stuart's officers said: "It was a tight place, General. I expected the column to be attacked at any moment, and we might have been destroyed without the possibility of retreat!" "One thing was left," replied Stuart. "What?" "To die game!"

Stuart's gauntlets.

After the battles of Richmond, when Jackson was about to make his famous advance on Manassas, Stuart was required to place his cavalry on his flanks. Leaving his pleasant headquarters in the grassy yard of the old Hanover Court House, he hastened to put his column in motion for the head-waters of the Rapidan. On Jackson's march to Manassas, Stuart was on the right of the Confederate column, with a cordon of pickets, and a network of scouting parties, scouring the whole region. To penetrate his chain of vedettes in any important movement was next to impossible, a task which the enemy often attempted without effect. But Gen. Stuart was not as careful of his personal safety as he might and should have been, and in this respect he was constantly running the narrowest risks.

One of these personal adventures happened on this expedition, and he barely escaped with his life.

Attended by only a portion of his staff, he had ridden to Verdiersville, a small settlement on the road from Orange Court House to Chancellorsville, where he expected to be joined by Fitzhugh Lee's brigade of cavalry. Awaiting this portion of his command Gen. Stuart, attended by his few companions, passed the night in the village, the commander sleeping in the porch of one of the houses. About this time the country was very much infested by prowling detachments of Federal cavalry.

In the early morning, Stuart, who had just awakened from his sleep, descried a body of cavalry coming up the road. He supposed it to be the head of Fitzhugh Lee's column, but, not without momentary uneasiness, he called to [Confederate] Capt. [John Singleton] Mosby (afterwards so famous as a partisan, and who kept some of the upper counties of Virginia so clear of the enemy that they were designated "Mosby's Confederacy") to observe the approaching horsemen. Mosby had just walked to the gate of the inclosure, when a volley of bullets whistled over his head, and gave all the information that was desired.

By the time the cavalrymen had galloped to the fence a few swift steps had brought Stuart to the side of his favourite mare "Skylark," grazing in the yard, and, seizing the halter, without bridle or saddle, on the bare back of the horse, he leaped the inclosure, cleared the open ground under a shower of bullets, and, digging the spurs into the sides of the noble animal, shot towards the forest with the speed of an arrow, and was soon lost in the cover of the woods. He left behind him, on the porch where he had rested, the cape of his overcoat; and, lying near it, a brown hat, looped up with a golden star, and decorated with a floating black feather, was evidence to the Federal cavalrymen of the strange and noble game that had escaped them.

Just one week after this adventure, when [Union Gen. John] Pope was hastily retiring before Lee's column, Gen. Stuart made an expedition to the enemy's rear, and struck the Orange and Alexandria Railroad at Catlett's Station. It was a complete surprise of the enemy in a dark and stormy night. Without light enough to see their hands before them, the attacking column plunged forward at full speed through ditches and ravines, overrunning the enemy's baggage train, burning his wagons, and creating an indescribable confusion.

As chance would have it, Stuart came upon Pope's headquarters just in time to find that that General had fled from the scene, in such hurry and disorder, however, as to leave his plans and papers, and among other things, his uniform coat, which Stuart at once seized in restitution for the cape and hat he had lost at Verdiersville. It was more than a fair equivalent for the adventure at the latter place. The captured papers were sent to Lee, and the coat reserved for exhibition in Richmond as a trophy of the raid. It was placed in a shop-window there, with a label attached to it, on which Stuart wrote: "Taken from the man who said he never expected to see anything but the backs of rebels."

After the exhausting campaign of the summer of 1862, terminating on the field of Sharpsburg, both armies rested for a brief period. Gen. Stuart had inaugurated a policy of raids in these intervals between the great contestants; and as it was advisable to beat up the quarters of the enemy, he was sent in October, with 1,800 men, and four pieces of artillery, to essay a second ride around McClellan. At daylight on the 10th October he crossed the Potomac, between Williamsport and Hancock, proceeded by a rapid march to Chambersburg, Pennsylvania, which he reached at dark on the same day, captured the place and destroyed the machine shops and railroad buildings, containing large numbers of arms and other public stores.

From Chambersburg Gen. Stuart decided, after mature consideration, to strike for the vicinity of Leesburg, as the best route of return, particularly as the enemy's presence would have rendered the direction of Cumberland, full of mountain gorges, exceedingly hazardous. The route selected was through an open country. Of course the wily commander left nothing undone to prevent the inhabitants from detecting his real route and object. He started directly towards Gettysburg, but, having passed the Blue Ridge, turned back towards Hagerstown [MD] for six or eight miles, and then crossed to Maryland by Emmitsburg, where, as his troopers passed, they were hailed by the inhabitants with the most enthusiastic demonstrations of joy.

Gen. John Pope, U.S.A.

Taking the route towards Frederick [MD], Gen. Stuart intercepted some dispatches directed to Washington, which satisfied him that his whereabouts was still a problem to the enemy. He now took the bold resolution of passing entirely around the Federal army, and cutting his way through to the ford near Leesburg. Moving with the utmost rapidity, he reached Hyattstown [MD], below Frederick, at daylight on the morning of the 12th, and pushing on towards Poolesville [MD], found that the road in that direction was barred by [Union] Gen. [George] Stoneman with about 5,000 troops, and that railroad trains were standing ready, with steam up, and loaded with infantry, to move instantly to the point where he attempted to cross.

Making a circuit through the woods, and guarding well his flanks and rear, Stuart avoided the town, and, pushing boldly forward, met the head of the enemy's force going towards Poolesville, at a point near White's ford. Quick as thought, Stuart's sharpshooters sprang to the ground, while the charging cavalry cut through the enemy's lines; and with Pelham's guns on a high crest screening the movement, Stuart made a bold and rapid stroke for the ford. The passage of the river was effected with all the precision of passing a defile on drill. All the results of the expedition were accomplished, without the loss of a single man killed.

The march, in respect of rapidity, is perhaps without a parallel in the record of the war. The distance from Chambersburg to Leesburg, ninety miles, was accomplished with only one hour's halt, in thirty-six hours, including a forced passage of the Potomac. In his official narration of his success, Gen. Stuart wrote:

> "We seized and brought over a large number of horses, the property of citizens of the United States. The valuable information obtained in this reconnoissance, as to the distribution of the enemy's force, was communicated orally to the Commanding General, and need not be here repeated. A number of public functionaries and prominent citizens were taken captive and brought over as hostages for our own unoffending citizens, whom the enemy had torn from their homes, and confined in dungeons in the North. The results of this expedition, in a moral and political point of view, can hardly be estimated, and the consternation among property-holders in Pennsylvania was beyond description. . . . Believing that the hand of God was clearly manifested in the signal deliverance of my command from danger, and the crowning success attending it, I ascribe to Him the praise, the honour, and the glory."

In the battle of Fredericksburg, Stuart's command was more conspicuous than it had ever before been on a single field. Acting in conjunction with [Stonewall] Jackson, his horse artillery was called into play; and it was at one time designed by Gen. Jackson, strengthened by this rapid and effective arm in his front, to make a final attempt to dislodge the enemy into the river. About the close of the day, when one of Gen. Lee's aides rode up to ascertain how things were going on in this direction, Stuart replied:

> "Tell Gen. Lee that all is right. Jackson has not advanced, but I have; and I am going to crowd them with artillery."

The attack designed by Jackson was not made; but Stuart did not retire his guns until dark, when no response could be elicited from the enemy's artillery, and the Confederates remained masters of the bloody field.

[Note by Pollard:] Fredericksburg was the ghastliest field of the war. One of Stuart's staff, who traversed the ground with the burial parties, has given a picture of it that has not been excelled in its vivid realization of the horrours of war. The reader, accustomed to brilliant views of war, interwoven with noble and chivalric deeds, will pause here to lift the embroidery and see what it covers:

"On a space of ground not over two acres we counted 680 dead bodies; and more than 1,200 altogether were found on the small plain between the heights and Fredericksburg, those nearest the town having mostly been killed by our artillery, which had played with dreadful effect upon the enemy's dense columns. More than one-half of these dead had belonged to [Union Gen. Thomas Francis] Meagher's brave Irish brigade, which was nearly annihilated during the several attacks. A number of the houses which we entered presented a horrid spectacle—dead and wounded intermingled in thick masses. The latter, in a deplorable state from want of food and care, were cursing their own [Yankee] cause, friends, and commander-in-chief, for the sufferings they endured. As we walked slowly along, [Confederate] Capt. Phillips suddenly pressed my arm, and, pointing to the body of a soldier whose head was so frightfully wounded that part of the brain was protruding, broke out with, 'Great God, that man is still living!' And so he was. Hearing our steps the unfortunate sufferer opened his glassy eyes and looked at us with so pitiable an expression that I could not for long after recall it without shuddering. A surgeon being close at hand, was at once called to the spot to render what assistance was yet possible; but he pronounced the man in a dying condition, and observed that it was totally opposed to all medical experience, and could only be considered in the light of a miracle, that a human being with such a wound should have lived through nearly sixty hours of exposure and starvation.

". . . I was painfully shocked at the inevitably rough manner in which the Yankee soldiers treated the dead bodies of their comrades. Not far from Marye's Heights existed a hole of considerable dimensions, which had once been an ice-house; and in order to spare time and labour, this had been selected by the Federal officers to serve as a large common grave, not less than 800 of their men being buried in it. The bodies of these poor fellows, stripped nearly naked, were gathered in huge mounds around the pit, and tumbled neck and heels into it; the dull 'thud' of corpse falling on corpse coming up from the depths of the hole until the solid mass of human flesh reached near the surface, when a covering of logs, chalk, and mud, closed the mouth of this vast and awful tomb."

In the battle of Chancellorsville, Stuart coöperated again with Jackson, his active horsemen concealing the flank movement on the enemy. When Jackson was shot down in the Wilderness, and A. P. Hill wounded about the same time, the command of the corps devolved upon [Confederate] General [Robert Emmett] Rodes, as the senior division commander upon the field; but he modestly concurred that Maj.-Gen. Stuart should be sent for, and requested to assume the direction of affairs until the pleasure of Gen. Lee should be known. When Gen. Jackson, wounded and removed from the field, heard that Stuart had taken command, he said:

> "Tell him to act upon his own judgment, and do what he thinks best; I have implicit confidence in him."

The Battle of Chancellorsville, May 3, 1863.

The next day Stuart fought over the ground won by Jackson, extending his line so as to approximate the Confederate troops on the south-east of Chancellorsville, and hurling the infantry impetuously against the enemy. An eye-witness of the attack says that he

> "could not get rid of the idea that Henry of Navarre had come back, except that Stuart's 'plume' was black! Everywhere, like Navarre, he was in front, and the men 'followed the feather.'"

At the risk, however, of spoiling this romantic picture, and passing from the sublime to what some persons may call the ridiculous, an additional fact may be stated, namely: That Gen. Stuart, attacking with Jackson's veteran corps, and carrying line after line of works, moved at the head of his men, singing "Old Joe Hooker, will you come out of the Wilderness."

When Stuart heard of Jackson's death tears gushed into his eyes. The friendship of these two commanders, so contrasted in the meditative air of the one, his serious, diffident temper in society, and the gay insouciant manner of the other, had been contracted in the first periods of the war, dated from the early campaigns of the Valley, and remained warm and constant to the last. It is said that Stuart was the only one of Jackson's companions in arms who ever ventured to joke the austere commander, and that Jackson, although reddening and confused at approaches of familiarity, and inapt to take a joke, always bore Stuart's facetious and high spirits in good part, and sometimes laughed, without restraint, at his own expense.

One of Stuart's staff-officers, Col. Heros von Borcke, a Prussian, relates that in attempting the English language to convey a compliment to Gen. Jackson, while intending to say, "It warms my heart when he talks to me," he had employed the expression, "It makes my heart burn," etc. Stuart, while calling upon Jackson with a number of visitors, rendered the compliment by making the Prussian chevalier say most absurdly that "it gave him the heartburn to hear Jackson talk," and set the whole company into a roar of laughter.

Dr. [Robert Lewis] Dabney, the biographer of Jackson, referring to a period when the army was in winter quarters, after the battle of Fredericksburg, says:

> "While Stuart poured out his 'quips and cranks,' not seldom at Jackson's expense, the latter sat by, sometimes unprepared with any repartee, sometimes blushing, but always enjoying the jest with a quiet and sunny laugh. The ornaments which the former proprietor of Moss Neck had left upon the walls of the General's quarters gave Stuart many a topic for badinage. Affecting to believe that they were of Gen. Jackson's selection, he pointed now to the portrait of some famous racer, and now to the print of some dog celebrated for his hunting feats, as queer revelations of the private tastes of the great Presbyterian. It was in the midst of such a scene as this, one day, that dinner was announced, and the two Generals passed to the mess-table. It so happened that Jackson had just received, as a present from a patriotic lady, some butter, upon the adornment of which the fair donor had exhausted her housewife's skill, and that the print impressed upon its surface was a gallant cock [rooster]. The servants, in honour of Gen. Stuart's presence, had chosen this to grace the centre of the board. As his eye fell upon it, he paused, and with mock

gravity pointed to it, saying, 'See there, gentlemen! If there is not the crowning evidence of our host's sporting tastes. He even puts his favourite game-cock upon his butter!' The dinner of course began with inextinguishable laughter, in which Gen. Jackson joined with as much enjoyment as any."

When Gen. Lee prepared for the Pennsylvania campaign, in the summer of 1863, all parts of his army were thoroughly reorganized, including the cavalry. This arm had been strengthened by several brigades from the South, and was now formed into a separate corps of three divisions, commanded by [Wade] Hampton, Fitzhugh Lee, and William H. F. Lee, the last a son of the Commander-in-chief; Stuart taking rank as Lieutenant-General, and commanding the corps, constituting the largest and most brilliant body of horsemen that had yet been assembled on the Confederate side at any time of the war. It numbered more than twelve thousand sabres, and the famous horse artillery had been increased to twenty-four guns. When this force was reviewed, and appeared drawn out in line a mile and a half long, in the open plain near Brandy Station, it was a magnificent spectacle; and the thousands of people who attended it looked with pride upon the glittering array that marched gaily through fields of sweet clover in the warm sun and balmy air of the month of June.

The brilliant and romantic effect of this review well suited Stuart's temper, his love of display, and his fondness of female admiration. He was this day in his glory.

Numerous visitors had been invited from Richmond; special cars with the battle-flag floating from the locomotive bore the official and distinguished persons who had agreed to honour the occasion with their presence; the general trains on the railroad brought in crowds of guests who were forwarded to their destinations in ambulances and wagons prepared for the purpose; the little village of Culpeper Court House was thronged with ladies from the neighbourhood, and, from the porches and verandas of the houses, flowers were showered down upon groups of officers who traversed the streets.

The review took place in open and picturesque ground. Gen. Stuart took his position on a slight eminence, whither many hundreds of ladies had gathered, and on a splendid charger, decked with bouquets, reviewed the whole corps as it passed in squadrons. Then came a sham charge by regiments, the artillery advancing at the same time at a gallop, and opening a rapid fire upon an imaginary enemy. The joyous and garish day wound up with a ball; and gay companies, that could not be elsewhere accommodated, danced in the open air on the turf, by the light of wood fires, and completed the animation of the scene.

Little thought was there then that in a few days this scene was to be reversed and changed into bloodiest battle, and that numbers of those who had gaily attended the review were to be stretched cold and lifeless on the same ground!

While [Union] Gen. [Joseph] Hooker, in command of the Federal army in front of Fredericksburg, was bewildered as to the main movement of Lee, he determined to send his whole cavalry corps (15,000 sabres) to break up Stuart's camp at Culpeper Court House, and to discover, if possible, the intent of his adversary in the disposition of his forces.

In the dawn of the 9th June, the alarm was given that the enemy was crossing at Beverly's Ford; and before Stuart, surprised, could get his forces well in hand, a dense mass of Federal horsemen had driven Jones' brigade a couple of miles. No sooner had he checked the enemy in this direction, by bringing up the brigades of William Lee and Wade Hampton, than he found his rear attacked by two brigades of the enemy which, crossing at Kelly's Ford, had taken a circuitous route along an unguarded bridle-path, and, advancing to Brandy Station, had taken possession of the plateau where the Confederate headquarters had been. Here a determined combat ensued, in which, for the first time in the war, on any considerable scale, cavalry fought in legitimate cavalry style. The men no longer dismounted and used their carbines; it was a fight with sabres, boot to boot. A few moments were sufficient to decide a contest so close.

Gen. Joseph Hooker, U.S.A.

As the scene of the short *mêlée* cleared, the ground was seen covered with dead and wounded; a Federal battery, every horse of which had been killed, stood abandoned; and far away a confused mass of fugitives hurried towards the river, with the shells of vengeful artillery bursting over their heads. The success of Stuart was four hundred prisoners, and three pieces of artillery. It was, we repeat, the only legitimate combat of cavalry in the war, on the scale of a battle, and in the novel trial Stuart, although much to blame for the surprise he suffered, and the disadvantage at which he was taken, bore off the palm [of success].

We have already stated in the narrative of Gettysburg the serious omission of Gen. Stuart in that campaign, in which in fact his whole magnificent force of cavalry was neutralized by the interposition between it and Gen. Lee of the enemy's main army. When Stuart, unable to impede the enemy's passage of the Potomac, deflected eastward and crossed the river at Seneca, it was to move from his proper place on the enemy's left to watch his movements, and to take a position where it was necessary to make a circuit of the entire Federal army to rejoin Gen. Lee. These circuits had been occasions of great newspaper sensations; they were admirable enough as independent movements; but in this instance, while Stuart was performing his accustomed feat, Gen. Lee was left without information of the enemy and was surprised by the battle of Gettysburg.

The sensation of the circuit was prodigious after the fashion of raids. Great consternation was occasioned; Stuart's troopers were known to have approached within twenty-five miles of Washington; the Washington and Baltimore Railroad was broken up, and for a few hours the Federal capital was isolated, not only from the army on which it depended for defence, but from communication with the North; stragglers and supply trains were captured; and thus the march around the Federal army was made, Stuart reaching Carlisle on 2nd July, not until the battle of Gettysburg had been opened, and the benefit of his information of the enemy's movements had been wholly lost to Gen. Lee. He had played only a brilliant episode when he should have performed a necessary and constituent part of the drama.

The last of Stuart's peculiar adventures in running the gauntlet of the enemy occurred in the campaign of manœuvres which terminated the third year of the war in Virginia. When in October of that year Gen. Lee made a flank movement, by which he hoped to get a position between the enemy and Washington, and force him to deliver battle, General Stuart took two brigades and several batteries and set out for Catlett's Station, to harass the enemy's flank and rear. Having passed Auburn, he at once discovered that he was between the advancing columns of the enemy. Enormous lines of [U.S.] infantry, cavalry, artillery, and baggage wagons were passing on both sides of him, and to have attacked them would have resulted in heavy loss. Nothing was left for Stuart but to conceal his force in the pine thickets; and orders were accordingly issued that no sound should be uttered throughout the command. He was completely hemmed in; and the heavy tramp of the enemy's infantry and the rumble of his artillery sounded plainly in the ears of the concealed soldiers. The accidental report of a fire-arm would have disclosed their position, and, in view of the overwhelming force of the enemy, nothing awaited them but destruction or surrender. The latter was not to be thought of.

An Antebellum photo of Stuart from 1854, owned by his wife Flora.

Three scouts were disguised in the Federal uniform, and instructed to cross the enemy's line of march, report the situation to Gen. Lee, and request him to attack the enemy's left flank at the next daybreak, when Stuart, breaking cover, would attack in the opposite direction, and complete the confusion. The adventure succeeded.

At dawn [Confederate] General [Robert Emmett] Rodes opened on the enemy as suggested; and Stuart, hurling the thunders of his artillery from an opposite direction, in the very pitch of the confusion, limbered up his guns, and dashed with cavalry and artillery through the hostile ranks, giving them a complete surprise, and inflicting upon them a loss of several hundred in killed and wounded. Having proceeded to Manassas and thence to Gainesville, Stuart, with a portion of his command, was falling back from the latter place, when [Union] Gen. [Hugh Judson] Kilpatrick came down from Bull Run, determined, as he said, to make short work of "the rebel raid." The Federal commander was described as "furious as a wild boar." He declared to a citizen, at whose house he stopped, that "Stuart had been boasting of driving him from Culpeper, and now he was going to drive Stuart." He was about to sit down to an excellent dinner as he made the observation, when, suddenly, the sound of artillery attracted his attention. Gen. Stuart had played him one of those tricks which are dangerous. He had arranged with Fitzhugh Lee, whose division was still towards Manassas, to come up on the enemy's flank and rear, as he pursued, and when he was ready, Stuart would face about and attack. Everything took place as it was planned. The signal-gun roared, and Gen. Stuart, who, until then, had been retiring before the enemy towards New-Baltimore, faced around and charged. At the same moment Fitzhugh Lee came up on the enemy's flank, and what was called the "Buckland Races" took place, Kilpatrick and his dispersed command flying for their lives. To add to the misery of the fugitive General, he lost his race-horse "Lively," a thorough-bred mare, which flew the track on this occasion, and became the prize of some of Mosby's men.

The perils to his person which Gen. Stuart encountered in a long series of adventures were sufficient to give one of less imagination a certain idea of immunity from danger, and he was heard frequently to say he was afraid of no bullet "aimed at him." His hairbreadth escapes were numerous and remarkable. His clothing had been frequently cut by bullets in various battles, and one of his staff-officers gives an amusing account of Stuart's extreme distress at the loss of half of his magnificent moustache, which on one occasion, in a spattering fire in the woods, a minié ball had clipped off as neatly as the scissors of a barber. But at last came the fatal bullet, the winged messenger of Death.

It was in the early days of the memorable May of 1864, when the two great armies were locked in deadly struggle on the lines of Northern Virginia, that Richmond was thrown into a state of especial and immediate alarm by the rapid advance against it of the Federal cavalry under [Union] Gen. [Philip Henry] Sheridan, who had managed to march around the Confederate lines. The indefatigable Stuart, however, had followed in track of the enemy; and while the people of Richmond momentarily expected that the outer lines of the city fortifications would become the scene of desperate conflict, the sound of light guns was heard, and the following cheerful, characteristic dispatch, told of Stuart's whereabouts and reassured the alarmed capital:

> "Headquarters, Ashland, May 11, 1864, 6:30 A.M. To [Confederate] General [Braxton] Bragg: The enemy reached this point just before us, but were promptly whipped out, after a sharp fight, by Fitz Lee's advance, killing and capturing quite a number. Gen. [James Byron] Gordon is in the rear of the enemy. I intersect the road the enemy is marching on at Yellow Tavern, the head of the turnpike, six miles from Richmond. My men and horses are tired, hungry, and jaded, but all right. J. E. B. Stuart."

The next day the prostrate, bleeding form of the commander

was brought into Richmond, and the glad city subdued to tears as her brave defender died in the midst of the people who loved and honoured him. For six hours he had fought the enemy with 1,100 men, and completed at Yellow Tavern the defeat of Sheridan's eight thousand. In the ardour of pursuit he had become separated from his men, discharging his revolver at some dismounted Federal cavalry who were running away on the opposite side of a high fence; and he had just fired his last shot when one of the fugitives turned upon him, and, steadying his aim by the fence, gave him a ball in the stomach that traversed the whole body. Thinking himself mortally wounded, Gen. Stuart turned his horse, rode back half a mile to the rear, and fell exhausted from the loss of blood. He was taken in an ambulance to Richmond, and died there the next day.

The last moments of the illustrious warrior were of touching and noble interest. Beneath the gay manners of the cavalier, and in the secret chambers of his soul, there was a deep, abiding religious sentiment, which now shone forth, illuminating the hero's character, and giving dignity to the last moments of life. He repeatedly asked that the hymns of the Church should be repeated to him. He was neither afraid nor loth to die; and when President [Jefferson] Davis, approaching his bedside, and taking his hand, asked, "General, how do you feel?" he replied: "Easy, but willing to die, if God and my country think I have fulfilled my destiny and done my duty."

As night approached, he asked his physician if he thought he would live through it; and being told that death was rapidly approaching, he nodded, and said: "I am resigned, if it be God's will; but I should like to see my wife. But God's will be done." The unfortunate lady was in the country at the time. He then made his last dispositions, and calmly took leave of all around him. He directed that his golden spurs, the gift of some ladies of Baltimore, should be given to Mrs. Gen. R. E. Lee, as a memento of love and esteem for her husband. To his staff-officers he gave his horses and other mementoes. To his young son he left his sword. He finally prayed with the minister and friends around him; and, with the words, "I am going fast now; I am resigned; God's will be done," yielded his fleeting spirit to Him who gave it.

The still form of the hero was laid in a simple grave on the hill-side in Hollywood Cemetery, in the midst of the roaring of the enemy's cannon at Drury's Bluff; and while the sound of battle smote the ears of the funeral cortége, men thought painfully that the voice which had so often startled the enemy with stirring battle-cry, was silent forever. Near the grave a short slight mound of earth told where rested a little daughter that had been the idol of the soldier's heart.[154]

The military character of Gen. Stuart may be briefly summed up.

He was the model of an excellent soldier, but deficient as an officer. He was splendid in action; he had a magnetic presence and a superb personal gallantry. But he knew but little of the art of war. There was much in his conduct that was volatile and lacked of sufficient seriousness. His character, indeed, is exceptional in balancing a disposition so gay with the real virtues of the man, and in presenting in manners so light the stern stuff of heroic souls. The bright blue eye that could beam with laughter looked into the very face of death without a quiver of the lid. Ambitious, fond of glory, and sensitive to blame or praise, he was yet endowed with a bold and independent spirit which enabled him to defy all enemies. Light-hearted from his very indifference to danger, he has been likened to some chevalier of olden days, riding to battle with his lady's glove upon his helm, humming a song, and determined to conquer or fall. No braver spirit, no simpler heart, ever expired in liberty's cause.[155] — SOUTHERN JOURNALIST EDWARD ALFRED POLLARD

Monument to the Confederate dead, Hollywood Cemetery, Richmond, VA.

Our "dashing Knight of the Black Plume," Confederate Gen. James Ewell Brown Stuart; bust by sculptor Edward V. Valentine, 1866.

SECTION TWO

*Military Recollections
& Personal Observations*

TEACH YOUR CHILDREN THE TRUTH
☛ . . . Moses, the world's great law-giver, commanded his people to teach the laws he had been directed to give them unto their children, in the house and by the wayside, to bind them as a sign upon their hands, and as frontlets between their eyes. May we not, in imitation of the great law-giver, tell our fathers, mothers, daughters and teachers to teach the children committed to their care and instruction the principles of American liberty, State and national, not as taught by the precept and example of the multitude, but as delivered by the fathers of the republic, and for which our comrades died that fell in battle. To tell and teach them that the dead, in honor of whom this monument has been erected, were not traitors, but true citizens, who gave their lives in defense of the truth, as they understood it, and of their altars and their homes: that [Robert E.] Lee, [Stonewall] Jackson, [Jeb] Stuart, [Turner] Ashby and [Ambrose P.] Hill, and their soldiers, were not rebels, nor traitors, but patriots, loving God and their fellow-men, and that they did their duty to their country. Teach them also to look upward to the Great Ruler of all things, truth and untruth, and forward to the duties in life that may be before them; to do their duty as our brave soldier did; to do it under all circumstances—to themselves, to their country and their God—and then come what may, success or failure, they will receive the plaudits of good men, the approval of their own consciences and the approbation of their God.[156] — CONFEDERATE COLONEL RICHARD HENRY LEE

THRILLING SCENES
☛ . . . I never shall forget the thrilling scene in [Stonewall] Jackson's corps as A. [Ambrose] P. Hill's guns opened at Mechanicsville on that memorable afternoon of the 26th of June, 1862, and the "foot cavalry" made the hills and valleys and woods ring with their Confederate yells as they eagerly pressed forward with anticipation of coming victory. Hill moved forward in fine style and drove the enemy from their position at Mechanicsville, thus opening the way for [James] Longstreet and D. [Daniel] H.

[Harvey] Hill, whose divisions were thrown across the Chickahominy [River] at that point.

In the early morning of the 27th of June the Confederate troops on the north side were in motion, and the Federal forces, under gallant [General] Fitz John Porter, awaited them in positions naturally strong, but which had been fortified with all the appliances of engineering skill and ample material.

"Gen. Lee at the Battle of the Wilderness."

It was my privilege to see that day a number of our leading generals. Our grand old chieftain, R. E. Lee, clad in a uniform of simple gray, and having the bearing of a king of men; Stonewall Jackson, in his dingy uniform, mounted on "Little Sorrel" sucking a lemon and evidently very impatient at the delay in the advance of his column; stern old [Richard Stoddert] Ewell, who impressed one as being every inch a soldier; Jeb Stuart, in his fighting jacket, and with the bearing of the "flower of cavaliers," and others who were "winning their spurs."

. . . [Later, with] Jackson on his march to Chancellorsville and flank-march to [Union General Joseph] Hooker's rear, he [A. P. Hill] was moving his division into line of battle to take the advance when Jackson was shot down by his own men, and, after giving his chief needed personal attention, Hill hurried to assume command of the corps and finish the brilliant movement which Jackson had so auspiciously begun, but he was wounded himself soon after and compelled to relinquish the command, and leave to "Jeb" Stuart—dashing, glorious Jeb Stuart—who was sent for and put in command, the glory of carrying line after line of the enemy's breastworks, as he gave the old corps the watchword, "Charge, and remember Jackson," and rode at the head of the charging columns, singing in clear notes that were heard above the din of battle: "Old Joe Hooker, won't you come out of the wilderness?"[157] — CONFEDERATE SOLDIER DR. JOHN WILLIAM JONES

THE DEATH OF JEB STUART: A POEM
☞ Night wraps the slumb'ring camp about
    With fast increasing gloom,
When on the silence breaks a shout
    That speaks of pending doom.
Hoarse sentry's challenge, rude alarms
    Of cries and tramping feet;
The drowsy troopers fly to arms
    Expected foes to meet.
But see, a friend! the countersign
    Is given, picket passed,
And breathless, foaming, down the line
    He rushes, lightning fast:
"Ye Southern men, our city fair,
    The Mecca of our land,
Is doomed within a day to bear
    The weight of foeman's hand.
Phil. Sheridan, the ruthless, rides
    With twenty thousand horse,
And, lest some accident betides
    To stop him in his course
To-morrow's sun will set upon
    Our city given o'er
To foes whom even women shun.
    Remember Shenandoah!"
To Stuart thus the rider spake,
    Then turned and rode away.
While they prepared the race to make
    Against the dawn of day.
The bugle sounds, and weary men
    Mount quick their jaded steeds;
No thought of sleep nor hunger then,
    They go where Stuart leads.

Their leader's face new life imparts
    In battle's fiery wrath;
Nor wounds nor death such rock-ribbed hearts
    Can fright from duty's path.
On, on! the dreaded foe doth knock
    At Richmond's very gates!
To-morrow brings the battle's shock,
    Scorn him who hesitates!
Day breaks; the battle gains apace,
    The sun is screened from sight,
While Stuart, 'gainst a kindred race,
    Does battle for the right.
Now strike for "Dixie," home and friends,
    While "Stuart" is the cry
That to each arm uplifted lends
    The strength to do or die.
The serried ranks advance, retreat,
    The earth shakes 'neath their tread,
They trample 'neath their horses'
    The corpses of the dead.
Sore pressed, the line of gray gives way
    Before the stronger blue.
Their chieftain dies; they hear him say,
    "Brave men, stand fast and true!"
While spurring hotly to the front
    Thro' hissing, leaden air,
He seeks the battle's very brunt
    To lead in person there.
He wins, but gives his precious life
    Our liberty to save;
This bitter, fratricidal strife
    Hath filled a hero's grave.
"Go back! each one your duty do
    As I mine own have done!"
Immortal words! Ye show how true
    This dying Southern son.
Our nation weeps with covered head
    While freedom's sadd'ning groan
Proclaims the peerless Stuart dead—
    God taketh back his own,
But lives heroic, lives sublime,
    End not with fleeting breath;
They are as jewels set in Time,

    Whose luster o'ercometh death.
Forever thro' the years that lapse
    Shall ghastly banners wave,
While glory's bugle sounds the "taps"
    O'er deathless Stuart's grave.[158] — A. S. MORTON, ST. PAUL, MINN., AUGUST 9, 1893

LETTER TO *CONFEDERATE VETERAN*
☛ It does my old Confederate heart good to know we have a paper by which we can communicate with each other. I belonged to the 3rd Virginia cavalry, under J. E. B. Stuart; was wounded twice, and still don't get a pension.[159] — CONFEDERATE SOLDIER J. R. WILES, PEMBROKE, KY

SOUTHERN CAVALIERS
☛ . . . Virginia, the grand old mother of the South, has gathered to her bosom the mightiest of the sons of valor. In the shadow of her lofty mountain pines sleeps Robert E. Lee, the kingliest soul that ever drew sword in the cause of truth and justice. In her arms also nestles the lofty Christian hero, Stonewall Jackson, who murmured when dying, "Let us cross over the river and rest under the shade of the trees.'" Here, too, sleeps the Prince Rupert of Southern cavaliers, [Jeb] Stuart, the gay and gifted cavalryman, one of Stonewall's band in life, and sleeping under the same green coverlid in death. And what pen could describe in fitting terms the numberless green hillocks whose only designation are the mystic letters, " C.S.A." How wonderful, how passing strange, that those letters, so proudly, so fondly worn and cherished once, should now represent only the shadow of an empire. What deeds of sacrifice, of valor, and of honor wrought for them, "C.S.A." It was no shadow to those who followed Lee, and the Johnstons, and Stonewall Jackson, and Bedford Forrest, for four long and bloody years. It was no shadow to those who, dying, blessed it with their latest breath, believing that victory, like an overshadowing halo, had crowned the offering of their lives.[160] — MISS CAMILLE WILLIAMS, JACKSON, TENN.

Gen. Nathan B. Forrest, C.S.A.

SERVING IN A. P. HILL'S SIGNAL CORPS

☞ . . . Gen. Lee would come up and spend hours studying the situation with his splendid glasses; and the glorious Stuart would dash up, always with a lady, and a pretty one, too. I wonder if the girl is yet alive who rode the General's fine horse and raced with him to charge our station. When they had reached the level plateau, and Stuart had left her in care of one of us and took the other off to one side and questioned the very sweat out of him about the enemy's position, he was *Gen.* Stuart then, but when he got back and lifted the beauty into the saddle and rode off humming a breezy air, immortalized by Swiney and John Esten Cook, he was Stuart the *beau.*

The next day his command was on the enemy's flank thirty miles away. The great [Confederate Gen. James Byron] Gordon came up and showed us how to steady the eyes with the fingers so as to look a long time. Old [Confederate] Gen. [Richard Stoddert] Ewell, with his old flea-bitten gray and crutches, was a frequent visitor.[161] — CONFEDERATE SOLDIER H. W. MANSON, ROCKWALL, TEXAS

THE GENIAL CAMP

☞ . . . A day or so previous to the date given above [August 19th, 1862] General Stuart had ordered his cavalry to move in the direction of Raccoon Ford. He expected that General Fitzhugh Lee with his brigade would be in the neighborhood of Verdiersville, on the plank road to Fredericksburg, on the 17th of August; and on the evening of that day he rode with his staff to that point to meet his troops. Finding that Lee's brigade was not there, and being unable to learn anything about it from the people of the vicinity, he sent Major [William Henry] Fitzhugh [Lee], of his staff, on the road on which he had expected Lee to move, to look for him. General Stuart remained at Verdiersville.

At an early hour next morning he was aroused by the noise of moving horses and wagons, and on going to the road he ascertained that they were coming along the route that he had expected General Fitzhugh Lee to take. He took the approaching troops for his own men, but sent out two officers to ascertain the facts. He was soon undeceived, as these officers were fired upon, turned about hurriedly, and were pursued. General Stuart, bareheaded and without his cloak, ran for his horse, mounted, rode rapidly to the rear, jumped a high fence, and, with several of his staff, sought shelter in a neighboring body of woods. Stuart was not the man, however, to go very far unnecessarily. He says in his report:

"Having stopped at the nearest woods, I observed the party approach and leave in great haste, but not without my hat and the cloak which had formed my bed. Major [W. H.] Fitzhugh [Lee] in his search for Fitz [Fitzhugh Lee]. Lee was caught by this party and borne off as a prisoner of war."

This misadventure of General Stuart was the subject of many a joke at his expense, but none laughed more heartily over the recollection of his hasty departure from Verdiersville than he did.

Gen. William H. F. Lee, C.S.A.

What a splendid fellow Stuart was! Of fine physique, possessing great powers of endurance, courageous to an exalted degree, of sanguine temperament, prompt to act, always ready for fight—he was the ideal cavalryman.

How genial he was! There was no room for "the blues" around his headquarters; the hesitating and desponding found no congenial atmosphere at his camp; good will, jollity, and even hilarity, reigned there. The banjoist was almost as indispensable an adjunct to the headquarters of the cavalry as was the adjutant-general. Songs and laughter often revealed Stuart's bivouac when other signs failed in the darkness of night. And what happiness was his if circumstances caused his tent to be pitched within calling distance of lovely women! How many happy hours were passed by him and his staff at the beautiful "Bower" in the Valley of Virginia! It was a refreshing sight to see him as he moved off from camp followed by his staff, and to catch the merry glance of his eye as he pointed with pride to a garland of flowers, or autumn leaves, decorating his horse's neck, the work of sweet woman's hand!

Let it not be supposed, however, that there was no sober nor serious side to the character of this gallant soldier. Behind and underlying all this freedom from care and light-heartedness there was a vein of earnest conviction and of deep devotion to principle, a recognition of man's dependence upon his Maker, and an abounding faith in the promises of his Redeemer, as proclaimed in the gospel of peace. While no soldier was ever more ready than he for the fray, none ever realized more fully the personal danger it involved, nor faced more courageously the issue of life or death that attended his every movement in response to the call of duty.[162] — WALTER HERRON TAYLOR

MAJ. JOHN PELHAM & GEN. JEB STUAREN

☛ . . . Young [John] Pelham [the "boy artillerist"] . . . excelled any man of his age, on either side, in the great conflict. . . . [He] was at West Point, and would have received his commission in a week, but he resigned and came South to enlist for his section. As a cadet he had dash and soldierly Bearing. He always walked straight as a "bee line," and never looked back, no matter how much noise the other cadets made in his rear. He was considered the best athlete at West Point, and was noted for fencing and boxing.

Then as now, at the academy, a cat, with its reputed plurality of lives, would be dead a dozen times in taking half the chances those laughing cadets would eagerly seek in the cavalry drill, but Pelham excelled them all. The Prince of Wales was struck with his horsemanship when he visited the academy in 1860. His horseback riding was marvelous, and went down from class to class as a sort of tradition, and years afterward the cadets would talk of John Pelham's wonderful riding.

It is said he got through the lines into Kentucky by a fair Indiana maiden whose affections he won, which were stronger than her true patriotism. He reported at Montgomery, the Confederate capital, and was sent to Virginia. At Manassas he so interested "Jeb" Stuart that he had him organize a six-gun battery. Of this battery were forty men from Talladega, under Lieut. Wm. McGregor, now living in Texas, and others, in charge of his "Napoleon" gun, from Mobile. This six-gun battery became the nucleus of "Stuart's Horse Artillery."

At Cold Harbor he advanced one gun a third of a mile to the front, and for more than an hour it was the only gun on the Confederate left firing, drawing the attention of a whole Federal battery, until Stuart said to Stonewall Jackson: "General, all your artillery on the left is idle; nobody is firing except Pelham." After the battle the warm pressure of Jackson's hand told how well he had demeaned himself. Shortly after this Pelham drove a gunboat from the "White House" with one gun. He again received the thanks of Stonewall at second Manassas, where he thrust his guns forward almost into the enemy's columns, and used them with bloody effect. During this fight Jackson said to Stuart, pointing to

Maj. John Pelham, C.S.A.

the young artillerist at his guns: "General, if you have another Pelham, give him to me." He was then twenty-three years old.

[When the young soldier was killed in action on March 17, 1863, Gen. Stuart announced the tragic loss in the following words:] "The noble, the chivalric, the gallant Pelham is no more. . . . How much he was beloved, appreciated, and admired, let the tears of agony we have shed and the gloom of mourning throughout my command bear witness. His loss is irreparable.[163] . . . His eyes had glanced over every battlefield of this army from the first Manassas to the moment of his death; and, with a single exception, he was a brilliant actor in all. The memory of 'the gallant Pelham,' his many virtues, his noble nature and purity of character are a sacred legacy in the hearts of all who knew him. His record was bright and spotless, and his career brilliant and successful."[164] — JOHN D. RENFROE (AND *CONFEDERATE VETERAN*)

SHELBY & STUART

☛ . . . [Confederate Gen. Joseph Orville Shelby was] to Arkansas and Missouri what [Jeb] Stuart was to Virginia, [Nathan Bedford] Forrest to Tennessee, and [John Hunt] Morgan to Kentucky.[165] — *CONFEDERATE VETERAN*

CAPT. FRANK P. GRACEY & STUART

☛ . . . Frank Gracey was one of the most gallant men of the Confederate army. He had the same sort of individual courage that distinguished Forrest, Stuart, Morgan and [Turner] Ashby. He was a born leader of men, and he allowed none to go before him into danger; and he was as generous as he was brave.[166] — E. B. ROSS

CONFEDERATE WAR HEROES

☛ . . . the instances of personal bravery and incredible daring [during the War] are countless; they fill the world's eye and challenge its admiration. The roll of honor is interminable; its cherished names crowd the temple of fame. In its carved niches stand for all time the proud but pallid forms of [Confederate icons]

[Nathan Bedford] Forrest, [Jeb] Stuart, [P. G. T.] Beauregard, [John Bell] Hood, [William Joseph] Hardee, [Thomas Carmichael] Hindman, [Braxton] Bragg, and the gallant Hills [Ambrose Powell Hill, Daniel Harvey Hill, and Benjamin Jefferson Hill], [John Hunt] Morgan, [John Bankhead] Magruder, [Richard Stoddert] Ewell, [Jubal Anderson] Early, [George Edward] Pickett, [Sterling] Price, Harvey, fearless Wheat of Zouave memory, [Albert] Pike, [Arnold] Elzy, [William Nelson] Pendleton, [Cadmus Marcellus] Wilcox, [Henry Alexander] Wise, [Jones Mitchell] Withers, dashing [Earl] Van Dorn, [Barnard Elliott] Bee, [Francis Stebbins] Bartow, and the noble [Lucius Quintus Cincinnatus] Lamar and Cobbs [Howell Cobb and Thomas Reade Rootes Cobb] of this Empire State [i.e., Georgia], [John Sappington] Marmaduke, and [John Cabell] Breckinridge, Gustavus [Woodson Smith], and lovable Edmund Kirby-Smith, who has so lately joined the illustrious band! "When can their glory fade?"[167] — MRS. C. HELEN PLANE, PRESIDENT GEORGIA DIVISION, UNITED DAUGHTERS OF THE CONFEDERACY [U.D.C.].

THE COURAGEOUS IRISH

☛ I recently had the pleasure of meeting Maj. F. A. Dangerfield, one of the bravest of the brave, who often commanded the famous Eleventh Virginia Cavalry, under Gen. J. E. B. Stuart. Our conversation naturally drifted to the war, and he told me of the remarkable exhibition of personal courage by [Confederate soldier] Jim O'Mera.

Near nightfall on the 6th of May, 1864, the second day of the fighting in the Wilderness at Spotsylvania, the General (Stuart) desired to ascertain whether or not the line of Federal earthworks in his front had been abandoned. Gen. Stuart sent to Maj. Dangerfield, whose regiment was close by, for a man who would "perform a hazardous duty." Private Jim O'Mera was selected and reported to Gen. Stuart. In reply to his salutation, Gen. Stuart simply said, "You see that line of earthworks; I want to know if it is manned. Ride within seventy yards of it, then turn to the left and gallop parallel with it to the end of the line. If the enemy is there, ride rapidly and they will shoot behind you." Jim simply

Gen. John S. Marmaduke, C.S.A.

replied, "All right, Gin'ral, I know it," with an appreciative gesture. Jim rode within seventy yards of the works and started on his run, parallel with the line. The works being well manned, were immediately illuminated by a terrific fusilade. It did not swerve Jim, however. When he had gone half the length of the line a bullet went through his horse's nose midway between the eye and the nostril. Jim then stopped his horse, unslung his carbine, and with as much deliberation as if aiming at a squirrel, he fired upon the enemy. He [Jim] then spurred his horse and ran parallel with the line to the end; then hurried to Gen. Stuart, who had watched the wonderful feat, saluted and reported: "They'er thar yit, Gin'ral." . . . There is no braver nor more patriotic race than the Irish.[168] — W. A. COLLIER, ESQ., MEMPHIS, TENN., DEC. 1, 1895

MORGAN & STUART
☛ In all our civil war no soldier was more admired and loved by his command [than Confederate General John Hunt Morgan]; none better illustrated the strategic genius, the military daring, the genial disposition, the patriotic pride, the soldierly sacrifice and endurance of the Kentucky Confederate cavalry. Gen. [Basil Wilson] Duke, who served under him, and was in his deepest councils, is surely a competent critic, and he declares him "the greatest partisan leader the world ever saw, unless it were the Irishman, Sarsfield." History may not accept this opinion, but I think will include him in the first three Southern cavalry commanders, whose names will live through coming ages, and perhaps, in this order: [Nathan Bedford] Forrest, Morgan, [Jeb] Stuart.[169] — REV. JOHN R. DEERING

ONE COMPANY IN 57 BATTLES
☛ On the 19th day of April, 1861, Company D, of the Clark Cavalry, marched to Harper's Ferry. It was composed of as gallant and true spirits as ever went forth to battle. Col. J.E.B. Stuart was in charge of it—and all the Cavalry—while Brigadier General T. J. ["Stonewall"] Jackson was in command of all the forces there. Our officers were Captain Joseph R. Hardesty; Lieutenants Wm. Taylor, David H. Allen and George Mason. We were assigned to the First Regiment Virginia Cavalry. In the first battle of Manassas, our Company and one other lost twelve killed. Among the slain was the gallant Lieut. D. H. Allen. After the battle Stuart was made Brigadier General, and Capt. Wm. E. Jones was made Colonel and assumed command of the regiment. The Sixth Regiment was then forming, and lacked two companies of having a quota, while the

First had too many.

In August, 1861, Gen'l. Stuart permitted the Clark and Rockingham Companies to decide, by vote, whether to go to the Sixth or to remain in the First. They elected to go in the Sixth. Its officers were Colonel Chas. W. Field; Lieutenant, Col. Julian Harrison; Major J. Gratton Cabell, and John Allen Adjutant. Fields shortly afterwards was made Brigadier General and assigned to the command of an infantry brigade, Maj. Thos. S. Flournoy was made Colonel, and Cabell E. Flournoy was made Major. In 1863, Julian Harrison was made Colonel, but being badly wounded the day he took command at Brandy Station, never came back to the regiment. Colonel Cabell Flournoy was killed two days before the second Cold Harbor light, when Richards became Colonel, Grimsley Lieutenant Colonel, and J. A. Throckmorton, Major. These gallant officers were leading their men to battle when the banner of the Confederacy was forever furled.

Acting Brig. Gen. Thomas T. Munford, C.S.A.

The Company had several Captains. On the 21st of July, 1861, Captain Hardesty resigned and Hugh M. Nelson was elected Captain, but not being present, Lieut. Wm. Taylor—than whom no braver man ever lived—led the Company that awful day.

Of all the officers that commanded Company D. from April. 1861, to April 1865, but three are living, and Colonel Grimsley is the only survivor of the commanding officers of the Sixth Virginia Cavalry. Our brigade commanders were Generals J.E.B. Stuart, Fitz [Fitzhugh] Lee, Beverly Robinson, Wm. E. Jones, L. L. [Lunsford Lindsay] Lomax and Wm. H. Payne.

Company D. had enrolled from April 1861 to April 1865, one hundred and seventy men, fought fifty-seven pitched battles, had eighty-three men killed, thirty-live to die after the war from wounds received, and disease contracted in prison and exposure, only fifty-two out of one hundred and seventy are alive to-day. Such is the record of this company. We all hope to have a reunion at Richmond the first and second of July.[170] — CONFEDERATE SOLDIER T. J. DEMENT, POSTMASTER AT CHATTANOOGA, TENN.

THE MEN WHO FOLLOWED STUART
☞ . . . The marvelous endurance of the men who followed . . . Stuart . . . [as well as the other Confederate cavalry leaders] has never been equalled. Storms and floods had no terror for these. No enemy was safe from their avenging hand and no vigilance could defy their enterprise. There were no alarms in any work for these brave and tireless riders. Single riders and even small troops of cavalry had made marches of a hundred miles in a day, but it remained for generals like Wheeler and Morgan and Forrest and Stuart and Hampton and Shelby and Marmaduke and Green to demonstrate the potency and tremendous value of cavalry in war, and lengthen the possibility of a day's march.[171] — BENNETT HENDERSON YOUNG

Bennett H. Young.

STUART & THE WOUNDING OF STONEWALL JACKSON
☞ On May 2, 1863, I was in the vicinity of old Verdiersville near the house of Mrs. Sidney Bledsoe, when a little before 3 o'clock I was directed by Gen. W. H. F. [William Henry Fitzhugh] Lee to carry a dispatch to Gen. J. E. B. Stuart. He told me not to go down the turnpike, as the Yankees were reported between there and the Rapidan River; so I went through the fields and woods and came out at Old Salem Church (in Orange County). As I left them at the Culpeper plank road, one of Hill's men said to me: "Come, buddy, go this way and we will show you the Yankees; there ain't any on that road." After this I found Gen. J. E. B. Stuart near Mr. Ned Easley's, and, close by, a battery of artillery in position. I delivered the papers to him in person. He asked me what time I left General Lee, and when I told him, he said: "You have been a long time coming." I told him then of my round about way and the trouble of not being able to pass the Infantry on Brock's road. He replied, "That accounts for it," and asked me if I knew the country about there. Thomas Chancellor, who happened to be standing near, said: "He knows every hog-path." General Stuart then asked me if my horse was all right for another ride. I assented, and he said, "I want you to carry a dispatch to General Jackson." And after a few minutes he delivered to me a large envelope, sealed, and said: "You will find General Jackson on the plank road somewhere between the Brock road and the line of battle. Keep behind the firing and

don't let them capture you," and added, "If General Jackson wants you for a guide, stay with him."

 Before I left General Stuart the fight had commenced; it was after 6 o'clock. I went towards Chancellorsville on the Easley road, then through the woods to the Lacy Mill; then I bore to my left, coming out on the turnpike in sight of Mr. James Talley's house, and on to the junction of the pike and plank road. Here I met some officers, who told me that General Jackson was certainly to the front, where the fighting was then going on. Putting spurs to my horse, I rode to the old Dowdall Tavern, where the Rev. Melzil Chancellor lived at that time. There I met Mr. Chancellor, who had just come back from General Jackson, having served him as a guide, and he directed me to him. I urged my horse on and was soon abreast with the General. I saluted, and said, "General Jackson, I have a dispatch for you from General Stuart," handing the envelope to him. He halted his horse, read the papers quickly, turned to me, and said, "Do you know all of this country?" I answered that I did, and he said, "Keep along with me."

 We were then between Powell's old field and the schoolhouse. There were many dead horses in the road and by it. I learned that it was where the Eighth Pennsylvania Cavalry charged. From here General Jackson moved on until he got opposite the schoolhouse. There he halted for a few minutes and had a conversation with some officers. Then he started on, two of the officers riding by him. After leaving the schoolhouse and going about two hundred yards in the curved road, we came up on a line of Infantry standing obliquely across the road. General Jackson stopped a few minutes in conversation with the officers of this Command, then passed on through its front, going nearly a hundred yards further, and just behind a battery which was supported by a very thin line. As we passed I asked whose command it was, and they said it was Field's Brigade. I asked what Regiment, and one man said his was the Fifty-fifth Virginia, and another said his was the Twenty-second Virginia Battalion. We bore obliquely to the left and went to the left of the Battery, where there was an open space at the fork of the roads—to Bullock's and the Old Mountain roads—which intersected the plank and turnpike roads here. General Jackson asked for me. I went forward and he asked me where those roads led to. I told him that the left-hand one led to the Bullock farm behind Chancellorsville, and the other ran somewhat parallel with the plank road and came out on it a half mile below, towards Chancellorsville. He told me if I knew it to lead the way, which I did for about two hundred yards, when he rode abreast of me and kept so until we halted.

We went down the Old Mountain road some four hundred yards, when we came in hearing of the Federals, I suppose some two or three hundred yards distant. It seemed that the officers were trying to form their men in line. We stayed there a few minutes, when the General turned his horse around and started back the road we had come, a little in advance of me. When we were some fifty or seventy-five yards from where General Jackson turned back, four or five officers rode in between my horse and the General's. We were about half way back, and nearly opposite the Van Wert house when General Jackson turned his horse's head towards the south, from a westerly course, and, facing the front of our own line of battle, he started to leave the Old Mountain road.

Just as he was crossing the road there was a single shot fired to the right of the Van Wert house in our line. In an instant it was taken up, and nearer there were five or six shots, like a platoon, and then suddenly a large volley, as if from a Regiment, was fired.

Gen. Stonewall Jackson, C.S.A.

General Jackson's horse wheeled to the right and started to run obliquely across the Old Mountain road, passing under the limb of an oak tree that extended across the road, which came near pulling him off his horse. The horse went to the opposite side of the road, some twenty-five yards from where the General was wounded, before he got control of him. He turned the horse and came back ten or twelve yards before he was taken down by some officers.

After getting General Jackson off his horse, he was taken by four men and carried to the plank and pike road running here side by side, where he was laid down with his head resting on some officer's left leg as he knelt on his right knee I think it was Gen. A. P. Hill—until a litter was brought from the Twenty-second (Va.) Battalion. It was unfolded and General Jackson put on it. Four men carried him across the pike and plank roads for the road that led to Stoney Ford. When in about twenty-five yards of that road the front left hand litter bearer, J. J. Johnson, Company H,

Twenty-second Virginia Battalion, was struck in the left arm by a piece of shell from a Federal battery, which caused him to let loose the litter, causing General Jackson a very hard fall. The other three litter bearers ran to the cover of the woods on the south side of the plank road, but soon rallied and came back, and with the assistance of an officer, not very high in rank, wearing bars, they lifted General Jackson up and laid him on the litter just over the embankment of the road where it had been carried by one of the bearers in his flight. They raised the litter up on their shoulders with General Jackson on it, and started to the woods on the Stoney Ford road, and carried him back some distance before they met an ambulance. After getting him into the ambulance they took the Hazel Grove road to the plank road that comes out at the corner of the Dowdall field, and up the plank road to the old Dowdall house, where Rev. M. S. Chancellor supplied the doctors with some spirits for General Jackson. They halted there a very few minutes, then drove on up the pike to the Wilderness Old Tavern, where Mr. W. M. Simms lived at the time. They drove out on the right of the pike in the field to a hospital tent, where they took General Jackson out of the ambulance and carried him into the tent, which was the last I ever saw of him.[172] — CONFEDERATE SOLDIER DAVID J. KYLE, OF VIRGINIA

STUART'S FAMOUS RIDE AROUND MCCLELLAN'S ARMY
☛ At your request I undertake, after an intervention of more than thirty-four years, to write (from memory) my recollections of Stuart's famous ride around [Union Gen. George Brinton] McClellan's army in the early summer of 1862; and also of the death of Capt. William Latane, of the Essex Light Dragoons, who fell in a charge made by his squadron upon the enemy near the "Old Church" in Hanover County, Va.

Capt. Latane, a son of Henry Waring and Susan Allen Latane, was born at "the Meadow" on the 16th of January, 1833, and grew to man's estate surrounded by home influences not inferior to any in Virginia. After receiving such training as the surrounding educational institutions could afford, he began the study of medicine at the University of Virginia in October, 1851. In the fall of 1852 he transferred the scene of his studies to the Richmond Medical College, where he graduated in the spring of 1853. The following winter he spent in Philadelphia, taking a postgraduate course at one of the medical schools of that city. In the spring of 1854 he located at "the Meadow," and at once became a candidate for the practice of medicine. His practice soon became extensive, he doing a large amount of charity practice among the poor around him. He gave successful attention also to his large farm and to the management of the labor on this farm.

Early in 1861, when [big government liberal, U.S. President] Mr. [Abraham] Lincoln made his call for troops to put down what he termed "the rebellion," there was a rush to arms all over Virginia, and soon a cavalry company called the Essex Light Dragoons was formed, electing as their officers Dr. R. S. Cauthorn, captain; William L. Waring, first lieutenant; William A. Oliver, second lieutenant; and William Latane, third lieutenant. The company was soon mustered into the Confederate service for one year. In the spring of 1862 it became necessary to reenlist the men and reorganize the company, and in this reorganization, by common consent, William Latan was made captain. About this time I made his acquaintance. He was of small stature and quiet demeanor, but quick to perceive the wrong and very assertive in his opposition to it. He commanded the confidence of his men by his even handed justice to all, but he never brooked disorder.

Soon after the reorganization Capt. Latane was ordered to report with his company at Hicks's Hill, near Fredericksburg, to become one of the constituent companies of the Ninth Virginia Cavalry, of which W. H. F. Lee, a son of Gen. R. E. Lee, was colonel; R. L. T. Beale, lieutenant colonel; and Thomas Waller, major. The Essex Eight Dragoons became Company F of that famous regiment, and in the years that followed few of the recruits knew the company by its original name.

The month of service around Fredericksburg amounted to little except picket and drill duty, but McClellan's landing on the

Gen. George B. McClellan, U.S.A.

peninsula and his march on Richmond made it necessary for us to retire to the lines around that city. Our regiment found a camp near Young's mill pond and not far from the Brook turnpike, occupying a position on the extreme left of the army defending Richmond.

On Thursday, June 12, came orders to prepare three days' rations and hold ourselves ready to march at a moment's notice. There was naturally suppressed excitement and speculation as to what we were to do or where we were to go. About one o'clock p.m. the regimental bugler sounded "Saddle up," which was caught up by the company buglers, and soon the camp was in commotion. "To horse" was soon sounded, and through the whole camp could be heard the command of the officers: "Fall in, men!" Our regiment marched out of camp to participate in the most memorable and daring raid that was made during the war. We marched in the direction of Hanover Court House, and went into camp after dark, having marched some fifteen miles. Early dawn on the following morning found us in the saddle, the Ninth Virginia in the front, and our squadron—composed of the Mercer Calvary, of Spotsylvania, and our company—being in the front of the regiment, the Mercer being in advance. Capt. [Stapleton] Crutchfield being absent, Capt. Latane commanded the squadron, riding in front, immediately in the rear of Col. Lee and staff.

Our march proceeded via Hanover Court House and on toward the Old Church. Our first indication of an enemy was the bringing in of a Yankee by one of our scouts. Soon thereafter Capt. Latane rode to the rear and ordered four of his own company to advance and form the first set of fours. This had scarcely been accomplished before Col. Lee ordered Capt. Latane to throw out four flanks, two on either side, and four members of his company were at once ordered to proceed, two to the right and the others to the left, and march a little in advance of the regiment. I was one of those on the left. Moving forward, not seeing an enemy or supposing one to be near, I suddenly heard the command to charge, and then came the clash of arms, with rapid pistol shots. Riding rapidly toward the firing, I found our squadron occupying the road and two companies of the Fifth United States Regulars attempting to form in a field near at hand, and Lieut. Oliver urging his men to charge them. This was promptly done and the enemy driven to the woods. Just before reaching the timber I overtook Lieut. McLane, of the Federals, and he, seeing the utter futility of resisting, surrendered. As I was taking him to the rear I met Col. Lee, and was told by him of the death of Capt. Latane.

Stuart's famous ride around McClellan's army.

He ordered me to turn my prisoner over to the guard and go and look after my captain. I soon found his body, surrounded by some half dozen of his men, one of whom was his brother John, who was afterwards elected a lieutenant in the company, and the following year he too sealed his devotion to his country with his life; another was S. W. Mitchell, a sergeant in the company, and as gallant a spirit as ever did battle for a country. Mitchell, being the stoutest man present, was selected to bear the body from the field. He having mounted his horse, we tenderly raised the body and placed it in front of him. John Latane then mounted his horse, and he and Mitchell passed to the rear, while the rest of us hurried on to join our command on its perilous journey. I wish I could write my feelings as I looked upon the form of him who but a few moments before was the embodiment of life and duty. I wish I could describe to you the beautiful half-Arabian horse that he rode, "the Colonel," and how splendidly he sat him. John R. Thompson, in his beautiful poem, "The Burial of Latane," and William D. Washington, in his painting of the same name, have by pen and brush so enshrined the name of Latane in the hearts of the people of our Southland that it will endure as long as men are admired for their devotion to duty and for risking their lives upon "the perilous edge of battle" in defense of home and country.

The glorious Stuart continued to ride grandly on his way, the Ninth Virginia still holding the post of honor at the front. Passing the Old Church, we hastened on toward the York River railroad. Soon it was crossed and night came on, but no halting. On we marched into the county of New Kent. All that long night was spent in the saddle pushing our way toward the Lower Chickahominy, which we reached in the early morning, only to find that the bridge over which we intended to pass had been burned; but Gen. Stuart was equal to the emergency. He soon had his rear guarded and the men swimming their horses over, while others were tearing down an old barn, out of which a temporary bridge was constructed. On this the artillery and the few horses that remained were taken over. The bridge was burned in order to prevent pursuit. Again there was an all-night march, as we hurried up through the county of James City and on to Richmond, which city we reached about midday on Sunday, June 15, and went back to our camp that afternoon.

We brought back many trophies of our raid, consisting of several hundred prisoners and as many horses.

As the years have crept on and I have called back to memory one incident after another of the deeds of daring and the scenes of danger through which the cavalry of the Army of Northern Virginia passed in the four years of conflict, I recall none more splendidly conceived, more dashingly executed, and showing more favorable results than Stuart's raid around McClellan at Richmond.[173] — HON. WILLIAM CAMPBELL, OF COMPANY F, NINTH VIRGINIA CAVALRY, C.S.A.

Mrs. Cordelia Powell Odenheimer, of Maryland; President General United Daughters of the Confederacy, 1915. The women of the U.D.C. have always been some of Gen. Stuart's most enthusiastic champions.

CHAPTER 6

STUART AS DESCRIBED BY A YANK
☛ Stuart was undoubtedly the most brilliant and widely known *sabreur* of his time. The term is used advisedly to describe the accomplished horseman who, while often fighting dismounted, yet by training and the influence of his environment was at his best as a leader of mounted men.

Stuart as a cadet at the Military Academy is thus described by General Fitzhugh Lee:

> "I recall his distinguishing characteristics, which were a strict attention to his military duties, an erect, soldierly bearing, an immediate and almost thankful acceptance of a challenge to fight from any cadet who might in any way feel himself aggrieved, and a clear, metallic ringing voice."

In the Indian country as a subaltern in the cavalry, his commanding officer, Major Simonson, thus wrote of him:

> "Lieutenant Stuart was brave and gallant, always prompt in the execution of orders, and reckless of danger or exposure. I considered him at that time one of the most promising young officers in the United States army."

As a Confederate colonel at the first Bull Run battle, General [Jubal Anderson] Early reported:

> "Stuart did as much toward saving the battle of First Manassas as any subordinate who participated in it; and yet he has never received any credit for it, in the official reports or otherwise. His own report is very brief and indefinite."

In a letter to [Confederate] President [Jefferson] Davis, General J. E. Johnston recommended Stuart's promotion, which was made September 24, 1861:

> "He is a rare man, wonderfully endowed by nature with the qualities necessary for an officer of light cavalry. Calm, firm, acute, active, and

enterprising, I know of no one more competent than he to estimate the occurrences before him at their true value. If you add a real brigade of cavalry to this army, you can find no better brigadier-general to command it."

In an account of the raid into Pennsylvania (October, 1862) Colonel Alexander K. McClure speaks of the behavior of Stuart's command in passing through Chambersburg:

"General Stuart sat on his horse in the center of the town, surrounded by his staff, and his command was coming in from the country in large squads, leading their old horses and riding the new ones they had found in the stables hereabouts. General Stuart is of medium size, has a keen eye, and wears immense sandy whiskers and mustache. His demeanor to our people was that of a humane soldier. In several instances his men commenced to take private property from stores, but they were arrested by General Stuart's provost-guard. In a single instance only, that I heard of, did they enter a store by intimidating the proprietor. All of our stores and shops were closed, and with very few exceptions were not disturbed."

General John B. Gordon, in his "Reminiscences" relates:

"An incident during the battle of Chancellorsville [illustrates] the bounding spirits of that great cavalry leader, General 'Jeb' Stuart. After Jackson's fall, Stuart was designated to lead Jackson's troops in the final charge. The soul of this brilliant cavalry commander was as full of sentiment as it was of the spirit of self-sacrifice. He was as musical as he was brave. He sang as he fought. Placing himself at the head of Jackson's advancing lines and shouting to them 'Forward,' he at once led off in that song, 'Won't you come out of the Wilderness?' He changed the words to suit the occasion. Through the dense woodland, blending in strange harmony with the rattle of rifles, could be distinctly heard that song and words, 'Now, Joe Hooker, won't you come out of the Wilderness?'"[174] — UNION GEN. THEOPHILUS FRANCIS RODENBOUGH

STUART AT THE "BOWER"
☛ After the battle of Chancellorsville our battalion, Alexander's Artillery, of [James] Longstreet's Corps, was moved down to Milford, Caroline County, to refit. We were in fine spirits, for we had taken an active part in the great victory, and the losses in our battalion had been very small. Our confidence in Gen. [Robert E.] Lee was greatly increased, but our joy was modified by the death of Stonewall Jackson.

On June 3 [1863] we left Milford and commenced a forward march, which ended only at Gettysburg. We got to Culpeper Court

House on the 5th, and stayed there until the 15th. During that time we were summoned hastily, marched out, and lay all day listening to the near sounds of the battle of Brandy Station, which was solely a cavalry fight. We were hid behind the hills because Gen. Lee did not wish to disclose the presence of his infantry and artillery, and we were only there to be called upon in an emergency; but the cavalry did the work, and we were not called into action.

Marching from Culpeper on the 15th, we went, via Sperryville and Gaines Roads, over Chester Gap, on the Blue Ridge, into the valley, and got to Milwood, about ten miles below Winchester, on the 18th.

At this beautiful place we stayed a week, and called upon to do the same work at Ashby's Gap that we had done at Brandy Station, the enemy trying hard to penetrate our line of march and our cavalry preventing it. The cavalry was marching all along on our right flank, keeping Gen. Lee informed of the enemy's movements and preventing them from knowing ours.

At this place I obtained permission to leave the march and visit the "Bower," in Jefferson County [originally in Virginia, now in West Virginia], the beautiful and well-known home of my mother's cousin, A. S. [Alexander Spottswood] Dandridge.[175] I found Gen. "Jeb" Stuart encamped [that is, headquartered] there, it being a favorite place for the cavalry. It was on Saturday, and that night there was a dance to the music of [Joe] Sweeney's banjo. The "Bower" was the home of four pretty and attractive Dandridge girls, and others were sheltered there from time to time. It was many times alternately in the hands of the enemy and in our own lines. This region was rescued from the reign of the despotic and contemptible [Union Gen. Robert Huston] Milroy by our advent. Milroy was successful in his warfare against women and children, but failed ignominiously when he met men. On this account our gay and gallant cavalrymen were welcomed with even more than the usual enthusiasm, and it was "on with the dance; let joy be unconfined;" but when midnight struck Gen. Stuart called a halt. He would fight on Sunday, but he would not dance on that day. Gen. Stuart was a consistent Christian. His gay [upbeat] and hilarious air conveyed the opposite impression to some, but he was a Cavalier, not a Puritan. When, a year later, he was dying from a wound at Yellow Tavern, he said: "If it is God's will that I shall die, I am ready." Much of his life was passed amidst "war's wild alarms," but "the end of that man was peace."[176] — CONFEDERATE CAPT. F. M. COLSTON, OF BALTIMORE, MD.

A page from a letter written by Gen. Stuart to his wife Flora.

INDUCING THE MEN TO ADVANCE

☛ [After the Battle of Hagerstown we] were flushed with victory, and retired to our side of the town, where we were soon joined by reenforcements, and two pieces of artillery were added to my command. The enemy dismounted their sharpshooters and skirmished on the left of the town, and we dismounted a few men to meet them, and drove them back. In doing this Soper Childs and his brother, Buck Childs, displayed conspicuous bravery. About 4 P.M. there appeared upon our left front a body of mounted men I could not account for, but after what I considered careful investigation I opened fire upon them with the artillery, and I think I never saw shells better placed, but was horrified to find, a few minutes later, that it was the staff and escort of Gen. J. E. B.

Stuart. It was a miracle that no lives were lost.

I withdrew from the field and went into Hagerstown [MD] to find the dinner that I had been hurried away from several hours before. I was at the hospitable home of Dr. Harvey, waiting for supper, when a staff officer of Gen. Stuart appeared, and, presenting the General's compliments, requested that Capt. Bond [the writer] would join him at the front, as he needed his assistance badly. This was irresistible, and I hurried to the company, and at a trot went out the Williamsport pike about three miles. I left the company in the road, and went on alone with an orderly (Lechlider), and found Gen. Stuart. He had about two hundred dismounted cavalry on the right of the pike in a hollow, and was endeavoring to induce them to charge a battery on a hill several hundred yards in advance, which, by the way, they did not appear to be anxious to do. He said: "Bond, I want to see you; but first help me here. We want to drive that battery off. Do you take one end of this line, and I will take the other." By a good deal of galloping up and down in front and by voice and action we induced the men to advance, at first slowly, and then at a run, and the Yankees limbered up and galloped away.[177] — CONFEDERATE CAPT. FRANK A. BOND

CONFEDERATE GEN. JAMES BYRON GORDON

☛ . . . Gen. Gordon's old regiment was incessantly engaged, as a part of [Jeb] Stuart's Cavalry, in the seven days' battle below Richmond, in the Maryland campaign at Sharpsburg, in the Pennsylvania campaign at Gettysburg, and in numerous cavalry battles in Virginia. In all the operations of the cavalry during these years he had borne a conspicuous part as a brave, daring, and skillful officer. Among the many distinguished cavalry officers from North Carolina he stood at the head.

Gen. Gordon's brigade, from this time till the death of its commander, participated in the principal cavalry battles of the Army of Northern Virginia. A detailed account of these numerous

Gen. James B. Gordon, C.S.A.

engagements would comprise a history of Stuart's Cavalry.

In May 1864, while Gen. Lee was confronting [Union] Gen. [Ulysses S.] Grant, at Spotsylvania Court House, [Union] Gen. [Philip Henry] Sheridan attempted to capture Richmond by a movement in the rear of Lee's army. He approached within three miles of the city on the Brook turnpike, and was only prevented from taking it by the desperate fighting of Stuart's Cavalry. This fighting cost the life of Gen. Stuart at [the Battle of] Yellow Tavern and of Gen. Gordon at [the Battle of] Brook Church.[178] — CONFEDERATE SOLDIER HON. KERR CRAIGE, SALISBURY, N.C.

TRICKING MCCLELLAN

Gen. Fitz J. Porter, U.S.A.

☞ ... Lee's project was to overwhelm [Union Gen. Fitz John] Porter's corps and seize McClellan's communications, and his base at White House, while the First Corps [Irvin] (McDowell) was over toward the Shenandoah, whither it had been sent against Jackson. Preparatory to the movement [Jeb] Stuart was sent to reconnoiter the rear of the Union position . Starting out toward Hanover Court House on the 12th of June [1862] with 1,000 troopers, Stuart made a daring and successful raid, completely encircling the Union army, gaining valuable information of its dispositions, and destroying large quantities of its property. He marched nearly 150 miles, crossed the Chickahominy [River] fifteen miles below Bottom's Bridge, and rejoined Lee at Richmond by way of the James River Road on the 15th. He captured a good many prisoners, and lost but one man. By turning this reconnaissance into a raid, however, and riding entirely round the Union army, Stuart "seriously alarmed McClellan for his rear," and probably caused him to have his transports at White House loaded and ready to start with his supplies for Harrison's Landing, when the occasion befell a few days later.[179] — MATTHEW FORNEY STEELE

REMEMBERING BREATHED OF STUART'S ARTILLERY
☞ Do you remember the brave Breathed, commanding a battalion of the Stuart Horse Artillery? I first spoke to him on the night preceding Chancellorsville, when he came to see [Jeb] Stuart. At that time he was already famous for his "do or die" fighting. A Marylander by birth, he had "come over to help us." He had been the right-hand man of [John] Pelham, the favorite of Stuart, and the admiration of a whole army for a courage which the word "reckless" best describes. And now his familiar name of "old Jim Breathed," bestowed by Stuart, who held him in high favor, had become the synonym of stubborn nerve unsurpassed by that of [famed French military commander Joachim] Murat.

To fight his guns to the muzzles or go in with the saber best suited Breathed. When he failed in anything it was because reckless courage could not accomplish it. He was young, of vigorous frame, with dark hair and eyes, and tanned by sun and wind; his voice was low and deep, his manners simple and unassuming; his ready laugh and offhand bearing indicated the born soldier; his eyes were mild, friendly, and full of honesty. . . .

In the last days of winter a force of Federal cavalry came to make an attack on Charlottesville, crossing the Rapidan high up toward the mountain and aiming to surprise the place. Unfortunately for him, [Union] Gen. [George Armstrong] Custer, who commanded the expedition, was to find the Stuart horse artillery in winter quarters near. So sudden and unexpected was Custer's advance that the artillery camps were entirely surprised.

Breathed had been lounging like the rest, laughing and talking with his men. Peril made him suddenly king, and saber in hand he rushed to the guns, calling to his men to follow. With his own hands he wheeled a gun around, drove home a charge, and trained the piece to bear upon the Federal cavalry, trampling in among the tents within fifty yards of him. "Man the guns!" he shouted in a voice of thunder. "Stand to your guns, boys; you promised me you would never let the guns be taken!"

A roar of voices answered him. Suddenly the pieces spouted flame, and shell and canister tore through the Federal ranks. Breathed was everywhere, cheering on the cannoneers. Discharge succeeded discharge; the ground shook, then the enemy gave back, wavering and losing heart. Breathed seized the moment. Many of the horses had been caught and hastily saddled. Breathed leaped upon one of them and shouted: "Mount!" The men threw themselves into the saddles, some armed with sabers, others with clubs, and others with pieces of fence rails caught up from the fires.

Maj. James Breathed, C.S.A.

"Charge!" thundered Breathed. And at the head of his men he led a headlong charge at the Federal cavalry, which broke and fled in the wildest disorder, pursued past Barboursville (now in West Virginia) to the Rapidan without pause.

That night Stuart went after them. . . . In passing Barboursville one of the Federals stopped to get a drink of water at the house of a citizen. "What's the matter? [asked the citizen.]

"We are retreating" he answered.

"Who is after you?"

The reply was: "Nobody but old Jim Breathed and his men, armed with fence rails."

On the back of a splendid picture [of Breathed] there is copied:

> "Headquarters Army Northern Virginia, July 7, 1864. Maj. James Breathed, Richmond, Va.: I heard with great regret that you were wounded and incapacitated for active duty. I beg to tender you my sympathy and to express the hope that the army will not be long deprived of your valuable services. The reports I have received from your superior officers of your gallantry and good conduct in action on several occasions have given me great satisfaction, and while they increase my concern for your personal suffering, render me desirous that your health will soon permit you to resume a command that you have exercised with so much credit to yourself and advantage to the service. Very respectfully, your obedient servant. R. E. Lee, General."

. . . J. E. B. Stuart wrote of him: "I will never consent for Capt. Breathed to quit the Horse Artillery, with which he has rendered such distinguished service, except for certain promotion, which he has well earned."[180] — JOHN ESTEN COOKE

UPON THE DEATH OF PRES. DAVIS' DAUGHTER VARINA

☞ . . . No other woman in the history of the world ever held such a place as our Daughter of the Confederacy. The adopted child of the greatest war heroes, the idol of those who followed Lee, Jackson, the Johnstons, Forrest, [Jeb] Stuart, and Morgan—the men who, though refused final victory by fate, have been crowned with a glorious immortality; she had all that noblest sentiment, faithfulest loyalty, and most chivalrous devotion could bestow, and neither affection nor ambition could add anything to the superb

crown which Confederates have placed on her brow.[181] —
CONFEDERATE HISTORICAL COMMITTEE

BLACK CONFEDERATE SOLDIER PRAISES STUART

☛ *Uncle Isaac; or Old Days in the South*, is written by William Dudley Powers, a Virginian, who, living all of his early life in Virginia, and among the scenes which belong to Virginia's happy past, is eminently qualified to bring back those recollections of the South's glorious days in a pleasant story to those who have come into life later. It is from the presses of the B. F. Johnson Co., Richmond, Va.

Uncle Isaac begins with a romantic but true sketch of the days when the old darky lived in Virginia, and the author allows the old man to tell his story in his own way.

He tells his young "Marse Charley" and his "Mis' Kate" of what sort of a Christmas they had in the days that are gone; of how his "Mars [Master] Ran' got kilt" in [George Edward] Pickett's charge at Gettysburg. He glorifies the "Powhatan Troop," and so the Fourth Virginia Cavalry, remembering especially in his talk the Major and others. He tells them also of Gin'rul [Jeb] Stuart, "de fines' cav'lry gin'rul dat dis worl' did eber see,"[182] and he recalls seeing [Confederate] Gen. [Richard Brooke] Garnett fall.[183] —
CONFEDERATE VETERAN

Uncle Isaac, one of the many black Confederates who praised Gen. Stuart.

EQUESTRIAN STATUE TO GEN. J. E. B. STUART

☛ T. W. Sydnor, Chairman of the Education Committee, sends this circular letter from Richmond, Va.:

> To the Surviving Members of the Cavalry and Horse Artillery and All Other Soldiers and Citizens Who Admire the Splendid Career of a Great Soldier.

It was unanimously decided, at a meeting of the Executive Committee of the Veteran Cavalry Association recently held in the city of Richmond, to proceed with the erection of an equestrian statue to Maj. Gen J. E. B. Stuart.

Years ago the preliminary steps were taken for this purpose, but further action was postponed on account of the financial depression then prevailing.

The substitution of the command, "Forward!" for that of "Mark Time," then given, is because the dark days of the past have been succeeded by a more prosperous period. In consequence, the resolve has been taken to press promptly to a successful completion the erection of a monument to the great cavalry chieftain who fell at the gates of Richmond.

We earnestly request all soldiers, whatever the arm of service, and all citizens who sympathize with or are willing to cooperate with the Veteran Cavalry Association in their noble purpose to send at once their names and post office addresses to Mr. W. Ben Palmer, Secretary of Veteran Cavalry Association, Richmond.

President, Fitzhugh Lee; Vice Presidents, Wade Hampton, L. L. [Lunsford Lindsay] Lomax, M. C. Butler, W. H. Payne, W. P. Roberts, T. T. [Thomas Taylor] Munford, H. B. McClellan.[184] — *CONFEDERATE VETERAN*

IN MEMORIAM—THE RAID, THE CHARGE, AT REST
(To Maj. Gen. J. E. B. Stuart.)

☛ Forward's the watchword to-night, my men. New spurs are to be won,
For a blow must be struck with a will and with might ere the morrow's rising sun—
A blow for Virginia's heroes famed on history's honored page,
Who left to worthy scions here a princely heritage.
A blow for our fallen comrades, for liberty and right.
I'll lead, and who'd be near me must be foremost in the fight,
For 'twill be no long-drawn combat, with rifle range between.
But breast to breast and blow for blow with saber swift and keen.
Then on, my lads! No song to-night; no saber's noisy clank—
For a fettered tread must our squadrons lead to the invaders' watchful flank.

The Southron knight kept well his word when his bugle rang from afar.
And his troop charged down to the welcomed fray with a shout and wild huzza,

Like the storm down an Alpine gorge, with its blasting, blighting breath,
Leaving wild waste behind it and heaping the spoils of death.
At its head, with flashing falchion, rode a cavalier—to life—
A man of mirth for a merry mood, but a foe to be feared in strife.
When the beacon blaze of his watchful eye swept o'er the opposing field,
And the menace flashed from his lifted steel bade the foe to die or yield;
When a stubborn will and a fierce resolve the unstained gauntlet threw
To the countless host of the Northern brave from the peerless Southern few.
For he charged in the van of his cavaliers—this "Rupert of sable plume"—
And who measured his blade with "The Pearl of the Gray" but courted a soldier's doom,
Where the stroke of his trusty saber fell with the force of the vernal flood,
As the eagle swoops from his eyrie down when his young ones cry for food.

'Tis an envied thrill the statesman feels as he bends o'er the enraptured throng,
On the impetuous tide of his eloquence to his purpose borne along;
'Tis a cherished pride the mariner boasts as he curbs mad old ocean's sport
And pages his fame on each homestead hearth as his bark safely rides to port.
But give me the sense that courses his frame and wraps every, nerve chord with fire
As the patriot leaps to his country's call in the glow of a sacred ire;
As he gauges each thrust of his trusty steel by the depth of his country's wrong;
Yields, drop by drop, a patriot's blood his country's foes among;
Reclaims with each blow from his lusty arm every footstep his childhood trod,
And offers his life for the land of his birth as a saint yields his soul to God.
So he brooked not to follow, who was born to lead, this Cavalier bold at their head,
Nor danger deterred nor death dismayed, where the still voice bade him tread;

For his soul's rich pride was the State's true weal, and his duty
    performed and well.
As he lived, so he died. As he fought, so he fell; at the front,
    freedom's faithful sentinel.

Now is hushed the neigh of his martial steed, and his bugle call is
    still;
Nor his guidon floats in the battle's van on the crest of each
    blood-bought hill;
And his saber rests by its master's side in the vale of peace and rest.
Where the arms to his own so tried and true lie folded across his
    breast.
But list! whilst a comrade stoops to drop a tear o'er his hero's
    grave,
Where the sweet white rose of his firstborn sleeps by the side of
    the parent brave,
From fair Richmond's spires steal the church bell chimes as they
    tell down the twilight air
Of Virginia's homes, now redeemed from the dust, and of rose
    wreaths clustering there;
While as long as Virginia's name shall last and her soil betrod by the
    free
Sire to son shall tell how bold Stuart fell and shall treasure his
    memory.[185] — CHARLES BOWER, M.D., TRENTON, N.J.

A RIDE WITH STUART

☛ Booted and spurred and mounted,
    Away at the bugle call;
And now for a ride by Stuart's side,
    To conquer, or fighting fall.

In the cold gray dawn of the morning,
    Ere the flush of the coming sun,
We ride with the dash of an arrow's flash
    To the spot where the pass is won.

And we hold it, too, 'til the shadowy forms
    Of the men who are dressed in gray,
Like some phantom host on a cloud-wrapped coast
    Sweep grimly into the fray.

And then once more to saddle
    And away with the hurricane's speed

To strike the flank of the foeman's rank
    Till it bends like a broken reed.

Afar in the thick of the battle,
    Half hid by the smoke and the gloom,
Strikes a knight full brave 'neath the beckoning wave
    Of Stuart's snow-white plume.

Hurrah! The field is ours!
    The routed foemen flee!
And we follow the lead of the charging steed
    Of the flower of Southern chivalry.[186] — CLIFFORD MCKINNEY TAYLOR

THE OLD JACKET OF GRAY

☛ . . . O heroes of Dixie, one and all—
The living and dead—on you I call,
    Who wore the old jackets of gray!
On the living to teach by tongue and pen;
On the dead, by those who loved them then,
Our youth to glory in the men
    Who, like Morgan, once led the way.

To glory in Lee and old Stonewall,
In the Johnstons, Hampton, [Jeb] Stuart, and all
    Who wore the dear jackets of gray;
In the privates who joined the hero band
From Maryland to the Lone Star's strand,
In the stars and bars of Dixie's land,
    And in Davis, who led the way.[187] — MRS. ANNIE BARNWELL MORTON, OF BEAUFORT, S.C.

STUART'S GREAT RIDE AROUND THE ENEMY

☛ Late in June, 1863, a large proportion of the cavalry of the Army of Northern Virginia was detached, and, under the command of J. E. B. Stuart, was sent on that march, wherein, after passing entirely around the Army of the Potomac, it was again united with the Army of Northern Virginia upon the disastrous field of Gettysburg. The march was long and tedious, but was enlivened by many extraordinary occurrences.

    I was at that time the clerk of the adjutant of the Ninth Virginia Cavalry, and, being on the march, had very few duties, so I frequently went out on reconnoitering expeditions or along with some of the scouts attached to the command.

One of these scouts, J. S. Curtis, was directly under orders of Gen. R. E. Lee. He is now in Texas. To him I became specially attached for his many manly qualities. He was from Stafford County, Va. Of all the men in that noble command, I should have selected J. S. Curtis to perform the most desperate of deeds. He was calm and courageous, and when necessary would risk any danger. But I started out to tell one or two incidents that happened on that memorable ride.

James Ewell Brown ("Jeb") Stuart in uniform, circa 1862 or 1863.

On the 28th of June, 1863, I went with a party to Fairfax Court House, when some of our scouts brought in six [Yankee] prisoners. They wore broadcloth, beaver hats, kid gloves, and "boiled" shirts.

They were quartermaster and commissary clerks, just out from Washington, and had spent the night in the city. When captured they were starting out to join their respective commands. They were dismounted and turned over to guards. We did not see them again until just before sunset near a ford on the Potomac.

One of the prisoners protested against wading, as he did not want to soil his fine clothes. About this time Gen. Stuart rode up and inquired the cause of their delay. On being told he promptly ordered them to enter the water, and he watched them plunge with evident amusement.

Early the next morning Curtis and I rode out from camp in search of breakfast, which we soon found at a farmhouse, where they treated us to the best they had. When we reached camp we found my command on the march, our regiment in advance and near the enemy. We (Curtis and myself) were ordered to select a few men and ride to the front, feeling our way until we reached Rockville. There we learned that a large train of wagons on the way to [Union Gen. George Gordon] Meade's army had turned, and was hurrying back to Washington.

Seeing the necessity of prompt action if we captured this train, we sent a man back to Col. [Richard Lee Turberville] Beale, of the Ninth Virginia Regiment, for a squadron to charge the train, but before the squadron reached us Gen. Stuart arrived and asked for volunteers to join us in the charge we had offered to lead, and several promptly volunteered.

We soon rode upon a platoon of [Union] cavalry, who fired at us and ran, but we held our fire for closer game. Curtis advanced on the left and I on the right. Now and then we would shoot, and over would topple a driver, but we could never tell whether he was hit or scared to death; but I am quite sure many a poor fellow went to his long home, for Curtis was one of the best shots I ever saw.

The train was a very long one, and when we neared the end we were in sight of the steeples of Georgetown. The quartermaster in charge of the train endeavored to escape, but we secured him, his fine horse, and trappings. J. S. Curtis, after these thirty-five years, is still living, active and useful, helping to build up the resources of the Lone Star State.[188] — WILLIAM J. CAMPBELL, OF DANVILLE, VA

THE WESTERN ARMY

☛ . . . I yield to no man in admiration of what the Army of Northern Virginia accomplished. It was led by Lee, Jackson, J. E. Johnston, the Hills, [Jeb] Stuart, and by Gordon, and won a renown that is as deserved as it is imperishable. Its operations were confined within narrow limits, no navigable streams pierced its borders, and two hundred miles square witnessed its operations, its magnificent successes, and its unsurpassed gallantry.

He must be a traitor to the glorious memories of the Confederacy who utters a single word in depreciation of its splendid worth and its superb work. The achievements of the Army of Northern Virginia have rendered illustrious its officers and its men, and they met every requirement that purest patriotism, heroic self-denial, and undaunted courage could either demand or accomplish.

Gathered in defense of the capital of the Confederacy, the preservation of which was held to be its very life, it suffered losses and evinced a valor which are among the most priceless treasures of the bravest and most chivalrous army which ever battled for human rights or defended the sacredness of native land. The very position it held, the very purpose it was marshaled to accomplish, gave it a prominence which had a tendency to overshadow the other armies of the South and to eclipse by its splendor the performances of other portions of the Confederate hosts.[189] — CONFEDERATE COL. BENNETT HENDERSON YOUNG

STUART AS AN EDUCATOR OF YANKS

☛ . . . [Jeb] Stuart, [Turner] Ashby, [Wade] Hampton, [John Hunt] Morgan, [Nathan Bedford] Forrest, and [Joseph] Wheeler soon taught the Union generals lessons in [the] . . . great department of military science . . .[190] — CONFEDERATE COL. BENNETT HENDERSON YOUNG

A GOOD CAPTURE BY SEVEN CONFEDERATES

☛ At the age of nineteen years I became a scout for Gen. J. E. B. Stuart, and at the end of one year was promoted to army headquarters, where I served Gen. Lee in the same capacity until the surrender.

On the 28th of June, 1863, Gen. Stuart, seeing a force of the enemy at a distance from our advance between Rockville and Georgetown, Md., requested a demonstration, at which I called for volunteers, and William [J.] Campbell and five others, whom I never knew, came forward. We, the seven of us, captured [Union Gen. George Gordon] Meade's wagon train, consisting of 900 mules, 175 wagons, a number of ambulances and private conveyances under a guard of 50 or 75 men. On account of this demonstration I was promoted and publicly complimented by Gen.

Lee.[191] — J. S. CURTIS, SHERMAN, TEX.

STUART'S REPLY TO A CRIMINAL-MINDED YANK
☞ The following correspondence speaks for itself. The letter of a Federal officer illustrates the infamous character of some officials in the great war. The answer of Gen. Stuart has the ring of the true metal.

The following message is from Union officer J. Irvine Gregg, Colonel Commanding, to "the officer commanding Confederate troops, near Gaines' Cross Roads, Va.":

> Union Headquarters Second Division, C.C., September 1, 1863. Sir: My patrol was fired upon last evening by a concealed party of Confederate troops, near the mill between Corbin's and Newby's Cross Roads, and one man wounded and four captured. If the same should again occur I will hold the inhabitants of the country in the immediate vicinity responsible, and cause all houses, barns, or other property, to be destroyed.

The following is Gen. Stuart's reply to Col. Gregg:

> [Confederate] Headquarters Cavalry Division. Army of Northern Virginia, September 3, 1863:
> Sir: Your communication of the 1st inst., addressed to "the officer commanding Confederate troops near Gaines' Cross Roads, Va.," has been referred to me. It caused no surprise. I expect such from those who, baffled in legitimate warfare, seek to turn their weapons against helpless women and children and unarmed men. Your threat is harmless. For any such acts as you propose, I will now know whom to hold responsible. My government knows how to protect her citizens; and justice, though sometimes slow, will be sure to reach the perpetrators of such barbarities as you desire to inaugurate. Our citizens are accustomed to your bravado; our soldiers know their duty.[192] — CONFEDERATE VETERAN

BRIEF DESCRIPTION OF STUART
☞ . . . [We will never forget] J. E. B. Stuart, "the flower of cavaliers," who ended his brilliant career in a heroic fight which saved Richmond from capture, and who left a strong testimony to his simple, Christian faith, when he said to President [Jefferson] Davis in his dying hour: "I am ready and willing to die if God and my country think that I have fulfilled my destiny and done my duty."[193] — CHAPLAIN GENERAL JOHN WILLIAM JONES

IN HONOR OF MORGAN, FORREST, STUART, & LEE

☛ . . . [Let us] celebrate the achievements of the men who followed the dash of Morgan's war horse, the ringing battle cry of Forrest, the white plume of [Jeb] Stuart, and the starry banner of Lee under the blue skies of old Virginia.[194] — MISS ANNA CAROLINE BENNING

THE TRUE CHARACTER OF OUR GENERALS

☛ [Before the War, the] great majority of the people of Southwest Virginia were not slaveholders, but their sympathy was with the Southern people, and they were intense believers in the doctrine of State rights. Their paramount allegiance, they regarded, was to their State. With them Virginia was first; all else was subservient to her wishes and demands.

Gen. Fitzhugh Lee, C.S.A.

The Southwest Virginians who had been educated at West Point and were still officers in the Union army, resigned their commissions and offered their swords to their own States. Joseph E. Johnston joined Robert E. Lee and became general-in-chief and the great organizer of the Confederate forces. J. E. B. Stuart continued with his friend, Fitz [Fitzhugh] Lee, and became the dashing leader of the Confederate cavalry. The silent Scotch-Irishman left his professor's chair at Lexington, and in less than four months' time the name of "Stonewall" Jackson had become immortal. The judge left his bench, the preacher his pulpit, the physician his patients, the farmer his lands, the mechanic his tools, and all hied over the mountains to the standards of their clansmen, Johnston and Jackson and Stuart and [William Edmundson] Jones and [John Buchanan] Floyd, and committed their lives and their fortunes to the hands of that best beloved and most incomparable man of them all, the great cavalier chieftain, Robert E. Lee. Thenceforward we were one people, having but one thought, the service of our mother, and through her the establishment of the rights and independence of the Southern States.

Thanks to God, we came out of that contest with our honor untarnished, and the reputations of our generals fixed among the great warriors of the world, and the bravery and devotion of the private soldiers became likened unto the Spartans of old.

Calumny cannot stain the character of the Lees nor of the Johnstons, Jackson or Longstreet, the Hills, Hood, or [Jeb] Stuart, nor dim the luster of their followers. The narrow-minded call them rebels in vain. When they say the soil of this country is too pure to furnish a base to their monuments, not we alone, but the civilized world cries: "Fools and bigots!" They, however, need no monument of stone to perpetuate their memories; their names will live as long as valor and personal worth have an admirer.[195] — JUDGE J. H. FULTON

WHAT MADE OUR CONFEDERATE GENERALS?
☞ . . . the Confederate war was a time when the spirit of the private equaled the gallantry of the officer, and when the courage of the rank and file made immortal fame for their great leaders. In their great victories Caesar made the Roman army, Napoleon [III] made the army of France, and [Arthur] Wellington made that of England and her allies; but the Confederate sailor made Admiral Semmes, the Confederate cavalrymen made James E. B. Stuart, the Stonewall Brigade made Jackson, and the Confederate private made Lee.[196] — ATTORNEY ROBERT SAYERS, JR.

STUART'S EQUESTRIAN MONUMENT
☞ A Monument to J. E. B. Stuart.—The Richmond *Times* of recent date states: "A rally of those interested in the erection in Richmond of a monument to Gen. J. E. B. Stuart will be held in Lee Camp Hall, it is expected, the second Monday in December. It is planned that Gen. Fitzhugh Lee, the President of the Association, will be here and preside. This was all arranged at an adjourned meeting of the Executive Committee of the Association. The committee also discussed possible locations for the monument. The Executive Committee found out that it would lake about $12,000 in addition to the funds already in hand. It is the decision that the statue should be equestrian. There has been some talk about having a pedestrian monument, owing to the lack of funds, but it is positively decided that it be equestrian."[197] — *CONFEDERATE VETERAN*

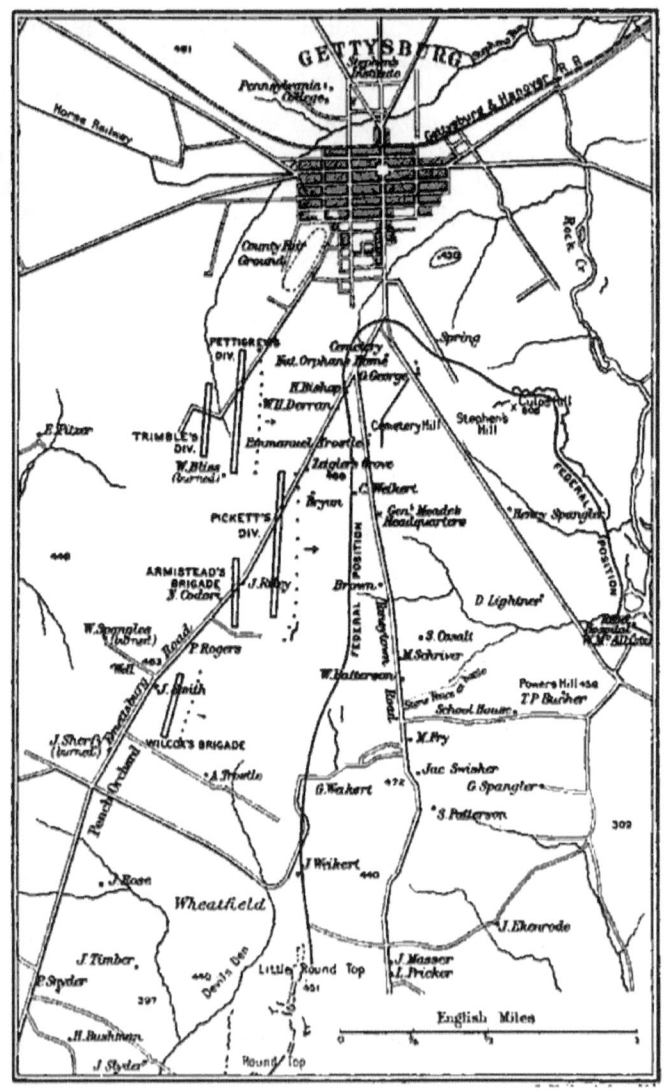

"Attack on Federal position at Gettysburg by Confederate infantry, 2:30 P.M., July 3, 1863."

CHAPTER 7

VIRGINIA MONUMENT TO J. E. B. STUART
☛ The Virginia Legislature has passed a bill giving the Veteran Cavalry Association, A. N. V., ten thousand dollars for an equestrian statue of Gen. "Jeb" Stuart, provided the Association will raise a like amount. W. Ben Palmer, Secretary V. C. A., Richmond, Va., hopes that veterans who read this notice will feel inclined to contribute for this monument to "one of the bravest cavalry leaders the world has known."[198] — *CONFEDERATE VETERAN*, 1903

ANOTHER S.C.V. CAMP NAMED AFTER STUART
☛ A Camp of Sons of Veterans was organized at Staunton, Va., on June 9, [1903] and given the name of the beloved J. E. B. Stuart. W. S. Kerr was elected Commander; V. K. Christian, Lieutenant Commander; H. S. Gilkeson, Adjutant; Dr. Roller, Surgeon; Rev. W. N. Scott, Chaplain; B. F. Kennedy, Color Sergeant.[199] — *CONFEDERATE VETERAN*

FATAL SHOT OF "JEB" STUART
☛ I was stationed on the right of our line, near the Telegraph or Brook road, with my company (K) dismounted, numbering about seventy men, and the first I knew about our troops being whipped and driven back on the left was when Gen. Stuart came down to my position with a view of ordering me back, and just as he rode up to the company the Yanks charged. He halted a moment and encouraged the men with the words (his saber above his head) "Bully for old K! Give it to them, boys!" And just as K had repulsed the Yanks he was shot through the stomach, reeled on his horse, and said, "I am shot," and then, "Dorsey, save your men."

I caught him and took him from his horse, he insisting that I should leave him and save my men. I told him we would take him with us, and, calling Corporal Robert Bruce and Private Charles Wheatley, sent him to the rear. No other troops that I saw were near Gen. Stuart when he was shot. I do not know the exact position of the mounted men of our regiment. I tell you in those

heated fights a fellow did not have much time to look around.[200] —
CONFEDERATE CAPTAIN FRANK DORSEY, FROM THE
MARYLAND JOURNAL

RECKLESS & WICKED WORDS Of SHERMAN
☛ I see that [Union Gen. William Tecumseh] Sherman has characterized our cavalrymen and their leaders in a manner much more discreditable to himself than to them, so preposterously unjust it is. He says in his "Memoirs":

> "The young bloods of the South, sons of planters, lawyers about town, good billiard players, and sportsmen, who never did work and never will. . . . They care not a sou for niggers, land, or anything—the most dangerous set of men this war has turned loose upon the world." (If he had said "upon my men," I should not dispute it, and that was just what was nettling him.) "They have no past, present, or future. They are splendid riders, first-rate shots, and utterly reckless. These men must all be killed or employed by us before we can hope for peace. [Jeb] Stuart, John [Hunt] Morgan, [Nathan Bedford] Forrest, and [Stonewall] Jackson are the types of this class. They have no property or future, and therefore cannot be influenced by anything but personal considerations."

Gen. William T. Sherman, U.S.A., 1864.

If they were sons of planters or farmers, how is it that they had no property or hope of ever having any? If they cared "nothing for niggers, land, or anything," how was it that they could be influenced by personal considerations—bribes? Are these nothing in the ordinary sense of the term? And how could he say that such sensible, industrious, high-toned, honorable gentlemen as Stuart, Morgan, Forrest, and Jackson were types of the men he so loosely describes? He writes like a crazy man.

Both Morgan and Forrest were industrious business men of means; and were they alive, they would be well off and enjoying a wonderful fame and popularity, and with Stuart and Jackson they would have had a brilliant future, even had they come out of the war penniless. Insurance companies, etc., even in the North, would have given them fine salaries simply for the weight their names would carry.[201] — COL. JAMES W. BOWLES, LOUISVILLE, KY.

I WAS WITH "JEB" STUART WHEN HE WAS SHOT

☛ My memory to-day is very clear on the main points. I was a member of Company K (a Maryland company), which, with Company D, formed the First Squadron of the First Virginia Cavalry, and on May 11, 1864, we were in the thicket of woods to the right of Chickahominy River.

Gen. Sheridan, late in the afternoon, made a charge and broke through our lines. In that charge Gen. Stuart, leading eight companies of the First Virginia Cavalry down the Chickahominy road, was mortally wounded. We were fighting in the woods when the Federal cavalry charged us, on horseback, and drove us back. Orderly Sergeant William Wright, of Company K, killed a Federal soldier and captured his horse. When we were driven back, I was on the extreme left of our line, at which place Gen. Stuart appeared suddenly, when I took off my hat to cheer him and I discovered that he was wounded. I helped him off his horse; just then Gen. Fitzhugh Lee and Capt. [Gustavus "Gus" W.] Dorsey came up, and Gen. Lee ordered us to take him away. We put him on the horse that we had captured from the Yankees, took him back and put him in the ambulance of [Confederate] Gen. [Lunsford Lindsay] Lomax's command at the bend of the road, about half a mile distant. I led the horse, and Charlie [Charles] Wheatley, Fred [L.] Pitts, and J. D. Oliver held him on the horse. Between the place that we started and the ambulance, Gen. Stuart was suffering such pain that he insisted upon getting off the horse and lying down on the ground. We kept him on the horse until we got him to the ambulance. Charlie Wheatley went to Richmond with him, and I returned to my company.

Charlie Wheatley has crossed the river, Fred Pitts lives in Philadelphia and Capt. Dorsey in Montgomery County, Md.

Gen. Stuart at that time was riding a horse that belonged to Ben Weller, who was a member of the First Virginia Regiment and was detailed as a courier for Gen. Stuart.[202] — THOMAS JACKSON WATSON, OF NO. 2 WALL STREET, NEW YORK

THE J. E. B. STUART MONUMENT

☛ The Veteran Cavalry Association of the Army of Northern Virginia has asked the assistance of the women of Virginia in raising the fund necessary to complete the monument to Gen. J. E. B. Stuart. The Association has raised the ten thousand dollars required to secure the appropriation from the Legislature, but more must be had to erect the pedestal and complete its surroundings. Do you not think that we, the women, as well as the men, owe this monument to the memory of the man who gave his life for the defense of Virginia and of Richmond, the capital of the Confederacy? Virginians everywhere should feel it a privilege, as well as a duty, to respond at once to this appeal. Five thousand loyal Virginians, giving the small amount of one dollar each would complete the work. Contribute liberally, but even the smallest amount will be received. Contribute in memory of the comrade dead as well as in honor of the gallant leader of the Veteran Cavalry Association.[203] — MRS. N. V. RANDOLPH, PRESIDENT RICHMOND CHAPTER, U.D.C.

The J. E. B. Stuart Monument.

LEE & LONGSTREET AT GETTYSBURG

☛ [July 1, 1863] . . . About 4 : 30 o'clock that afternoon I was sent to Gen. Lee with some information. I found him standing alone on an eminence in an open field, some distance to the right of Heth's Division, with the bridle rein of [his warhorse] Traveler thrown over his right arm and looking anxiously through his field glasses at either [Confederate] Gen. [James Byron] Gordon's or [Robert Emmett] Rodes's command retiring from Cemetery Ridge. While I remained standing within a few feet of him I heard the clatter of horses' feet. I turned and saw Gen. Longstreet galloping up, with his long black beard floating over his shoulders and an orderly following a few paces in his rear. He dismounted, stepped to the front of Lee, and gave him the regular military salute.

Lee responded and instantly said: "General Longstreet, where is your command?" Both faced about, and Longstreet, pointing, said: "General, there comes the head of my column where you see that dust rising." It was three or four miles in our rear. Gen. Lee replied quickly with flushed cheek: "I am sorry, sir, you were not up sooner, as I had ordered you." Longstreet replied: "I hope, General, I am not too late." Lee said: "If you had come up sooner, as I expected you, I intended to send you in the rear of those hills, and we would have captured those people (he always called the Yankees ["those] people") this evening, but you are too late, sir; I hope they will be there in the morning."

Longstreet insisted two or three times that he could have at least two of his brigades up in time to go in the rear of the enemy, or "those hills"; but Lee repeated again: "You are too late, sir, to go on this evening."

It was then about 5 p.m. Lee ordered him to bring his command up on his right and let it get something to eat and a good night's rest and, pointing to what afterwards proved to be Little Round Top, said, "I want you, sir, to occupy that point at daylight in the morning," evidently not knowing its name at that time; but he well knew that it commanded the whole ridge. Cemetery Ridge, three or four miles around to Culp's Hill. Longstreet then mounted his horse and started back to his command; but, when he had ridden about fifty paces, he wheeled and came back, saluted Gen. Lee without dismounting, and asked: "Where is Gen. Stuart?" Lee replied earnestly, with uplifted hands: "I have not heard one word from Stuart since we crossed the Potomac River. I have lost my eyes and ears" (meaning his cavalry).

I have given you almost verbatim every word which passed between Lee and Longstreet on this occasion. They are indelibly engraved on my mind, and I remember them as distinctly as if they had been spoken yesterday.[204] — MAJ. J. COLEMAN ALDERSON, CHARLESTON, W. VA

LEE ON THE DEATH OF JEB STUART

☛ The death of his dashing chief of cavalry was a great blow to Gen. Lee. He was on Traveler when a courier dashed up with the news that Stuart was mortally wounded. Gen. Lee was evidently greatly affected, and said, slowly, as he folded up the dispatch: "Gen. Stuart has been mortally wounded; a most valuable and able officer." Then, after a moment he added in a voice of deep feeling,

"He never brought me a piece of false information," turned, and looked away.[205] — CONFEDERATE CAPT. ROBERT E. LEE (JR.), SON OF THE GEN.

SLAVERY *NOT* THE CAUSE OF THE WAR

☛ . . . If it is charged that slavery was the corner stone of the Southern Confederacy, what are we to say of the Constitution of the United States? That instrument as originally adopted by the thirteen colonies contained three sections which recognized slavery.

But after all that may be said we are told that slavery was the cause of the war and that the citizen-soldiers of the South sprang to arms in defense of slavery.

Yes, my comrades, calumny, masquerading as history, has told the world that that battle flag of yours was the emblem of slave power, and that you fought not for liberty but for the right to hold your fellow-men in bondage.

Gen. Albert S. Johnston, C.S.A.

Think of it, soldiers of Lee! Think of it, followers of Jackson and [Jeb] Stuart and Albert Sidney Johnston! You were fighting, they say, for the privilege of holding your fellow-men in bondage! Will you for one moment acknowledge the truth of that indictment? Ah, no! that banner of the Southern Cross was studded with the stars of God's heaven. You could not have followed a banner that was not the banner of liberty! You sprang from the loins of freemen! You drank in freedom with your mothers' milk! Your revolutionary sires were not inspired by a more intense devotion to liberty than you were!

Tell me, were you thinking of your slaves when you cast all in the balance, your lives, your fortunes, your sacred honor, in order to endure the hardships of the march and the camp and the peril and suffering of the battlefield? Why, it was but a small minority of the men who fought in the Southern armies—hardly one in ten—that were financially interested in the institution of slavery.[206]
— REV. RANDOLPH HARRISON MCKIM

BATTLE OF BRANDY STATION

☛ The 8th of June, 1863, was a gala day with the cavalry corps attached to the Army of Northern Virginia. It was the day of grand review at Brandy Station, when Jeb Stuart's cavalrymen passed in review before Gen. Robert E. Lee and staff. For some days previously there had been unusual bustle in the camps of the several brigades composing this famous corps. There was a general polishing up of sabers, guns, and revolvers, the rubbing and currying of horses, the dusting of blankets and saddles, all in preparation for a grand display when to be passed in review before the eyes of the commander in chief. Every cavalryman who could be spared from the picket line along the Rappahannock had been called into camp to participate in the brilliant maneuvering. It was the preliminary preparation for the invasion of Pennsylvania, and at a time when Gen. Stuart's corps had probably reached the maximum, both as to number and equipment. There were about eighteen thousand men in the saddle that day, and for the most part the horses and equipment were in first-class condition. They presented a magnificent spectacle, and were highly complimented by Gen. Lee.

The corps was composed of the very flower of our young Southern manhood. In every saddle was seated a gentleman, proud of his family name, and intense in his devotion to his native Southland. No knightlier band ever followed a more chivalric leader than the men under Jeb Stuart. And it was observed that Gen. Stuart's personal charms never showed to better advantage than on that day. Young, gay [upbeat], and handsome, dressed out in his newest uniform, his polished sword flashing in the sunlight, mounted on his favorite bay mare in gaudiest trappings, his long black plume waving in response to the kisses of the summer breeze, he was superb in every movement, and the personification of grace and gallantry combined. Such was our Chevalier Bayard of the South. He was surrounded by a galaxy of subordinate officers who have carved their names with bright sabers upon Fame's monument. There were Fitz Lee and Wade Hampton, division commanders, and [William Henry Fitzhugh] "Rooney" Lee, Tom [Thomas Lafayette] Rosser, William E. [Edmundson] Jones, Pres Young, M. C. [Matthew Calbraith] Butler, [Richard Lee Turberville] Beale, [Lunsford Lindsay] Lomax, [Richard Henry] Dulaney, [Thomas Taylor] Munford, and others who had contributed to the fame of the great cavalry corps.

Brandy Station is on the Old Virginia Midland (now Southern) Railway, about six miles northeastwardly from Culpeper Court

House, and a mile south of the Rappahannock River. The surrounding country is admirably adapted to cavalry maneuvers, being an undulating plain spreading out for six or eight miles.

It was the early morning after the grand cavalry review before the sun was risen, when the camp was startled by a sharp picket firing at Rappahannock Ford. The bugles rang out "boots and saddles," and by the time the men nearest the river were in line, the enemy were upon them in great force. Just across the Rappahannock, on the north side, the Federal General [Alfred] Pleasanton had concentrated his cavalry corps about twenty thousand in number—a fine body of troops and splendidly mounted. Doubtless he had information through his scouts and signal corps that some extraordinary movements among the Confederate cavalry were in progress on the south side of the river, so he determined to cross over with his full corps to ascertain the meaning of these movements. Gen. William E. Jones was in immediate command of the Confederate picket line along the Rappahannock, and Gen. Jones had his headquarters on the bluff above the river in close proximity to the ford. The Seventh Virginia Cavalry, under Col. Dulaney, was on duty at this place. The enemy made such a sudden dash at the picket line, and in overwhelming numbers, that they were across the river and were galloping up the slope on the south side before the Seventh Regiment had scarcely time to form its line. Gen. Jones, awakened from a sound slumber by the firing, did not take time to put on either coat or boots, but in shirt sleeves and stocking feet leaped to the saddle, and, putting himself at the head of his troops, gave the enemy such a stiff fight that he held them in check until the remainder of the corps could be mounted and Gen. Stuart form his line of battle. Thus began the most famous cavalry battle of history, lasting from sunrise until sunset of the 9th day of June, 1863.

Col. Richard H. Dulany, C.S.A.

While the artillery, the revolver, and the carbine played their part, it was mainly a saber fight from start to finish. There were charges and countercharges with alternating success. Pleasanton made a brilliant dash and handled his troops with consummate skill, but Stuart and his troopers stubbornly contested every inch of ground and finally became the aggressors, driving Pleasanton and his famous fighters back across the river.

   In numerical strength the combatants were nearly equal, a slight preponderance in favor of the Federals, while the ground was an ideal spot for cavalry movements. On either side it was the largest body of cavalry ever brought into action at one time. Both Stuart and Pleasanton had won their spurs as cavalry leaders, and each commanded a superb organization. It was a soft summer day, and the balmy air was laden with the perfume of the early June roses, which filled the gardens surrounding the neighboring farmhouses until the aroma was dispelled by the sulphurous fumes of the battle smoke, which later in the day rolled in great clouds over the battle-scarred fields. Gen. Stuart was in finest mettle that day, and apparently ubiquitous. He was here, there, and everywhere. There was scarcely a rift in the smoke, but you could see his black plume floating in that part of the field where the battle was fiercest, and above the huzzas of the Federals and the wild yells of the Confederates you could hear Stuart's voice, from time to time, ringing out the words of command.

   Speaking of Stuart's plume, it was an object of great pride with him. He lost it once, and it fell into the hands of the enemy, but he could not rest until he had recovered it. It was in the summer of 1862, and down at the old Verdiersville tavern on the plank road between Orange and Fredericksburg. He had appointed a meeting with Gen. Fitz Lee at Verdiersville that day; but, being the first to arrive after partaking of a good dinner, he had lain down on a bench on the front porch for a summer siesta while awaiting Fitz Lee's arrival. When, half an hour later, he was told that a body of horsemen were coming up the road, he naturally supposed it was Fitz Lee and his troopers; and, quickly arising, walked out to the gate bareheaded, leaving his hat on the porch. Casting his eyes down the road, he was astonished to see a cavalcade of blue-coated gentry rapidly approaching. There was no time to return to the house for the hat; so, quickly mounting his unbridled horse, grazing in the yard close by, over the picket fence he went, up the road like a bullet shot from a gun, with the enemy in hot pursuit. But "Highfly" was too speedy for any Yankee horse, so Stuart made his escape; but the enemy carried off the hat and black plume as a trophy of their raid. A few nights afterwards Gen. Stuart placed himself at the head of a detachment of picked men, and, slipping through the enemy's lines, made a bold dash upon [Union] Gen. [John] Pope's headquarters at Bristoe Station. In the darkness, Pope barely escaped capture, but his flight was so sudden that he left behind his dress uniform, which fell into Gen. Stuart's hands. The next day, under flag of truce, an exchange cartel was arranged whereby Gen. Stuart recovered his hat and plume in exchange for Pope's uniform.

Gen. Lunsford L. Lomax, C.S.A.

Returning from this digression to the battle field of Brandy Station, it would seem invidious, when all performed their parts so nobly, to mention special acts of gallantry. As a matter of fact, the individual soldier has very little knowledge of the movements in detail during a great battle beyond the movements of his own immediate command. Usually there is enough going on in his own vicinity to focus his observation. However, there was one performance at Brandy Station which had such important effect on the final result I feel impelled to refer to it. There was a Federal battery of artillery planted on an elevation, near a little white church, which was giving great annoyance to our troops. Galloping down the line. Gen. Stuart rode up to Col. Lomax, of the 11th Virginia Cavalry, and asked if his regiment could silence that battery. "I will do it or lose every man in the attempt," replied Lomax. Then turning to his troopers, and pointing his sword toward the belching artillery, Lomax called out, "Men, we want those guns; follow me." They were off up the hill like a whirlwind, then, quickly charging the line so as to give a full front. Lomax swept down upon the battery on a side swipe. This necessitated a shifting of the guns, in which the gunners lost their range, so that the volley of grape and canister was not so effective as it might otherwise have been. A regiment of New York cavalry had been dismounted to support the battery. They made the fatal mistake of attempting to remount to meet the oncoming charge. Before half of them were in the saddle, Lomax and his men of the bloody Eleventh were among them, slashing right and left. The New Yorkers were routed, and the battery of six pieces captured. In this charge the volley of grape and canister had torn into shreds the battle flag of the Eleventh Regiment, had broken the flagstaff, and swept it from the hands of the color bearer. A few days afterwards the regiment was delighted to receive a brand-new silken battle flag, a personal gift from Gen. Stuart, in commemoration of their services at Brandy Station. It was Stuart's chivalrous way of rewarding bravery.

Pardon another slight digression. On the 9th day of June, 1893, on a street corner in the city of Portland, Oregon, I met Gen. H. B. Compson, then a prominent citizen of the Pacific Coast. After an exchange of greetings, some remark was made about the warmth of the weather. "I was just thinking, as I came up the street," said Gen. Compson, "that thirty years ago to-day was the hottest day I ever saw." When asked what torrid event had made such an indelible impression upon him, he replied: "It was at Brandy Station, where the great cavalry battle was fought. At that time I was in command of the Seventh New York Cavalry, supporting a battery which you Rebels took from us, and for a little while I thought it about the hottest place a mortal man ever got into." And at the recollection of it he began to wipe the perspiration from his brow. When told that I belonged to the regiment which captured his guns, there was another handshake. Pretty soon afterwards, two old soldiers, of opposing armies, had found a shady nook, where they sat down and were good-humoredly fighting over the old battles again. When a soldier meets a soldier, regardless of his belongings, it is not long until a bond of sympathetic friendship has been established.

While Pleasanton was defeated at Brandy Station, he made a masterly withdrawal of his forces. It had been a long and hard day's fight, and both sides were pretty well exhausted. It was late in the afternoon, almost sunset, before Pleasanton's lines began to waver under Stuart's aggressive attacks. The enemy retired slowly, but in good order, toward the river, and at last under the friendly darkness effected a retreat across the stream. Evidently it had been Pleasanton's design to locate the position of Lee's main army and to feel his strength, but he had failed. Very soon after this Gen. Lee began that movement which culminated in the battle of Gettysburg.[207] — GEORGE H. MOFFETT, PARKERSBURG, W. VA.

JAMES EWELL BROWN STUART: A POEM
☞ Of all our knights, he was the flower
  Of armies clad in hodden gray;
Of all our knights he was the flower,
  Always gay.
As joyous as he led the dance,
  And singing oft a roundelay,
He for Virginia couched his lance
  And plunged into the battle fray.
Kindly and courteous, temperate, great,
  Unawed by threats or war's alarms,
He fell at Richmond's very gate,
  And sleeps in old Virginia's arms.[208] — MRS. H. S. TURNER, WASHINGTON, D.C.

THE UNVEILING OF STUART'S STATUE IN RICHMOND
☞ . . . The first day of the [Confederate veterans] Reunion, May 30, [1907], is Memorial Day and [a] legal holiday throughout the country. A morning session of the United Confederate Veterans is provided for organization and to allow Gen Stephen D. Lee, the presiding officer, an opportunity to announce the appointment of his committees.

At 2 p.m. of that day will come the great parade of the Veteran Cavalry Association, of which Col. John W. Gordon will be chief marshal. At the conclusion of this parade will occur the unveiling of the monument to the memory of Gen. J. E. B. Stuart with appropriate services. The address on this occasion will be delivered by Judge Theodore S. Garnett, who was a member of General Stuart's staff, and the monument will be accepted on behalf of the city by Mayo McCarthy.

Following the unveiling exercises, in which the two grandchildren of General Stuart will take part, the parade will be re-formed, and will move on to Hollywood [Cemetery], where, in accordance with the usual custom, the graves of the Confederate dead will he decorated, and an address will be delivered in the cemetery by the Rev. Dudley Powers.[209] — *CONFEDERATE VETERAN*

JEB STUART CAMP ERECTS BATTLE MARKERS
☞ The committee of the J. E. B. Stuart Camp decided to place granite markers at the following places, where engagements were fought . . . :
The Battle of Cool Spring, July 18th, 1864, near Castleman's Ferry.

Fight at the Double Tollgate, Aug. 11th, 1864.
Fight at Berry's Ferry, July 19th, 1864.
Battle of Berryville, Sept. 3rd, 1864.
The Buck Marsh fight, near Berryville, Sept. 13th, 1864.
Fight at Gold's Farm, Sept. 3rd, 1864.
Fight at Col. Morgan's Lane, Aug. 19th, 1864.
Fight at Mt. Airy, Sept. 15th, 1864.
The Vineyard Fight, Dec. 16th, 1864.
Mt. Carmel Fight, Feb. 19th, 1865.[210] — THOMAS DANIEL GOLD

CONFEDERATE WOMEN & THE GRAPEVINE TELEGRAPH

☛ . . . It was wonderful how quickly news of the movements of the enemy could be discovered and disseminated and spread abroad by means of the grapevine telegraph. There were some families who were appointed by Gen. Jeb Stuart himself to collect information, and it is safe to say he picked out the loveliest, brainiest, most devoted and patriotic among all the fair women in the Confederacy. These ladies received and entertained Federal officers at their homes, and they were ostracized all during the war by the whole community, for their mission was kept a profound secret. These Circes invariably wormed out every military secret from their visitors, and by the time the bluecoats were springing buoyantly to the bugle's blare of "boots and saddles" there were several Paul Reveres of every age and sex speeding through Mosby's Confederacy, and the flying Federal column might sweep through the country without seeing a living thing and return to report that the country was literally a desert, harboring neither man nor beast.[211] — ALEXANDER HUNTER

To aid the Southern Cause Confederate women sometimes acted as spies for Gen. Stuart, eagerly and surreptitiously collecting information from Yanks.

DEDICATION OF THE STUART MONUMENT

☛ The dedication of the J. E. B. Stuart monument [May 1907, Richmond, Virginia] caused an outpour of people that must have gratified those who were most intimate with the wonderful cavalryman and a man who was so light-hearted and gay, and yet in whose life there were such deep and undying Christian virtues. "Jeb" Stuart will ever be a study in human nature. The unveiling of the monument was by his little granddaughter [Miss Virginia Stuart Waller], whose modest but splendid face is here presented. She was with Mrs. J. E. B. Stuart.[212] — *CONFEDERATE VETERAN*

Virginia Stuart Waller.

UNVEILING OF THE STUART MONUMENT

☛ Leaving home on May 28, [1907] I arrived in Richmond on the 30th, and was made aware of the great care Mr. Frye, his clerks, and every employee of the Jefferson [Hotel] have for the comfort and pleasure of their guests by being shown immediately to the beautiful room engaged several months before by the Jefferson Davis Monument Association, whose guest I was. I have been in most of the best hotels in this country, and I have never met with such care for the comfort and pleasure of every guest as is exercised by every employee of the Jefferson Hotel, Richmond. Its spacious lobby, halls, corridors, writing and dining rooms, parlors, drawing-rooms, and libraries will accommodate more people comfortably than any hotel I have ever seen. And the perfect cleanliness and the fresh air all through every place made it an ideal place for the immense crowd which was there for a week.

Having lost twelve hours on my way there, I did not witness the very impressive ceremonies of the unveiling of the monument to Gen. J. E. B. Stuart, which was on the morning of the 30th. I heard General Lee say that there were as many as two hundred and fifty thousand people out that day. The monument is a handsome equestrian statue of him as his old soldiers loved to see him—leading his soldiers into the thick of the fight. His wife and daughter were in Richmond all through the Reunion, thus adding to the pleasure of us all, for what Southern man and woman is there among us all who is not proud of the record of "Jeb" Stuart? The weather was beautiful, and everything passed off as his cavalry corps must have wished.

I feel sure that those who have been in the habit of attending the Reunions will agree that the Richmond [Confederate Veterans] Reunion of 1907 was the grandest ever held. I suppose there never was one at which there were present so many of the families of the great Confederate leaders. First, there were Mr. and Mrs. J. [Joel] Addison Hayes. Mrs. [Margaret Howell Davis] Hayes is the only surviving child of President [Jefferson] Davis. Mr. Hayes is himself a Confederate veteran. For a few months ago Mrs. Davis wrote to me that Mr. Hayes ran away and joined the Confederate army when he was so little that he could not carry a musket, so they allowed him to carry water to the other soldiers.

Their oldest son, Jefferson Hayes Davis, on whom we Mississippians were very glad to bestow his grandfather's name by an act of our Legislature, and who gives promise now of making us still gladder that we did it, was there. I believe he knows what it means to bear the name of Jefferson Davis. He is yet young—twenty-two, I think—but I thought I saw in his general bearing that he realized that the man who bore the name of Jefferson Davis must be upright, honorable, true, and generous; must think of his country and the preservation of her rights before he does of any good which might come to himself; that he must be great in power and success, must be unselfish in his country's service, and must

Confederate soldiers, circa 1862.

be greater still should misfortune and maligning attend his latter days. And, being all this, he may, as his illustrious grandfather did, rest in his old age in the love and confidence of the people, who cherish the memory of his grandfather.

The young daughter, Lucy White Hayes, though brought up in the Far West, is just as sweet and just as modest and just as altogether attractive as any Southern girl you ever saw. The youngest son, William Howell Davis Hayes, is an upright, frank-mannered boy of seventeen, and bids fair to make us all glad of the Davis in his name. Mr. Hayes is a gentleman of the old school in his beautiful demeanor toward all with whom he comes in contact. And, to my mind, and as far as I could hear, it seemed to be the opinion of all who met her that Mrs. Hayes is just the dignified, courteous, and altogether attractive Southern gentlewoman we would all wish for her to be.

Miss Mary Lee, the daughter of Gen. R. E. Lee, was there, and I was introduced to her too, but did not have an opportunity of seeing or talking to her afterwards, the veterans surrounded her so.

Mrs. Stonewall Jackson [maiden name: Mary Anna Morrison] and her granddaughter, Julia Jackson Christian, were there. I had the good fortune to be seated next to Mrs. Jackson one day at dinner, and Miss Christian was just opposite me. You know we U.D.C.'s feel that Mrs. Jackson belongs to us, as she is the President of one of our Chapters and is one of the Honorary Presidents of the U.D.C. She is as lovely and sweet and gentle and womanly as you rarely in life find a woman. Her granddaughter is what you would expect her to be with such a grandmother.

Mrs. A. P. [Ambrose Powell] Hill [maiden name: Kitty Morgan, a sister of John Hunt Morgan] and her daughter, Mrs. Magill, were there. Mrs. Hill, one can see on a very short acquaintance, is a big-hearted, whole-souled, hospitable Southern lady, and is Confederate to the least part of her. And her daughter is a handsome woman of about my own age (the only safe thing to do when you speak of a woman's age is to liken it to your own) who knows how to make those who are not Virginians feel at home in Virginia.

Battle-scarred ruins around Richmond, VA., circa 1865.

Miss Hampton, the daughter of General [Wade] Hampton, was there, and just as handsome and attractive as she was when I knew her when we were both young ladies in Washington.

Mrs. [William] Mahone [maiden name: Otelia Butler], a dear, sweet, motherly little woman who wins your heart as soon as you meet her, was there.

I only met Mrs. Stuart [maiden name: Flora Cooke] and her daughter, but one could see at a glance that they were typical Southern ladies.

Mary Anna Randolph Custis Lee, wife of Gen. Robert E. Lee.

And now I come to one whom I fell in love with, and I do believe it was natural, so I am claiming her as a friend always hereafter—Mrs. W. H. Fitzhugh Lee [maiden name: Mary Tabb Bolling]. Virginians love to call her Mrs. "Rooney" Lee. I knew her slightly when I was a girl in Washington. She was regal-looking then; but her face is more lovely now, softened by her sorrow and advancing years. Such a pure, beautiful soul looks at you through her eyes, that you feel the better for knowing her. You know the world must be better to hold such as she is; so true and so illustrative of the real meaning of *noblesse oblige* that you like to be near her, and always leave her with an inspiration to make the world better because of your life. And you are not surprised that her son, with such a mother and his inheritance on his father's side, is fast becoming the most popular man in Virginia, and that he has such sentiments and expresses them so beautifully that he made the "Rebel Yell" almost take the roof off the building when he spoke to the Confederates in Convention assembled. We [United] Daughters [of the Confederacy] who met him and who heard of the record he is making are expecting one day to see Robert E. Lee, Jr., the President of these United States.

Every man and woman in Richmond strove to make the Reunion one which could not be forgotten, and all who were there know that they succeeded. The Governor of Virginia and his charming wife gave each and every one of us just the welcome you would expect from a Governor of Virginia, the mother of States. In fact, they were so kind and so cordial that if the Virginians see them as we saw them there will be no rotation in office when it comes to the Governor in that State.

The Confederates were entertained in tents near the Soldiers' Home, and their meals were cooked and served right on the tenting grounds; and although it rained most of the time, they were so comfortable that when one of the pastors, whose church was near the tents, had the fire built in the Church and sent carriages to bring those there who wanted to leave the tents, they would not go, saving they were comfortable enough. It is very queer, but I was wishing for that very thing for them in discussing the Reunion with my husband last fall. Nothing can he so comfortable or so nice for them as tents, and I hope Birmingham will "follow suit" next year. It seems that there were no accidents and very little sickness among the veterans.

The horse show building, where the great ball was, was finely arranged for it, and the girls in their pretty dresses and the men in their uniforms were a very pretty sight. The reception given at the Museum to Richmond's guests, the Confederate veterans, was crowded, despite the fact that a steady downpour continued throughout the whole afternoon. The citizens of Richmond gave so many entertainments that it was impossible for one to be present at all, with only twenty hours in each day to do it in, for none of us thought of giving more than four hours out of each twenty-four to sleep. The memorial services were very inspiring, conducted jointly by the U.C.V. [United Confederate Veterans] and C.S.M.A. [Confederate Southern Memorial Association]. It made us glad to be there; for, although the men whom the orators spoke of and the times which they bid us to contemplate in retrospect are with us no more, we lifted our heads higher and our hearts beat quicker when we heard of the great leaders and the great deeds of the men from whom we are proud to have sprung.[213] — MRS. LIZZIE GEORGE HENDERSON, PRESIDENT U.D.C.

BAD LUCK, GOOD LUCK

☞ . . . On August 15th, Lee met his generals at Gordonsville [VA]. He had there, or ready to join him shortly, an army superior to [Union Gen. John] Pope's troops immediately opposed to him. His plan was that [Stonewall] Jackson should engage the Federal front while [Confederate Gen. James] Longstreet, moving round their left front, cut their communications. Pope was in grave danger when an accident saved him. Stuart leading the advance was all but captured. He lost his famous plumed hat, a subject of much chaff on both sides, and, what was of greater importance, his despatch box containing a letter conveying the information that more troops from Richmond had joined Jackson. Pope, warned in the nick of time, fell back speedily and skilfully behind the Rappahannock [River].

Again Lee planned to turn his flank; this time it was the right he aimed at; again Fortune intervened to save Pope. Heavy rains brought the river down in flood, and Jackson, to whom the turning movement had been entrusted, was unable to cross.

But Fortune was not wholly unkind. Stuart got over the river and in a raid had his revenge, for he captured some of Pope's papers which disclosed the fact that part of McClellan's army had reached Aquia Creek, and that within a few days Pope's strength on the Rappahannock would be formidable. Lee, who now had with him 55,000 men, at once ordered up the remaining troops from Richmond. The arrival of part of the [U.S.] Army of the Potomac had brought Pope's numbers to over 70,000.[214] — SIR FREDERICK MAURICE

THE DEATH OF STUART
☛ It has been said that Lee was the brain of the Confederate army, Jackson was its arm, but Stuart was its soul. The great cavalry leader was part of the history of an age that dazzled the world for a space, going out in darkness. The carriage of a noble person, the manners of a kind heart awakened interest, enthusiasm, wherever he was seen. His deeds, his exploits illuminated the gloomy scenes of war—all that was chivalric gleamed as light about the name of J. E. B. Stuart. In the saddle he was the picture of the warrior; out of the saddle the man in him was devout at times, full of prayer; at other times gay with laughter, light of heart, full of song, full of music, which was a passion with him.

Gen. Philip H. Sheridan, U.S.A.

Stuart fell in a skirmish near Yellow Tavern in 1864. . . . At Ashland they were led to believe that [Union] Gen. [Philip Henry] Sheridan was moving on Richmond. General Stuart divided and placed his cavalry on three roads leading to Richmond, with directions to watch the movements of the enemy and engage him at all hazards, in order to prevent his entrance into the city, and with the understanding that the Confederate cavalry should reunite at Yellow Tavern. Stuart accompanied the march of the brigade. Upon reaching the vicinity of Yellow Tavern he found a strong picket of the enemy in front, which he succeeded in driving before him. He shortly encountered two brigades of Federal cavalry drawn up in line to support the picket. This was morning, and the fighting continued incessantly with varied success until high noon. It could be seen by the Confederates that the enemy had been reenforced. From high noon till three o'clock the fighting, which had been severe, seemed to stop by common consent. Field hospitals were established and the men rested. At three o'clock it was announced that the enemy was advancing in stronger numbers, a larger force than had hitherto been seen. The artillery was immediately placed upon an eminence by General Stuart's order for the purpose of commanding the approach of the Federals. The cavalry was hurriedly mounted and moved to the support of the artillery.

Upon that eminence many brave men were lost, and the star of a great and glorious leader went down. As soon as the artillery opened fire the enemy could be distinguished by the naked eye preparing to charge in full force. Every effort was made by the little brigade to meet this charge gallantly, but it was thrown back again and again by overwhelming numbers.

Gen. Joseph Wheeler, C.S.A.

Stuart held his position by the artillery, never leaving his post except to rally the men or lead them back to the charge with flaming sword. Nothing could have surpassed the supreme courage displayed by him. He was cool and clear as his command went forth clear and determined. Stuart fought without respect to numbers until a shot cut him down where he stood battling for the guns. Crash on crash pealed forth. One malignant shell touched the "bravest and the tenderest." The first intimation the men received of the truth was to see him dismount from his iron-gray horse, hold it by the reins, his black plume tilting to one side as he staggered and fell down among the ranks of the enemy. The enemy seemed unconscious of the presence of the cavalry hero, who had been a target for their bullets and who had met them with such daring on so many contested fields.

In the meantime another brigade of the division moved to the support of the little brigade, when it was made known for the first time along the line that General Stuart had been shot and was perhaps dead in the hands of the enemy. The effect of these tidings upon a body of men already overpowered by continuous hard fighting can hardly be imagined. Deep grief, despair was pictured upon the face of every living man. The command was rallied and formed to make a final charge for the recovery of General Stuart's body, alive or dead. Captain Dorsey, commanding a company of Maryland cavalry, requested that he might have the honor of leading the charge. This was granted. The charge was made amidst a fierce storm of bullets.

General Stuart was found lying by the side of the iron-gray prostrate, rational, but completely disabled by a gunshot wound through the center of his body. Every eye moistened as it fell upon the graceful form outstretched, the golden hair blood-stained, the long plume, which had never been lowered by danger or despair, trailing beside him. All entreaties to induce him to leave the field were useless. He begged to be allowed to die where he had fallen within hearing of the guns. He was first in the hearts of his followers. They would not leave him. His men lifted him gently, laid him across the saddle, and bore him sorrowfully away from the scene of terrible conflict.[215] — ELIZABETH WINTER (NÉE PAYNE), WIFE OF CONFEDERATE GENERAL LUNSFORD LINDSAY LOMAX, EXCERPTED FROM THE *PHILADELPHIA TIMES*, 1882

Gen. Ambrose P. Hill, C.S.A.

A Victorian montage of 97 Confederate generals (and Pres. Jefferson Davis). How many can you identify? Gen. Stuart, number 85, is located just below Gen. Robert E. Lee. Note: Gen. John S. Preston is number 1 (top), Gen. Lee is number 97 (center). (Oddly, one of my favorite generals, Southern icon Nathan Bedford Forrest, was not included.)

CHAPTER 8

STUART'S VETERANS AT HIS MONUMENT
☛ Boys! of that gallant time, near half a century ago—
Troopers of Stuart! In that heroic day
When hostile cannon vainly sought to mow,
Your charging columns headed victory's way.
Horsemen of Black Horse fame! We meet again;
Hampton's and Fitz Lee's squadrons fill the plain.
Once more we meet, once more we greet, once more
With throbbing hearts we close round Stuart's form
Far, far behind us lie life's years—two score
Have passed since last we faced the battle storm.
With all things changed and in the calm of peace,
We, bent survivors of war's strenuous game,
Are met, as if to claim a brief surcease
Of age and sorrow at the shrine of Fame.
Well may we come. Your story is as great
As any battle legend of our war-scarred State.
Your Stuart rode with black horse to the fray;
On Death's pale horse you saw him ride away.
On Fame's immortal bronze he rides to-day.
The world remembers. Now behold in view
The tribute that Virginia pays to you.
His fame is yours—without you it were naught;
With your blood, as with his, that fame was bought.
The shaft, to him of heart so strong and true,
Yet what he was and is he owes to you.
Whoever here uncovers to his fame
Honors your valor, knowing not your name.
For Stuart, glorious leader that he was,
Was but trustee of glory that was yours.
This shaft to him shall speak through all the years
Not of his splendid leadership alone,
But of a blessed memory, embalmed in tears,
Needing no monument of bronze or stone
Of that devoted band of cavalry

Which braved all dangers both by day and night,
Guarded the front and flank and rear of Lee,
First in assault, and last at close of fight;
Instant and constant even till their foes
Yielded the generous tribute of their praise;
Last to surrender—battling till the close
At Appomattox. And for this the minstrel's lays
Have made the names your gallant leaders bear
The synonyms of courage and devotion everywhere—

Yours is the deathless tale that men so dearly love
Of rank and file as true as officers above.[216] — I. S. W.

AMONG STUART'S LAST WORDS . . .
☛ "I am shot. Dorsey, leave me here and save your men."[217] — *CONFEDERATE VETERAN*

GEN. J. E. B. STUART'S LAST BATTLE
☛ From time to time there have appeared in various papers and magazines accounts of the wounding of Maj. Gen. J. E. B. Stuart at Yellow Tavern May 11, 1864, these accounts placing him in different parts of the field while leading different commands and doing different things, and of what he said to the many different men who helped him when wounded. Without trying to account for these many statements, I will give you as briefly as possible a true account of that great calamity to the South—the mortal wounding of "Jeb" Stuart.

Gen Jeb Stuart, C.S.A.

Late on the morning of May 11, 1864, General Stuart reached Yellow Tavern with Fitz Lee's Division (Lomax's and [William C.] Wickham's Brigades), numbering about twenty-four hundred men, with ten guns, horse artillery, consisting of one section of Hart's South Carolina Battery, Breathed's Battery (four guns), and the Second Maryland Battery (four guns)—all commanded by the famous Maj. Jim Breathed, of whom gallant Tom Munford, the usual commander of Wickham's Brigade, said: "He was as brave an officer and the hardest fighting soldier that the war produced."

The fatal wounding of Gen. Stuart at the Battle of Yellow Tavern, May 11, 1864.

General Stuart posted his command with Lomax on the left and Wickham on the right, the two brigades forming an obtuse angle, with an interval of about two hundred yards between Lomax and the prolongation of Wickham's lines, both brigades facing the advance of [Union] Gen. [Philip Henry] Sheridan, who was approaching from the northwest by the Mountain or "Three Notch" road.

The Yankee cavalry consisted of Torbett's Division, commanded by Brigadier General [Wesley] Merritt, with the brigades of [George Armstrong] Custer, Merritt, and Devins facing Lomax, and Wilson's Division, composed of McIntosh's and Chapman's Brigades, supported by Davies's Brigade of Gregg's Division, facing Wickham, with the usual proportion of horse artillery, the very best artillery in the Yankee army. This force, according to General Sheridan's report on May 14, 1864, after the Yellow Tavern and Meadow Bridge fights, still numbered twelve thousand men.

About 3 or 4 p.m. Custer with his brigade charged and captured one section of the Baltimore Light Artillery, which was unsupported on the left and in advance of Lomax. Chapman's Brigade charged at the same instant as Custer, and Lomax was broken and driven back, and it was after this charge that "Jeb" Stuart was wounded.

In that splendid work, *The Campaigns of Stuart's Cavalry*, by Maj. H. B. McClellan, Stuart's chief of staff, there is an account of the mortal wounding of General Stuart as written by the author to Mrs. Stuart shortly after the General's death, which was published in Volume VII, *Southern Historical Society Papers*. It states that General Stuart when wounded was caught and helped from his horse by Capt. Gus [Gustavus Warfield] Dorsey, Company K, First Virginia Cavalry, and that while waiting for another horse General Stuart ordered Captain Dorsey to return to his command and drive back the enemy, although there was hardly a handful of men between that little group and the advancing enemy. This was old Troop K, commanded by Gus Dorsey.

Capt. Gus W. Dorsey, C.S.A.

Lieut. Col. John Esten Cooke, of Stuart's staff, says: "Stuart reeled in his saddle, and would have fallen had he not been caught by Capt. Gus Dorsey." N. W. Harris, Company G, First Virginia Cavalry, much quoted for coolness and courage by B. B. Vaughan, one of G's best troopers, in his address on the cavalry campaign of May, 1864, before the A. P. Hill Camp in Petersburg, Va., said:

> "Our company was resting immediately on the telegraph road, Troop K to our right. The Yanks were advancing along the road. Stuart was there and ordered Captain Hammond to charge with his squadron, which he did gallantly, and was killed. We were ordered to dismount, and the last words I ever heard from 'Old Jeb' were, 'Boys, don't stop to count fours. Shoot them! Shoot them!' and we did shoot them. We had an excellent position. There was a deep cut in the road with a good fence to the left and in front of us. The Yanks were charging with sabers and slashed at us over the fences, but we soon piled them up so as to completely blockade the road with dead horses and men. As soon as General Stuart saw we had blockaded the road and stopped their advance he rode off in the direction of Troop K, and that was the last I ever saw of him. I am sure Captain Dorsey will sustain me in the statement that there was not a member of Stuart's staff with him when he was shot, not even a courier."

Lieut. Col. Gus W. Dorsey, then captain of Troop K, First Virginia Cavalry, says:

> "I was stationed on the right of our line near the telegraph road with my company (K), numbering about seventy men dismounted, and the first I knew of our troops being whipped and driven back on the left was when General Stuart came down to my position to order me back,

and just as he rode up to the company the Yanks charged. He halted a moment and encouraged the men with the words (his saber above his head): 'Bully for old K. Give it to them, boys!' And just as K had repulsed them he was shot through the stomach, reeled on his horse, and said, 'I am shot,' and then said, 'Dorsey, save your men!' I caught him and took him from his horse. He insisted that I should leave him and save my men. I told him we would take him with us; and calling Corporal Robert Bruce and Private Charley Wheatley, we sent him to the rear. No other troops were near General Stuart when he was shot that I saw. When we were in those heated battles, a fellow had not much time to look around."

M. J. Billmyer, the gallant captain of Company F, First Virginia Cavalry, Shepherdstown, W.Va., says:

"I was on the extreme left of the First Virginia (main body), K about one hundred and fifty yards to our left."

W. S. Purnell, Company K, who when captured escaped from Fort McHenry, Baltimore, Md., back to K, says:

"I distinctly remember that Captain Dorsey helped General Stuart from his horse when wounded, and that Fred L. Pitts's horse was used to carry General Stuart to the rear."

Fred Pitts says:

"I am certain that when General Stuart joined us he was entirely alone. I saw him speak to Captain Dorsey, and then lost sight of him for a few minutes on account of a little trouble we were having with the people in front of us. It was a pretty hot place. I saw him reel in his saddle, and heard him tell Captain Dorsey he was hit or wounded. He either dismounted himself or was taken down by Captain Dorsey, and for a few moments was left on the ground. It was evident we could hold the position only a few moments, and Captain Dorsey directed me to get my horse for General Stuart to ride, because he was a quiet animal, and for me to ride the General's, which had become very restive, and ordered us to hurry to the rear while he held the position to enable us to get away. I remember meeting the ambulance just as we got to the main road; but at that moment we repelled a charge of cavalry, and the ambulance people got away with General Stuart. Our gallant old Captain Dorsey, our beau ideal of a dashing cavalryman, was the finest soldier I ever saw. But for his prompt and gallant action we could not have gotten General Stuart away, and I believe that to accomplish this he would have held his position as long as he had a man left."

By an order from our War Department August 6, 1864, Troop K, all Marylanders, was transferred from the First Virginia Cavalry to the First Maryland Cavalry, of which Gus W. Dorsey was made lieutenant commanding.

On April 9 the "Old Brigade" was composed of the First Maryland and the First, Second, Third, and Fourth Virginia Cavalry. It was the brigade that cut its way through the Yanks at Appomattox, and was disbanded by Brig. Gen. Thomas T. Munford, Virginia's greatest living soldier, April 28, 1865, because of Gen. Joe Johnston's surrender on the 26th.[218] — CONFEDERATE CAPTAIN FRANK DORSEY, BALTIMORE, MD.

A YANKEE SOLDIER WHO ADMIRED STUART

☛ . . . The generous Union soldier believes that there was equal sincerity and equal courage on both sides. On both sides the highest attributes of a military people were undeniably demonstrated. No magnanimous Union soldier demands that the Southern people shall level the graves of their heroic dead and eliminate from their memories the reminiscences of the battlefield, the camp, the hospital, and the death chamber with which many of their kindred have been immemorially associated. Their right to erect monuments to perpetuate the memory of their bravery he does not impugn.

Gen. Stuart's pistol.

The soldier in blue does not challenge the fame of those whose valor and skill made them the idols of the Southern armies. The fame of Lee, Stonewall Jackson, [Jeb] Stuart, the Hills, and the Johnstons is just as much a part of the national heritage as is the fame of Grant, Thomas, Sheridan, Sherman, and Custer. Ex-Confederates are all our heroes.[219] — A FORMER UNION SOLDIER, ANONYMOUS, 1911

J. E. B. STUART'S FATE AT YELLOW TAVERN

☛ In the February *Confederate Veteran*, 1909, a Mr. Frank Dorsey writes of the fatal wounding of Maj.-Gen. J. E. B. Stuart at Yellow Tavern. There has been so much controversy in the papers during the many intervening years as to how the wounding and death of our noble General occurred. Please allow an eyewitness who participated in that memorable engagement at Yellow Tavern to give to the public what occurred as he saw it.

Mr. Dorsey's statement is nearer correct than any other I have yet seen. I was in a position to know every particular of that memorable fight on May 11, 1864. I belonged to Company K of the First Virginia Cavalry, Companies D and K forming our squadron. Company D was made up of men from Washington County, Virginia, commanded by Captain [Connally Trigg] Litchfield; and Company K, of Maryland, commanded by Lieut. Gus Dorsey. The First Virginia on that day was in line of battle on the extreme left of Wickham's brigade, with Companies D and K forming the left of the regiment, resting on the Yellow Tavern road. Just across the road was General Lomax's brigade. Companies D and K were deployed along a line of fence in the woods—a position they, together with the regiment, had held nearly all day.

About 5 o'clock in the afternoon General Stuart came riding slowly through the woods, whistling and entirely alone. He took a position directly between Fred Pitts (a young man from the eastern shore of Maryland) and myself, with his horse's head extending over the fence. My left elbow was touching the boot on General Stuart's right foot, while Pitts was equally as close to the General on his left. He had been with us in this position but a few minutes when some of General Lomax's mounted men made a charge up the road and were driven back by a regiment of Federal cavalry, which, when they got to our line of battle, filed to the left along the fence in front of our command, passing within ten or fifteen feet of General Stuart. They fired a volley as they passed, one shot of which hit the General in the side. I saw him press his hand to his side and said to him: "General, are you hit?" "Yes," he replied. "Are you wounded badly?" I asked. "I am afraid I am," he said. "But don't worry, boys, Fitz [i.e., Gen. Fitzhugh Lee] will do as well for you as I have done."

As we were taking him back Tom Waters, of Baltimore, led his horse while Fred Pitts and myself, one on either side of him, went back about one hundred yards. Then Pitts and I left him in charge of Waters and some men from the ambulance corps and returned to our position at the fence, as it was of the greatest importance to hold this position to prevent him from being captured. When General Stuart had been removed from the field, our regiment slowly retreated. When Pitts and I left him, the General was still sitting on his horse. When wounded, he was near the center of Company K, with no other troops near him. He took neither a courier nor any member of his staff with him. Who took him off his horse, I do not know.[220] — J. R. OLIVER, 235 WEST PRESTON STREET, BALTIMORE, MD.

THE DASHING GEN. J. E. B. STUART

☛ On May 12, 1864, as the shadows of the night gathered fast upon a day filled with deepest gloom, in the house then standing on this spot, the heroic spirit of a true and brave Confederate soldier put on immortality. I am directed to give some personal recollection of him, the great cavalryman, to whom I was as a devoted son and to whose memory you would this day do great honor. At the very suggestion a flood of memories rushes in upon me and overwhelms the power of utterance with a sense of intolerable grief.

The last three days of General Stuart's life were filled with all the elements of the tragic drama.

This devoted city [Richmond, VA], the object of all the enemy's assaults, the citadel in whose defense Stuart exerted his supreme efforts, was then beset by the most formidable array of arms ever brought against her. The vast army with which [Union Gen. Ulysses S.] Grant had marched into the Wilderness had lost in one short week of battle nearly 50,000 men, and yet he had replaced them with an equal number of fresh troops, leaving him free to send Sheridan with his 12,000 cavalry unopposed to the very gates of Richmond, confident then of its capture and destruction.

One of Stuart's men at work.

On May 9 at three o'clock in the afternoon, parting with General Lee at Spotsylvania Court House, never to meet in this world again, General Stuart moved rapidly with two brigades of his command (Fitz Lee and Lomax), leaving orders for [James B.] Gordon with the North Carolina brigade to follow.

Reaching Yellow Tavern with one brigade (Lomax's) about ten o'clock on the morning of the 11th, just as the head of Sheridan's heavy columns arrived there, a brisk skirmish commenced which soon developed into a severe battle, lasting until after midday. Then a long silence ensued until near four o'clock, when a sudden mounted charge by the enemy, in column of regiments, broke the left of our line and captured our only battery, our gun alone escaping. In the melée near the battery General Stuart, while encouraging his brave men in their hand-to-hand fight over the guns, was shot by a Federal sergeant who had passed him in the charge and was then returning close by him on the main (Telegraph) road.

To Captain [Gustavus W.] Dorsey, of Maryland, commanding Company K (Marylanders), First Virginia Cavalry, belongs the honor of having saved the General from capture by the advancing enemy. Captain Dorsey, seeing him wounded and his horse unmanageable, placed him on the horse of Private Pitts, who, with Private [Charles] Wheatley, of Company K, led him to an ambulance, in which he left the field under the charge of Major [Charles Scott] Venable. Attended by his chief surgeon, John B. Fontaine, and two others of the staff, and Couriers Ellis, Carpenter, and Thompson, of his escort—after ordering his faithful adjutant general, Maj. Henry B. McClellan, to report to General Fitz Lee—he was driven by way of Atlee and Mechanicsville, avoiding the enemy and reaching Richmond about eleven o'clock that night. From Mechanicsville he sent me ahead into the city to have a bed ready for him and to report to [Confederate] General [Braxton] Bragg.

Here at the house of Dr. Charles Brewer, his brother-in law, he lingered until nightfall of the 12th of May, his powerful frame and resolute will fighting against the mortal wound, such as few men could have withstood even for an hour.

[Among my personal remembrances:] I recall his reply to a suggestion made by one of his brigade commanders on the march, that it would be impossible to overtake and stop Sheridan. "No," said Stuart with hot impatience, "I would rather die than let him go on."

As we approached the battle field that morning his chief bugler (a noncombatant, you know), riding close by him, mildly protested against the General's habit of exposing his life in every battle, saying to him: "General, I believe you love bullets." Turning sharply to the bugler, Stuart said: "No, Fred, I do not love bullets any better than you do; I go where they are because it is my duty, and I do not expect to survive this war."

During the battle he deplored the absence of Gordon's North Carolina brigade, who were attacking Sheridan's rear far away on the Mountain Road. But alas! within a few days after the battle Gordon was united with him in death.

The Battle of Yellow Tavern, May 11, 1864; Stuart (right) vs. Sheridan (left).

Here in his death chamber about noon on the 12th I was alone at his bedside, watching and holding his pulse as it throbbed fast and faster to the inevitable end. Suddenly a loud shout arose from a crowd of men and boys passing along Broad Street. Awakening with a startled look, he said: "Go and see what that means." Hastening to the street, I saw an ambulance moving slowly through the rain toward the capital, and was told that a wounded general—a captured Yankee general—was being driven to a hospital. Returning to General Stuart's bedside, I found him nearly asleep, and refrained from telling him the rumor. It was, in fact, a wounded general; but, sad to say, it proved to be none other than Stuart's gallant friend and companion, Gen. James B. Gordon, of the North Carolina brigade, who was shot that morning near Brookhill, and died here only a week later.

During the day President [Jefferson] Davis visited General

Stuart's bedside, and with deep emotion bade him a long farewell. The Rev. Joshua Peterkin, that saintly man of God if ever there was one on earth, with prayer and supplication and Stuart's favorite hymn, "Rock of Ages, Cleft for Me," administered to him the consolation of our holy Church, in whose communion he died.

Realizing that death was very near, be prepared to meet it as he had so often faced it before—"without fear and without reproach." "I am ready to go," he said, and his last fervent wish was for his beloved wife, then hastening to his bedside. His last thought was of duty done so faithfully to God and his country.

> "For how can man die better than facing fearful odds,
> For the ashes of his fathers and the altars of his gods?"

Eight general officers were his pallbearers, among whom I recall Gens. George W. Randolph and Joseph R. Anderson. The services at St. James Church and the burial in Hollywood were attended, without military display, by many devoted friends and comrades in the midst of falling rain, the very clouds in sympathy with our troubled souls, accompanied not only by the artillery of heaven, but by the booming of our guns then driving the enemy beyond our reach. So true is it as Percy Greg sang: "The cannon of his country pealed Stuart's funeral knell."

. . . Captain [Cecil] Battine, of the 15th King's Hussars, in his book, *The Crisis of the Confederacy*, states:

> "James Stuart, or J. E. B., as he was called in the army, from his first initials, proved himself in his short career the greatest warrior among the great men who have been so called. Whether or no he was really descended from Robert the Bruce, he certainly inherited the kingly talent for leading men and making war. He won the great battle of May 3, 1863, which was decisive in this campaign, by skillful and gallant leading. He was but thirty years old when he took Jackson's place at the head of the Second Corps."[221]

And again, in describing Chancellorsville, Battine said:

> "The signal was then given for an assault. While the guns swept the road and the clearing on either side of it, Stuart led his infantry once more across the ravine, singing at the top of his voice and waving his sword. His blonde beard, blue eyes, and noble figure on horseback recalled the Norman hero who led the van at Hastings, singing the songs of Roland."

The city of Richmond, in grateful recognition of his sacrifice of

Lieut. Theodore S. Garnett, C.S.A.

life in her defense, voted him an equestrian statue, and yonder monument bears eloquent testimony as well to the fulfillment of that pledge as to his undying fame. His name is inseparably linked with that of his great commander and of his immortal lieutenant. Lee, Jackson, and Stuart form a trinity of Confederate faith, honor, and glory.

My comrades, this stone is well placed here by the hands of ever-faithful and devoted Confederate women. While it honors the dead, may it never lose its significance for the living! The graves at Hollywood are marked with many distinguished names of our Confederate dead. But history will search in vain for a nobler tomb than that of the brave, the joyous, the skillful, and beloved commander who died here.[222] — JUDGE THEODORE S. GARNETT, AID-DE-CAMP TO GENERAL STUART

STUART THE ECCENTRIC

☛ ... The people love a hero about whom they can tell a good joke now and then. That is one feature of hero worship. The plume which Jeb Stuart wore in his hat (there is a good joke about that plumed hat) and his passion for the banjo music of [Joe] Sweeney, whom he kept by his side, are eccentricities of a great man; but how delightful they are to talk of and to read about! And they show one phase of his character. They are the outcroppings of that perpetual gaiety and those high spirits with which Stuart was endowed above all other generals of the army, which kept his men from dejection in the camp and on the march, and were a tonic to them when they heard the round, full notes of the cavalier hero's voice as he went singing into battle. Let Stuart wear his plume. I like it.[223] — A. J. EMERSON

CONFEDERATE GIRLS DURING THE WAR

☛ ... The War Department [in Richmond, VA] was just across the street from us, and we often sat at the windows and watched the coming and going of the officers. We could see Gen. J. E. B. Stuart with his waving plume on his wide-brimmed hat, his clanking spurs sounding loudly on the pavement as he dismounted from his fine horse.[224] — MRS. MARK VALLENTINE, LITTLE ROCK, ARK.

THE SOLDIERS' LOVE OF GEN. STUART
☛ . . . It was on a June morning something more than a month after [the Battle of] Chancellorsville when General Lee reviewed Stuart's Cavalry on a wood-set plain to the north of Culpeper Court House. Death was forgotten on that early summer's day, and the zest of victory was in the air. The "army lifted its eyes to the crimson banner with its thirteen stars, and June was in every soldier's heart. To the right and left there sprang a rustling. The sun strengthened, the mists began to lift, and the bugles blared together. Into the very atmosphere sifted something like golden laughter." A shout arose: "Jeb Stuart! Jeb Stuart!" "Out of the misty forest, borne high, a vivid square in a sea of pearl, came a battle flag crimson and blue and thirteen-starred. Forth it paced, held high by a mounted standard bearer."[225] — MARY JOHNSTON (AND *CONFEDERATE VETERAN*)

STUART'S DEATH WOUND
☛ Having seen so many accounts of the wounding of General Stuart, all different and none correct, I feel that I would be derelict in my duty were I to fail to tell what 1 know about it. I was orderly sergeant of Company E, First Virginia Cavalry, Wickham's Brigade. I was never wounded, captured, or sick, consequently was never absent from my command except to procure fresh horses. I followed General Stuart as colonel first and then as brigadier and until his death. I have been waiting for a wiser head and abler pen than mine to tell of General Stuart's death; but as I am now in my seventy-fourth year, I will not procrastinate longer.

The starting point, Spotsylvania Court House, is well known. [Union Gen. Philip H.] Sheridan was on the Old Mountain road. Stuart was just in the rear, and he had several skirmishes with Sheridan's rear guard; but finding that nothing could be accomplished by following in the rear, Stuart sent a small force to retard Sheridan's movements as much as possible. With the rest of his command Stuart turned to the left and marched rapidly parallel with the Cincinnati and Ohio Railroad in order to gain Yellow Tavern. He struck the Brook road, turned to his right, and reached Yellow Tavern in advance of Sheridan, then turned on the mountain road and met him at the point where the fight took place. General Lomax was in advance, and when his column met the enemy the fight commenced.

The head of General Wickham's column was at a point on the Brook road, and he was turned across the field up a short steep hill. On reaching the top of the hill the Second, Third, and Fourth

Regiments were marched on to the battle ground, and the First was marched back down the hill and put in position near the Brook road, with the right of the regiment resting against a body of old field pines in order to be ready to strike the enemy should they repulse Lomax and pursue him to that point. However, instead of coming back by way of the tavern, as they went, they fell back in the angle formed by the two roads. After the fighting was all over on the mountain road and things had quieted, heavy firing was heard up the Brook road in the direction of Yellow Tavern.

Union headquarters, Sixth Army Corps, near Yellow Tavern, VA., February, 1865.

Being an orderly sergeant and not confined closely to ranks, I rode up to the edge of some pines to see if I could make any discovery, but the pines were so dense that nothing could be seen through them. I had been there but a very short time when General Stuart rode up right by my side and seemed deeply interested in the firing, which was getting closer every second. Suddenly the bullets commenced to come through the pines thick and fast all around us. As the place was not healthy and I had gone there without orders, I hurriedly left and joined my command, thinking we would have to charge. I had been at my post only a minute or two when word was passed down the line that General Stuart was wounded.

Now, you will observe that he, standing near the pines, was directly in line with the straight part of the road toward the tavern and that the man who shot him had no knowledge of his presence.

I learned afterwards that he had come over from the battle field to where the First was stationed and, not being satisfied with his day's work, had sent Capt. Wesley Hammond with his squadron up in the direction of the tavern to attack and draw the enemy down so that the First could get a chance at them, but failed, as they came only as far as the crook in the road, then retired.

The only Federals seen by the First Regiment that day were a few mixed up with Captain Hammond's men. He was killed, and his men came back at full speed. Cooke says in *Mohun* that the General seemed to be desperate after being repulsed and rushed into the enemy's lines, firing right and left with his pistol, when a Federal put a pistol to his side and fired the fatal shot. The fighting was all over at that point before he came over to our position.

Another account is that Stuart gathered a handful of men and charged Custer's Brigade and was taken back like chaff before the wind, when the First Regiment appeared and charged Custer and took him back dying; but a Yankee close to Stuart fired and killed his horse, and the second shot struck him. When a lieutenant ran to him and said, "General, you are wounded," he replied: "Yes, I am done for, but don't let my men know it. Get me another horse." They soon had another horse for him, but in attempting to rise he was unable to do so; so they put him on the horse and rode on each side of him to hold him on, and in that way he kept the field and continued to give orders. I shall contradict none of this, except to say that the First did not charge Custer or anybody else that day. The only fighting done by the First was what Captain Hammond's squadron did in trying to draw them down to give us a chance at them.

Mrs. Lee says in her little school history that Stuart was shot by a man who took rest on an iron fence. Now, I have ridden over the greater part of Virginia and portions of Pennsylvania and Maryland and have no recollection of seeing an iron fence in all my travels.

I am very much of the opinion that I was the last man who saw General Stuart before he was shot. He was very near the rear of the First, but behind them. The enemy were charging Captain Hammond, coming right toward us, and of course every eye was fixed on the road in front of them. Stuart was entirely alone, not one of his staff with him, and there were no troops anywhere in sight of us.[226] — B. J. HADEN, UNION MILLS, VA.

CONFEDERATE PRIVATE MEETS STUART ON THE FIELD

☞ . . . [On May 7th, 1864] our lines were reconstructed, advanced a little, and the afternoon passed in burying our dead and making breastworks. The losses on both sides were heavy, but necessarily heaviest on the Federal side. The nature of the ground made it impracticable to use artillery to advantage, and I remember well that during the whole battle of the Wilderness I heard only two cannon shots. In the re-formation of our lines on the 7th our brigade was placed on the extreme right and my own regiment, the Second South Carolina, on the right of the brigade. Quietness prevailed during the afternoon, but a little after sunset we heard, off to our right front, some sharp rifle-firing, followed by a Rebel yell. It lasted but a few minutes, and then all was quiet again. We made a fair supper on the contents of the haversacks of the dead enemy, and as darkness came on we began to "go to bed" between earth and sky.

But the "dull god" sleep was not to preside over us that night. At about half past seven a mounted officer dashed along the line and in sharp but suppressed speech said: "Attention, men! Fall into line!" Of course we privates jumped into line of battle and were sure the enemy was creeping up to us through the bushes. But the next moment the command, "By the right flank, march!" was given, and away we went in quick time through the thickets as best we could.

Stuart's cavalry boots.

Never before nor afterwards did I experience such a trying night march. On we went, with never a halt, over rough places, little streams, swamps, and through next to impenetrable thickets. The stars were bright, but there was no moon. A little before dawn we struck a road at a left oblique angle and followed the left end, thence on to a bridge over a little stream, and thence on to a crossroads, where at the first show of dawn we found Gen. J. E. B. Stuart and staff in the saddle.

Stuart was smiling, and in a moment he was all action. He turned the head of our regiment at right angles to the left and into the road leading north up a gentle slope. Open fields were on the right and thick pine woods on the left. Halfway up the slope Stuart and his staff wheeled our brigade into line of battle and double-quicked us up to the top of the low hill. There we found some of Stuart's cavalry dismounted behind fence rail breastworks in the open on both sides of the road, and advancing up the other side of the hill there was a heavy Federal line of battle. The dismounted cavalry quickly fell back through our ranks, and we as quickly occupied their position behind the rails. Our regiment, the Second, was on the left and the Third on the right of the road. Large fields were in our front, except some open pines on the right, where the Third Regiment took post. In the field directly in our front were a large two-story farmhouse and outbuildings.

At this time Stuart was the only Confederate general officer in sight and, figuratively speaking, just as cool as a piece of ice, though all the time laughing. He rode right along the lines and, with the help of his staff, personally posted all the regiments of the brigade. On rushed the solid lines of the enemy with every apparent confidence of rushing over us and capturing that hill, which was in truth the key of that route to Richmond. Stuart rode along our line, continually cheering us and telling us to hold our fire till the Federals were well in range. "And then," he said, "give it to them good and hold this position to the last man. Plenty of help is near at hand." He also told us that we had been sent to him to hold that hill at all hazards.

The position of the Third Regiment on the opposite side of the road was a little in advance of ours, and when the Federal line got up to a large wild cherry tree on the right side of the road the Third fired a solid and withering volley into it, and this was quickly followed by a similar volley by our regiment. The Federals seemed completely surprised, staggered, and as we continued our rain of lead into their ranks broke and retreated in great disorder down the hill and took shelter in a woods in their rear. But before they got back to the woods we saw one of their men turn back and run up the road toward us, and when he got near the cherry tree he stooped down and picked up the body of one of his comrades, put it on his shoulder, and rapidly walked back into his own lines. No Confederate gun was trained on that man. We all admired his pluck and imagined the picked-up body was that of his kinsman or friend. If he is still living or any of his comrades who saw this incident, I would like to hear from him or them.

The field in our front was blue with the dead and wounded Federals. They were Grant's van, under [Union Gen. Gouverneur Kemble] Warren, with orders to seize these heights of Spotsylvania Court House, and as prisoners they told us they imagined that the hill was held by a small force of our cavalry. And that was about where the little fight we heard the evening before took place. Stuart during this sharp fight was riding back and forth along our lines, cheering us with such words as, "Give it to them, boys!"

In this first fight at Spotsylvania the Third Regiment lost one killed, and the Second had three wounded. After the bloody repulse of the Federals some of the Third called over to us and said: "Nance's death is avenged." But very soon after this the forces of both armies began to arrive and take position under the eyes of skilled engineers. A strong Federal line of battle developed in the woods back of the farm buildings, marched up to them, and at once put into them a force of sharpshooters to annoy us. Up to this time no artillery had been used by either side, but a moment later a Confederate battery of four Enfield guns and one brass howitzer, personally directed by Stuart, dashed up and, planting their guns at intervals along our line, opened a rapid fire into the advancing enemy, and this checked them near the farmhouses, behind which many of them crowded for refuge. Then Stuart ordered the artillery to burn the buildings, and the very first incendiary shell from the brass cannon fired the main building. And then I saw a sight I never wanted to see again. A woman bareheaded, her long hair streaming behind, ran out of the big house and across the field to the left between the two fighting armies and reached shelter in the woods on the Po River.

Gen. John Bell Hood, C.S.A.

Now both sides rushed their legions to this great key to the route to Richmond. [Confederate Gen. John Bell] Hood's old division, under [Confederate Gen. Charles William] Field, arrived in line of battle and joined our left in the woods on the Po, and this completed the Confederate left. Entirely against his will, Grant found his objective again here at old Spotsylvania. By the middle of the afternoon, thousands of troops of both sides having arrived, we took position, began to build breastworks, and settled down to a death struggle. Bullets and shrieking shells filled the air, and one had to be very careful or stand a good chance of being picked off.

Stuart, after the arrival of other general officers, flew away to foil a Federal cavalry raid elsewhere and, a few days afterwards, to meet his death at Yellow Tavern. In every way Stuart was a grand man and every inch a true soldier. In the early morning of that day we privates thought him more than the equal of any other living man in cool bravery, dashing heroism, manly beauty, and all that went to make up our ideal of a military chieftain. He wore a full red beard, had searching eyes, a towering presence, was quick and ubiquitous in a fight, and sat his horse to perfection. I shall never forget the inspiring effect his presence had on our men on that bloody early morning and our regret when he galloped away to other fields.[227] — CONFEDERATE PRIVATE JOHN COXE, LILLIA'S LAKELET, GROVELAND, CAL.

VIRGINIA'S CONTRIBUTION TO THE CONFEDERACY
☛ . . . The Confederate cavalry in Virginia was commanded by J. E. B. Stuart. Though he was able at Chancellorsville to take Stonewall Jackson's place and successfully handle infantry, he loved cavalry service better and well deserved the name "Chevalier of the Southern Cause." He was untiring in the service and inspired his men with a devotion that made them willing to share the dangers into which his exacting orders carried them. It has been said that the supreme compliment to a company was its assignment to extra hazardous or fatiguing duty. The love between him and his men was a personal affection. His wish that he might be killed leading a cavalry charge was almost literally granted. He died May 12, 1864, of wounds received at the head of his troopers in an encounter on the road to Richmond May 10 between Stuart's Cavalry and a portion of Sheridan's command under Custer and Merritt. What wonder that the memories of his meteor-like flights haunted the dreams of John Esten Cooke's *Surrey*, and he exclaimed in his vision: "How the ghost of Stuart rides!"[228] — MISS MARGARET L. VON DER AU, ATHENS, GA.

STUART & THE BATTLE OF BRANDY STATION
☛ The greatest cavalry engagement of the war was fought on June 9, 1863, between [C.S.] Gen. J. E. B. Stuart, commander of the cavalry of the Army of Northern Virginia, and [U.S.] General [Alfred] Pleasanton, commanding the Federal cavalry of the Army of the Potomac. General Stuart's command at that time was composed of the following cavalry brigades: Turner Ashby's old brigade, commanded by Gen. W. E. Jones; W. H. F. Lee's, Wade Hampton's, Fitzhugh Lee's, and Beverly [Holcombe] Robertson's. General Pleasanton commanded [John] Buford's and [David McMurtrie] Gregg's Federal divisions of cavalry, two brigades of infantry, and four batteries of artillery. Four batteries of horse

artillery under General Stuart made the artillery on each side about equal.

Fitzhugh Lee's brigade had been advanced up the Rappahannock to Oak Shade as the advance guard of the army of Gen. R. E. Lee, which was then on the march to Pennsylvania, while General Stuart was left with the remainder of his command to guard the flank and protect the rear of the army. On the morning of June 9 General Pleasanton, with Buford's Cavalry Division and a brigade of infantry and two batteries, crossed the river at Beverly's Ford with this force, with a brigade of cavalry under Colonel [Benjamin Franklin] Davis in the advance. Company A. of the Sixth Virginia Cavalry, was on picket at the ford. My brother, S. W. Young, and Frank Alder, who were on the picket at the time, were both captured. The company was surprised, yet contended for every foot of ground between them and the camp of Jones's and W. H. F. Lee's brigades, near St. James Church, with the battalion of horse artillery. The Sixth Regiment, which was out on the road, got off first; the Seventh Regiment next, just as the Federals were getting up in our midst. Many of our men had not finished their breakfast and had to mount their horses bareback and rush into the fight. We succeeded in driving the Federals back at this time; and Colonel Davis, commanding the Federal advance, was killed. About this time the Federals were reenforced by a fresh brigade, which charged the Sixth and Seventh Regiments, driving them back past the artillery. Just then Hampton's Brigade came up, and by a combined effort the Federals were driven back and the artillery saved.

The firing in our front had almost ceased, except that of the

The Battle of Brandy Station.

sharpshooters on the skirmish line. General Gregg, commanding a division, had been ordered by General Pleasanton to cross the river at Kelly's Ford, four miles below, and attack General Stuart in the rear. Apprehending this, General Stuart ordered General Robertson with his brigade to take the road to Kelly's Ford and to hold General Gregg in check. General Robertson took the wrong road and went too far to the right and missed Gregg's command entirely, which allowed Gregg to pass on and gain Stuart's rear. Lieutenant Carter, with one gun of [Roger Preston] Chew's Battery, was the only obstacle in Gregg's way. He had gone to the rear with this gun because his ammunition was exhausted with the exception of a few damaged shells. These he managed to fire sufficiently to check Gregg in his advance until other troops could be sent back to his assistance. General Jones, who was one and a half miles in advance on Fleetwood Hill, the position occupied by Carter with his gun, and which point Gregg was trying to make, ordered the Twelfth Regiment of Virginia Cavalry to gallop at once to Fleetwood Hill to meet Gregg's advance.

When Col. A. [Asher] W. Harman reached Fleetwood Hill and met the Federals who were coming up, his regiment was badly scattered along the road. Those on the fastest and best horses were in the lead. Colonel Harmon did not wait for his men to close up, but went "at 'em." He was badly wounded in the fray. Just at this time the "Comanches," or Thirty-Fifth Battalion of Virginia Cavalry, came up to the assistance of the Twelfth Regiment, and their combined efforts drove the Federals back to a battery of theirs which was shelling our men, when Colonel [Elijah Viers] White charged this battery, driving the Federals from it. They soon rallied and came back, and at this time Colonel Lomax came gallantly up with the Eleventh Virginia Regiment, which, by the help of Hampton's Brigade, drove the Federals off and left three guns of the Federal battery in our hands. While this was being done in Stuart's rear, W. H. F. Lee with his brigade attacked Buford's command on his right and held him in check during the engagement at Fleetwood Hill. Gregg then fell back and joined Buford on his left, and the whole command of General Pleasanton fell back across the river. Night closed the scene of one of the greatest cavalry engagements of the war.

This battle was fought by fifteen regiments on the Confederate side, composing Jones's, Lee's, and Hampton's Brigades, and one regiment of Fitzhugh Lee's brigade, all cavalry and artillery. General Stuart had no infantry in this battle. Robertson's Brigade was at no time engaged, having missed the road to Kelly's Ford and being unable to get back in time to take part in the battle. The Federal forces under General Pleasanton consisted of cavalry and infantry amounting to 10,981 effective men, while General Stuart had about 7,000 men. Pleasanton lost 936 officers and men and three guns of the Sixth New York Battery, while General Stuart lost 523 men and officers. General Stuart fought this battle under great disadvantage, being surprised by Buford in the morning at Beverly's Ford and then being surprised by Gregg in the rear. Charging and countercharging continued during the whole day.[229] — CONFEDERATE CAPT. T. J. YOUNG, AUSTIN, ARK.

Title page, sheet music for the popular Confederate song, *The Bonnie Blue Flag*.

CHAPTER 9

LAST ORDERS OF JACKSON, STUART, & LEE

☛ At Chancellorsville on the first evening of the battle, about an hour before [Stonewall] Jackson was killed, he met Gen. R. E. Lee at the Block House on the Plank Road leading from Orange Court House to Fredericksburg by Chancellorsville, and this was their last meeting. Jackson was placing his infantry line for the night after leaving General Lee and coming on his own line. Gen. Fitz [Fitzhugh] Lee's line of cavalry was in front of Jackson's. There Jackson met Gen. J. E. B. Stuart for the last time. Jackson's first words to General Stuart were: "Have you a man that knows the country here? I have lost sight of Major Johnson with my ordnance and supply train, and I cannot locate him. I must have him here by four o'clock in the morning sharp." General Stuart said to me: "Weller, have you a man that knows this country?" "No one so well as myself." "Then you report to General Jackson." Jackson said to Stuart: "Can you spare Weller to-night?" "Certainly," said General Stuart. General Jackson said to me: "This is an important mission. I have lost sight of Major Johnson in the fight this evening. Now, I want you to have him at the Block House at four o'clock in the morning with my ordnance and supply train." And Jackson repeated to me: "This is an important mission, and may God speed you!" These were his last words to me. He started up his line and in less than one hour was killed. He got between his and the cavalry line of Fitz Lee, which we had just left for the night. He extended his line a little too far, and, returning on Lee's line in the dark, he got in front of his own line and was killed [by friendly fire].

Gen. William E. Jones, C.S.A.

I rode for Johnson, which was a dismal ride over the country in the night, and I could not get even a negro to tell me anything; but about twelve o'clock I found the train by a dim light and delivered my message to Major Johnson. I was tired and so was my horse. I procured some corn for my horse, then the next was for myself. I went to Jim, the Major's cook, and he gave me some cold biscuits and a piece of beef. I laid down by my horse and thought I would let him eat, then I would return to General Stuart by daylight but, to my surprise, there came a courier from General Stuart for me to come back at once and meet him on the Plank Road just beyond the Block House toward Chancellorsville. This Block House was a little schoolhouse in the forks of the road. When I arrived there, Stuart told me what had happened, that we had lost Jackson, that he was in command of Jackson's Corps of Infantry, and that we would be in the infantry. Gen. Fitz Lee was in charge of the cavalry, and Stuart wanted me to stay with him.

The line of battle was across the main road toward Chancellorsville, with [Confederate] General [Robert Emmett] Rodes's division on the right and [Confederate] General [Raleigh Edward] Colston's division on the left. The enemy had felled timber all night, which made it difficult to get through, but the boys went through. The Federals had thirty-eight pieces of artillery in position to play upon that road, but with all that they could not stop us. Soon their line began to break, and then their thirty-eight pieces were silenced, and they began to retreat by Chancellorsville toward the river. Just as soon as they came to the Chancellorsville house they set fire to it. There were many soldiers in it. General Stuart saw the fire and said to me: "Weller, you go to General Rodes and get thirty men and put out the fire." I got my men and formed a skirmish line, but lost four before I could reach the fire. They made it hot for us, and when we got there we could get no water. The water had to come from a well, and I knew the men would be killed at the well; so we had to let the house burn. I got my men behind the house and tore down the building connecting the house with the stables and saved the men in the stables and yard, the Federals still keeping it warm for us, though they were retreating as fast as they could. Just at that time General Stuart appeared. He saw the situation and that our line was moving forward, and he said to me: "Take your men and try to locate the enemy's position." They retreated north on the Culpeper road to Mrs. Kiles's farm, in the direction of their pontoons, where they made the second stand. I reported their position to General Stuart, and the whole of our line moved forward for the final result.

That evening in the advance Stuart saw from where he was that the third brigade of Colston's left was not moving. He said: "Weller, see what the trouble is with that brigade." I went and found no field officer. They were all killed or wounded. I came back and reported this, when General Stuart said: "You go and take charge of it yourself and form a line on Colston's left. You will have to travel quick to get into line, and stay there until I relieve you." That was as hot a place as I want to get into; but that was the close of the day's fight, and we lay on the battle field that night, where there was great suffering among ten thousand men on both sides. After the field was cleared, General Stuart resumed his cavalry command.

Gen. Robert E. Lee, C.S.A.

I don't remember just what turn we made; but, anyway, I must not forget to tell of making fifty-five Yanks run, and I did it easily at that. We were marching for Gettysburg in two lines by the Bull Run route. Gen. Fitz Lee was on the right of Fairfax Court House, on the Alexander road to Centerville, I don't remember dates; but one bright morning, when Gen. J. E. B. Stuart was leading with his staff, we came to Fairfax Station, on the Orange and Alexandria Railroad. As daylight began to dawn, General Stuart said to General [Wade] Hampton, whose brigade led, "We will stop and let our command rest a couple of hours," which we did. Then Stuart said: "Captain Weller, take ten men and go to the courthouse and see if everything is clear." I started with my men. It was light when I struck the town. Right in front of me I saw a door partly open, and a man's hand waved to me. When I went to him, he said: "You had better be careful. Fifty or sixty Yanks went by here last evening toward Centerville, and I think they camped at the water just out of town." At that the Yanks caught sight of my men. We heard a few shots. There they were, all clerks from the department. I had a good horse, and my only chance to escape was to outwind them. They captured my men and left them under guard, and then all started after me. The idea struck me that if they did not kill me I would run them into General Hampton's brigade, which I did. General Stuart heard us coming and ordered Hampton to mount his brigade and form a line. I was coming, with my fifty Yanks after me, and at close range; so Stuart kept undercover of the timber. I soon saw the situation; and as they seemed determined to get me, I went right on past Hampton's command, when he just made a left turn and swiped them all on the spot, and it was a great relief to me. I escaped with a few scars to my horse and myself. Then Gen. Fitz Lee marched into the east end of town and recaptured my ten men. That ended the race, and we needed the fifty horses for our men that were afoot.

The march was resumed toward Rockville, on the Potomac, where we crossed over into Maryland. Just before we got to the river General Stuart sent me to the front of the line of march. General Hampton's brigade was in front and also Hampton's old company, commanded by Lieutenant Hampton, the General's son. General Stuart told me to help young Hampton get some videttes across the canal. Just as soon as we struck the towpath I told Hampton that we were all right; there was a boat coming, which was captured at once. The driver hallooed out, "Here is the damn Rebels," and we made the boatman turn the boat crosswise of the canal and throw out his gang plank. Hampton dismounted twenty men, and over they went to the Maryland side as videttes. I left Hampton's company there. We could cross the canal only by bridging the lock, which was narrow, and could go only by fours so it took us all night, and during that time forty-two boats collected there, some going up and some down. They were all freight boats, but two of the packet boats had soldiers from Grant's army going to Washington, some of them sick and wounded. Hampton's men took charge of the boats and got plenty of grain to feed all of our horses, and they gathered all the prisoners in the little town of Rockville.

I was working to get the command across the lock, and just at daylight General Stuart sent me an order to burn all of the boats there. That was hard, but I delayed until I could investigate. I found that all of the boats were private property, and the men had their families living there. They had their mules to draw the boats, their milch cows, pigs, geese, and chickens with them. They were people that had been there since the Chesapeake and Ohio Canal was built. I told the boys to hold. I could not burn the boats until I saw General Stuart. I found Stuart, Hampton, Morgan, and Wickham all together, and I said: "General Stuart, I have disobeyed your order for the present." "Why did you?" he said. When I explained the situation, General Stuart said: "How can you put them out of commission?" "I propose to turn all boats crosswise in the canal and then cut the sluice gate to the river. That will tear out such a big opening that it will leave them high and dry for sixty or ninety days." General Stuart said to the other generals: "What do you think of Weller's proposition?" General Hampton said: "Weller is right." He then told me to line up all of the prisoners and administer the oath and turn them loose and follow up the command as fast as I could.

Col. Elijah V. White, C.S.A.

Then the curtain rolled up for Gettysburg. We played many trying scenes behind the footlights until we came to Spotsylvania Court House about May 9, 1864, where General Stuart's last order was given to me by himself. That morning all of his staff were with him, consisting of Maj. H. B. McClellan, Capt. John Esten Cooke (author of *Surrey of Eagle's Nest*), Captain White, of Maryland, and Capt. B. [Ben] Weller, chief of couriers [the writer]. We were coming down the road from the Wilderness, and General Stuart was humming his old favorite song, "Old gray horse, get out of the Wilderness, bully boys, hey."

[Confederate] General [George Thomas] Anderson, who was in command of General Longstreet's corps of infantry, passed just at that time. There came a courier from Gen. Fitz Lee with a dispatch stating that he was on the Todd Tavern road, and the enemy was pressing him with their infantry, and he was losing heavily. General Stuart turned to me and said: "Weller, you go to General Anderson and get a brigade of infantry and relieve General Lee and stay there until I relieve you." The colonel had reported to me who was in command of the brigade. I took up a little ravine near the turn of the road, placed the men behind an old fence, where I told them to lie down close to the ground, and when the enemy got within a hundred yards to let them have it, which they did, the enemy coming in regular line of battle. We repulsed them the third time before they would turn, and they then turned toward the courthouse to our right. Being the only man on a horse and the second on the charge, I got a piece of shell through my left arm, but did not leave my line. As it bled profusely, I got one of the men to tie my handkerchief around my arm, put a stick through it, and twist it tightly.

General Stuart found out that I was wounded, and he relieved me. Then the big fight was on. I went south past the Block House, and there at a farmhouse I found Dr. Eliason, our division surgeon, who dressed my arm. I had washed some of the blood off and fixed myself for the night, when about sunset General Stuart rode up and inquired where I was. I was sitting on my saddle blanket, and he rode to where I was, got down and sat by me, and began to ask me about the roads east of Spotsylvania Court House. I took a piece of paper and made him a diagram as nearly as I could, and then I said: "General, I will be with you to-morrow." "No; I have a more important mission for you to perform which will be of more benefit to the Confederacy than for you to try to ride with me. I will have all the necessary papers for you to go to Staunton, in Augusta County, and relieve Col. M. C. Herman, our quartermaster, and put some one else in his place. This is an important mission. Go there first and then go down home and get well. I want you with me." I thanked him. He got on his horse and said that if anything should come up in the morning to prevent his being at the Block House with the papers, Major McClellan would be there with them for me at 9 a.m. sharp. McClellan was there, but I never saw General Stuart again. He was killed at Yellow Tavern the day I reached Staunton. There the curtain fell with one of our headlights.

Col. Roger P. Chew, C.S.A.

We had many rough rehearsals behind the footlights until we reached Appomattox, April 9, 1865. After Stuart was killed, I returned to Gen. Fitzhugh Lee and remained with him until the surrender at Appomattox. We arrived there the night of the 8th, and about 4 a.m. the next morning up rode a courier to Fitz Lee's headquarters under a tree with a dispatch stating that the enemy had taken possession of the Lynchburg road in front of us. General Lee turned to me and said: "Weller, you go and find Gen. R. E. Lee and give him my compliments and say to him that the enemy has taken possession of the Lynchburg road and shall I open it." General Lee said: "Give Gen. Fitz Lee my compliments and say to him that if the enemy does not press him to remain where he is." But while I was making the ride Gen. Fitz Lee drove the enemy back with the loss of some men, and when I delivered R. E. Lee's order Gen. Fitz Lee said: "Go back to Gen. R. E. Lee with my compliments and tell him that I have opened the road." Gen. R. E. Lee then said: "Wait; I will answer." During the time I was by his side, and we had crossed over the road to an old fence, when up rode [Union] General [George Armstrong] Custer with the papers in regard to the meeting with General Grant. Then General Lee turned to me and said: "Weller, give Gen. Fitz Lee my compliments and say to him that there are no further orders."

Then the curtain fell. That communication of orders through me ended the war at Appomattox April 9, 1865.[230] ⎯ CONFEDERATE CAPT. BEN WELLER, COMPANY E, FIRST VIRGINIA CAVALRY, LOS ANGELES, CAL.

CRITICISM OF STUART AT GETTYSBURG

☛ . . . I have said that this battle [the Battle of Gettysburg] was the result of accident, and due to the absence of the Confederate cavalry, which should have been at hand to inform General Lee of the movements and position of the Federal army. Where was it?

When General Lee determined upon the campaign, General J. E. B. Stuart was directed to place all the cavalry on the right flank of the army, and, by moving east of the Blue Ridge, to watch and follow the enemy across the Potomac. When General Lee reached Chambersburg [PA] with Longstreet's and Hill's corps, Ewell's being in advance at Carlisle and York, he had received no direct communication from Stuart and he was ignorant of his whereabouts. Stuart, however, after leaving two brigades of his cavalry to hold the gaps of the Blue Ridge, with no enemy in front of them, had crossed the Potomac at Seneca Creek, above Washington, and was on "one of his wild raids" around the rear of the Federal army. At Rockville [MD] he captured a wagon train, which he attempted to carry along with him. Reaching Hanover, he found himself opposed by a strong force of Federal cavalry, and, as his horses and men were nearly worn out, he undertook to join the main army or some part of it. He accordingly made a night march to York, but [Jubal Anderson] Early had gone; and, pushing along to Carlisle, he found it occupied by a Federal force.

After throwing some shells into the town and setting fire to the barracks located there, fearing that the army was engaged in a battle at Gettysburg, he hurried as best he could with his jaded troopers to lend a tardy assistance to the army from which he had been so long absent.

Stuart's carbine.

There was no good result from this raid—a wagon train and a paltry score of paroled prisoners not compensating for the embarrassment which General Lee had experienced. I never heard, however, that General Lee ever reproved General Stuart for this futile raid, although it will go down in history as the cause of the failure of this great campaign.

What the feeling was in the Union army that night I am unable to say; but that of the Confederates was one of exultation, for they had nearly accomplished the end in view, and confidently rested on their arms in the hope of a successful issue on the following day.[231]

— SOUTHERN HISTORIAN ROBERT ALONZO BROCK

THE BATTLE OF CHANCELLORSVILLE

☛ On the morning of April 27, 1863, the boom of cannon awoke me from my pleasant slumbers and dreams of peace. I was a member of Company B, First Regiment of South Carolina Volunteers, and was with a detail guarding a man's premises to keep the soldiers from trespassing on the fowl house and pig pens. We had been there several weeks, faring sumptuously, being well fed by the owner of the plantation. Not long after the first shot I saw a courier dashing down the road, toward the farmhouse. He handed me an order which read: "Sergeant [J. M.] Hood [the writer] will report with his men at once to his company, which is under marching orders."

When we reached the camp the command was marching toward Deep Bottom, on the Rappahannock River, near Fredericksburg. [Union] General [Joseph] Hooker had sent a part of his army across at this point as a feint, the main army having crossed at United States Ford and other fords above and formed a line of battle at Chancellorsville.

On the early morning of the 1st of May, 1863, Gen. Stonewall Jackson's corps was ordered to march up the plank road toward Orange Court House. This corps marched all day and late in the evening, when we formed a line of battle and advanced to the works of the enemy, which we battered until dark. Early the next morning General Jackson left a mere skirmish line and marched the rest of the corps toward Richmond, as we thought. We were on a forced march all day, until nearly night, when we crossed the plank road about two or three miles from where we had left it that morning. My brigade, under command of Brigadier General [Samuel] McGowan, marched down the plank road right after the Yankees, who, finding themselves flanked, broke ranks and fled. All we had to do was to load, shoot, raise the Rebel yell, and charge them.

Gen. Samuel McGowan, C.S.A.

After this little skirmish, General Jackson ordered us out to the right of the road. By this time it was quite dark; in fact, because of the dense undergrowth it soon became so dark that I could not see my hand before me. I remember lying flat on the ground while the shells from the Yankee battery were cutting off the tops and limbs of trees, which were falling all about us. I did not know what moment the limb of a tree might fall upon me.

As soon as their battery became silent General Jackson marched us out to the right of a little old blind road and placed us in line of battle. After ordering us to lie with our guns in our hands, he placed videttes on the road with instructions to fire immediately on any one coming down that way. With his aids General Jackson went to reconnoiter. In the darkness they lost their way and came down this protected road themselves. The videttes fired at once, wounding General Jackson and some of his staff. I heard the guns that may be said to have cut off the "right arm of General Lee." We did not know of the sad affair until the next day. General Jackson died ten days later, and the army of the Confederacy lost one of the greatest generals that the world has ever seen. Gen. J. E. B. Stuart was assigned to the command of our corps.

Sunday morning, the 3rd of May, dawned bright and fair. Along the line came the order to advance. Slowly and cautiously the line of battle moved forward. The works of the enemy came into view. With a great Rebel yell we charged them, but, behold! when we captured them there were no Yankees there. Still yelling, we crossed the works and mounted the top of a hill, looking down into a ravine. There we found them massed just in our front, and they accommodated us with a considerable volley of small arms. The first one of our number killed on that Sabbath day was a boy of sixteen years, very much out of place in that terrible carnage. On the march up to Chancellorsville this boy, Jimmie Hunter by name, kept saying that he was going to a May ball. Noticing across the river a balloon sent up by the enemy to watch our movements, Jimmie laughingly said: "Mr. Hooker, you have looked at my hand, and I won't play." He played his last hand that day.

After considerable fighting the Yankees began to retreat. General Stuart came trotting along our line whistling "Old Joe Hooker, Git Out o' the Wilderness." The soldiers took it up and sang it lustily as they ran in pursuit of the enemy. We followed them past the Chancellorsville Court House, crossed the plank road, and stacked arms. Just as we left the plank road we noticed that a battery of the enemy had been blown up, with the caissons loaded with shrapnel, killing a great many horses and men. Never had we seen a forest so badly torn up. Every tree was literally torn into shreds.

The Battle of Chancellorsville, April 30 to May 6, 1863.

After resting until late in the afternoon, we moved farther to our left. As we marched along we noticed that a great many soldiers had been burned, the woods having caught fire from bursting shells. Near some of the soldiers there was evidence that they had made an effort to clear a space around them, where they lay with gaping wounds; but the fire was unmerciful. In line of battle we lay quiet until after dark, when the enemy sent a few volleys among us, which were returned with interest.

On the following day, Monday, we built breastworks and lay in them until Tuesday, when the Yankees crossed to the north bank of the Rapidan River. We then marched down the plank road to Hamilton's Crossing and went into camp, remaining there until late in June, when we started on the memorable trip to Gettysburg, Pa.[232] — CONFEDERATE SGT. J. M. HOOD, ATLANTA, GA.

A JOKE ON STUART'S CAVALRY

☛ I think it was soon after the return of Lee's army from the Gettysburg campaign that Stuart had the grand review of his cavalry division; at least there was such a review.

A few days before the review, while we of Lane's Brigade were quietly resting in camp, we were surprised to see cavalrymen dash through our camp, some of them without hats, completely stampeded. We asked what was the matter, and they said the Yanks had run them out of their camps. We were [then] rushed off some ten miles to intercept this cavalry raid, at some point, I think, on the Rappahannock, and stayed all night, returning to camp the next day.

A few days after [this] we went out to witness the grand review. Before starting some one suggested that we had better take our arms and accouterments, which we did. As we trudged along squadrons of cavalry kept passing us, and we were hailed with: "Boys, where are you going?" The reply was: "Out to the grand review." "What are you doing with your guns and accouterments?" Our reply was: "Why, to keep the Yankees off till you get through, of course." I think I heard some muttered imprecations, and I don't think I imagined it, either.[233] — REV. H. H. STURGIS, HOMESTEAD, FLA.

LEE'S EYES & EARS

☛ [Fortunately for General Robert E. Lee, he could obtain important information concerning vital military questions from] the commander of his cavalry, James Ewell Brown Stuart, commonly called Jeb Stuart from the three first initial letters of his name.

This distinguished cavalryman was a native of Patrick County, Va., a graduate at West Point of the class of 1854, and a soldier from the feathers in his hat to the rowels of his spurs. He was twenty-nine years old when Lee ordered him to locate McClellan's right flank and in the full vigor of a robust manhood. His brilliant courage, great activity, immense endurance, and devotion to his profession had already marked him as a cavalry commander of unquestioned merit. He had the fire, zeal, and capacity of Prince Rupert, but, like him, lacked caution; the dash of Murat, but was sometimes rash and imprudent; was as skillful and vigorous as Frederick the Great's celebrated cavalry leader, and, like [Prussian military leader Anton Friedrich von] Seidlitz, was willing to break the necks of some of his men by charging over rough ground if he made bold horsemen of the rest and gained his object. He would have gone as far as Cardigan, with "cannon to right of him, cannon to left of him, cannon in front of him."

Gen. Fitzhugh Lee, C.S.A.

He was a Christian dragoon—an unusual combination. His Bible and tactics were his text-books. He never drank liquor, having given a promise to his mother to that effect when a small boy, but when wet from the storm and wearied from the march he would drink, without cream or sugar, the contents of a tin quart cup of strong coffee. Duty was his guiding star. Once when on the eve of an expected battle he was telegraphed that his child was dying and urged to go to her, he replied: "I shall have to leave my child in the hands of God; my duty requires me here."

Lee knew him well. He had been a classmate at the United States Military Academy of his eldest son, and was his aid-de-camp when [socialist] John Brown was captured. Such was the man who stood before his commander on June 11, 1862, to receive his instructions.[234] — CONFEDERATE GEN. FITZHUGH LEE

FOLLOWING THE FEATHER

☛ . . . Stuart was near Ely's ford with the cavalry and the Sixteenth North Carolina Infantry, having gone there after dark to hold Averell still, who, having returned from his raid, was reported to be at that point. At 10:30 P.M. Captain [Richard Henry Toler]

Adams, of Hill's staff, summoned him to the command of Jackson's corps. Upon his arrival upon the battlefield, Jackson had been taken to the rear, but A. P. [Ambrose Powell] Hill, who was still there, turned over the command to him. With the assistance of Colonel E. P. [Edward Porter] Alexander, of the artillery, he was engaged all night in preparations for the morrow.

Gen. Isaac R. Trimble, C.S.A.

At early dawn on the 3rd, Stuart pressed the corps forward—Hill's division in the first line, [Isaac Ridgeway] Trimble's in second and [Robert Emmett] Rodes' in rear. As the sun lifted the mist, the ridge to his right was found to be a commanding position for artillery. Quickly thirty pieces, under Colonels T. H. Carter and Hilary P. Jones, were firing from it. Their fire knocked a piece of the door or pillar of the apartment [Union Gen. Joseph] Hooker was occupying at Chancellorsville against him, and struck him down senseless. [Union Gen. Alfred] Pleasanton says when he saw him about 10 A.M. that day, "he was lying on the ground, usually in a doze, except when I woke him up to attend to some important dispatch." [Union Gen. Darius Nash] Couch was then temporarily called to the command.

Stuart pressed onward. At one time his left was so strongly pressed that his three lines were merged into one while holding his position. He replied to a notice sent him that the men were out of ammunition, that they must hold their ground with the bayonet.

About this time Stuart's right connected with [Richard Heron] Anderson's left, uniting thus the two wings of General Lee's army. He then massed infantry on his left, and at 8 A.M. stormed the enemy's works. Twice he was repulsed, but the third time Stuart placed himself on horseback at the head of the troops, and ordering the charge, carried and held them—singing, with a ringing voice, "Old Joe Hooker, won't you come out of the Wilderness?" An eye-witness says of him that he could not get rid of the impression that "Harry of Navarre" led the charge, except that Stuart's plume was black, for everywhere the men "followed his feather."^{235} —
CONFEDERATE GEN. FITZHUGH LEE

A PERSONAL ENCOUNTER

☛ ... [On May 3, 1863, a] little after dawn the next morning the battle [of Chancellorsville] opened. A six-gun battery planted just in front of the brick Chancellorsville house received our special attention, and General [Jeb] Stuart, taking position about twenty yards on our right, sat for some time witnessing the duel, seemingly much interested. I had never been so near him before and was much impressed by his fine presence and his absolute indifference to the rain of shell and shrapnel to which he was exposed. He was mounted on a trim light bay, which had received a slight wound in the neck from which the blood trickled in a tiny, steady stream. I remember being relieved when I saw that it was not flowing in jets. He sat his horse with an easy grace, reminding me of the perfect seat of General [Wade] Hampton and of Col. Alex C. Haskell. Soon he galloped off to the right toward McGowan's Brigade, which was then charging the enemy's fortified line, and we saw him no more.[236] — J. W. BRUNSON

THE TRUE SPIRIT OF CHIVALRY

☛ ... One of the remarkable things about the war and which was one of the important factors in prolonging the resistance of the South against such tremendous odds was the large number of military leaders of very great ability. Napoleon [III] was not supported by an abler body of lieutenants, and among them was none abler than [Richard Heron] "Fighting Dick" Anderson. There was something in the life of the Old South that gave interest in and fitness for military affairs. As Senator [George Frisbie] Hoar, of [Concord] Massachusetts, once put it: "The institutions of the South promoted the aptness for command and the spirit of generous hospitality." Not that our people loved war, but they felt the obligation to defend at any cost their heritage of liberty and civilization won in war by their fathers. It was this spirit that led such men as Lee, Jackson, the two Johnstons, Anderson, [Jeb] Stuart, Forrest, Wheeler, and their fellow officers to sacrifice all earthly advantages for the beleaguered South. It was the true spirit of chivalry.[237] — JAMES HUGH MCNEILLY, D.D., NASHVILLE, TENN.

A PLEASANT REMINDER

☛ I was [recently] reminded of an interesting conversation I had with Gen. J. E. B. Stuart at the headquarters of the cavalry corps near Orange Court House just before the opening of the campaign of 1864.

I was doing staff duty with the General at the time, and we were sitting in his hut descanting upon the probabilities and possibilities of the coming campaign. Suddenly his face glowed with old-time recollections, and he said: "There is a Yankee general, a corps commander, whom I know well, and if by any chance he should fall into my hands at any time I will share my blanket with him."

"Who is it, General?" I asked.

"Why, old Sedg," said he. "He was my instructor at West Point, and I was very fond of him."

Strange to say, both died within three days of each other, [Union Gen. John] Sedgwick being killed on the 9th and Stuart dying on the 12th of May in Richmond from wounds received at Yellow Tavern on the day previous.

This incident goes to show the kindly feeling evinced by some of the old West Pointers for each other which the deadly strife they were engaged in on opposite sides could not utterly eradicate. And it shows the eminently grand and noble soul of Stuart in thus proclaiming his feeling toward his old preceptor and proving his knighthood, which always "was in flower."[238] — MAJ. WILLIAM M. PEGRAM, OF BALTIMORE, MD.

FROM ONE GENERAL TO ANOTHER

☛ Jeb Stuart was the greatest cavalryman America ever saw.[239] — CONFEDERATE GEN. JAMES LONGSTREET

THE BRILLIANT CIRCUIT

☛ . . . Lee's first duty upon assuming command of the Army of Northern Virginia was the unpleasant one of having to resist the general wish and advice of his officers to fall back upon a stronger position nearer to Richmond. He felt that such action was unnecessary and impolitic, but he also felt that he did not yet have the confidence of his officers and troops.

Under such circumstances it was a bold thing for him, in opposition to the judgment of those whom he usually trusted, to decide to stand his ground; but he did it with excellent results. His decision once reached, he set about obtaining reenforcements in his usual vigorous fashion. He also sent out that brave cavalryman, General J. E. B. Stuart, to obtain information as to McClellan's forces and situation. Stuart executed a brilliant circuit of the whole Union army, and Lee knew that he had another great lieutenant besides Jackson. He now prepared to take the offensive.[240] — WILLIAM PETERFIELD TRENT

ANOTHER VIEW OF STUART'S CIRCULAR RIDE

☛ . . . McClellan had no correct idea of the number of Lee's men. Lee then summoned that dashing young cavalryman, "Jeb" Stuart, who had assisted him in the capture of [socialist] "Old John Brown," and asked him to scout around the right wing of the enemy [George Brinton McClellan], and find out his strength. Stuart's response to this request was one of the most daring cavalry raids ever recorded.

With 1200 men he set out, circled the Federal right, attacked and scattered several bodies of cavalry that tried to stop him, and made his way to the rear of the Federal army, thus learning exactly its size and strength. Then, as the enemy were now aroused along the track he had just passed over, he boldly continued his headlong ride, circled the Federal left wing, and came victoriously into camp, having lost but one man from his entire troop, and after being in the saddle more than forty hours. Jeb Stuart was now prepared to give Lee full and exact information.

At one point in this daring raid, which astonished North and South and nearly paralyzed McClellan, Stuart had found his force confronted by a swollen river, the bridge having been carried away. Near by stood a barn. The resourceful leader promptly directed that this structure be torn down and a bridge built from its materials. This was done, and the marvelous raid was triumphantly completed.[241] — BRADLEY GILMAN

HONOR TO WHOM HONOR IS DUE

☛ . . . The cause that gave to the world Robert E. Lee, Stonewall Jackson, Joseph E. Johnston, Albert Sidney Johnston, Nathan Bedford Forrest, Joseph Wheeler, John H. Morgan, J. E. B. Stuart, Wade Hampton, and John B. Gordon cannot and will not be forgotten.

If those who were actors in the conflict or descendants of those who made such marvelous record should fail or refuse to honor the Confederate cause [Americanism] and those who battled for the rights of the South, the world will and ought to reckon them as ingrates and cravens.[242] — CONFEDERATE· COL. BENNETT HENDERSON YOUNG, LOUISVILLE, KY.

Gen. John B. Gordon, C.S.A.

HEROISM IN WAR
☞ . . . For skill, strategy, generalship, and leadership I am persuaded that unbiased, unprejudiced history must willingly accord full meed of praise, appreciation, and applause to such military leaders as Lee, . . . Jackson, Johnston, Forrest, Stuart, and many others whose names and fame will echo down the paths of the ages, sung by poets and proclaimed by sages.²⁴³ — JUDGE JOHN T. GOOLRICK, FREDERICKSBURG, VA.

THE MORALE OF THE CONFEDERATE SOLDIER
☞ . . . Inasmuch as the Southern soldier fought so impressively for a principle, the hidden springs of his morale were without doubt spiritual—that is, founded in human character.

Perhaps an army, like a nation, can be judged from its leaders. Throughout the South many officers, comprising the cream of the staff, were known as "praying" soldiers—Robert E. Lee, "Stonewall" Jackson, D. H. Hill, J. E. B. Stuart, [Edmund] Kirby Smith, W. N. [William Nelson] Pendleton, John B. Gordon, and President Jefferson Davis.²⁴⁴ — C. R. SPENCER, JR., WHITEVILLE, N.C.

IN STUART'S OWN WORDS
☞ Gen. J. E. B. Stuart issued an order on June 13 [1863] in which he said: "With an abiding faith in the God of battles and a firm reliance on the saber, your success will continue." He was a firm believer in the saber, but some experts to-day say a club would answer the same purpose.

In his report of the Gettysburg campaign General Stuart says: "In retiring from Middleburg [Pennsylvania] one of our guns had the axle broken by one of the enemy's shots, and the piece had to be abandoned. This is the first piece of my horse artillery which has ever fallen into the enemy's hands."²⁴⁵ — *CONFEDERATE VETERAN*

STUART'S JOY RIDE IN THE GETTYSBURG CAMPAIGN
☞ [Matthew Forney] Steele's (an Alabamian) *American Campaigns* tells us that Stuart's Confederate Cavalry was out of place at the critical time, and its raid around the Federal army was a fatal mistake, which is a fact, as events turned out. There is no doubt in the world that the march was ordered, but left entirely to Stuart as to the conduct of same, with the result as noted above. On the morning of July 1 [1863] Stuart reported: "Reaching Dover, Pa., I was unable to find our forces, and the whereabouts of our army was still a mystery." General Lee said: "The movements of the army

preceding the battle of Gettysburg had been much embarrassed by the absence of the cavalry." But Stuart went within a few miles of Washington and captured a wagon train.[246] — JOHN C. STILES

COMPANY Q
☛ Gen. J. E. B. Stuart published an order on July 29 [1863] which started as follows: "The nondescript, irregular body of men known as Company Q, which has so long disgraced the cavalry service and degraded the individuals resorting to it, is hereby abolished."[247] — JOHN C. STILES

LEE'S LETTER TO HIS WIFE MARY
☛ I reviewed the cavalry in this section yesterday. It was a splendid sight. The men and horses looked well. They have recuperated since last fall. [Jeb] Stuart was in all his glory. Your sons and nephews were well and flourishing. The country here looks very green and pretty, notwithstanding the ravages of war. What a beautiful world God, in His loving kindness to His creatures, has given us! What a shame that men endowed with reason and knowledge of right should mar His gifts.[248] — FROM A LETTER BY CONFEDERATE GEN. ROBERT E. LEE, DATED JUNE 8, 1863.

STUART, THE SOUTH, & THE SLAVERY MYTH

Mrs. Varina H. Davis.

☛ . . . I maintain that the Southern States did not go to war for the perpetuation of slavery, but for the preservation of the principle of self-government. To say that the battle flag of the Confederacy was the emblem of slave power and that Lee and Jackson and their heroic soldiers fought not for liberty, but for the right to hold their fellow men in bondage, is to contradict the facts of history. Jefferson Davis, the President of the Confederacy, declared that the South was not fighting for slavery; and, in fact, he embarked on the enterprise of secession believing that he would as a consequence lose his slaves, for he wrote to his wife [Varina Howell] in February, 1861, "In any case our slave property will eventually be lost"—that is to say, whether successful or not in establishing the Southern Confederacy.

Lee, the foremost soldier of the South, long before the war had emancipated the few slaves that came to him by inheritance; whereas his Union antagonist, General Grant, held on to those that had come to him through marriage with a Southern woman until they were freed by the Thirteenth Amendment. Stonewall Jackson never owned more than two negroes, a man and a woman, whom he bought at their earnest solicitation. He kept account of the wages he would have paid white labor, and when he considered himself reimbursed for the purchase money (for he was a poor man) he gave them their freedom. Gen. Joseph E. Johnston never owned a slave, nor did Gen. A. P. Hill, nor Gen. Fitzhugh Lee. Gen. J. E. B. Stuart, the great cavalry leader, owned but two, and he rid himself of both long prior to the war.[249]

To this testimony of the most puissant men engaged in the conflict *I add the testimony of the common soldiers of the Confederacy. With one voice then and with one voice now the Southern soldiers avowed that they were not fighting and suffering and dying for slavery, but for the right of self-government* [my emphasis, L.S.].[250]

I was a soldier in Virginia in the campaigns of Lee and Jackson, and I declare I never met a Southern soldier who had drawn his sword to perpetuate slavery. Nor was the dissolution of the Union or the establishment of the Southern Confederacy the supreme issue in the mind of the Southern soldier. What he had chiefly at heart was the preservation of the supreme and sacred right of self-government. The men who made up the Southern armies were not fighting for their slaves when they cast all in the balance—their lives, their fortunes, and their sacred honor—and endured the hardships of the march and the camp and the perils and sufferings of the battle field. Besides, it was a very small minority of the men who fought in the Southern armies who were financially interested in the institution of slavery.[251] — REV. RANDOLPH HARRISON MCKIM

THAT TRUE KNIGHT

☛ . . . It was [June 1, 1862] when that skillful and gifted soldier, Joseph E. Johnston, to whom justice has not yet been done, fell wounded at the close of the first day's fight at [the Battle of] Seven Pines that Lee was summoned to take command of the force opposing [Union Gen. George Brinton] McClellan's army, then so close to Richmond that the church bells could be heard in their camps. In assuming command of that Army of Northern Virginia, which he never left and which never left him, Lee's grasp of the conditions was shown in activity which was immediate and in effect which was electrical.

First happened the daring raid of Stuart, sent out by Lee to locate the right flank of McClellan's army. Stuart did this and more. He rode clear around the rear of McClellan's army and delivered his report of what existed to Lee in Richmond, raising himself once and forever to the eminence which abides with him to-day. Thenceforward the black plume of that true knight was seen waving at the front whenever daring of the man on horseback was demanded.[252] — HON. LEIGH ROBINSON

Flags of the Southern Confederacy. Display them with pride.

CHAPTER 10

THE BATTLE OF KELLY'S FORD

☛ This article is written only to describe some incidents that came under my personal observation during one of the fiercest cavalry fights witnessed by me during the War between the States.

As a boy of seventeen I left the Virginia Military Institute, and in December, 1862, I joined Company C, Fourth Regiment of Virginia Cavalry, Wickham's Brigade. We were then in camp off the Rappahannock River a few miles above Fredericksburg, Va., the town in which my mother lived during her girlhood. About the 1st of March, 1863, we moved our camp to John Minor Botts's

Gen. William W. Averell, U.S.A.

farm, near Culpeper Court House. Just about daybreak on the morning of March 17 we were aroused by the sound of the bugle call. "Boots and saddles!" Each regiment rapidly formed into line and marched off in the direction of Kelly's Ford, on the Rappahannock River.

The gray mist of the morning had given way to the crimson light of the rising sun. General [William Woods] Averell, in command of the Federal cavalry, had succeeded in crossing the Rappahannock after driving in our pickets of the Fauquier Black Horse Company. He had several thousand cavalry and a few pieces of artillery, while Gen. Fitz [Fitzhugh] Lee had only eight hundred troopers and three pieces of horse artillery, under Major [John] Pelham. We had passed Fleetwood Hill and Stevensburg when the gray columns of Fitz Lee moved rapidly into line of battle and threw out sharpshooters all along the front.

Just then I was ordered up from my company to report to

Maj. William A. Morgan, C.S.A.

[Confederate] Major [William Augustine] Morgan, of the First Virginia Regiment, who afterwards became lieutenant colonel. He was in command of the picket line of sharpshooters, who were dismounted and lying down about two hundred yards from the rock fence, behind which were stationed the Federal batteries. Major Morgan and I were mounted and riding together in a gallop along and in the rear of the sharpshooters, while the crack of the carbines from the Federals in our front was music to our ears. The Major halted and gave me a verbal order to be taken at once to General Lee, whom I soon found on the crest of a hill near the line of battle surrounded by a few of his staff officers. I delivered the message and was about to return when he ordered me to remain for a few minutes. One of his staff asked him why he was waiting. Turning quickly in his saddle and raising his glasses to his eyes, he replied to the question asked him by the officer: "He is coming now."

We turned our eyes toward Culpeper Court House and saw a single trooper coming toward us. The long strides of his horse were lessening the distance between us and him, and as he approached nearer I noticed that his horse was champing the bit, while the white foam was dripping from his flanks as he was urged on by his daring rider. General Lee's eyes sparkled as he suddenly exclaimed: "It is Jeb Stuart!" He was alone and near enough by then for us to hear his voice as it rang out upon the stillness: "If you want to have a good time, jine the cavalry."

Stuart's blue eyes flashed. His gray cloak was thrown back over his shoulders and showed plainly the red lining, a black plume floated back from his soft felt hat, and a handsome Confederate uniform adorned his person.

It seems that Stuart had heard of Averell's contemplated attack on Lee and had taken the train at Fredericksburg, gotten off at Culpeper Court House, mounted a horse, and by hard riding reached us in time for the fight. General Lee said to him that there was a little fun brewing, and he was glad to see him, and added: "Where is Pelham? Tell him to crowd them with his artillery." After a good joke and a hearty laugh, Stuart said: "Fitz, are you ready? Don't let Averell get you." Lee received the remark with a laugh, and off they went, drawing their sabers at the sound of the bugle to charge. They led the First Regiment into a hand-to-hand fight. The Yankees stood their ground with unusual courage, and numbers on both sides fell from their horses, pierced by saber and pistol balls.

I had returned to Major Morgan under a terrific fire, and when passing General Lee I saw his horse reel and fall, shot through by a ball. Just then Major Morgan suddenly checked up his horse and said to me: "There lie a brace of beautiful pistols and a sword. Don't you want them?" I remarked to him: "You will excuse me."

While our batteries were pouring shot and shell into the advancing enemy young Pelham left his pieces and joined Stuart and Lee in the desperate charge, and in the act of cheering on his men he fell, pierced by a Minie ball. Just before sunset the Rebel yell was heard above the rumbling sound of the wheels of Averell's artillery retreating toward the Rappahannock River. The death of Pelham was a sad blow to General Stuart . . .[253] — WILLIAM B. CONWAY, M.D., ATLANTA, GA.

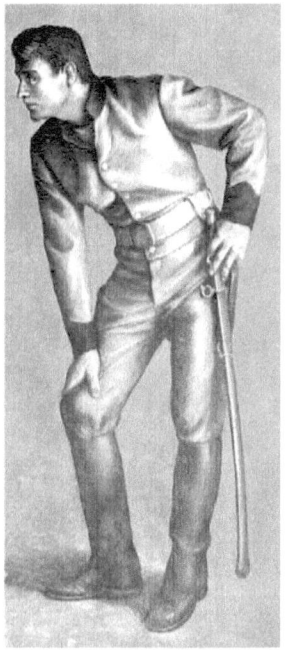

A 1939 oil painting of Confederate Maj. John Pelham, by Jared French, originally displayed at Court House Annex, Richmond, VA.

IN DEFENSE OF STUART'S RIDE AROUND MCCLELLAN

☛ In looking over the old numbers of the *Confederate Veteran*, which I frequently do (and taken as a whole, it is one of the most interesting histories of the War between the States), I find an article in the number for October, 1917, by John Witherspoon DuBose in reply to an address delivered by the Rev. W. H. Whitsett before the R. E. Lee Camp of Confederate Veterans at Richmond, Va., published in the August number of that year, in which he severely criticizes, by implication at least, the Confederate War

Department, including Mr. [Jefferson] Davis and also some of our most prominent Southern generals, and more particularly Jeb Stuart and General Forrest.

While not so familiar with the unwritten or inside history of those who were prominent in the War between the States as the writer of that article, an author of considerable repute, one of his books being *Joe Wheeler and the Army of the Tennessee*, and who in all his writings makes Joe Wheeler *par excellence* the greatest cavalry leader developed by the war, and which seems to be more than anything else his object in this article, still, having served under General Wheeler for one year and under General Forrest for two years and six months of my life as a soldier, I believe that I am as competent as he to judge of their respective ability, or the "military genius," as he would put it, of the two generals; and perhaps I should have as good idea of Jeb Stuart's military genius, although I never served under him.

He brushes Stuart aside by saying that "in the summer of 1862 General Stuart rode around [Union Gen. George Brinton] McClellan in the peninsula, an expedition fruitless and almost bloodless." As a parallel to this he says:

> "Colonel Wheeler made his first raid by going into North Mississippi and West Tennessee, around [Don Carlos] Buell, Grant, and others at Corinth, with some one hundred thousand troops. He succeeded so well that [Braxton] Bragg, only forty miles from Corinth and Buell, reached Chattanooga unmolested, without firing a gun or losing a wagon. Perhaps comparison is invidious."

If the word "invidious" is here used in the sense of "a state of being envious," I believe he is right. What does history tell us about it? It says:

> "At the time this raid was made [the raid by Jeb Stuart around McClellan] General McClellan was within a few miles of Richmond at the head of the most numerous and the best-equipped army that had ever assembled on American soil. More than 150,000 troops were encamped on the banks of the Chickahominy [River], and the arsenals and machine shops of the North had left nothing to be desired in their armament and equipment for the great struggle before them."

Over this large army was placed the ablest and most accomplished soldier the North had yet produced, and the Federal authorities confidently expected to defeat Lee and capture Richmond in a very short time. Gen. J. E. Johnston had been wounded "while reconnoitering with General Stuart" a few days before near Fair Oaks, and General Lee had been given the command of the Army of Virginia. In order to ascertain the defenses and the strength of McClellan's army, he directed General Stuart, with 1,500 men, to make a reconnoissance in McClellan's rear, and in which he entirely encircled McClellan's army. And it is said:

> "The raid around McClellan was long remembered not only by those who took part in it, but by the entire people, who were delighted with its audacity and pleased with the annoyance which it caused the enemy."

And history tells us:

> "The result of this reconnoissance decided General Lee to bring on the battle of Cold Harbor. And General Jackson was promptly directed to move his corps to the Chickahominy for an attack on the enemy on flank and in reverse."

So the battle of Cold Harbor was fought and resulted in a great victory for Southern arms, and there the sun of Lee arose never to set, but to shine on with increasing splendor through the ages, while the star of McClellan went down in blood.

Then was Stuart's raid around McClellan in 1862 "fruitless and almost bloodless"? Let the facts of history answer.

I should like to follow Jeb Stuart, the Chevalier Bayard of the South, through his meteoric career—to the Wilderness, where the mantle of the immortal Jackson fell upon his shoulders, and on the next day to Chancellorsville, and in fancy see him riding up and down the lines of Jackson's old brigade in order to dispel the gloom from the minds of those brave men caused by the fall of their great commander, moved by that exuberance of spirits peculiar to him which even in the turmoil of battle never failed him, and in fancy hear him break out in that rollicking impromptu song made to fit the occasion, "Old Joe Hooker, come tearing out of the wilderness"! Then as they approach near the enemy see him rise in his

Monument at Yellow Tavern, marking the spot where Stuart was wounded.

stirrups, with drawn saber and flashing eye, and hear him give the command in a voice that rang up and down the line like a bugle blast. "Charge, men, charge, and remember Stonewall Jackson!" Then see Hooker, with his broken, discouraged, and bleeding army, fleeing in disorder to the north bank of the Rappahannock.

So the results of Jeb Stuart's raid around McClellan's army in the summer of 1862 were not so "fruitless and bloodless" as one might be led to suppose. And I should like to follow him on through his many engagements and achievements to the place where he fell, just a short time before the close of the war, a glorious sacrifice to his country's cause.

It is unkind at least to bring up at this late day a lot of table talk that is not history (for it is certain that General Lee trusted Jeb Stuart as implicitly after Gettysburg as he did before), and for no other apparent purpose than to cast reflection on the phenomenal "genius" of one Southern general in order to magnify that of another.[254] — J. G. WITHERSPOON, CROWELL, TEX.

Confederate cavalry charge on the enemy.

SHERMAN'S OPINION OF STUART

☛ I must confess that I have little respect for the Union men of the South. They allowed a clamorous set of demagogues to muzzle and drive them like a set of curs. Afraid of shadows, they submit tamely to anything that the enemy do, but are loud in complaints of the smallest excesses of our soldiers. I account them as nothing in this great game. The young bloods of the South, sons of planters, lawyers about towns, good billiard players and sportsmen—men who never did work and never will—war suits them, and the rascals are brave.

They are fine riders and bold to rashness and dangerous subjects in every sense. They care not a sou for niggers, land, or anything. They hate Yankees and don't bother their brains about the past, present, or future. As long as they have good horses, plenty of forage, and an open country they are happy. They are splendid riders, shots, and utterly reckless. [Jeb] Stuart, John Morgan, Forrest, and Jackson are the types and leaders of this class. They must all be killed or employed by us before we can hope for peace. They are the best cavalry in the world, but it will tax [Union Chief Justice of the U.S.] Mr. [Salmon Portland] Chase's genius of finance to supply them with horses. At present horses cost them nothing, for they take where they find and don't bother their brains who is to pay for them.[255] — UNION GEN. WILLIAM T. SHERMAN

STUART'S LETTER TO A SOLDIER'S MOTHER
☛ Gen. Stuart wrote the following letter to the mother of his young male courier Jaquelin S. Ware, of Clarke County, Virginia: "Headquarters Second Cavalry Corps, A.N.V., February 20, 1864. My Dear Madam: You need have no apprehension about your son Jaquelin, who is still with Major Fitzhugh [Lee], and has won golden opinions with all who knew him. If it should ever be in my power to assist him, be assured it will be cheerfully done. I have the honor to be, very respectfully yours, J. E. B. Stuart."[256] — *CONFEDERATE VETERAN*

STUART'S CHRISTIAN CHARACTER
☛ Gen. J. E. B. Stuart, brave, dashing, and daring officer, in his early boyhood dedicated his life to the Master's [i.e., Jesus] cause. When he fell mortally wounded, seeing panic-stricken followers dashing past, he called out: "Go back, men! Go back and do your duty as I have done mine, and our country will be free!" A few hours later with dying lips he exclaimed: "If God and my countrymen think I have done my duty, I am ready to go."[257] — MRS. EUGENIA HILL ARNOLD, ELKINS, W. VA.

THE *ESPRIT DE CORPS* OF THE CONFEDERATE CAVALRY
☛ . . . though our camp equipage and equipment were so inferior to those of our antagonists, we do not think any experienced soldier, watching our marching columns of infantry or cavalry, or witnessing our brigade drills, could fail to be thrilled by the spectacle they presented. Here, at least, there was no inferiority to

the army in blue. The soldierly qualities that tell on the march, and on the field of battle, shone out here conspicuously. A more impressive spectacle has seldom been seen in any war than was presented by "Jeb" Stuart's brigades of cavalry when they passed in review before Gen. Lee at Brandy Station in June, 1863. The pomp and pageantry of gorgeous uniforms and dazzling equipment of horse and riders were indeed absent; but splendid horsemanship, and that superb *esprit de corps* that marked that veteran legion, and which, though not a tangible or a visible thing, yet stamps itself upon a marching column—these were unmistakably there. And we take leave to express our own individual opinion that the blue-gray coat of the Confederate officer, richly adorned with gold lace, and his light-blue trousers, and that rakish slouch hat he wore made up a uniform of great beauty. Oh, it was a gallant array to look upon—that June day, so many years ago![258] — RANDOLPH HARRISON MCKIM

SAVED BY A PRECIPITATE FLIGHT

☛ Gen. J. E. B. Stuart reported on September 7 [1863]: "I organized a party of twelve men to go within the enemy's camps at New Baltimore and endeavor to capture [Union] General [Joseph Jackson] Bartlett. They succeeded in getting possession of his headquarters at one o'clock at night, but the general had made a precipitate flight in his nether garments."[259] — FROM THE "OFFICIAL RECORDS"

RECOLLECTIONS OF CHANCELLORSVILLE

☛ . . . We all loved General Stuart; he was so nice and had always a pleasant word for every one. . . [One] evening there was a rendezvous at our house of Generals Anderson, Posey, and Stuart, with some of their aids. My sisters, who know that the servants had gone did everything themselves, prepared a good supper and took great pride in waiting on the table and having everything nice. While we were all at the table enjoying the good things suddenly a courier came with dispatches saying that the enemy was crossing at United States Ford. Immediately all was confusion. Hastily the generals bade us good-bye, but General Stuart, always so charming, took time to say to my sister: "Thank you, Miss Fannie, for the good supper; and as it is always my custom to fee the waitress, take this from me as a little remembrance." And he gave her a tiny gold dollar. I have it yet, [it is] one of my most cherished possessions.[260]
— MRS. SUE CHANCELLOR, FREDERICKSBURG, VA.

THE BATTLE OF FREDERICKSBURG

☛ . . . This narrative would be incomplete if I did not mention the heroic conduct of Gen. J. E. B. Stuart, commander of the cavalry, and his men. He was a man born to lead, and his conduct inspired every man under him with the same daring spirit. In winter the weather was never too severe to hinder his activities, and in summer the heat was never too great to check his operations. The nights were never too dark, but rather seemed to favor his movements. No force brought against him was equal to his stratagem and courage. His resourcefulness served him in every emergency. His confidence in his men was only equal to theirs in him. His love for his country [The C.S.A.] and its cause [Americanism] was dearer to him than his life, which he gave up freely in its defense. His regard for his commander in chief [Robert E. Lee] was like that of an obedient and loving son to a father. While the infantry was held in camp snowbound, he and his men were watching the enemy's outposts or operating within their lines. Without him General Lee could never have maneuvered his infantry so successfully, for he screened his movements from the eyes of the enemy and kept him informed of their every movement. If he accomplished so much with a force so small, we naturally ask ourselves what he would have done with an army equal to the task assigned him. While Longstreet and Jackson were leisurely moving their infantry from the Valley to take position at Fredericksburg, Stuart and his men were fighting daily battles with the enemy, and nothing they did escaped his observation, for he was always on their flank and rear.[261] — I. G. BRADWELL, BRANTLEY, ALA.

The Battle of Fredericksburg, December 13, 1862.

STUART'S LETTER COMMENDS HIS SCOUTS
☛ Headquarters Cavalry Corps, Army of Northern Virginia, April 20, 1864: Lt. Col. W. H. [Walter Heron] Taylor, Ass't Adj't General. Colonel: I have the honor to report the following affair (petite guerre), which occurred in the operations within the enemy's lines near Catlett's Station on the 16th inst:

Privates Channing M. Smith, Richard Lewis, and Lowe, of Company H, Fourth Virginia Cavalry, acting as scouts in Fauquier county, met and attacked a party of five of the enemy, killing four, one escaping. This affair reflects great credit on the valor and skill of the gallant scouts who executed it, and too much praise cannot be awarded, them.

Their operations serve to inspire confidence in our men and keep our enemies in a state of constant and wholesome terror. The attention of the Commanding General is called to these young men, who are continually giving evidence of their gallantry and daring by similar exploits. I have the honor to be, very respectfully your obedient servant, J. E. B. Stuart, Major General.[262] — CHANNING M. SMITH, DELAPLANE, VA.

WHY STUART WAS LOVED BY HIS MEN
☛ . . . Stuart was a great leader and fought for the love and excitement of fighting. His men caught the spirit of their great commander and emulated his example. He never sent his men into danger, but was always found in the lead and in the thickest of the fighting. He did not seem to need discipline to control his men, for all followed him, charmed by his manner and ever ready to do his will.[263] — I. G. BRADWELL, BRANTLEY, ALA.

HOW STUART FOUND LEE
☛ An incident which was recalled vividly was the important mission that this squad [Company D, First Maryland Cavalry, C.S.A.], under command of Corporal Edwin Selvage, executed just before the battle of Gettysburg.

Late on the afternoon of July 1 [1863], Corporal Selvage, of Company D, with the eight men, was ordered by their commanding officer to report to [Confederate] General [Richard Stoddert] Ewell, who directed Selvage to take the road to Cashtown, Pa., and from there the most direct road to Carlisle, Pa., and take a dispatch to Gen. J. E. B. Stuart.

Upon asking where Stuart could be found, Selvage was told that it was thought he was somewhere near Carlisle, and he was directed to find him, and lose no time in doing so. History shows that Stuart, who was left in the rear of Lee's army to harass the enemy, could never be located or communicated with during the first part of the battle of Gettysburg. These men were given the work to find the General and deliver the dispatch, which later brought Stuart and his command to the scene of action.

Corporal Selvage gave the following account of their experience in finding General Stuart:

> "When we left headquarters, we inquired the shortest way to Carlisle, but, being in hostile territory, we could get little or no information that would be of service to us, and we were left to our own resources in finding the road.
>
> We continued, however, until about 11 o'clock at night, when we were challenged and found ourselves directly in front of the Union pickets. How to get past without being recognized was the puzzling question. It lay with "Buddy" Obenderfer, the "kid" of the squad, as he then was called, to get us through the lines. Obenderfer said: "Corporal, I'll bluff them, and you rush past." Obenderfer rode up to the picket, without heeding the challenge to dismount, and engaged the sentinel in conversation. The rest of the squad, taking advantage of the distraction, dashed through the line, Obenderfer following in the rear. We were pursued for about five miles, but by cutting across fields we outwitted the Yanks.
>
> We continued on and, when a short distance out of Carlisle, we came upon the outpost of the cavalry, and, upon inquiry, found the pickets to be of Stuart's command. The rest was easy, and about 1 A.M. we found Stuart's adjutant, and to him we delivered the dispatch.
>
> We were directed by the adjutant to stay there and rest. Some hour and a half later, Stuart himself rode up and inquired who was in command of the squad which had delivered the dispatch. I reported, and Stuart asked if I could lead his command to the place of the engagement. I replied that I could, and, toward daybreak, at the head of Stuart's column, I reported to Ewell, and was warmly commended for the service rendered the cause."

This tells the story of how Stuart found General Lee when he came on the battle field of Gettysburg. This is only one of many courageous and daring deeds of the members of Company D.[264] — *CONFEDERATE VETERAN*

STUART'S BATTALIONS

☛ A few days later General Lee, on the same ground [Savannah, GA], reviewed General Stuart's cavalry corps, consisting of three divisions, whose ranks were very much depleted by constant contact with the enemy and hard service. This was very evident from the appearance of the men and their horses. The wonder is that their general, with so poor a force and equipment, could perform such achievements against such overwhelming odds. Surely Stuart and his men were little less than superhuman. But how proudly rode "The Knight of the Black Plume" that day before his chief!

All who followed Stuart exhibited the same martial spirit that characterized their leader. What they had lacked in number and equipment they made good by their rapid movements, watchfulness, and bravery; for Stuart's men were always everywhere to head off any attempt of the enemy and to return blow for blow, or even to assume the offensive when expedient.

They were the eyes of the army; the sun was never too hot nor the air too cold to check their activities, and they and their horses seemed immune to hunger and fatigue. The nights were never too dark nor the roads too bad to delay their excursions, and they always managed to get there on time, or ahead of time, to checkmate any movement on the part of the enemy. Their leader, as well as his men, seemed born for the saddle and at his best when fighting sword and pistol in hand in a "mix-up" with the enemy, or flying across ditches or over fences pursued by the foe.

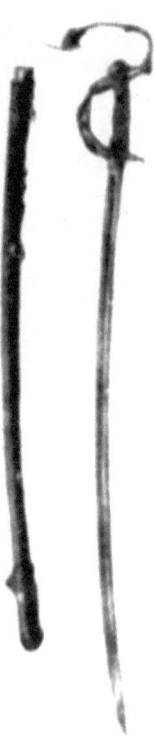

Stuart's sword.

Even after the subsequent exhausting campaign in which Stuart was killed, these decimated battalions, under the wise leadership of the noble [Wade] Hampton, were able utterly to rout a select force many times larger than their own under [Union Gen. Philip H.] Sheridan at Trevilian Station, when the latter and a few of his men barely escaped into Grant's lines below Richmond, after losing their entire equipment. They were true to the cause of the South to the last . . . .[265] — I. G. BRADWELL, BRANTLEY, ALA.

STUART'S RIDE THROUGH THE ENEMY'S COUNTRY

☛ Maj. Gen. James Ewell Brown Stuart, commanding the cavalry corps of the Army of Northern Virginia, exercising the discretion given him by General [Robert E.] Lee, had the men of [Wade] Hampton's, Fitzhugh Lee's, and William Henry Fitzhugh Lee's brigades to prepare three days' rations, and, on the night of June 24, 1863, to secretly rendezvous near Salem Depot. His purpose was to so maneuver as to pass around the rear of the Federal army, and cross the Potomac River between that army and Washington. He left [Beverly Holcombe] Robertson's and Jones's brigades, under the command of the former, in observation of the enemy on the front, with full instructions as to following up the enemy, in case of withdrawal, and rejoining the army. Stuart carried six pieces of artillery, with caissons and ambulances, and these were the only vehicles accompanying him.

At 1 o'clock on the morning of June 25, Stuart's force moved out in noiseless march. After maneuvering under great difficulties, making several detours to avoid the Federal forces, the command reached the Potomac River on the evening of June 27. The river was two feet higher than usual, from the effect of recent rains, and the command, under great difficulties, effected a crossing at Seneca Falls [NY], about twenty miles above the city of Washington. The cavalry had but little trouble in reaching the opposite shore, but the artillery and ambulances were not so fortunate. The deep water threatened the destruction of the ammunition. In spite of this apparent insuperable difficulty, the indomitable energy and resolute determination of the artillerymen won, and the entire command bivouacked on Maryland soil.

Realizing the necessity of joining the army in Pennsylvania, Stuart resumed his march northward early on the morning of June 28. After encountering and brushing aside several small cavalry detachments, the command reached Rockville, a village situated on the road from Washington to the Federal army. Stuart found the latter had preceded him across the Potomac River, and was located between his force and the Confederate army. This condition was an unexpected obstacle. However, it did not prevent him from attacking and capturing a train of wagons eight miles long, approaching from the direction of Washington, loaded with army supplies. As soon as the presence of the Confederate force was discovered, those in charge of the train attempted to turn the wagons and to escape at full speed. The farthest wagon was within three or four miles of Washington. Not one escaped, though many were turned over and broken, which necessitated burning them. The splendid teams, with excellent rigs, were secured and driven off.

The capture of this train caused the troops to become scattered, and delay followed. The burden of caring for and conducting this train, for there were still two hundred wagons, made the progress of the column necessarily slow. In addition to caring for the train, when the column came in contact with telegraph and railroad lines, time was consumed to destroy them. The head of the column reached Westminster about 5 P.M., on the 29th. Here its progress was obstinately disputed for a short time by a [Union] squadron of the First Delaware Cavalry. In the brief engagement here Lieuts. Pierre Gibson and John W. Murry, of the Fourth Virginia Cavalry, were killed. "The ladies of this place begged to be allowed to superintend their interment, and, in accordance with their wishes, the bodies of these young heroes were left in their charge." Such of the opposing squadron as were not killed or captured were pursued a long distance on the Baltimore road and created a great panic in that city, as they impressed the authorities with the belief that the Confederates were at their heels.

Looking up the Potomac River from Fort Sumter.

Several flags and a piece of artillery without a carriage were captured. The piece of artillery was spiked and left. For the first time since the command left Rector's Crossroads in Virginia, it obtained a full supply of forage. It bivouacked on the night of the 29th a few miles north of Westminster, the head of the column halting at Union Mills, midway between Westminster and Littlestown [PA], on the Gettysburg road. Early on the morning of the 30th, the march was resumed by a cross route to Hanover, Pa. When the head of the column reached Hanover, it came in contact with [Union Gen. Hugh Judson] Kilpatrick's Division of Cavalry passing through, and it made a demonstration toward attacking Stuart. The leading regiment of Stuart's column made a gallant charge, which repulsed the enemy and drove him pell-mell through the town, capturing his ambulances and a large number of prisoners, all of which were carried safely to the Confederate train. Owing to the great elongation of Stuart's column, by reason of the two hundred wagons and the broken country, his command could not deal as advantageously with this column of the enemy as it would have otherwise done.

 While Stuart was having reinforcements brought up, Kilpatrick regained possession of the town, but the heights by which the town was surrounded were soon crowned with Confederate artillery. Kilpatrick's column was cut in twain, and the Confederate force fell upon the rear portion, driving it and capturing a number of Kilpatrick's staff and many other prisoners. The wagon train had become a serious embarrassment, but this did not deter Stuart from exerting himself to save it. Another serious embarrassment was that the ammunition of the command had become greatly diminished from the numerous skirmishes in which it had engaged. The command was in the enemy's country, near a hostile army, and, besides, about four hundred prisoners had accumulated since last paroling. Nothing daunted, Stuart had the train closed up and parked, and Hampton, who was far behind at the outset, arrived and engaged the Federal forces farther to the right. Finally his sharpshooters dislodged the Federals from the town, but moved toward the Confederate column, on its left, with dismounted men.

 The train, however, was pushed on through Jefferson for York, Pa. The march was continued during the night and over a very dark road, which made it exceedingly hard on the command. With the many previous combats and night marches, it was a severe tax on the men and horses. Whole regiments slept in the saddle, the faithful horses keeping the road unguided. In some instances the men fell from their horses overcome with fatigue and want of sleep. Reaching Dover on the morning of July 1, Stuart gained no satisfactory information concerning the Confederate army. It cannot be denied that he was lost. After a brief rest, he pushed on to Carlisle, which he knew was one of the points in the itinerary of the army. He reached that city in the afternoon of July 1. His rations were entirely out and he wished to levy a contribution on the inhabitants for rations, but before reaching the town he was informed that it was held by a considerable force of militia, who were concealed in the buildings with a view to entrap him upon entering the town.

Stuart soon found that his information was correct, and, though he disliked to subject the town to the consequences of attack, yet it was essential he should procure rations for his men and forage for his mules and horses. It must be remembered that his retinue consisted of thousands of cavalry and artillery horses, and probably an extra thousand animals captured with his train, and all, men and animals, needed food. Stuart, therefore, directed Fitz Lee to send in a flag of truce, demanding an unconditional surrender or to be subjected to a bombardment. The surrender was refused. He made preparations to shell the town and repeated the demand. It was again refused. He then threw a few shells, but his limited supply of ammunition prevented him from enforcing his threat. The whereabouts of the Confederate army was still a mystery.

But during the night of July 1, he received a dispatch from General Lee (in answer to one sent from over on [Jubal Anderson] Early's trail) that the army was at Gettysburg and had been engaged on the 1st with the Federal advance. He immediately issued orders for his force to move that night, with the view to reaching Gettysburg early next day, and started himself that night. His advance reached Gettysburg on July 2, in time to meet a move of the Federal cavalry on the Confederate rear by the way of Hunterstown, when Hampton's Brigade, after a fierce engagement, compelled the Federals to leave the field and abandon their purpose.

Gen. Jubal A. Early, C.S.A.

Thus ended one of the most remarkable rides by cavalry that history records. With less than three thousand troopers and artillerymen, Stuart had made a march almost continuous, day and night, for eight days and nights, entirely in country in possession of an enemy, conducting a wagon train not less than eight miles long, consisting of approximately two hundred wagons. Considerable of the time the men and horses were without food. A large part of the time the horses had no food except such as they obtained during brief periods of stop to graze. Notwithstanding the great achievement by Stuart and his gallant troopers, many of his associates have indulged in sharp criticism because of his failure to reach the army in time to give the necessary information of the movements of the Federal army; some have actually charged that he is responsible for the failure of the Pennsylvania campaign.[266] — JOHN PURIFOY, MONTGOMERY, ALA.

OBITUARY OF STUART'S WIFE FLORA STUART

☞ Nearly threescore years after the death of her famous husband [Jeb], Mrs. J. E. B. Stuart died in Norfolk, Va., on May 10 [1923], at the age of eighty-eight years. The death of General Stuart in May, 1864, left his young wife, as brave as she was beautiful, to face the future alone, the only dependance of three small children. After the war was over she opened a girls' school at Staunton, Va., which she conducted successfully for many years. For the past thirty years she had lived in Norfolk at the home of her son-in-law, R. Page Waller. She is survived by one son, Capt. J. E. B. Stuart [II], U.S.A., retired, of New York City.

Quite a romance is woven about Lieutenant Stuart's courtship of the beautiful Flora Cooke, daughter of Col. Philip St. George Cooke, U.S.A., in charge of the post at Fort Riley, Kans., when that State was opened. Lieutenant Stuart was then connected with Fort Leavenworth, and when it was reported that the prettiest girl in the State was then visiting her father at Fort Riley, he contrived to be a messenger to Colonel Cooke, and there met her. The acquaintance quickly ripened into love, and they were soon married. She had been his wife ten years when the War between the States came on. Lieutenant Stuart resigned his commission in the Federal army and threw in his lot with Virginia, but her father, then Major General Cooke, retained his command with the Union forces, and she bade farewell to soldier husband and soldier father with a prayer that they would never meet in battle. But she was a soldier's wife and never wavered in her allegiance to the cause for which her husband was fighting [Americanism]. As the conflict swept across Northern Virginia, she would follow the trail of Stuart's Cavalry that she might be with him in the intervals of battle; and she was hastening to the side of her gallant husband after he was mortally wounded at Yellow Tavern in May, 1864, but he passed away before she could reach him. After the more than a half century, they are again united, and she rests by his side in beautiful Hollywood [Cemetery] at Richmond, Va.[267] — *CONFEDERATE VETERAN*

FLORA STUART: IN MEMORIAM

👉 The last of a distinguished line of women who shared through those trying days of 1861-65 the companionship of the great leaders of the Confederacy has passed to her reward. In the death of Mrs. J. E. B. Stuart, the South closes one of its pages in history, as she was the last surviving widow of a member of General Lee's staff. That no flower could be purchased on the day of her funeral in the city of Richmond is sufficient comment to indicate the admiration and devotion in which she was held. This is an unprecedented tribute to a life that has left a lasting impression upon its generation.[268] —
LEONORA ST. GEORGE ROGERS SCHUYLER

STUART

👉 There's a name that the Southland will never forget,
Or the halo of romance that clings round it yet;
On the hearts of her sons it is graven in glory,
In letters of gold on the page of her story;
Through her hills and her valleys 'twill echo for aye—
Stuart! Jeb Stuart! Dashing, and gallant, and gay!

He was handsome and gallant—a *preux chevalier*—
Matchless audacity, supreme capacity
To dazzle, and baffle, and confound the foe;
Uneasy their slumber when Stuart was near—
He struck, and they scarce knew whence came the blow,
He cowed their audacity, curbed their rapacity,
As he rode round their camps and their armies at will,
    Till to their minds loomed he thus:
    A grim, gray, ubiquitous
Demon portentous of daring and skill.

O'er the clashing of armies far thundered his fame;
And gray-bearded warriors heard Jeb Stuart's name,
And hailed the great trooper the peer of all time,
From Murat—beau sabreur—to bold Pappenheim.
Peerless in leading and fearless in fray—

They swore that he rode round an army each day—
Stuart! Jeb Stuart! Dashing, and gallant, and gay!

Sweet to his ear was the bugle call ringing
When, as the "Charge!" rang out, thundered the battle shout,
And his gaunt, gallant squadrons rushed over the plain
To the shock of the onset, with bright sabers swinging,
Till the meadow ran red with the blood of the slain!
But when, with victorious shout, they drove the foe in rout,
Then Stuart shone forth at his noblest revealed;
    Never more valiant foe
    Ever gave blow for blow,
Or victor more generous e'er won a field!

The thunder of battle to him was delight,
As with garlanded steed he dashed into the fight,
With a song on his lips, as at Chancellorsville,
When with youth's gay insouciance, a great leader's skill,
He led "Stonewall's" gaunt veterans into the fray
Until victory crowned that fierce, terrible day,
And Hooker's blue legions reeled back in dismay
Before Stuart! Jeb Stuart! Dashing, and gallant, and gay!

And Virginia! Dear mother, Virginia! With pride
She hailed the adored one! her dashing, gallant son!
Flung him the garlands he loved so to wear
(Dear as the saber he wore at his side
Was to Stuart a wreath from the hands of the fair).
And when his day was done, his glorious course was run,
Fast fell her tears o'er the grave of her slain;
    Nor wept she alone, for the Southland was weeping
    O'er the tomb where the hero forever was sleeping,
Deaf to the bugle call—calling in vain.

But could he have chosen, that day he lay low,
So would he have died, with his face to the foe,
In the forefront of battle, his sword in his hand,
For the Southland he loved, for his dear motherland!
And his fame shines untarnished and dimless for aye—
Peerless in leading and fearless in fray—
Stuart! Jeb Stuart! Dashing, and gallant, and gay![269] — ARTHUR LOUIS PETICOLAS, CHICAGO, ILL.

AFTER THE BATTLE OF BRANDY STATION

☛ I saw General Stuart that day riding out on the field where shot and shell were raining around, and he didn't seem to bat an eye.[270]
— H. M. STRICKLER, LURAY, VA.

"Sponsors and Maids of the United Sons of Confederate Veterans."

CHAPTER 11

STUART'S CAVALRY AT GETTYSBURG, JULY 3, 1863

☛ Gen. R. E. Lee, commanding the Army of Northern Virginia, reached the vicinity of Chambersburg, Pa., on the 27th of June, 1863. On the morning of the 1st of July, he proceeded in the direction of Gettysburg, the Corps of Longstreet and Hill having been previously ordered to move in the same direction, and Ewell's Corps was moving in the same direction from Carlisle and York. When Lee reached Cashtown, eight or nine miles northwest from Gettysburg, an occasional cannon shot was heard. After a brief pause to learn the conditions which would follow, and finding that the cannonade continued and increased, he moved rapidly forward. Arriving near the crest of an eminence, more than a mile west of Gettysburg, he dismounted and, leaving his horse under cover, proceeded to a position overlooking the field. This was about 2 P.M., and the battle was raging with considerable violence. Soon after Lee reached the vicinity of the fighting the Confederate force succeeded in forcing their Federal contestants to abandon the field, and, as he followed, he saw the enemy retreating through the town of Gettysburg to an eminence beyond.

Lee was now confronted with an expected condition. Both armies seemed to have blundered into a battle. Lee soon learned that a fierce encounter had occurred between two divisions of Hill's Corps and two of Ewell's Corps with [Albert Gallatin] Jenkins's cavalry brigade, on the part of the Confederate army, and the First and Eleventh Federal Army Corps and [John] Buford's cavalry division, of the Federal army. That the losses were heavy in both armies; the Federal army having been forced from the field, its losses exceeded those of the Confederates. He soon became possessed with the information that Maj. Gen. J. E. B. Stuart, with three brigades of cavalry, was at Carlisle, Pa., thirty or more miles distant, and that [Beverly Holcombe] Robertson's command, left in the Virginia mountains, had not reported to that part of the army. He immediately dispatched messengers to each, with information that a battle had been fought at Gettysburg and with instructions that both commands repair immediately to that point.

Confederate Gen. Robert E. Lee astride his favorite warhorse, "Traveller."

Here was an unusual and peculiar condition. While the cavalry accompanying an army is required to discharge a variety of duties when actively campaigning and on the move, it is supposed to perform all necessary preliminary work to keep in touch with the commanding general, and promptly inform him of the movements and probable intentions of his adversary. In this case neither commander of the two main bodies of cavalry knew the location of the commanding general nor the location of the army. The commanding general was sending out scouts to hunt up and escort the cavalry to the army.

Stuart received his message during the night of the 1st of July and immediately put his troops in motion to march to Gettysburg. Gen. Wade Hampton, of his command, reached the vicinity of Gettysburg on the evening of the 2nd of July, in time to meet and check a movement of Federal cavalry which was attempting to pass around the Confederate left flank, to reach and destroy the trains of the Confederates. [Then came] Stuart's great ride through the enemy's country . . .

Comparatively few readers of the history of the battle of the 3rd of July, 1863, at Gettysburg are aware that a cavalry attack on the rear of the Federal army was part of General Lee's plan of battle on that date. In his report he pays this brief eulogy to the prowess of the cavalry and makes brief mention of the battle, but does not state that he authorized it in any other way;

> "The ranks of the cavalry were much reduced by its long and arduous march, repeated conflicts, and insufficient supplies of forage, but the day after its arrival at Gettysburg it engaged the enemy's cavalry with unabated spirit and effectually protected our left."

Though Stuart's troopers had been in the saddle, practically night and day, since the night of the 24th of June, eight days, and the horses and riders were badly jaded, and had previously been active in covering the movements of the army since the 16th of June, when they crossed the Rappahannock River and moved along the east side of the Blue Ridge, covering the advance of the infantry and its accompanying artillery, after conferring with General Lee, Stuart moved forward to a position left of Ewell's left, and in advance of it, where a commanding ridge completely controlled a wide plain of cultivated fields stretching toward Hanover, on the left, and reaching to the base of the mountain spurs, among which the Federal forces held position, preliminary to beginning active operations. His command was increased by the addition of Jenkins's Brigade, who, he says, here in the presence of the enemy allowed themselves to be supplied with but ten rounds of ammunition, although armed with the most improved Enfield carbines.

Stuart moved Jenkins's and W. H. F. Lee's Brigades, the latter commanded by [Confederate Gen. John Randolph] Chambliss [Jr.], through the woods to a position and hoped to effect a surprise upon the Federal rear; but Hampton's and Fitz [Fitzhugh] Lee's Brigades, which had been ordered to follow him, unfortunately debouched into the open ground, disclosing the movement and causing a corresponding movement of a large force of Federal cavalry.

He sent for Hampton and Fitz Lee to come forward, so that he could show them the situation at a glance from the elevated ground he held and arrange for further operations. His message failed to find Hampton promptly, and he never reached Stuart; so Lee remained, as it was deemed inadvisable at the time the message was delivered for both to leave their commands.

Hampton went to hunt Stuart, but before he found him the Federal cavalry had deployed a heavy line of sharpshooters and were advancing toward the Confederate position. The Confederate artillery, however, had left the crest which it was essential for it to occupy on account of being too short range to compete with the longer range Federal guns; but Stuart sent orders for it to return. Jenkins's Brigade was employed chiefly dismounted and fought with decided effect until the ten rounds were expended and then retreated under circumstances of difficulty and exposure which entailed the loss of valuable men.

Confederate forces attacking Cemetery Hill at Gettysburg, PA., on the night of Thursday, July 2, 1863.

The left, where Hampton's and Lee's brigade were, by this time became heavily engaged as dismounted skirmishers. Stuart's plan was to employ the enemy in front with sharpshooters and move a command of cavalry upon their left flank from the position lately held by him; but the falling back of Jenkins's men caused a like movement on the left, and the enemy, sending forward a squadron or two, was about to cutoff and capture a part of the Confederate dismounted sharpshooters.

To prevent this Stuart ordered forward the nearest cavalry regiment, one of W. H. F. Lee's, quickly to charge this force of cavalry. It was gallantly done, and about the same time a portion of Fitz Lee's command charged on the left, the First Virginia Cavalry being most conspicuous. In these charges, the impetuosity of these gallant fellows, after two weeks of hard marching and hard fighting on short rations, was not only extraordinary, but irresistible. The enemy's masses vanished before them like grain before the scythe, and that regiment elicited the admiration of every beholder and

eclipsed the many laurels already won by its gallant veterans.
    Their impetuosity carried them too far, and the charge being very much prolonged, their horses, already jaded by hard marching, failed under it. Their movement was too rapid to be stopped by couriers, and the Federal troops seeing it, turned upon them with fresh horses. The First North Carolina Cavalry and Jeff Davis Legion were sent to their support, and gradually this hand-to-hand fighting involved the greater portion of the command till the Federal troops were driven from the field, which was now raked by their artillery, posted about three quarters of a mile off, the Confederate officers behaving with the greatest heroism throughout. The Confederate artillery commanding the same ground, no more hand-to-hand fighting occurred, but the wounded were removed and the prisoners taken to the rear. General Hampton was wounded in this action.

Gen. Edward P. Alexander, C.S.A.

    Though the results obtained were favorable, according to Stuart's conclusion, he would have preferred a different method of attack, but he soon saw that entanglement was unavoidable, and he determined to make the best fight possible. Both Fitz Lee and the First Virginia begged Stuart (after the hot encounter) to allow them to take the Federal battery, but Stuart doubted the practicability of the ground for such a purpose. During the day's operations, Stuart held such a position as not only to render Ewell's left entirely secure, where the firing of his command, mistaken for that of the enemy, caused some apprehension, but commanded a view of the routes leading to the Federal rear. Had the enemy's main body been dislodged by the infantry assault, as was confidently hoped and expected, Stuart was in precisely the right position to discover it and improve the opportunity. He watched keenly and anxiously the indications in his rear for that purpose, while by the attack which he intended the Federal cavalry would have separated from the main body, and gave promise of solid results and advantages.
    Some writers refer to the failure of Custer's Brigade to join Hugh Judson] Kilpatrick on the Federal left, the Confederate right,

on July 3, as a mistake. [Confederate] Col. E. [Edward] Porter Alexander, in his excellent work, *Military Memoirs of a Confederate*, permitted himself to drop into such an error. He says:

> "By some mistake, surely a fortunate one for the Confederates, Custer's Brigade had already been sent to Gregg's Division on the other flank."

Kilpatrick, to whose division Custer's Brigade belonged, reporting, said: "By some mistake, General Custer's Brigade was ordered to report to General [David McMurtie] Gregg and did not join me during the day." Colonel Alexander may have been led into his erroneous conclusion by Kilpatrick's report.

General Gregg's report gives a different view for Custer's absence, as will be seen. He reported:

> "At 12 M., I received a dispatch from the commander of the Eleventh Army Corps to the major general commanding the Army of the Potomac, that large columns of the enemy's cavalry were moving to the right of our line. At the same time I received an order from Major General [Alfred] Pleasanton, through an aide-de-camp, to send Custer's Brigade, of Kilpatrick's Division, to join Kilpatrick on the left. The First Brigade of my division was sent to relieve Custer's Brigade. This change having been made, the enemy's cavalry gained our right and were about to attack, with the view of gaining the rear of our line of battle. The importance of successfully resisting an attack at this point, which, succeeded in by the enemy, would have been productive of the most serious consequences, determined me to retain the brigade (Custer's) of Kilpatrick's Division until the enemy were driven back. General Custer, commanding the brigade, fully satisfied of the intended attack, was well pleased to remain with his brigade."

It was the threatening and dangerous aspect of Stuart's demonstrations that caused Gregg to order Custer to remain and allow his brigade used in meeting Stuart's determined assault. As this story proceeds, it will be readily seen that Custer's troops were needed and were very active against Stuart's brave Confederate troopers, and his absence from the Federal left was not a mistake, but a necessity.

Continuing, Gregg said:

> "The very superior force of dismounted skirmishers of the enemy advanced on our left and front required the line to be reenforced by one of General Custer's regiments."

At this time the skirmishing became brisk on both sides, and an artillery fire was begun by the Confederate and Federal troops. During the skirmish of the dismounted men, the Confederates brought a column upon the field for a charge. The charge of this column was met by the Seventh Michigan Cavalry, of Custer's Brigade, but not successfully. The advantage gained in this charge was soon wrested from he Confederates by the gallant charge of the First Michigan, of the same brigade. This regiment drove the Confederates back to their starting point. Other charges were made by the Confederate columns, but in every instance they were driven back. Defeated at every point, the Confederates withdrew to their left, and, on passing the wood in which the New Jersey Cavalry was posted, that regiment gallantly and successfully charged the flank of the Confederate column. They retired their column behind their artillery and at dark withdrew from their former position. At that time Gregg felt himself at liberty to relieve Custer's Brigade.

Union Gen. George A. Custer (seated left) with his wife Elizabeth Bacon Custer and his brother Thomas W. Custer (standing).

Capt. William E. Miller, Third Pennsylvania Cavalry, has written a lucid story of the operations of the cavalry division commanded by Gen. D. [David] McM. [McMurtie] Gregg during the Pennsylvania campaign, and which is published in *Battles and Leaders*. The following matter, pertaining to the cavalry battle, at Gettysburg, July 3, is obtained from it.

The cavalry command of Gen. J. E. B. Stuart occupied what is known as Cress's Ridge, in the vicinity of Gettysburg, July 3, 1863. The place was admirably adapted to the massing and screening of troops. Behind the woods, Stuart, who had come from the direction of Gettysburg along the York Pike, concentrated his troops on what is the Stallsmith farm. Gregg's troops were not so favorably situated. Occupying a line about three miles long from Wolf's Hill to Lott's house, through an open country, they were in full view of the Confederates.

A party of Confederate skirmishers, thrown out from the front of Stuart's center, occupied the Rummel farm buildings, which were situated in the plain about three-fourths of a mile northwest of Lott's house, near the base of Cress's Ridge. About 2 o'clock [Union Gen. John Baillie] McIntosh dismounted the First New Jersey and moved it forward in the direction of Rummel's. To meet this advance the Confederates pushed out a line of skirmishers and occupied the fence south of Rummel's. The First New Jersey soon adjusted their line to correspond with that of their antagonists and firing began. At the same time a Confederate battery appeared on top of the ridge and commenced shelling.

[Union officer Alexander Cummings McWhorter] Pennington [Jr.], Pennington's battery, in position in front of Spangler's house on the Hanover road, instantly replied. A section of [Alanson Merwin] Randol's battery, under Lieutenant [James] Chester, was placed in position a little southwest of Lott's house. Pennington and Chester soon silenced the Confederate battery, and finding Rummel's barn filled with Confederate sharpshooters, who were picking off the Federal soldiers, they turned their guns on it and drove them out. In the meantime the Federal front line was advanced and drove back that of the Confederates. A lull in the firing now ensued, during which Custer's Brigade returned.

After the engagement opened, McIntosh had discovered that the force in his front was too strong for his command, and consequently he had sent word to General Gregg to that effect, requesting that Irvin Gregg's Brigade be forwarded to his support. As this brigade was some distance in the rear, and therefore not immediately available, Gen. D. McM. Gregg, meeting Custer, who was about to begin his march in an opposite direction, ordered him to return, and, at the same time, sent word to Irvin Gregg to concentrate as much of his command as possible in the vicinity of Spangler's house. Custer, eager for the fray, wheeled about and was soon on the field. (Here is additional evidence that Custer's failure to join his division was at Gen. D. McM. Gregg's instance, under a peremptory order to remain.)

General Gregg, at this juncture, appeared and took command in person. Custer, as soon as he arrived, extended the left of his line along Little's Run, with a portion of the Sixth Michigan, dismounted, and at the same time Randol placed in position to the left and rear of Chester the second section of his battery, in command of Lieutenant [Ernest L.] Kinney. At this stage the Fifth Michigan was ordered to relieve the Third Pennsylvania and the First New Jersey. The Fifth Michigan was dismounted, and while it was moving to the front a dismounted regiment from W. H. F. Lee's Brigade came to the support of the Confederate skirmishers. A heated contest followed, in which the First New Jersey and Third Pennsylvania remained to take part.

The Battle of Gettysburg, July 3, 1863, with Confederate troops on the right.

After the firing abated, these regiments attempted to withdraw, but they were followed so closely that they were obliged to face about and resume the conflict. The short supply of ammunition of the Fifth Michigan having by this time given out, and Maj. Noah H. Ferry, who was in command of the line, having been killed, the whole line was driven in. Improving this opportunity, Fitz Lee sent forward the First Virginia, which charged the right and center. The Seventh Michigan at once moved forward from the Reever house, in close column of squadrons, and advanced to the attack. The right of the Fifth Michigan swung back, and the Seventh pressed forward to a stone-and-rail fence and opened fire with their carbines. The First Virginia advanced with steadiness, and soon the two regiments were face to face, the fence alone separating them.

Miller's squadron, which occupied the right center, and which up to this time had not been engaged, opened a flank fire on the Virginians, which aided in materially in holding them in check. The First North Carolina and the Jeff Davis Legion coming up to their support, they crowded the Seventh Michigan back, and it was obliged to give way, the Confederates following in close pursuit. "A more determined and vigorous charge than that made by the First Virginia it was never my fortune to witness."

But they became scattered by the flank fire they received, together with the shells from the Federal artillery, and were in the end obliged to fall back on their main body.

About half a mile distant from the last-mentioned fence, where the crossroad passes through the woods on the Stallsmith farm, there appeared moving toward us a large mass of cavalry, which proved to be the remaining portions of Hampton's and Fitz Lee's brigades. They were formed in close columns of squadrons and directed their course toward the Spangler house. A grander spectacle than their advance has rarely been beheld. They marched with well aligned fronts and steady reins. Their polished sabers glittered in the sun. All eyes turned upon them. Chester on the right, Kinney in the center, and Pennington on the left opened their fire with well-directed aim. Shell and shrapnel met the advancing Confederates and tore through their ranks. Closing their gaps as though nothing had happened, on they came. As they drew near, canister was substituted by the Federal artillerymen, and horse after horse staggered and fell. Still they came on.

The Federal mounted skirmishers rallied and fell into line; the dismounted men fell back, and a few of them reached their horses. The First Michigan, drawn up in close column of squadrons near Pennington's battery, was ordered by Gregg to charge. Custer, who was near, placed himself at its head, and off they dashed. As the two columns approached each other, the pace of each increased, when suddenly a crash, like the falling of timber, betokened the crisis. So sudden and violent was the collision that many of the horses were turned end for end and crushed the riders beneath them. The clashing of sabers, the firing of pistols, the demands for surrender, and cries of the combatants filled the air. As the columns were drawing nearer to each other, McIntosh sent his adjutant general, [Frederick C.] Newhall, to the left with orders to [Charles] Treichel and [James] Rogers to mount and charge, and also sent Captain Wagner, of his staff, to rally the headquarters staff, buglers and orderlies, while he himself rode to the Lott house for the First Maryland. As the First Maryland had been moved, and failing to find it where he had expected it, McIntosh gathered up what loose men he could, joined them to the headquarters party, and charged.

At this stage of the conflict, without orders, Captain Miller "sailed in," striking the Confederate left flank about two-thirds down the column. [James H.] Hart, of the First New Jersey, whose squadron was in the woods to Miller's left, soon followed, but directed his charge to the head of the Confederate column. When Newhall reached Treichel and Rogers, he joined them in their charge, which struck the right flank of the Confederate column, near the color guard. The standard bearer, seeing that Newhall was about to seize the colors, lowered his spear, which caught his opponent on the chin, tearing and shattering his lower jaw, and sending him senseless to the ground. Every officer of the party was wounded. Miller's command swept through the Confederate column, cut off the rear portion and drove it back.

Gen Richard S. Ewell, C.S.A.

In the charge, Miller's men became somewhat scattered. A portion of them, however, got into Rummel's lane, in front of the farm buildings, and there encountered some of Jenkins's men who seemed stubborn about leaving. Breathed's battery, unsupported, was only one hundred yards away, but Miller's men were so disabled and scattered that they were unable to take it back.

The losses in this fighting were: Federal, 30 killed, 149 wounded, 75 missing; total, 254. Confederate, 41 killed, 50 wounded, 90 missing; total, 181. The Confederate losses do not include the losses in Jenkins's Brigade.

In going over the field, Mr. Rummel, who aided in removing the dead, found two men, one a private in a Federal command, the other a Confederate, who had cut each other down with their sabers, and were lying with their feet together, their heads in opposite directions, each with the blood-stained saber still tightly in his grip. At another point he found two men, one a Virginian and the other a Pennsylvanian, who fought on horseback with their sabers until they finally clinched and their horses ran from under them. Their heads and shoulders were severely cut, and their fingers, though stiff in death, were so firmly imbedded in each other's flesh that they could not be removed without the aid of force. Mr. Rummel told Captain Miller that he had dragged thirty dead horses out of his lane.

The following is related by Captain Miller as coming under his personal notice: In the midst of the engagement, and immediately in front of Rummel's house E. G. Eyster, of Company H, Third Pennsylvania Cavalry, captured a dismounted Confederate and covered him with his carbine. Eyster's attention becoming drawn off by the firing around him, the Confederate drew his revolver, shot Eyster's horse, and held the rider a prisoner. Just then Sergeant Gregg, of Company A, came upon the scene and cut the Confederate to the ground. Before Gregg had time to turn, another Confederate came up, and, with a right cut, sliced off the top of Gregg's scalp. Gregg, who subsequently rose to a captaincy in his regiment, and who died in 1886, had only to remove his hat to show a head as nicely tonsured as a priest's.

Eyster and Gregg were both taken prisoners in the fight. Gregg, being wounded, was removed in an ambulance, and Eyster was compelled to walk with other prisoners. They were separated on the field. Eyster was sent to prison; Sergeant Gregg was sent to the hospital, and was soon afterwards exchanged. It so happened that when one came back to the regiment the other was absent, and vice versa, so that they never met again until sixteen years afterwards at Gettysburg, where the regiment was holding a reunion. In going over the field, Eyster was relating the story to Col. John B. Bachelder on the very spot where the above scene had occurred, when Gregg came up and they met for the first time since their separation on the ground.[271] — JOHN PURIFOY, MONTGOMERY, ALA.

THE COURIER TRICK

☛ In May, 1864, when a large Federal cavalry force approached Richmond with the idea of capturing the city, Gen. Jeb Stuart, realizing the large force of the enemy, sent a courier with a false, or fake, order, directing him to ride at once into the enemy's line and get captured. The contents of that fake order were such as would deceive the Federal forces in regard to the disposition of General Stuart's command. The courier was captured, his papers read, the enemy's plans changed, and in the fight near Yellow Tavern, the Federals were repulsed and Richmond saved. Had that courier failed to be captured, the result of the fight that day might have been different.[272] — AN ANONYMOUS COURIER, ARTILLERY, SECOND CORPS, A.N.V.

AN ENGLISH CONFEDERATE WHO LOVED STUART

☞ At different times during the past years, there have been references in the *Confederate Veteran* to an Englishman, Mr. Gerald Smythe, of Hastings, England, who kept the Confederate flag flying at his home. Such loyalty and devotion to the memory of a nation that "fell so pure of crime" aroused general appreciation, and Mr. Smythe is regarded as really one of us. He made a visit to this country some years ago and was entertained by Capt. Robert E. Lee, son of General Lee, and was made an honorary member of R. E. Lee Camp of Richmond, Va. He made many friends by his visit to Virginia, and he writes that in 1913, while living at Tunbridge Wells [UK], he entertained in his home

> "the late Col. W. Gordon McCabe and the late Col. H. W. Feilden, of the British Army, who was on the personal staff of General Beauregard at Charleston from 1862 to 1864. The last previous meeting between those two gallant veterans had taken place on the ramparts of Fort Sumter during the Yankee bombardment in 1863. This was one of the most interesting experiences I had met with up to that time, and except for having received Miss Mary Custis Lee, the General's granddaughter, as a guest in this house, it has not since been surpassed. If, in the course of a military performance by a military band during our summer season, *Dixie* comes into any selection played, I always come to 'attention' and remove my hat. I regard that air at least as one of my 'National Anthems.'"

The following lines were written by Mr. Smythe on the death of "Gen. J. E. B. Stuart, commanding cavalry, A.N.V."

"Weep, women of the South, and strew fresh garlands on our hero's grave.
For 'neath this verdant, grassy mound lies Stuart, bravest of the brave.
No lingering illness laid him low, old age enfeebled not his might,
But death, in battle, struck him down, he fell to rise no more in fight.
No more will he, with flashing steel, fierce blows in deadly conflict rain;
No more his charger in the van will trample down the foe like grain.
Although no more he'll lead the charge in the dread battle's fiercest hour,
His spirit still will haunt the fray, still o'er the muddy plain will scour.
Think not, ye Northern leaders, now, though gallant Stuart lieth low,
His comrades bold will timid be; more fiercely will they fight the foe;
Bravely will they avenge his death, and this will be their battle cry:
'Remember Stuart and strike home!' Then will the foe in terror fly." June, 1864.[273] — *CONFEDERATE VETERAN*

REMEMBERING STUART'S BIRTHDAY IN 1926

☞ The 6th day of February marks the anniversary of the birth of a baby, ninety-three years ago, who grew to be one of the greatest of the heroes of the War between the States. He is formally known as

Gen. James Ewell Brown Stuart, and affectionately known as "Jeb" Stuart and "The Eyes and Ears of the Army." Dashing, gay, debonair, he left a cheery memory and a blessed memory, too, for he lived purely and fell in honor, dying with words of submission to God upon the lips that sang in midst of peril and oft breathed a prayer from his happy heart.[274] — MYRTLE HARWOOD WILKINSON, HISTORIAN, U.D.C. CHAPTER, MINERAL, VA.

STONEWALL JACKSON'S "GRIM HUMOR"

☛ I was sitting on a fence, with a chum, on the old Warrenton road just before the Second Manassas battle, when Stonewall and his staff rode up from the east, while General [Jeb] Stuart approached from the west, stopping directly in front of us. General Stuart had just made a raid around [Union Gen. John] Pope's army, capturing his headquarters. General Stuart had little of the West Point etiquette, and, as he approached General Jackson, he called out: "Hello, Jackson! I've got Pope's coat; if you don't believe it, there's his name," holding up a magnificent new major general's coat, which made General Jackson's old gray look like second-hand clothing. Stuart's staff evidently expected a loud laugh, but General Jackson, with his hand at salute, said: "General Stuart, I would much rather you had brought General Pope instead of his coat."[275] — CONFEDERATE SOLDIER CHARLES STRAHAN

Gen. Thomas J. Jackson, C.S.A.

A CAVALRYMAN IN STUART'S DIVISION

☛ ... [Stonewall] Jackson moved to Port Republic, crossed the river, burned the bridge, met [Union Gen. James] Shields in Luray Valley, and in a short time had him moving. Jackson left the cavalry in the Valley, went east, and [Turner] Ashby's old brigade was commanded by Gen. B. H. Robertson—such a contrast! Shortly we came east and joined in the fight of Slaughter (Cedar) Mountains, and in a very short time the Yankees were north of the Rappahannock River.

Our brigade was in Gen. J. E. B. Stuart's Division. Stuart was a famous raider. One night, the darkest and rainiest I ever experienced, he led us to Catlett's Station in the rear of [John] Pope's army, and got the boasting general's headquarters' wagons, his uniform, etc. Soon after we returned, we struck out again far in the rear of Pope, went through Thoroughfare Gap of the Bull Run Mountains, and kept on until we arrived at Bristoe on the Orange and Alexandria Railroad within five miles of Manassas and quite twenty-five miles in Pope's rear. His large railroad yards were holding us back. Looking back the route we had come, we could see a fog of dust for miles and we were sure it was Pope's army. Nearer and nearer it came! But we had no orders from Stuart to prepare to fight them, and when they were near enough to us, we all holloaed, "Why, it's Stonewall Jackson and his whole army!" His men had marched quite forty miles at that. It did not take long to get all of the stores of everything at Manassas. In the two days' fight near Manassas, Stuart's cavalry was in some engagement with the enemy nearly all of the time. During the war I never thought our cavalry got the credit they deserved in the large battles.

"Catlett's Station, where Stuart made a raid and captured Gen. Pope's baggage."

. . . About the 25th of June, when we were only a few miles from Aldie, Stuart sent me with a dispatch to General Lee, saying: "You will find me near Berryville, west of the Blue Ridge." I knew then it was about a thirty mile ride. I found General Lee near where Stuart told me, and I shall never forget it. That great chieftain was sitting on a camp stool. He got up. I dismounted and saluted and handed him Stuart's large envelope. Holding it in his hand, he said: "You have been riding your mare hard." I said: "Yes, General; I did not know how important it was." I then asked: "General, can I get a feed of corn for my horse?" Pointing to a plot, he said: "We have no corn for our horses; there is some good grass. Take your saddle off, lie down, and take a sleep. I want you to go back to General Stuart to-night." His words were like a father talking to his child. to- night." His words were like a father talking to his child. It is my belief that there was but one Man who ever came into this world greater than General Lee, and he died on the cross. It did me good to carry a dispatch from General Lee.[276] — JOHN W. PEAKE, SIXTH VIRGINIA CAVALRY, C.S.A.

MUSIC ON THE HOOF

☛ ... There were many other good bands in the different brigades of Lee's army. Even the cavalry had their bands. Stuart was fond of music and always on the march he had a fellow riding behind him singing and playing on an old banjo.[277] — I. G. BRADWELL, BRANTLEY, ALA.

STUART AT THE BATTLE OF CHANCELLORSVILLE

☛ Stuart's battle on the May 3rd [1863] was superb, and he is entitled to great credit for his brilliant achievement. It should not be overlooked, however, that he had a brave and efficient helper in Gen. E. Porter Alexander, whose previous service had been confined almost wholly to looking after the army ordnance. To his skill and energy is due, largely, the excellent part rendered by the Confederate artillery. Stuart's historian, Col. H. B. McClellan, makes the following acknowledgment:

> "General Alexander's reconnoissance convinced Stuart that Hazel Grove was the key to the Federal line, and to this part of the field Stuart directed a large share of his personal attention on the morning of the 3rd. Had General Lee been present on the left during the Sunday morning (3rd) attack, and seen Stuart's energy and efficiency in handling his reserves, inspiring the men by his contagious spirit, and in the cooperation of the artillery with the infantry, he might have rewarded Stuart on the spot by promoting him to the now vacant command of Jackson's Corps. Stuart's qualities were just what was needed, for he was young and had boldness, persistence, and magnetism in very high degree."[278] — JOHN PURIFOY, MONTGOMERY, ALA.

STUART & SECESSION

☛ Was it disloyal for Gen. Robert E. Lee, Stonewall Jackson, J. E. B. Stuart, and others to resign from the United States Army?
No.
Why not?
Because the Constitution of the United States provided for a

union of independent and self-governing States, and a citizen's first duty was to his State. Secession was a legal right.[279] — FROM THE CATECHISM FOR THE CHILDREN OF THE CONFEDERACY

WHERE STUART EXCELLED
☛ Stuart had excelled every cavalry leader that ever lived, I suppose, in the work of screening an army from the enemy's observation.[280] — ROBERT W. BARNWELL, FLORENCE, S.C.

DAVIS & STUART
☛ When Stuart lay wounded and dying, Mr. [Jefferson] Davis knelt and prayed that "this precious life might be spared to our needy country."[281] — DR. W. L. FLEMING, LOUISIANA STATE UNIVERSITY

JEB STUART'S TRIBUTE TO HIS HORSE
☛ From Alexander L. Tinsley, of Baltimore, MD: "As illustrative of the versatility of Gen. Jeb Stuart, the following stanzas to his horse, 'Maryland,' are submitted. They were composed on the spur of the moment, just after one of his famous raids, I understand, and a copy of them was given to me many years ago by my aunt, at whose home in Shepherdstown, W. Va., they were written. She was the widow of Lieut. Col. William F. Lee, of the Thirty-third Virginia Infantry, who was mortally wounded at the battle of Bull Run, and who had been an old army friend of General Stuart":

I hear your old familiar neigh,
    Maryland! My Maryland!
Asking for your corn and hay,
    Maryland! My Maryland!
But you must wait till break of day,
And Bob will then your call obey,
And make you look so sleek and gay,
    Maryland! My Maryland!

Upon your proud old back I'll sit,
    Maryland! My Maryland!
When last night's bivouac I quit,
    Maryland! My Maryland!
To use my spur I'll not omit,
And minding ditches not a whit,
I'll yield to you the willing bit,

Maryland! My Maryland!

I've seen you rear that noble crest,
    Maryland! My Maryland!
When battle brings its stirring zest,
    Maryland! My Maryland!
When duty calls you have no rest,
But o'er the fields from east to west,
You yield to every hard behest,
    Maryland! My Maryland!

I feel secure upon your back
    Maryland! My Maryland!
When danger howls upon your track,
    Maryland! My Maryland!
You bore me o'er the Potomac,
You circumvented Little Mac,
O, may I never know your lack,
    Maryland! My Maryland![282] — *CONFEDERATE VETERAN*

A CONFEDERATE SCOUT, STUART, & LEE

☛ . . . Riding south, the Confederate pickets halted us, but the officer in command, Lieutenant Pendleton, of Clarke County, was an old acquaintance, and he permitted us to proceed to General Stuart's headquarters, which were at Rapidan Station, about four miles from the picket post and twelve miles from Culpeper.

When we reached the station, Wiltshire and Shephard, tired and hungry, concluded to forage on their company quartermaster, and I proceeded to General Stuart's headquarters, on a small eminence across the railroad from the Taliaferro mansion and commanding a magnificent view on both sides of the beautiful Rapidan Valley.

By this time the sun was up, and it was a splendid autumn morning. Riding direct to General Stuart's tent, I dismounted and my horse was given to an orderly to be fed and groomed. To General Stuart I made verbal report of the success of the expedition, and drew out the written memorandum, which he eagerly perused. After a brief conversation, he had a short consultation with his adjutant general, and in a little while one of his staff rode rapidly off in the direction of Orange Court House.

Then, turning to me, General Stuart asked if I had eaten my breakfast. When informed that I had been a stranger to solid food for thirty-six hours, he ordered his cook to prepare breakfast for me. That I got away with a "square meal" I need hardly say, particularly to old soldiers who could eat a half dozen meals a day and still vow they "hadn't eaten anything for forty-eight hours."

Breakfast over, General Stuart again engaged me in conversation, and was profuse in expressions of thanks for the prompt and satisfactory manner in which our mission in the rear of the enemy had been discharged. Noticing my exhausted appearance, for I had been in the saddle over twenty-four hours, he ordered a robe spread before the fire used for cooking breakfast. I well recollect that the late Rev. Dabney Ball, who was on General Stuart's staff, spread the robe and kindly bade me take a morning snooze. It required no rocking to put me to sleep. With recollection of duty at least faithfully discharged and the approval of the great cavalry captain of the Army of Northern Virginia, I soon dropped into a sleep, both sweet and refreshing, from which I was aroused an hour or two later by the tramp of horses near by, when I saw Gen. Robert E. Lee, the great Confederate chieftain, mounted on his famous iron-gray war horse, in earnest conversation with General Stuart.

The front hall of General Robert E. Lee's home in Richmond, VA.

A moment later General Stuart called me, and I was introduced to General [Robert E.] Lee. He questioned me closely, reread the memorandum, looked me squarely in the eye, and then placing his hand on my shoulder said: "Young man, you have done a good night's work. I thank you." This was the proudest day of my life, though I may have felt a little more of a flutter about my heart when a certain black-eyed girl in the "Hill City" finally said "yes" after my importunities of two long years. When introduced to the great general, I measured six feet even in my stocking feet, but the gracious recognition seemed to augment my stature several inches.

Later in the day, when I went to take leave of General Stuart with a view, of again reporting to my command, to my great surprise he told me to consider myself permanently detailed for scout service under his direction; that I could go to my company, but need not be subject to company duty, and that Major [Henry Brainerd] McClellan, his adjutant general, would take my address and send for me when wanted. This was done, and when General Stuart was killed at Yellow Tavern, I was on scouting duty for him on the line of the Baltimore and Ohio Railroad, watching the movements of the Federal troops.[283] — CONFEDERATE SCOUT H. D. BEALE, FROM THE *WEEKLY SUN*

GENERAL STUART'S SPURS

☞ At least two pairs of spurs were presented to Gen. Jeb Stuart by his admirers. One pair was the gift of a number of Baltimore ladies; the other, and with which this article is concerned, was the gift of some of his friends in St. Louis, near which city, at Jefferson Barracks, he had been stationed shortly before the War between the States.

This latter pair was entrusted to his friend, Lieut. William Fitzhugh Lee, to carry to him in the East. Lieutenant Lee, however, was placed under arrest at Jefferson Barracks for certain pro-Southern utterances, pending the acceptance of his resignation as an officer of the United States Army. In the meanwhile, his wife, my aunt, returned to her home in Shepherdstown, Va., taking the spurs with her.

No opportunity presented itself for some time to deliver the spurs to the General, and it was not until after the battle of Antietam that this could be done. This battle was fought within three miles of Shepherdstown, to which place General Lee had his wounded removed. My father, Assistant Surgeon Alexander Tinsley [Sr.], but lately there on hospital duty in Richmond, was directed to prepare the town for the reception of the Confederate wounded and was left in charge of the more dangerously wounded. He was captured when the town was occupied by the Federals and was sent as a prisoner of war to Baltimore. He was accompanied to Baltimore by his wife, my mother, who was the sister of Mrs. Lee, and who took the spurs with her.

Not very long afterwards, my father was exchanged and was sent to Richmond on a flag of truce boat and was accompanied by my mother, who had concealed the spurs in the bustle of her dress, and she gave them to the General. It was these spurs that, on his deathbed, General Stuart directed be given to my aunt, whose husband Lieutenant Colonel Lee, had been mortally wounded at the battle of Bull Run while leading the charge of the Thirty-third Virginia, Jackson's Brigade, which, with a loss of forty per cent of its men, succeeded in capturing two batteries of Federal Regular Artillery just on the point of enfilading Jackson's line. The spurs are now in the possession of the family of Colonel Lee's grandson, the late Maj. W. F. Lee Simpson, U.S.A.[284] — ALEXANDER L. TINSLEY [JR.], BALTIMORE, MD.

A sampling of Confederate generals, including Beauregard, Ewell, Longstreet, Jackson, A. P. Hill, A. S. Johnston, and Stuart (at the 4:00 o'clock position).

Gen. J. E. B. Stuart's Ride Around McClellan, June 1862.

CHAPTER 12

ANNOUNCING THE DEATH OF JEB STUART'S SON
☛ Capt. J. E. B. Stuart [II], son of that illustrious cavalryman of Confederate fame, died at Istokpoga, Fla., on November 26 [1930], aged seventy-one years.[285] — *CONFEDERATE VETERAN*, DECEMBER 1930

ON THE DEATH OF GEN. STUART
☛ [Having been told that he had been shot] General [Fitzhugh] Lee and I went as rapidly as possible back to General Stuart. When we got there, a half dozen men had dismounted and were helping General Stuart into the ambulance. The enemy, seeing that something of unusual interest had occurred, pressed up even closer to our line, and the fighting there was almost hand to hand, the fighting lines being not over fifteen or twenty yards apart at some places, and even closer. The mules attached to the ambulance became unmanageable, and notwithstanding the coolness and courage of the driver, dashed down over the steep embankment with General Stuart in the ambulance. The right hind wheel flew up in the air, and I thought, "My God, he is going to be dragged to death!" but to my great joy when the ambulance struck the road it righted itself, and down the road back to Chickahominy it went.

I followed with my horse's head right in the ambulance, for I was a mere youth of eighteen summers and did not know what I was doing. I was completely demoralized, and followed the ambulance to the Chickahominy River before it dawned upon me that I ought to go back to the firing line.

The last thing I saw of him he was lying flat on his back in the ambulance, the mules running at a terrific pace, and he was being jolted most unmercifully. He opened his eyes and looked at me, and, with the faintest expression, shook his head from side to side as much as to say, "It's all over with me." Then he peacefully closed his eyes and folded his arms with a look of complete resignation.

And thus, our comrades, ebbed out the life of our beloved chieftain—the Navarre of our Southland, a man who, by his love for everyone of us individually, by his unswerving fidelity to the

Southern cause, by his unequaled heroism and generalship, has won for himself the fame of the greatest cavalry general of the nineteenth century. Who can gainsay it?

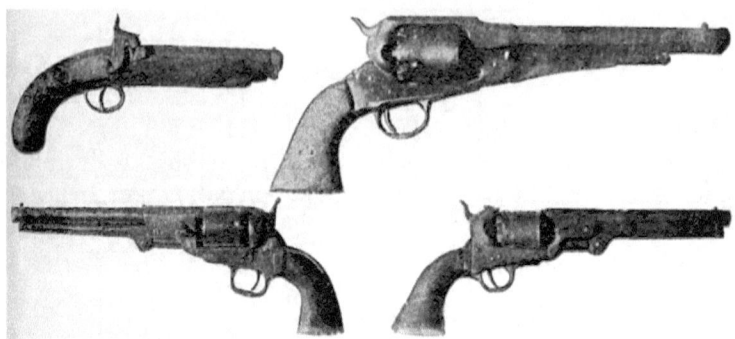

Examples of Confederate arms. Top left: Navy pistol, with belt hook. Top right: Confederate revolver, brass frame, 36-caliber. Bottom left: Confederate revolver, Colt model, 36-caliber. Bottom right: Confederate revolver, Colt model, 36-caliber, with 12 cylinder stops.

I cannot close without drawing a comparison between Stuart and the much vaunted [Union Gen. Philip Henry] Sheridan of the Northern army. Stuart was, and is, the only man known to the wide world who ever made a raid around an army. With a little band of about 1,200 horsemen, this daring cavalry leader actually rode clear around McClellan's army numbering 280,000 splendidly equipped troops. Why, he actually got them so confused—in the language of the old Tar Heel—they "didn't know 'zackly what regiment they did belong to." On the other hand, look at the future attempts of Sheridan to imitate him. He never started out anywhere that he wasn't met, checkmated, and compelled to retreat. Let us push the comparison further. One a cruel, heartless, relentless libertine; the other a pure, Christian, chivalrous gentleman.

And so, as long as the Anglo-Saxon race lives and its language is spoken, the names of J. E. B. Stuart, Stonewall Jackson, and Robert E. Lee will be honored by all men in every clime and under every sun.[286] — DR. CYRUS MCCORMICK

STUART SAVED RICHMOND

☛ Somehow I always associate Jeb Stuart as the soldier who, by virtue of circumstances, should ever be held closest to the hearts of all who treasure sentiment in connection with our [Confederate] Capital [Richmond, VA]; for he gave his life defending Richmond

and thereby saved the city from capture. A captured city would have presented a very different military proposition from a capitulated city, and as my brother Eustace rode with Stuart on his memorable raid clear around McClellan's army, the fate of [Stuart's death at the Battle of] Yellow Tavern came close to our hearts.[287]
— MRS. WILLIAM LYNE, ORANGE, VA.

WHY SECESSION WAS JUSTIFIED

☞ . . . Men like Robert E. Lee, Jefferson Davis, Stonewall Jackson, Albert Sidney Johnston, Joseph E. Johnston, [Jeb] Stuart, [Josiah] Tattnall, and [Franklin] Buchanan were not rebels or traitors. They were patriots. They fought for the South, for its independence, for its clear right. They fought against invaders who, in violation of the Constitution, were endeavoring to subjugate their section and people. You [Confederate veterans] should be proud of a cause illustrated and defended by such men as Robert E. Lee, who had been offered the position of Commander in Chief of the Union Army [by Lincoln], had declined the offer and cast his lot with his own people. He knew the resources of the North and the odds against which the South would have to contend, but this gave him no pause. Believing the South was right, he went with the South and declared it was better to resist the wrong even although it was believed that resistance would be unsuccessful, than to tamely yield to the wrong without resistance. No cause could be a bad cause or an unworthy cause for which such men fought and struggled.[288] — SAMUEL B. ADAMS

POPE'S PLUNDER

☞ . . . In the meantime Stuart with his cavalry was engaged in harassing the enemy's rear. On the morning of the 22nd he crossed the Rappahannock at Waterloo Bridge and Hart's Ford, with all of his division except the Seventh and Third Virginia Cavalry and two pieces of artillery. He reached Warrenton in the afternoon and moved in the direction of Catlett's Station with the design of destroying the railroad bridge that crosses Cedar Creek at that point.

Col. Thomas L. Rosser, C.S.A.

Had the object of the expedition been accomplished, [Union Gen. John] Pope's line of communication would have been sundered, and the importance of success spurred Stuart to go forward, though a terrific thunderstorm drenched his troops and enveloped them with thick darkness. The downpour, too, threatened to make the streams impassable on his return.

Approaching Catlett's Station under cover of the stormy night, the Federal pickets were captured by the direction of Colonel [Thomas Lafayette] Rosser, who commanded the advance, and his bold horsemen were soon in the midst of the enemy's encampments.

Pope's headquarters were near by, and they were guided to the spot by a captured negro. Pope himself was away, but many of his official household were there, and most of them with much valuable plunder were taken possession of. Among the captured articles was Pope's despatch book, revealing his plans and describing his embarrassments.

The destruction of the railroad bridge, the main object of the expedition, was not accomplished on account of the darkness and the heavy rain, but Stuart returned with much plunder and 300 prisoners.[289] — CONFEDERATE CAPTAIN WILLIAM NAYLOR MCDONALD

STUART ON THE BATTLEFIELD

☞ . . . At daybreak, Stuart was going at full gallop to the front.

A rapid fire of skirmishers, mingled with the dull roar of cannon, indicated that Nighthawk had not been deceived.

All at once the sharp-shooters were seen falling back from the woods.

"Bring me a piece of artillery!" exclaimed Stuart, darting to the front.

But the attack of the enemy swept all before it. Stuart was driven back, and was returning doggedly, when the gun for which he had sent, galloped up, and unlimbered in the road.

It was too late. Suddenly a solid shot screamed above us; the gun was hurled from its carriage, and rolled shattered and useless in the wood; the horses were seen rearing wild with terror, and trying to kick out of the harness.

Suddenly one of them leaped into the air and fell, torn in two by a second round shot.

"Quick work!" said Stuart, grimly.

And turning round to me, he said, pointing to a hill in rear—"Post three pieces on that hill to rake all the roads."

The order, like the former, came too late, however. The enemy advanced in overpowering force—drove Stuart back beyond his head-quarters, where they captured the military satchel of the present writer—and still rushing forward, like a hurricane, compelled the Confederate cavalry to retire behind Goose Creek. On the high ground there, Stuart posted his artillery; opened a rapid fire; and before this storm of shell the Federal forces paused.

Confederate troops burning Yankee wagon trains, July 1862.

The spectacle at that moment was picturesque and imposing. The enemy's force was evidently large. Long columns of cavalry, heavy masses of infantry and artillery at every opening, right, left, and centre, showed that the task of driving back Stuart was not regarded as very easy. The sunshine darted from bayonet and sabre all along the great line of battle—and from the heavy smoke, tinged with flame, came the Federal shell. With their infantry, cavalry, and artillery, they seemed determined to put an end to us.

Stuart galloped to his guns, pouring a steady fire from the lofty hill. Captain Davenant directed it in person, and he was evidently in his right element. All his sadness had disappeared. A cool and resolute smile lit up his features.

"All right, Davenant! Hold your ground!" exclaimed Stuart.

"I will do so, general."

"Can you keep them from crossing?"

"I can try, general."

A whirlwind of shell screamed around the two speakers. For the hundredth time I witnessed that entire indifference to danger which was a trait of Stuart. The fire at this moment was so terrible that I heard an officer say: "General Stuart seems trying to get himself and everybody killed."

Nothing more inspiring, however, can be imagined than his

appearance at that moment. His horse, wild with terror, reared, darted, and attempted to unseat his rider. Stuart paid no attention to him. He had no eyes or thought for any thing but the enemy. His cheeks were flushed, his eyes flamed—he resembled a veritable king of battle.[290] — CONFEDERATE OFFICER JOHN ESTEN COOKE

STUART & THE LADIES

☛ . . . Middleburg [VA] is a pleasant little place, of some 1500 inhabitants, which, by reason of its proximity to the Federal lines, had often been visited by raiding and scouting parties of the enemy, and had suffered specially in the shameless barbarities committed by those Yankee robbers, [Union Gens. Robert Huston] Milroy and [John White] Geary. The citizens had awaited the result of our late combat with the greatest anxiety, and manifested their satisfaction at our success in loud expressions of rejoicing.

Riding up the main street of the village, I was brought to a halt by a group of very pretty young girls, who were carrying refreshments to the soldiers, and invited me to partake of them, an offer which I was not strong enough to decline. In the conversation which followed, my fair entertainers expressed the greatest desire to see General Stuart, and were

One of Stuart's many female admirers, rushing off to catch a glimpse of him at a public gathering in Richmond.

delighted beyond measure to hear that the bold cavalry leader was my personal friend, and that I should probably have little difficulty in persuading him to devote a quarter of an hour to their charming company. This spread like wildfire through the village, so that half an hour later, when Stuart galloped up to me, I was attended by a staff of fifty or sixty ladies, of various ages, from blooming girlhood to matronly maturity.

The General very willingly consented to remain for a while that everyone might have an opportunity of seeing him, and was immediately surrounded by the ladies, all eager to catch the words that fell from his lips, and many with tears in their eyes kissing the skirt of his uniform coat or the glove upon his hand. This was too much for the gallantry of our leader, who smilingly said to his gentle admirers, "Ladies, your kisses would be more acceptable to me if given upon the cheek."

Thereupon the attacking force wavered and hesitated for a moment; but an elderly lady, breaking through the ranks, advanced boldly, and, throwing her arms around Stuart's neck, gave him a hearty smack, which served as the signal for a general charge.

The kisses now popped in rapid succession like musketry, and at last became volleys, until our General was placed under as hot a fire as I had ever seen him sustain on the field of battle.

When all was over, and we had mounted our horses, Stuart, who was more or less exhausted, said to me, "Von, this is a pretty little trick you have played me, but in future I shall detail you for this sort of service." I answered that I would enter upon it with infinite pleasure, provided he would permit me to reverse his mode of procedure, and commence with the young ladies.

The General and Staff bivouacked with the cavalry near Middleburg, while for me was reserved the agreeable duty of riding on special business to Upperville, where, beneath the hospitable roof of Dr. Eliason, I passed some pleasant hours with the family circle, to whom I had to recite fully the events and adventures of the day.[291] — HEROS VON BORCKE

OLD JACK'S NEW UNIFORM

☛ On October 8th, I was honoured with the pleasing mission of presenting to Stonewall, as a slight token of Stuart's high regard, a new uniform coat, which had just arrived from the hands of a Richmond tailor. Starting at once, I reached the simple tent of our great general just in time for dinner. I found him in his old weather-stained coat, from which all the buttons had been clipped by the fair hands of patriotic ladies, and which, from exposure to sun, rain, and powder-smoke, and by reason of many rents and patches, was in a very unseemly condition.

When I had despatched more important matters, I produced General Stuart's present in all its magnificence of gilt buttons and sheeny facings and gold lace, and I was heartily amused at the modest confusion with which the hero of many battles regarded the fine uniform, scarcely daring to touch it, and at the quiet way in which at last he folded it up carefully and deposited it in his portmanteau, saying to me,

"Give Stuart my best thanks, Major; the coat is much too handsome for me, but I shall take the best care of it, and shall prize it highly as a souvenir. And now let us have some dinner."

Stonewall Jackson in 1847, as a U.S. First Lieutenant of Artillery.

But I protested emphatically against the summary disposition of the matter of the coat, deeming my mission indeed but half executed, and remarked that Stuart would certainly ask how the coat fitted, and that I should take it as a personal favour if he would put it on. To this with a smile he readily assented, and having donned the garment, he escorted me outside the tent to the table where dinner had been served in the open air. The whole of the staff were in a perfect ecstasy at their chief's brilliant appearance, and the old negro servant, who was bearing the roast turkey to the board, stopped in mid career with a most bewildered expression, and gazed in such wonderment at his master as if he had been transfigured before him.

Meanwhile, the rumour of the change ran like electricity through the neighbouring camps, the soldiers came running by hundreds to the spot, desirous of seeing their beloved Stonewall in his new attire; and the first wearing of a new robe by Louis XIV, at whose morning toilette all the world was accustomed to assemble, never created half the excitement at Versailles that was roused in the woods of Virginia by the investment of Jackson in the new regulation uniform.[292] — GEORGE FRANCIS ROBERT HENDERSON

A VIRGINIA GIRL & HER "COMRADE" GEN. STUART

☛ . . . It was from Petersburg that I [Myrta Lockett Avary] was summoned to Culpeper by [Confederate Major] Dan [Grey], who felt that the army might have a long enough breathing spell there for me to pay him at least a visit. When I got to Mr. Bradford's, where he had engaged board for me, I found General Stuart's headquarters in the yard, and his staff were boarders at Mr.

Bradford's, and I ate at the same table with the flower of the Southern cavalry. Unfortunately for me, Dan's command was stationed at a distance of several miles, and I could not see as much of him as I had hoped. He met me the day of my arrival, rode by once or twice, took one or two meals with me, and then it seemed that for all I saw of him I might as well have remained in Petersburg.

My seat at table was next to that of General Stuart, and for vis-à-vis I had Colonel John Esten Cooke. Colonel Cooke was a glum old thing, but General Stuart was so delightful that he compensated for everything. In a short time I was completely at my ease with him, and long before he left I had grown to love and trust him.

One day General Stuart asked me in a teasing way:

"You wouldn't really like to see Dan Grey, would you?"

"Oh, but I would, general," I said, in too dead earnest to give raillery for raillery.

"I don't believe you really want to see Dan Grey."

"Well, I don't, then," [I replied] a bit sullenly.

"What a pity! You might see him now, if you really wanted to."

I wouldn't notice such a frivolous remark.

Dinner over, we went out on the veranda, as usual, and General Stuart dropped into a chair beside me.

"I really thought you rather liked Dan Grey, but it seems I was mistaken. And you really don't want to see him? Sad—I must tell him and condole with him."

I tried to bury myself in a book I was reading, and to pay no attention to him. A miserable old book it was—*Children of the Abbey*, or something like it—that I had picked up somewhere at Mr. Bradford's. Hereafter, if I write "Aunt Sally's" instead of Mr. Bradford's, please understand that one and the same place is meant. Aunt Sally was Mr. Bradford's wife, and I reckon the first term best describes the place.

"You wouldn't really rather have Dan Grey sitting here in this chair beside you than me?" continued my tease.

I lifted to him eyes wet with vexation and longing.

"I'll make you smile now!" he said. "*Do* you want to see Dan?"

"Yes, I do. I want to see him dreadfully, but I am not going to tell you so again."

"You will if I command you to, won't you? If you are in the cavalry I am your superior officer, you know. I can even make Dan mind what I say, can't I? If you are refractory, I can command Dan to bring you to terms."

"I'd like to see Dan do it! You may be commander-in-chief of the cavalry, but you aren't commander-in-chief of me—you or Dan either."

"It seems not," he commented meekly. "You are the most insubordinate little rebel I ever saw. I have a great mind to court martial you—no, I believe I'll send for Dan and let him do it."

He called a courier, and wrote a despatch in regular form, ordering Major Dan Grey to report at once to General Stuart. Then he added a little private note to Dan which had for a postscript:

"Sweet Nellie is by my side."

"That will bring him in a hurry!" laughed Stuart.

Life in the Confederate "trenches."

The courier, not knowing but that the fate of the Confederacy depended upon that despatch, put spurs to his horse, galloped down the road and out of sight. I suppose he ran his horse all the way, and that Dan ran his all the way back, for before General Stuart left the veranda Dan galloped into the yard.

"I'll get the first kiss!" said General Stuart, still teasingly.

He leaped from the porch and ran across the yard, I tearing after him. I caught up and passed him, and looking back at him from Dan's arms, into which I had stumbled, breathless and panting, I laughed out: "I can beat the Yankees getting out of your way!"

Perhaps this race and General Stuart's love of teasing may seem undignified conduct for the chief of the Southern cavalry, but it is history and it is fun, and those who knew him did not fail in respect to Stuart. Many of us loved the ground he walked on. His boyish spirits and his genial, sunny temperament helped to make him the idol of the cavalry and the inspiration of his soldiers, and kept heart in them no matter what happened.

That was a lovely evening. General Stuart had [Joe] Sweeney, his banjo- player, in. Sweeney was a dignified, solemn-looking man, but couldn't he play merry tunes on that banjo, and sad ones too! making you laugh and cry with his playing and his singing.

"When the sad, chilly winds of December
Stole my flowers, my companions, from me."

That was one of his mournful favorites. And you heard the jingle of spurs in his rollicking:

"If you want a good time,
Jine the cavalry,
Bully boys, hey!"

We called for "Old Joe Hooker, won't you Come Out of the Wilderness?" . . . and "O Lord, Ladies, don't you mind Stephen!" and "Sweet Evelina," and—oh! I can't remember them all, but if you choose to read Esten Cooke, he will tell you all about Sweeney's songs and banjo. Stuart sang "The Dew is on the Blossom" and "The Bugles Sang Truce." He made Sweeney give, twice over, "Sweet Nellie is by my Side," and sat himself down beside me, and tried to tease Dan because he sat at table with me every day and Dan couldn't. In spite of everything I was very happy in those old days at the Bradfords'! I was not yet out of my teens, you know; so I hope I was not very much to blame because I was always ready for a romp across that lawn at Mr. Bradford's with the commander-in-chief of the Southern cavalry. His was the gentlest, merriest, sweetest-tempered soul I ever knew. He was always ready to sympathize with me, to tease me, and to help me. Whenever he teased me out of conceit with myself or him, he always would put me in a good humor by saying nice things about Dan, or sending a courier after him.

He had an idea that I was very plucky, and in after days when I was ready to show the white feather, Dan would shame me by asking, "What would General Stuart say?"

Mr. Bradford and his wife, "Aunt Sally," were characters. Mr.

Bradford was a very quiet, peaceable man; Aunt Sally was strong minded, and had a tongue and mind of her own. Mr. Bradford had a good deal of property and stayed out of the army to take care of it. I think Aunt Sally made him stay out of the war for this reason, but she made home about as hot for him as the field would have been. I can't think he stayed at home to keep out of war, for he was in war all the time. Aunt Sally continually twitted him with staying at home, although she made him do it. She was always sure to do this when the table was filled with Confederate officers.

"The place for a man," she would say, "is on the field. Just give me the chance to fight! Just give me the chance to fight, and see where I'll be!"

And General Stuart would convulse me by whispering: "I don't think she needs a chance to fight, do you?"

Sometimes when Aunt Sally's harangue would begin the general would whisper, "Aunt Sally's getting herself in battle array," or "The batteries have limbered up," or "Aunt Sally's scaled the breastworks," and Mr. Bradford's meek and inoffensive face would make the situation funnier. He would mildly help the boarders to the dish in front of him and endeavor feebly to turn the conversation into a peaceful and safe direction, though this never had the slightest effect upon his belligerent wife.

One day it was about the time of Stuart's historical grand review—Mr. Bradford invited all the cavalry generals whose forces were stationed around us to dine with the commander-in-chief of the cavalry. He would never have dared to do this if Aunt Sally had been at home, but Aunt Sally at this auspicious moment was in Washington, where we all hoped the fortunes of war and shopping would keep her indefinitely. Her niece, Miss Morse, and I sat down, the only ladies present, at a table with eighteen Confederate generals. Miss Molly and I were at first a trifle embarrassed at being the only ladies, but they were all refined and well-bred, and soon put us at our ease. General Wade Hampton led me in to dinner, and I sat between him and General [Stephen Dodson]

Gen. John H. Morgan, C.S.A.

Ramseur. General Ramseur was young and exceedingly handsome, and a paralyzed arm which was folded across his breast made him all the more attractive.

"If you sit next me, Mrs. Grey," he said with a little embarrassment, "you will have to cut up my dinner for me. I am afraid that will be putting you to a great deal of trouble. Perhaps I had better change my seat."

"Oh, no!" I said, "I will be very glad—if I can be satisfactory."

He smiled. "Thank you. I am always both glad and sorry to impose upon a lady this service. I am sorry, you know, to tax a lady with it, but then, she always does it better than a man."

I had been studying his face, and now, for want of something more sensible I said: "If I am to feed you, General Ramseur, I must measure your mouth."

It happened that there was dead silence at the table when this silly speech of mine was made. Everybody was listening.

"Madam," said the handsome general, blushing and smiling, "I am entirely willing that you should."

I caught a mischievous light in General Stuart's merry eyes, and blushed furiously. Then I followed his laugh, and the whole table roared.

"I will tell Dan Grey!" cried Stuart. "I will tell Dan Grey!" ran around the table like a chorus.

But I fed my handsome general all the same. It was while I was at Mr. Bradford's that one of the most stirring events in Confederate history occurred. This was the trampling down of John Minor Botts's corn. Very good corn it was, dropped and hilled by Southern negroes and growing on a large, fine plantation next to Mr. Bradford's; and a very nice gentleman Mr. Botts was, too; but a field of corn, however good, and a private citizen, however estimable, are scarcely matters of national or international importance.

The trouble was that John Minor Botts was on the Northern side and the corn was on the Southern side, and that Stuart held a grand review on the Southern side and the corn got trampled down. The fame of that corn went abroad into all the land. Northern and Southern papers vied with each other in editorials and special articles, families who had been friends for generations stopped speaking and do not speak to this day because of it, more than one hard blow was exchanged for and against it, and it brought down vituperation upon Stuart's head. And yet I was present at that naughty grand review—afterward writ in letters of blood upon hearts that reached from Virginia to Florida—and I can testify that

General Stuart went there to review the troops, not to trample down the corn. Afterward John Minor Botts came over to see General Stuart and to quarrel about that corn. All that I can remember of how the general took Mr. Botts's visit and effort to quarrel was that Stuart wouldn't quarrel—whatever it was he said to Mr. Botts he got to laughing when he said it. Our colored [servant] Abigail told us with bated breath that "Mr. Botts ripped and rarred and snorted, but Genrul Stuart warn't put out none at all."

Confederate Gen. Turner Ashby (pictured here), commander of Jackson's cavalry, had much in common with the knightly Stuart.

There had been many reviews that week, all of them merely by way of preparation and practise for that famous grand review before the battle of Brandy or Fleetwood, but it is only of this particular grand review I have many lively memories. Aunt Sally was away, and we attended it in state. Mr. Bradford had out the ancient and honorable family carriage and two shadowy horses, relics of days when corn was in plenty and wheat not merely a dream of the past, and we went in it to the review along with many other carriages and horses, whose title to respect lay, alas! solely in the past.

That was a day to remember! Lee's whole army was in Culpeper. Pennsylvania and Gettysburg were before it, and the army was making ready for invasion. On a knoll where a Confederate flag was planted and surrounded by his staff sat General Lee on horseback; before him, with a Rebel yell, dashed Stuart and his eight thousand cavalry. There was a sham battle. Charging and countercharging went on, rebels yelled and artillery thundered. Every time the cannons were fired we would pile out of our carriage, and as soon as the cannonading ceased we would pile back again. General Stuart happened to ride up once just as we were getting out.

"Why don't you ladies sit still and enjoy the fun?" he asked in amazement.

"We are afraid the horses might take fright and run away," we answered.

I shall never forget his ringing laugh. Our lean and spiritless steeds had too little life in them to run for anything—they hardly pricked up their ears when the guns went off.

How well I remember Stuart as he looked that day! He wore a fine new uniform, brilliant with gold lace, buff gauntlets reaching to his elbows, and a canary-colored silk sash with tasseled ends. His hat, a soft, broad-brimmed felt, was caught up at the side with a gold star and carried a sweeping plume; his high, patent-leather cavalry boots were trimmed with gold. He wore spurs of solid gold, the gift of some Maryland ladies—he was very proud of those spurs—and his horse was coal black and glossy as silk. And how happy he was—how full of faith in the Confederacy and himself!

My own cavalry officer [Dan Grey] was there, resplendent in his new uniform—I had had it made up for him in Richmond. Dan was very proud of the way I got that uniform. He was almost ready to credit himself with having put me up to running the blockade! He told General Stuart its history, and that is how a greatness not always easy to sustain had been thrust upon me. General Stuart thought me very brave—or said he thought so. The maneuvers of Dan's command were on such a distant part of the field that I could not see him well with the naked eye, and General Stuart lent me his field-glasses. The next morning, just as gray dawn was breaking, some one called under my window, and gravel rattled against the pane. I got up and looked out sleepily. My first thought was that it might be Dan. There was not enough light for me to see very well what was happening on the lawn, but I could make out that the cavalry were mounted and moving, and under my window I saw a figure on horseback.

"Is that Mrs. Grey?"

"Yes. What is the matter?"

"General Stuart sent me for his field-glasses. I am sorry to disturb you, but it couldn't be helped."

I tied a string around the glasses and lowered them.

"What's the matter? Where is the cavalry going?"

"To Brandy Station. Reckon we'll have some hot fighting soon," and the orderly wheeled and rode away.

I stayed up and dressed, and thought of Dan, and wished I could know if he was to be in the coming engagement, and that I could see him first. But I didn't see him all day.[293] — MYRTA LOCKETT AVARY

THE BUCKTOWN RACES

☞ In 1864, when Gen. J. E. B. Stuart was falling back, covering the retreat of General Lee after the battle of Bristoe Station, closely followed by [Union] General Kilpatrick, he left a brigade hidden in the woods on the flank of the advancing enemy. With this brigade he kept in communication by means of signal stations. In this way he was enabled to attack Kilpatrick's flank and front simultaneously and to achieve a success which was long known in cavalry circles as "The Bucktown Races." Kilpatrick's wagon train supplied the Confederate cavalry with enough genuine coffee and toothsome sutlers' stores to feast on for several weeks.[294] — DR. CHARLES E. TAYLOR OF N.C.

SOUTHERN WOMEN OBSERVE STUART'S BIRTHDAY

☞ A resolution was introduced by Miss Anna B. Mann, of Virginia, for special observance of February 6, 1833, the hundredth anniversary of the birth of Gen. J. E. B. Stuart. Adopted.[295] — 39th ANNUAL CONVENTION OF THE UNITED DAUGHTERS OF THE CONFEDERACY AT MEMPHIS, TENN., NOV. 16-19, 1932

THE CHRISTIANITY OF JEB STUART

☞ The number and influence of Christian officers in our army is a chapter which expands so widely as one comes to write it, that I find myself compelled to condense much of the material that it may be brought within proper limits; but there are other facts which must not be omitted.

[Let me speak now of General J. E. B. Stuart, Chief of Cavalry, Army of Northern Virginia.] He has been called "the flower of cavaliers," the "Prince Rupert" of the Confederacy, and "Harry of Navarre," and he has been described as a gay, rolicksome, laughing soldier, "always ready for a dance or a fight." And yet Stuart was an humble, earnest Christian, who took Christ as his personal Saviour, lived a stainless life, and died a triumphant death. He used to attend our Chaplains' Association when he could, took a deep interest in its proceedings, and manifested the liveliest concern for the spiritual welfare of his men.

Not long before his lamented death he sought a personal interview with me, and discussed with great interest and intelligent zeal plans for the better supply of the cavalry with chaplains and religious reading. He spoke of the active life the cavalry were compelled to lead, as at the same time a serious obstacle to regular services among them and an increased necessity for having men of God who would follow them on their rapid marches, or carry the bread of life to them on the outposts. He was especially anxious to get an efficient man at his head-quarters, who could always be found when a preacher was needed, and made a very liberal offer for the comfort and support of such an one. But he was very emphatic in saying:

> "I do not want a man who is not both able and willing to endure hardness as a good soldier. The man who cannot endure the fatigues, hardships and privations of our rough riding and hard service, and be in place when needed, would be of no earthly use to us, and is not wanted at my head-quarters."

He fell in battle at Yellow Tavern, in a heroic and successful effort to save Richmond from Sheridan's raid in May, 1864, and in the full tide of a brilliant career. But though thus cut down when full of life and hope, he said, when the surgeon expressed the hope that he would ultimately recover:

> "Well, I don't know how this will turn out; but if it is God's will that I shall die, I am ready."

He reached the house of his brother-in-law, Dr. [Charles] Brewer, in Richmond, and began to sink so rapidly that it was very evident to his friends and to himself that he must soon pass away. He calmly made disposition of his effects, and gave necessary directions. Hearing the sound of artillery, he said to his gallant and trusted adjutant, Major H. B. McClellan, who was with him, and whose valuable services in the field he so highly appreciated: "Major, Fitz. [Fitzhugh] Lee may need you," and expressed interest in how the battle was going.

But he quickly added, with a sigh: "But I must be preparing for another world."

About noon [Confederate] President [Jefferson] Davis visited his bedside, and tenderly, taking the hand of his great cavalry-man, asked him how he felt.

"Easy, but willing to die, if God and my country think I have fulfilled my destiny and done my duty."

To the surgeon later in the afternoon he replied, when told that he could not live long:

"I am resigned if it be God's will. I would like to see my wife. But God's will be done."

His noble wife [Flora] had been sent for, and was hastening to him, but she did not arrive until after his death.

To the doctor, who was holding his wrist and counting his pulse, he said:

"Doctor, I suppose I am going fast now. It will soon be over. But God's will be done. I hope I have fulfilled my destiny to my country and my duty to God."

Turning to Rev. Dr. Joshua Peterkin, of the Episcopal Church, of which General Stuart had long been a consistent member, he asked him to sing:

"Rock of Ages, cleft for me,
Let me hide myself in Thee,"

and he himself joined in the song with all the strength he could summon.

He joined with fervor in prayer with the ministers present, and again said, just before he passed away: "I am going fast now; I am resigned; God's will be done." And thus the dashing soldier quietly "fell on sleep," and left behind the record of a noble life, and a simple trust in Christ—the prophecy of a blissful immortality, where charging squadrons and clashing sabres never disturb the "rest that remaineth for the people of God."[296] — JOHN REVEREND WILLIAM JONES

THE IRREPARABLE LOSS OF STUART

☛ [Union Gen. Philip Henry] Sheridan's raid would have been the usual record of nothing accomplished and a broken-down command except that at Yellow Tavern the Confederate cavalry chieftain was mortally wounded and died the next day in Richmond. This sad occurrence was of more value to the Federal cause than anything that could have happened, and his loss to Lee was irreparable. He was the army's eyes and ears—vigilant always, bold to a fault, of great vigor and ceaseless activity. He had a heart ever loyal to his superior, and duty, was to him the "sublimest word in the language."²⁹⁷ — CONFEDERATE GENERAL FITZHUGH LEE

GEN. LEE TO MRS. STUART UPON STUART'S DEATH
☞ As I write, I expect to hear the sound of guns every moment. I grieve for the loss of the gallant officers and men, and miss their aid and sympathy. A more zealous, ardent, brave, and devoted soldier than Stuart the Confederacy cannot have.²⁹⁸ — CONFEDERATE GENERAL ROBERT E. LEE

GEN. LEE TO HIS SOLDIERS UPON STUART'S DEATH
☞ Among the gallant soldiers who have fallen in the war, General Stuart was second to none in valor, in zeal, and in unflinching devotion to his country. His achievements form a conspicuous part of the history of this army, with which his name and services will be forever associated. To military capacity of a high order, he added the brighter graces of a pure life guided and sustained by the Christian's faith and hope. The mysterious hand of an all-wise God has removed him from the scene of his usefulness and fame. His grateful countrymen will mourn his loss and cherish his memory. To his comrades in arms he has left the proud recollection of his deeds and the inspiring influence of his example.²⁹⁹ — CONFEDERATE GENERAL ROBERT E. LEE

Lee commanding his troops at Gettysburg.

GEN. HAMPTON TO HIS TROOPS UPON STUART'S DEATH
☞ In the midst of rejoicing over the success of our arms, the sad tidings come to us from Richmond of the death of our distinguished Chief of Cavalry. Death has at last accepted the offering of a life, which before the admiring eyes of the Army, has been so often, so freely and so nobly offered, on almost every battlefield of Virginia. In the death of Major-General J. E. B. Stuart the Army of Northern Virginia has lost one of its most brilliant, enthusiastic and zealous military leaders, the Southern cause [Americanism] one of its

earliest, most untiring and devoted supporters, and the Cavalry arm of the service a chieftain who first gave it prominence and value, and whose dazzling achievements have attracted the wonder and applause of distant nations. His spirit shone as bright and brave in the still chamber of death, as amid the storm of the battlefield, and he passed out of life the same buoyant hero he had lived. Blessed through a short but glorious career with many instances of almost miraculous good fortune, it was his great privilege to die with the consciousness of having performed his whole duty to his country. To his children he leaves the rich legacy of a name which has become identified with the brightest acts of our military history and, when the panorama of our battles shall be unfolded to posterity, in almost every picture will be seen the form of our gallant leader. His name will be associated with almost every scene of danger and of glory, in which the Cavalry of the Virginia Army has borne a part, and they will recount the exploits of Stuart with the pride which men feel in their own honorable records.

The Major General commanding hopes that this division will show by their own noble conduct their high appreciation of the character of their lost commander, and when the danger thickens around them and the cause of their country calls for heroic efforts they will remember the example of Stuart. No leader ever set a more glorious example to his soldiers on the battlefield than he did, and it becomes the men he has so often led, while they mourn his fall, to emulate his courage, to imitate his heroic devotion to duty and to avenge his death.[300] — CONFEDERATE GENERAL WADE HAMPTON

STUART'S FUNERAL

☛ While General Lee and his army continued to wrestle with the hosts of [Union Gen. Ulysses S.] Grant, the city of Richmond was in deep gloom and mourning. Once more the tide of battle had come near her gates; and this time the beloved and gallant Stuart had fallen. He had been the pride of her heart, her brave and chivalrous defender. But Stuart was to sleep his last long sleep upon her bosom, in beautiful Hollywood around whose promontories sweep the waters of the James as they rush onward to the Chesapeake and where the tall pine trees whisper of the life eternal. The city aroused herself from her grief to do homage to the noble dead.

The City Council of Richmond passed resolutions of respect and sympathy for the family of General Stuart and asked that the body of him who "yielded up his heroic spirit in the immediate defense of their city, and the successful effort to purchase their safety by the sacrifice of his own life," might "be permitted to rest under the eye and guardianship of the people of Richmond and that they might be allowed to commemorate by a suitable monument their gratitude and his services."

At five o'clock on the afternoon of May 13 [1864], the funeral of General Stuart took place from old St. James Church in Richmond. The coffin containing the remains of the brave soldier was carried up the aisle and, covered with wreaths and flowers, was placed before the altar.

Stuart's gravesite memorial, inscribed with the words: "Dead, yet alive; mortal, yet immortal."

The funeral service was conducted by Reverend Dr. [Joshua] Peterkin who had been with General Stuart during his last hours. The church was filled with officials of the Confederate government and citizens of Richmond. President [Jefferson] Davis sat near the front, with a look of great sadness upon his careworn face. His cabinet officers were around him and on either side of the church were the senators and representatives of the Confederate Congress. But the cavalry officers and soldiers who loved and followed Stuart were all absent. They were on the firing line, either in the Wilderness or on the Chickahominy—fighting in defense of Richmond which he had died to save.

No military escort could be spared from the front to accompany the funeral procession to Hollywood or to fire the usual parting salute to the dead commander. But as the body was lowered into the grave, the earth trembled with the roar of artillery from the battlefield where his old troops were obeying his last command and driving back the Federals. No better salute could have been given the gallant leader.

Leaving the body of their brave defender beneath the pines of Hollywood [Cemetery], the officials and citizens of Richmond returned to their homes to meet other sorrows. Before a year passed, the devoted city was overtaken by the fate which Stuart had so ably aided Lee in averting. Richmond fell into the hands of the Federals, General Lee surrendered, and the southern Confederacy was no more.

When the city arose from her ashes and again put on the garb of peace, one of her first works was to erect memorials in honor of the men who had fought so nobly in her defense.

In 1888, a monument was erected by some of Stuart's comrades to mark the place at Yellow Tavern where he received his mortal wound. Governor Fitzhugh Lee was the orator of the occasion. He had been one of Stuart's most trusted brigadier generals, and had known him since they were cadets together at West Point. In beautiful and touching language, he reviewed the chief events of Stuart's life, his brilliant campaigns, and his last hours.[301] — MRS. MARY LYNN WILLIAMSON

FOLLOWING STUART'S FEATHER AT YELLOW TAVERN

☛ . . . The *Standard Encyclopedia* puts the strength of Grant's army [at this time, Spring 1864] at 150,000, but does not state how many men Lee had. Perhaps 75,000 would be a fair estimate. The same authority gives Grant's losses at the battle of the Wilderness as 18,000; Lee's at 11,000.

The losses in the battle of Spotsylvania Court House, fought two days afterward, were as great, if not greater, than those of the Wilderness.

When the cavalry retired from the front the men mounted their horses, and almost Lee's entire cavalry force, headed by their chief, Gen. J. E. B. Stuart, started in a bee line for Richmond, without halting a moment.

[Union] Gen. [Philip Henry] Sheridan, commanding Grant's cavalry, had passed around our right wing with his whole command, and was heading toward the Confederate Capital.

I think it was about 4 o'clock in the afternoon when we started. Sheridan was several miles ahead of us. We marched all night. We overtook Sheridan at Hanover Junction, on the railroad leading to Richmond; not, however, until he had destroyed a large quantity of provisions stored there for Lee's army, a great loss to the Confederates at that time.

Sheridan had prepared for this expedition, and all of his men had well-filled haversacks, while ours were empty.

Gen. Stuart's grave monument, Hollywood Cemetery, Richmond, VA.

I cannot remember just when and where we got in front of Sheridan, but I know from Hanover Junction on we were in constant touch with his forces, and harassed them all we could.

At a place called "Yellow Tavern" several regiments of our cavalry (mine among them) were dismounted, formed across the fields, and moved forward in real line of battle style until we came upon the enemy, also dismounted. After a brisk encounter we fell back to a road that was somewhat sunken.

There we halted for the purpose of stopping the enemy's advance, for the sunken road furnished us some protection, but they did not stop. They marched on, firing as they came.

Their line was longer and thicker than ours, and it was evident that we were about to be surrounded. Some of our men mounted the fence in the rear and fled across the fields. Others stood their ground and were captured, I among them.

I was near Colonel [Henry Clay] Pate, the colonel commanding a regiment in my brigade. He was killed by a bullet striking him in the center of the forehead. Also near me was our captain, Bruce Gibson.

There was a little culvert across a ditch in the road that the farmers used in going from the road into the field. Some of our men crept under this culvert and escaped. Probably 200 of us were captured.

But the army sustained a greater loss than that, a loss second only to that of Stonewall Jackson.

Just behind our line in the field was Gen. Stuart with his staff. A bullet struck him somewhere about the stomach. He was held on his horse until it was led to a place of safety. Then he was taken from his horse, put into an ambulance and carried to Richmond. He died the next day.

Stuart was considered the greatest cavalry leader of the war on either side, and his death brought a very great loss to Gen. Lee, and also to the whole Confederacy.

The Confederacy had from the beginning attached greater importance to the cavalry arm of the service than had the North, and many had been the daring raids that Stuart made within the enemy's lines, capturing thousands of wagons laden with military stores, and many thousand prisoners. In fact, almost our entire cavalry was equipped with saddles, bridles and arms captured from the enemy; nearly all the wagons in Lee's army were captured wagons. But perhaps Providence knew that the time was near at hand when we would not need these things, so He permitted the one who had been the means of supplying our wants in this particular to retire from the field. He was buried in Hollywood Cemetery, Richmond, Va., and a magnificent equestrian statue marks the spot.

Many of Stuart's raids were made under the cover of darkness. He always wore a long ostrich feather in his hat, and was a splendid rider. The soldiers had a war song, the chorus of which was something like this: "We'll follow the feather of Stuart tonight."[302]
— CONFEDERATE SOLDIER LUTHER W. HOPKINS

A war-torn Confederate Battle Flag—because of what it stands for, the most beautiful banner in the world.

THE NOBLE CAVALIER

☛ ... [On June 8, 1864, we] moved camp this evening to the south side of the Chickahominy. We are now camped near the Brook Turnpike, in a section of beautiful, rich, and productive country of fertile land. The Brook Turnpike is an excellent macadamized road leading out of Richmond in a northwesterly direction through a gently rolling country of green fields and well cultivated farms and gardens. The pike proper is only six miles long and leads to the Yellow Tavern, where the road forks, one leading to Louisa Court House and the other, known as the Telegraph road, leading to Fredericksburg. The Yellow Tavern is six miles northwest of Richmond and is the spot that makes our memories bleed, for there a few weeks ago, on the eleventh of May, our gallant, brave, and dashing leader, General J. E. B. Stuart, fell, mortally wounded while fighting with his face to the foe. A braver and nobler cavalier never drew a sword or wielded a saber.[303] — CONFEDERATE GUNNER, STUART'S HORSE ARTILLERY, A.N.V., GEORGE MICHAEL NEESE

A 1939 oil painting of Confederate Gen. J. E. B. Stuart, by Jared French, originally displayed at Court House Annex, Richmond, VA.

AN UNEQUALED CAVALRY LEADER

☛ James Stuart, or Jeb as he was called in the army from his first three initials, proved himself in his short career the greatest warrior among the many great men who have been so called. Whether or no he was really descended from Robert the Bruce, he certainly had inherited the kingly talent for leading men and making war. He won the great battle of [Chancellorsville on] May 3 [1863] which was decisive in this campaign by skilful and gallant leading.

He was but twenty-eight years old when he took Jackson's place at the head of the Second corps, and it would perhaps have been well for the Southern cause [Americanism] if Lee had retained him at his side to share in the supreme command as he had used Jackson, instead of once again transferring him to the command of the cavalry which Fitz Lee, W. [H. F.] Lee, or [Wade] Hampton was qualified to hold. Stuart had, like [Union] Gen. [John] Sedgwick, served under Lee in the cavalry of the United States army, and the knowledge possessed by their former colonel of the two men's characters and capacities stood the Southern general in good stead on this critical field; he could take liberties with the over-cautious Sedgwick and give the rein to the offensive skill of Stuart.

The house in which Gen. Stuart died—since torn down; a plaque remains.

Soon after the outbreak of the war Stuart distinguished himself as a cavalry leader, and his strategical work in blindfolding the enemy and in enlightening his own army has never been surpassed. As a cavalry tactician he is not only the first, but hitherto the only, leader of the arm who understood how to combine the effects of fire and shock, how to render effective service in fighting on foot without losing the power to strike on horseback when opportunity offered, though his Federal opponents imitated his strategy and tactics with some success in the next campaign.[304] — BRITISH MILITARY CAPTAIN CECIL BATTINE

THE IRREPLACEABLE STUART
☛ . . . General Stuart had imprudently left the position mentioned above [a dirt round surrounded by forest on each side] and ridden in the direction of the enemy, when a Yankee who had been dismounted and who was running through the woods to escape to his friends, saw him and fired at him with his pistol, giving him a wound from which he died the following day. The loss of General Stuart was second only to that of General Jackson, as it was not possible to replace him.[305] — THOMAS DANIEL GOLD

STUART'S EQUESTRIAN STATUE AT RICHMOND
☛ The equestrian statue of the great leader of the Southern cavalry which was lately unveiled at Richmond is a testimony of the love and admiration of the men who followed him in battle and wept over his bier:

> "So sinks the day-star in the Ocean bed,
> And yet anon repairs his drooping head,
> And tricks his beams and with new spangled ore
> Flames in the forehead of the morning sky."[306]

— CONFEDERATE COLONEL JOHN SINGLETON MOSBY

THE TEXT ON STUART'S EQUESTRIAN MONUMENT
☛ The following resolution [as to what should be inscribed on Stuart's equestrian monument] was submitted to the Richmond City Council on May 14, 1864:

(East Side)
MAJOR GENERAL J. E. B. STUART
COMMANDING CAVALRY CORPS, ARMY OF NORTHERN VIRGINIA
THIS STATUE ERECTED BY HIS COMRADES AND THE CITY OF RICHMOND
A.D. 1907

(West Side)
BORN IN PATRICK COUNTY, VA., FEBRUARY 6, 1833
DIED IN RICHMOND, VA., MAY 12, 1864, AGED 31 YEARS
MORTALLY WOUNDED IN THE
BATTLE OF YELLOW TAVERN MAY 11, 1864
"He gave his life for his country and saved this city from capture."

(South Side)
"Tell General Stuart to act on his own judgment and do what he thinks best; I have implicit confidence in him." — *General T. J.*

(Stonewall) Jackson on turning over the command of his troops to Stuart, after being wounded at Chancellorsville, May 2, 1863.

(North Side)
"His grateful countrymen will mourn his loss and cherish his memory. To his comrades in arms he has left the proud recollection of his deeds and the inspiring influence of his example." — *General R. E. Lee announcing the death of General Stuart to his Army, May 20, 1864.*[307] — THEODORE STANFORD GARNETT

The End

Confederate General James Ewell Brown Stuart's equestrian monument, Richmond, VA., at it appeared around 1905.

Gen. Jeb Stuart, modeled by Virginia sculptor Edward Virginius Valentine.

Gen. Stuart as he looked during the War for the Constitution, circa 1863.

APPENDIX A

GEN. STUART'S OFFICIAL RECORD OF THE BATTLE OF DRANESVILLE, VA., DECEMBER 20, 1861

ON THE 20TH INSTANT I was placed in command of four regiments of infantry, 150 cavalry and a battery of four pieces of artillery, viz.: Eleventh Virginia, Colonel S. Garland, Jr.; Sixth South Carolina, Lieutenant-Colonel Secrest; Tenth Alabama, Colonel J. H. Forney, and First Kentucky, Colonel Thomas H. Taylor; making an aggregate force of 1,600 infantry; Sumter Flying Artillery (four pieces), Captain A. S. Cutts; One Hundredth [V.] North Carolina Cavalry, Major Gordon, and Fifty-second [V.] Virginia Cavalry, Captain Pitzer, for the purpose of covering an expedition of all the wagons of our army that could be spared (after hay) to the left of Dranesville.

I proceeded at once by the nearest route, at daylight, toward Dranesville.

Knowing the situation of the enemy's advance posts, I sent the cavalry forward far in advance of the infantry, to take possession of the two turnpikes to the right of Dranesville, leading directly to the enemy's advanced posts, so as to prevent any communication of our movements reaching them, and with the main body I followed on to take a position with two regiments and a section of artillery on each turnpike, also to the right of Dranesville, and close enough to their intersection to form a continuous line.

Such a position I knew I could hold against almost any odds, but as my cavalry came in sight of the turnpike Captain Pitzer discovered the enemy on the ridge and sent me word immediately. I galloped forward at once, and, reconnoitering for myself, found that a portion of the enemy was in possession of the ridge, and I could heard distinctly artillery carriages passing up the Georgetown turnpike in considerable numbers, and presently saw the cannons, mounted on limber boxes, passing up toward Dranesville. I knew, too, that the enemy's infantry were in advance, and I at once suspected that he was either marching upon Leesburg or had received intelligence through a spy of our intended forage expedition and was marching upon it. In either case our wagons would have fallen an easy prey to him, and I saw at once that my only way to save them was to make a vigorous attack upon his rear and left flank, and to compel him to desist from such a purpose.

I sent back for the infantry to hurry forward, and sent Captain Pitzer with his detachment of cavalry to gain the roads toward Leesburg, give notice to our wagons to return at once to camp and keep between them and the enemy, threatening his front and flank; and I will state here, parenthetically, that this duty was performed by Captain Pitzer and his gallant little detachment in the most creditable manner, all our wagons reaching camp safely.

In the meantime the enemy's skirmishers took possession of the dense pine in our front, and as our infantry was met by my messenger three-fourths of a mile back, it was some time coming up. Colonel Garland's regiment, leading, was directed to deploy two companies on each side of the road to clear the ground of the enemy's skirmishers. One of these companies, having mistaken its direction, went too far to the right, and Colonel Garland had to replace it with another. The pines were cleared at double-quick, and the battery was ordered in position and fired very effectively during the whole of the engagement to the front.

The infantry were placed in position as follows: Garland's regiment on the right of the road, a little in advance of the artillery; Secrest's (South Carolina) on the left of the road. Forney's regiment, arriving later, replaced Garland's, which moved by the flank to the right; and the First Kentucky, Colonel Taylor, at first intended as a reserve, was ordered to take position on the Sixth South Carolina.

As our infantry was well secured from the enemy's view, their artillery fire, which opened about fifteen minutes after ours began, had little effect upon the infantry, but played with telling effect along the road, as from its position and the straightness of the road in our rear, it raked the latter with shell and round shot completely. Their caissons and limbers were behind in a brick house, completely protected from our shot, while our limbers and caissons were necessarily crowded and exposed. There was no outlet to right or left for a mile back by which the artillery could change its position. When our forces took their position the fire of the artillery caused great commotion in the enemy's lines, and a part evidently took to their heels. The right wing was ordered forward, and the Tenth Alabama rushed with a shout in a shower of bullets, under the gallant lead of their colonel (Forney) and Lieutenant-Colonel Martin, the latter falling in the charge. A part of this regiment crossed the road and took position along a fence, from which the enemy felt the trueness of their aim at short range. The colonel was here severely wounded, and had to retire. In his absence the command devolved upon Major Woodward.

The Eleventh Virginia, holding position on the right of the Tenth Alabama, were not so much exposed to the fire of the enemy, and consequently suffered less. The Sixth South Carolina gradually gained ground also to the front, and being, together with the Tenth Alabama, exposed to the fire of the enemy's sharpshooters from a two-story brick house, suffered most. My orders to Colonel Taylor, First Kentucky, were given through Colonel Forney, and I soon knew by the commotion on my left that it was in place. The thicket where the Sixth South Carolina and First Kentucky operated was so dense that it was impossible to see either their exact position or their progress in the fight, and I regret to say that the First Kentucky and the Sixth South Carolina mistook each other for the enemy, and a few casualties occurred in consequence; but with that exception the whole force acted with admirable unison, and advanced upon the enemy with the steadiness of veterans, driving him several times from his position with heavy loss. When the action had lasted about two hours I found that the enemy, being already in force larger than my own, was recovering from his disorder and receiving heavy re-enforcements. I could not, with my small number, being beyond the reach of re-enforcements, force his position without fearful sacrifice, and seeing that his artillery, superior to ours in numbers and position only, was pouring a very destructive fire into Cutt's battery, I decided to withdraw the latter at once, preparatory to retiring from the field, judging, too, that I had given our wagons sufficient time to get beyond the reach of the enemy.

The battery suffered greatly. Its position was necessarily such that it could fire only to the front, and the caissons and limbers had no cover whatever from such a fire. Three or four cannoneers had been shot at their posts and several wounded, and every shot of the enemy was dealing destruction on either man, limber or horse.

The conduct of the brave, true and heroic Cutts attracted my admiration frequently during the action—now acting No. 1 and now as gunner, and still directing and disposing the whole with perfect self-command and a devotion to his duty that was, I believe, scarcely ever equaled. He executed my orders to withdraw his battery under a ricochet fire of great accuracy.

One piece I found it necessary to detail some infantry (Eleventh Virginia) to assist in conducting to the rear, which was done by them under great personal exposure.

Having secured the artillery, I sent orders to the four regimental commanders to disengage themselves from the enemy and retire slowly and in perfect order to the railroad, where a stand would be made. This delicate duty was performed admirably, and our troops marched back leisurely, bringing with them all the wounded that could be found.

The men gathered up their blankets as they passed the points where they had been deposited before the fight. I regret to say, however, that one of the regiments reached the road this side of their blankets and knapsacks, thus missing them entirely, a circumstance which the enemy will construe into precipitate flight. The enemy was evidently too much crippled to follow in pursuit, and after a short halt at the railroad I proceeded to Fryingpan Church, where the wounded were cared for.

Early next morning, with the two fresh regiments furnished me (the Ninth Georgia and Eighteenth Virginia) and a detachment of cavalry under Lieutenant-Colonel Baker, I proceeded toward the scene of action of the previous day, the cavalry being sent in advance. Learning that the enemy had evacuated Dranesville and had left some of our wounded there, I pushed on to that place to recover them and to take care of the dead. I found our dead on the field, and proceeded at once to remove them all to Centreville for interment. The wounded (about ten) were left by the enemy at a house at Dranesville, who intended to send for them the next day. They had been cared for with the utmost devotion by several of the ladies of the place. They were also removed to Centreville, except two, who were not able to survive the removal, and so, at their own desire and on the surgeon's advice, were left in charge of the ladies.

As to the strength of the enemy, if the concurrent statements of the citizens residing along his route of march can be credited, he had fifteen regiments of infantry, several batteries and seven companies of cavalry. The latter had started in the direction of our wagons just before the action began, but were then recalled.

Our wounded, who were for the time prisoners, say that the enemy's loss was acknowledged by them to be very heavy, and among the officers killed or mortally wounded was Colonel Kane, of Utah notoriety, and citizens living below declared that they carried off twenty wagon loads of killed and wounded, besides many dead before them on their horses, and that as soon as their dead and wounded were removed they left the field precipitately, leaving behind much of the material which we left on the field, but which we recovered next day.

I can not speak in too high terms of Colonel Forney, that gallant son of

Alabama, whose conspicuous bravery, leading his men in a galling fire, was the admiration of all; nor of his lieutenant-colonel (Martin), who, with the battle cry of "Forward!" on his lips, fell, bravely encouraging his men. Nor can I do more than simple justice to the officers and men of that regiment, who seemed determined to follow their colonel wherever he would lead.

Colonel Garland and Major Langhorne, of the Eleventh Virginia, behaved with great coolness under fire, and the men of that regiment, though deprived by locality from sharing as much of the danger of the engagement as the Tenth Alabama Regiment, yet acquitted themselves to my entire satisfaction.

The Sixth South Carolina and First Kentucky were, I regret to say, too much screened from my view to afford me the privilege of bearing witness by personal observation of individual prowess; but that the Sixth South Carolina, under the fearless Secrest, did its whole duty, let the list of killed and wounded and her battle flag, bathed in blood, with its staff shivered in the hand of the bearer, be silent but eloquent witnesses. Their major (Woodward) was painfully wounded, but bore himself heroically notwithstanding. From the sounds that I could distinctly hear from the left I felt assured that the First Kentucky, under the gallant Taylor, the intrepid Major Crossland and daring Desha, was all right.

Our batteries' loss in killed and wounded was great, and the men deserve great credit for their devotion to their pieces under such perilous circumstances. The detachment of North Carolina Cavalry, under Major Gordon, was of great service in watching the approaches to our flanks, though the ground was extremely unfavorable for cavalry.

Had we effected the safety of our wagons—constituting the greater part of the available means of transportation of this army—with great loss to ourselves, without inflicting much on the enemy, alone would have been a triumph of which the brave men of the four regiments under my command could be proud; but when it is considered what overwhelming odds were against us, notwithstanding which we saved the transportation, inflicted upon the enemy a loss severer than our own, rendering him unequal to the task of pursuit, retired in perfect order and bringing with us nearly all our wounded, we may rightly call it a glorious success. Our entire loss is as follows:

Eleventh Virginia Volunteers: 6 killed; 15 wounded; 0 missing.
Sixth South Carolina Volunteers: 18 killed; 45 wounded; 0 missing.
Tenth Alabama Volunteers: 15 killed; 45 wounded; 6 missing.
First Kentucky Volunteers: 1 killed; 23 wounded; 2 missing.
Cutt's Battery: 3 killed; 15 wounded; 0 missing.
Cavalry: 0 killed; 0 wounded; 0 missing.
Total: 43 killed; 143 wounded; 8 missing.

The list of killed has been materially increased by deaths which have occurred since the battle, as the number found dead on the field was only twenty-seven.
J. E. B. STUART, BRIGADIER-GENERAL COMMANDING.[308]

From *The Confederate Soldier in the Civil War*, 1897

APPENDIX B

FOUR YEARS OF THE WAR IN BRIEF

Compiled by Victorian Southerners

Abraham Lincoln elected President of the United States in November, 1860.
South Carolina seceded December 20, 1860.[309]
Mississippi seceded January 9, 1861.
Alabama and Florida seceded January 11, 1861.
Georgia seceded January 19, 1861.
Louisiana seceded January 26, 1861.
Texas seceded February 1, 1861.
The seceded States met in Congress at Montgomery, Ala., February 4, 1861.
National Peace Conference at Washington February 4, 1861.

THE CONFEDERACY

The Constitution of the Confederate States adopted February 8, 1861.[310]
Jefferson Davis elected President and A. H. Stephens Vice President February 8, 1861.
Jefferson Davis inaugurated President February 18, 1861.
Bombardment of Fort Sumter began April 12, 1861.[311]
Surrender of Fort Sumter April 13, 1861.
Virginia seceded April 17, 1861.
Baltimore riot, April 18, 1861.
Lincoln's blockade proclamation, April 19, 1861.
Federal evacuation of Harpers Ferry, April 19, 1861.
Norfolk Navy Yard abandoned by the Federals April 20, 1861.
Virginia admitted to the Confederacy May 6, 1861.
Tennessee seceded May 6, 1861.[312]
Arkansas admitted to the Confederacy May 18, 1861.
Seat of Confederate government removed from Montgomery to Richmond May 20, 1861.
North Carolina seceded May 21, 1861.
Federal occupation of Alexandria May 24, 1861.

BATTLES IN VIRGINIA IN 1861

Big Bethel, June 10, 1861.
Gen. J. E. Johnston abandoned Harper's Ferry June 13, 1861.
Rich Mountain, July 11, 1861.
[First] Manassas, July 21, 1861.
Carnifix Ferry, September 10, 1861.
Leesburg, October 20, 1861.
Dranesville, December 20, 1861.

BATTLES IN THE TRANS-MISSISSIPPI
Booneville, Mo., June 20, 1861.
Carthage, Mo., July 5, 1861.
Oak Hill, August 10, 1861.
Capture of Lexington, Mo., September 20, 1861.

NAVAL AFFAIRS IN 1861
Fight off Hatteras, August 28, 1861.
Off Port Royal, November 7, 1861.
[U.S.] Commodore [Charles] Wilkins forcibly took [C.S. envoys] [James] Mason and [John] Slidell from the English vessel *Trent* November 8, 1861.

BATTLES IN VIRGINIA & MARYLAND IN 1862
Johnston's retreat from Manassas and Centerville, March 8, 1862.
Battle of Kernstown, March 23, 1862.
Confederate conscript law, April 16, 1862.
Evacuation of Yorktown, May 4, 1862.
Battle of Williamsburg, May 5, 1862.
Battle of Front Royal, May 22, 1862.
Battle of Seven Pines, May 30, 1862.
Battle of Cross Keys, June 8, 1862.
Battle of Port Republic, June 8, 1862.
Battle of Mechanicsville, June 26, 1862.
Battle of Gaines's Mill, June 27, 1862.
Battle of Frazier's Farm, June 30, 1862.
Battle of Malvern Hill, July 1, 1862.
Battle of Savage Station, June 29, 1862.
Battle of Cedar Run, August 9, 1862.
Battle of Second Manassas, August 30, 1862.
Lee entered Maryland September 5, 1862.
Capture of Harpers Ferry, September 15, 1862.
Battle of Sharpsburg, September 17, 1862.
Battle of Fredericksburg, December 13, 1862.

BATTLES SOUTH & WEST IN 1862
Fishing Creek, Ky., January 19, 1862.
Surrender of Roanoke Island, N.C., February 8, 1862.
Surrender of Fort Donelson, Tenn., February 16, 1862.[313]
Surrender of Newbern, N.C., March 14, 1862.
Surrender of Island No. 10, April 7, 1862.
Battle of Shiloh, April 6, 1862.
Fall of New Orleans, May 1, 1862.
Fall of Memphis, June 6, 1862.
Battle of Baton Rouge, August 5, 1862.
Battle of Richmond, Ky., August 29, 1862.
Battle of Corinth, October 3, 4, 1862.
Battle of Perryville, Ky., October 8, 1862.
Battle of Murfreesboro, Tenn., December 31, 1862.

BATTLES IN THE TRANS-MISSISSIPPI
Battle of Elkhorn [Tavern], March 7, 1862.
Battle of Prairie Grove, December 8, 1862.

NAVAL AFFAIRS IN 1862
Fight at Hampton Roads, March 8, 1862.
Naval attack on Drury's Bluff, May 15, 1862.

BATTLES IN VIRGINIA & PENNSYLVANIA IN 1863
Battle of Chancellorsville, May 2, 3, 1863.[314]
Battle of Winchester, early in June, 1863.
Battle of Gettysburg, Pa., July 1, 2, 3, 1863.
Battle of Bristoe Station, October 14, 1863.
Fight at Germanna Ford, November 27, 1863.

BATTLES SOUTH & WEST IN 1863
Charleston, S.C., first attacked in April, 1863.
Battle of Baker's Creek, Miss., May 16, 1863.
Surrender of Vicksburg, July 4, 1863.
First assault on Fort Wagner, July 11, 1863.
Second assault on Fort Wagner, July 18, 1863.
Gillmore's bombardment of Fort Sumter, August 18, 1863.
Morris Island taken September 6, 1863.
Surrender of Cumberland Gap, September 9, 1863.
Battle of Chickamauga, September 19, 1863.[315]
Battle of Missionary Ridge, November 25, 1863.

TRANS-MISSISSIPPI, 1863
Battle of Helena, Ark., July 4, 1863.

BATTLES IN VIRGINIA, PENNSYLVANIA, & MARYLAND, 1864
Dahlgren's raid on Richmond, March 1, 1864.
Battles of the Wilderness, May 5, 6, 1864.
Battles of Spotsylvania Court House, May 8, 12, 1864.
General Stuart killed at Yellow Tavern May 10, 1864 [This is an error: Stuart was wounded on May 11, and died on May 12].
Battle of New Market, May 15, 1864.
Beauregard "bottled" Butler below Richmond, Ky., May 16, 1864.
Battle of Cold Harbor, June 3, 1864.
Capture of Staunton, June 5, 1864.
Butler's attack on Petersburg, June 9, 1864.
Hunter repulsed at Lynchburg June 16, 17, 1864.
The "mine" attempt on Petersburg, July 30, 1864.
Battle of Monocacy, Md. July, 1864.
Chambersburg, Pa., burned July 30, 1864.
Battle of Reams's Station, August 25, 1864.
Battle near Winchester, September 19, 1864.
Battle of Fisher's Hill, September 22, 1864.
Fall of Fort Harrison, September 29, 1864.

BATTLES SOUTH & WEST IN 1864
Battle of Ocean Pond, Fla., February 20, 1864.
Cavalry fight at Okolona, Miss., February 21, 1864.[316]
First battle of Sherman's march, Resaca, June 14, 1864.[317]
Battle of New Hope, June 28, 1864.
Battle of Atlanta, July 20, 22, 23, 1864.
Battle of Jonesboro, Tenn., September, 1864.
Fall of Atlanta, September 2, 1864.
[Battle of Spring Hill, Tenn., November 29, 1864.][318]
Battle of Franklin, Tenn., November 30, 1864.[319]
Battle of Nashville, Tenn., December 14, 15, 1864.[320]
Atlanta burned November 15, 1864.
Savannah evacuated December 28, 1864.

TRANS-MISSISSIPPI
Battle of Mansfield, La., April 8, 1864.
Battle of Pleasant Hill, April 9, 1864.
Battle of Big Blue River, Mo., October 23, 1864.

NAVAL AFFAIRS IN 1864
Fight in Mobile Bay, August 5, 1864.
Privateer *Alabama* sunk June 19, 1864.
Privateer *Florida* captured October 6, 1864.

BATTLES IN VIRGINIA IN 1865
Fortress Monroe conference [Hampton Roads], February 3, 1865.[321]
Battle of Five Forks, April 1, 1865.
Grant assaults Lee's line April 2, 1865.
Evacuation of Richmond, etc., April 2, 1865.
Lee begins his retreat April 2, 1865.
Federal occupation of Richmond April 3, 1865.
Army of Northern Virginia surrendered by General Lee at Appomattox Court House April 9, 1865.

BATTLES SOUTH & WEST IN 1865
Capture of Fort Fisher, N.C., January 15, 1865.
Columbia destroyed by Sherman February 17, 1865.
Charleston evacuated February 17, 1865.
Battle of Bentonville, N.C., March 19, 1865.
Mobile captured April 12, 1865.
Sherman and Johnston agree to a truce April 13, 1865.[322]

FROM THE *MACON* (GEORGIA) *TELEGRAPH*, 1912

NOTES

All footnotes, endnotes, & notes in general are mine, unless otherwise indicated. L.S.
(All Bible citations are from the KJV.)

1. Seabrook, *Abraham Lincoln Was a Liberal, Jefferson Davis Was a Conservative: The Missing Key to Understanding the American Civil War*, p. 55.
2. Schlüter, p. 23.
3. Woods, p. 47.
4. On Lincoln's socialistic, Marxist, and communist thoughts, ideas, and tendencies, see my books: 1) *Lincoln's War: The Real Cause, The Real Winner, The Real Loser*; 2) *Abraham Lincoln Was a Liberal, Jefferson Davis Was a Conservative: The Missing Key to Understanding the American Civil War*; 3) *Abraham Lincoln: The Southern View*. Also see McCarty, passim; Browder, passim; Benson and Kennedy, passim.
5. See J. W. Jones, TDMV, pp. 144, 200-201, 273.
6. Schlüter, p. 23.
7. Nichols, p. 59. (I have paraphrased this quote. L.S.)
8. *The Independent*, Vol. 102, No. 3724, June 5, 1920, p. 309. For more on this topic see my appendix, "Commies in the White House," in my book *Twelve Years in Hell: Victorian Southerners Expose the Myth of Reconstruction, 1865-1877*.
9. See Seabrook, *The Alexander H. Stephens Reader*, passim. See also, Pollard, LC, p. 178; J. H. Franklin, pp. 101, 111, 130, 149; Nicolay and Hay, ALCW, Vol. 1, p. 627.
10. *Confederate Veteran*, Vol. 12, 1904, p. 442.
11. *Confederate Veteran*, Vol. 35, 1927, p. 288.
12. Seabrook (ed.), *A Short History of the Confederate States of America* (J. Davis), p. 59.
13. Seabrook (ed.), *A Short History of the Confederate States of America* (J. Davis), pp. 55-56.
14. For more on this specific topic, see my book *Everything You Were Taught About the Civil War is Wrong, Ask a Southerner!*, pp. 34-39.
15. BISG (the "Book Industry Study Group"), for example—a Left-wing organization which describes itself as "the leading book trade association for standardized best practices, research and information, and events"—gives its BISAC ("Book Industry Standards and Communications") listing for works on the War for Southern Independence under the heading "Civil War Period, 1850-1877." Nearly all books published in the U.S.A. today are under the categorizational control of this progressive group located in New York City.
16. See e.g., Seabrook, *The Quotable Jefferson Davis*, pp. 30, 38, 76.
17. See e.g., Seabrook (ed.) *The Rise and Fall of the Confederate Government* (J. Davis), Vol. 1, pp. 55, 422; Vol. 2, pp. 4, 161, 454, 610. Besides using the term "Civil War" himself, President Davis cites numerous other individuals who use it as well.
18. See e.g., *Confederate Veteran*, Vol. 20, 1912, p. 122.
19. Minutes of the Eighth Annual Meeting, July 1898, p. 87.
20. See e.g., Fitzhugh, pp. 154, 287, 324; see also, e.g., Messer-Kruse, p. 103.
21. See Marx and Engels, passim.
22. For more on this specific topic see my book, *America's Three Constitutions: Complete Texts of the Articles of Confederation, Constitution of the United States of America, and Constitution of the Confederate States of America*.
23. For more on the nihilistic, atheistic, anti-life, anti-tradition, anti-American, anti-Constitution, anti-capitalism, anti-South agenda of the Victorian Republican Party (then the Liberal Party) and the modern Democratic Party (now the Liberal Party), otherwise known as "The Communist/Socialist Rules for Revolution," see Hasselberg, pp. 2350-2351; Lenin, passim; Marx and Engels, passim; B. Dodd, passim. Also see my book *What the Confederate Flag Means to Me: Americans Speak Out in Defense of Southern Honor, Heritage, and History*.
24. *Confederate Veteran*, Vol. 9, 1901, p. 318.
25. *Minutes U.C.V., Vol. 2. Proceedings of the Tenth Annual Meeting and Reunion of the United Confederate Veterans*, held at Louisville, Kentucky, May 30-June 3; 1900, New Orleans, LA: United Confederate Veterans, p. 25.

26. Gaslighting, one of the primary weapons of the Left, is defined as "deceiving a person or group of people through repetition of a constructed false narrative." Medically speaking it is defined as "a form of emotional abuse or psychological manipulation involving distorting the truth in order to confuse or create doubt in another person to the point where they begin to question their sanity or reality."
27. *Confederate Veteran*, Vol. 17, 1909, p. 106.
28. *Confederate Veteran*, Vol. 34, 1926, p. 445.
29. *Confederate Veteran*, Vol. 8, 1900, p. 134.
30. *Confederate Veteran*, Vol. 8, 1900, p. 134.
31. *Confederate Veteran*, Vol. 19, 1911, p. 480.
32. *Confederate Veteran*, Vol. 1, 1893, p. 204.
33. *Confederate Veteran*, Vol. 1, 1893, p. 235.
34. *Confederate Veteran*, Vol. 25, 1917, p. 135.
35. Pollard, *Lee and His Lieutenants*, p. 422.
36. *Confederate Veteran*, Vol. 19, 1911, p. 576.
37. *Confederate Veteran*, Vol. 19, 1911, p. 576.
38. *Confederate Veteran*, Vol. 20, 1912, p. 26.
39. *Confederate Veteran*, Vol. 19, 1911, p. 576.
40. *Confederate Veteran*, Vol. 36, 1928, p. 185.
41. *Confederate Veteran*, Vol. 29, 1921, p. 52.
42. *Confederate Veteran*, Vol. 19, 1911, p. 576.
43. *Confederate Veteran*, Vol. 22, 1914, p. 358.
44. *Confederate Veteran*, Vol. 25, 1917, p. 462.
45. *Confederate Veteran*, Vol. 11, 1903, p. 391.
46. McKim, p. 219.
47. *Confederate Veteran*, Vol. 28, 1920, p. 150.
48. *Confederate Veteran*, Vol. 15, 1907, p. 521.
49. Pollard, *Lee and His Lieutenants*, p. 439.
50. *Confederate Veteran*, Vol. 1, 1893, p. 235.
51. *Confederate Veteran*, Vol. 32, 1924, p. 415.
52. Pollard, *Lee and His Lieutenants*, p. 422.
53. *Confederate Veteran*, Vol. 20, 1912, p. 58.
54. *Confederate Veteran*, Vol. 1, 1893, p. 352 (b).
55. *Confederate Veteran*, Vol. 27, 1919, p. 98.
56. *Confederate Veteran*, Vol. 11, 1903, p. 391.
57. *Confederate Veteran*, Vol. 20, 1912, p. 58.
58. *Confederate Veteran*, Vol. 11, 1903, p. 391.
59. *Confederate Veteran*, Vol. 11, 1903, p. 391.
60. *Confederate Veteran*, Vol. 11, 1903, p. 341.
61. Pollard, *Lee and His Lieutenants*, p. 423.
62. *Confederate Veteran*, Vol. 40, 1932, p. 288.
63. *Confederate Veteran*, Vol. 9, 1901, p. 318.
64. *Confederate Veteran*, Vol. 29, 1921, p. 166.
65. *Confederate Veteran*, Vol. 26, 1918, p. 189.
66. Warner, *Generals in Gray*, s.v. "James Ewell Brown 'Jeb' Stuart."
67. *Confederate Veteran*, Vol. 35, 1927, p. 433.
68. *Confederate Veteran*, Vol. 31, 1923, p. 17.
69. Jones, *Life and Letters of Robert Edward Lee*, p. 70.
70. *Confederate Veteran*, Vol. 39, 1931, p. 261.
71. *Confederate Veteran*, Vol. 29, 1921, p. 253.
72. *Confederate Veteran*, Vol. 23, 1915, p. 15.
73. *Confederate Veteran*, Vol. 23, 1915, p. 68.
74. *Confederate Veteran*, Vol. 38, 1930, p. 49.
75. *Confederate Veteran*, Vol. 23, 1915, p. 69.
76. *Confederate Veteran*, Vol. 13, 1905, p. 21.

77. *Confederate Veteran*, Vol. 13, 1905, p. 60.
78. *Confederate Veteran*, Vol. 11, 1903, p. 509.
79. *Confederate Veteran*, Vol. 14, 1906, p. 74.
80. *Confederate Veteran*, Vol. 21, 1913, p. 427.
81. *Confederate Veteran*, Vol. 22, 1914, p. 358.
82. *Confederate Veteran*, Vol. 25, 1917, p. 303.
83. *Confederate Veteran*, Vol. 27, 1919, p. 293.
84. See Battine, p. 77.
85. *Confederate Veteran*, Vol. 20, 1912, p. 120.
86. *Confederate Veteran*, Vol. 28, 1920, p. 445.
87. *Confederate Veteran*, Vol. 19, 1911, p. 575.
88. *Confederate Veteran*, Vol. 20, 1912, p. 58.
89. *Confederate Veteran*, Vol. 14, 1906, p. 74.
90. *Confederate Veteran*, Vol. 14, 1906, p. 74.
91. *Confederate Veteran*, Vol. 1, 1893, p. 361.
92. *Confederate Veteran*, Vol. 12, 1904, p. 600.
93. *Confederate Veteran*, Vol. 7, 1899, p. 214.
94. *Confederate Veteran*, Vol. 7, 1899, p. 214.
95. *Confederate Veteran*, Vol. 10, 1902, p. 360.
96. *Confederate Veteran*, Vol. 1, 1893, p. 361.
97. *Confederate Veteran*, Vol. 8, 1900, p. 125.
98. *Confederate Veteran*, Vol. 8, 1900, p. 40.
99. *Confederate Veteran*, Vol. 27, 1919, p. 97.
100. *Confederate Veteran*, Vol. 18, 1910, p. 211.
101. *Confederate Veteran*, Vol. 16, 1908, p. 266.
102. *Confederate Veteran*, Vol. 30, 1922, p. 343.
103. *Confederate Veteran*, Vol. 20, 1912, p. 58.
104. *Confederate Veteran*, Vol. 19, 1911, p. 497.
105. *Confederate Veteran*, Vol. 14, 1906, p. 175.
106. *Confederate Veteran*, Vol. 17, 1909, p. 493.
107. *Confederate Veteran*, Vol. 14, 1906, p. 205.
108. *Confederate Veteran*, Vol. 15, 1907, p. 362.
109. *Confederate Veteran*, Vol. 29, 1921, p. 251.
110. *Confederate Veteran*, Vol. 26, 1918, p. 89.
111. *Confederate Veteran*, Vol. 33, 1925, p. 153.
112. *Confederate Veteran*, Vol. 15, 1907, p. 345.
113. *Confederate Veteran*, Vol. 27, 1919, p. 98.
114. *Confederate Veteran*, Vol. 36, 1928, p. 185.
115. *Confederate Veteran*, Vol. 33, 1925, p. 134.
116. *Confederate Veteran*, Vol. 34, 1926, p. 329.
117. Gold, pp. 181, 215.
118. *Confederate Veteran*, Vol. 33, 1925, p. 94.
119. *Confederate Veteran*, Vol. 33, 1925, p. 218.
120. *Confederate Veteran*, Vol. 30, 1922, p. 32.
121. *Confederate Veteran*, Vol. 18, 1910, p. 211.
122. *Confederate Veteran*, Vol. 11, 1903, p. 390.
123. *Confederate Veteran*, Vol. 2, 1894, p. 214.
124. Bradford, p. 51.
125. *Confederate Veteran*, Vol. 15, 1907, p. 209.
126. Stuart also had a warhorse named "Virginia."
127. *Confederate Veteran*, Vol. 40, 1932, p. 178.
128. *Confederate Veteran*, Vol. 33, 1925, p. 87.
129. *Confederate Veteran*, Vol. 35, 1927, p. 257.
130. Young, p. 13.

131. *Confederate Veteran*, Vol. 26, 1918, p. 89.
132. *Confederate Veteran*, Vol. 11, 1903, p. 174.
133. *Confederate Veteran*, Vol. 24, 1916, p. 56.
134. *Confederate Veteran*, Vol. 30, 1922, p. 260.
135. See *Confederate Veteran*, Vol. 19, 1911, pp. 575-576.
136. *Confederate Veteran*, Vol. 30, 1922, p. 18.
137. *Confederate Veteran*, Vol. 35, 1927, p. 438.
138. *Confederate Veteran*, Vol. 31, 1923, p. 381.
139. See e.g., *Confederate Veteran*, Vol. 1, 1893, pp. 7, 8, 61, 88.
140. See e.g., *Confederate Veteran*, Vol. 1, 1893, pp. 47, 86, 116, 143, 181, 218, 229, 283, 284, 315, 360.
141. See e.g., *Confederate Veteran*, Vol. 9, 1901, pp. 367, 400.
142. See e.g., *Confederate Veteran*, Vol. 4, 1896, pp. 4, 120, 356.
143. See e.g., *Confederate Veteran*, Vol. 7, 1899, p. 389.
144. *Confederate Veteran*, Vol. 23, 1915, p. 261.
145. *Confederate Veteran*, Vol. 30, 1922, p. 452.
146. *Confederate Veteran*, Vol. 5, 1897, p. 287.
147. Williamson, pp. 14-21.
148. McClellan, pp. 1-9.
149. *Confederate Veteran*, Vol. 27, 1919, pp. 96-98.
150. In some sources Sweeney's first name is given as Sam. See e.g., *Confederate Veteran*, Vol. 20, 1912, p. 112.
151. *Confederate Veteran*, Vol. 11, 1903, pp. 390-392. (The title of this entry is mine. L.S.)
152. *Confederate Veteran*, Vol. 40, 1932, pp. 176-178.
153. Bradford, pp. 35-62.
154. [Pollard's note:] Heros von Borcke, a Prussian officer on Gen. Stuart's staff, in some interesting memoirs of the commander, thus relates how the strong man was moved by the death of the little daughter by whose grave he now slept, war's fitful fever over, and its glory laid in the dust: "During the night of the 5th November, 1862, there came a telegram for Gen. Stuart, which, in accordance with his instructions, habitually observed by me, I opened with his other dispatches, and found to contain the most painful intelligence. It announced the death of little Flora, our chief's lovely and dearly-loved daughter, five years of age, the favourite of her father and of his military family. This sweet child had been dangerously ill for some time, and more than once had Mrs. Stuart summoned her husband to Flora's bedside; but she received only the response of the true soldier: "My duty to the country must be performed before I can give way to the feelings of the father." I went at once to acquaint my General with the terrible tidings, and when I had awakened him, perceiving, from the grave expression of my features, that something had gone wrong, he said, "What is it, Major? Are the Yankees advancing?" I handed him the telegram without a word. He read it, and the tenderness of the father's heart overcoming the firmness of the warriour, he threw his arms around my neck and wept bitter tears upon my breast. My dear General never recovered from this cruel blow. Many a time afterwards, during our rides together, he would speak to me of his lost child. Light-blue flowers recalled her eyes to him; in the glancing sunbeams he caught the golden tinge of her hair; and whenever he saw a child with such eyes and hair, he could not help tenderly embracing it. He thought of her even on his death-bed, when, drawing me towards him, he whispered, "My dear friend, I shall soon be with little Flora again."
155. Pollard, *Lee and His Lieutenants*, pp. 421-439. (The title of this entry is mine. L.S.)
156. *Confederate Veteran*, Vol. 1, 1893, p. 205. (The title of this entry is mine. L.S.)
157. *Confederate Veteran*, Vol. 1, 1893, p. 234. (The title of this entry is mine. L.S.)
158. *Confederate Veteran*, Vol. 1, 1893, p. 277. (The title of this entry is mine. L.S.)
159. *Confederate Veteran*, Vol. 1, 1893, p. 330. (The title of this entry is mine. L.S.)
160. *Confederate Veteran*, Vol. 1, 1893, p. 361. (The title of this entry is mine. L.S.)
161. *Confederate Veteran*, Vol. 2, 1894, p. 12. (The title of this entry is mine. L.S.)
162. Taylor, pp. 91-93. (The title of this entry is mine. L.S.)
163. *Confederate Veteran*, Vol. 6, 1898, p. 362.
164. *Confederate Veteran*, Vol. 2, 1894, pp. 74, 75. (The title of this entry is mine. L.S.)
165. *Confederate Veteran*, Vol. 3, 1895, p. 117. (The title of this entry is mine. L.S.)
166. *Confederate Veteran*, Vol. 3, 1895, p. 250. (The title of this entry is mine. L.S.)

167. *Confederate Veteran*, Vol. 3, 1895, p. 377. (The title of this entry is mine. L.S.)
168. *Confederate Veteran*, Vol. 3, 1895, p. 384 (I). (The title of this entry is mine. L.S.)
169. *Confederate Veteran*, Vol. 4, 1896, p. 89. (The title of this entry is mine. L.S.)
170. *Confederate Veteran*, Vol. 4, 1896, p. 155.
171. Young, p. xvii. (The title of this entry is mine. L.S.)
172. *Confederate Veteran*, Vol. 4, 1896, pp. 308-309. (The title of this entry is mine. L.S.)
173. *Confederate Veteran*, Vol. 5, 1897, pp. 53-54. (The title of this entry is mine. L.S.)
174. Rodenbough, pp. 266, 268, 270. (The title of this entry is mine. L.S.)
175. Dandridge was a close cousin of Martha Washington, wife of America's first president, George Washington.
176. *Confederate Veteran*, Vol. 5, 1897, p. 551. (The title of this entry is mine. L.S.)
177. *Confederate Veteran*, Vol. 6, 1898, p. 80. (The title of this entry is mine. L.S.)
178. *Confederate Veteran*, Vol. 6, 1898, p. 216. (The title of this entry is mine. L.S.)
179. Steele, p. 203. (The title of this entry is mine. L.S.)
180. *Confederate Veteran*, Vol. 7, 1899, pp. 167-168. (The title of this entry is mine. L.S.)
181. *Confederate Veteran*, Vol. 7, 1899, p. 252. (The title of this entry is mine. L.S.)
182. My translation: "Gen. Stuart was the finest cavalry general that this world did ever see." L.S.
183. *Confederate Veteran*, Vol. 7, 1899, p. 568. (The title of this entry is mine. L.S.)
184. *Confederate Veteran*, Vol. 8, 1900, p. 40.
185. *Confederate Veteran*, Vol. 8, 1900, p. 125.
186. *Confederate Veteran*, Vol. 8, 1900, p. 243.
187. *Confederate Veteran*, Vol. 8, 1900, p. 275.
188. *Confederate Veteran*, Vol. 9, 1901, p. 222.
189. *Confederate Veteran*, Vol. 9, 1901, p. 312.
190. *Confederate Veteran*, Vol. 9, 1901, p. 316. (The title of this entry is mine. L.S.)
191. *Confederate Veteran*, Vol. 9, 1901, p. 370.
192. *Confederate Veteran*, Vol. 10, 1902, p. 261. (The title of this entry is mine. L.S.)
193. *Confederate Veteran*, Vol. 10, 1902, p. 360. (The title of this entry is mine. L.S.)
194. *Confederate Veteran*, Vol. 10, 1902, p. 553. (The title of this entry is mine. L.S.)
195. *Confederate Veteran*, Vol. 10, 1902, p. 555. (The title of this entry is mine. L.S.)
196. *Confederate Veteran*, Vol. 10, 1902, p. 555. (The title of this entry is mine. L.S.)
197. *Confederate Veteran*, Vol. 11, 1903, p. 27. (The title of this entry is mine. L.S.)
198. *Confederate Veteran*, Vol. 11, 1903, p. 201.
199. *Confederate Veteran*, Vol. 11, 1903, p. 335. (The title of this entry is mine. L.S.)
200. *Confederate Veteran*, Vol. 11, 1903, p. 347.
201. *Confederate Veteran*, Vol. 11, 1903, p. 458.
202. *Confederate Veteran*, Vol. 11, 1903, p. 553.
203. *Confederate Veteran*, Vol. 12, 1904, p. 102.
204. *Confederate Veteran*, Vol. 12, 1904, p. 488. (The title of this entry is mine. L.S.)
205. *Confederate Veteran*, Vol. 12, 1904, p. 583. (The title of this entry is mine. L.S.)
206. *Confederate Veteran*, Vol. 13, 1905, p. 119. (The title of this entry is mine. L.S.)
207. *Confederate Veteran*, Vol. 14, 1906, pp. 74-75.
208. *Confederate Veteran*, Vol. 14, 1906, p. 549. (The title of this entry is mine. L.S.)
209. *Confederate Veteran*, Vol. 15, 1907, p. 197. (The title of this entry is mine. L.S.)
210. Gold, p. 133. (The title of this entry is mine. L.S.)
211. *Confederate Veteran*, Vol. 15, 1907, p. 262. (The title of this entry is mine. L.S.)
212. *Confederate Veteran*, Vol. 15, 1907, p. 294. (The title of this entry is mine. L.S.)
213. *Confederate Veteran*, Vol. 15, 1907, pp. 348-349.
214. Maurice, pp. 128-129. (The title of this entry is mine. L.S.)
215. *Confederate Veteran*, Vol. 15, 1907, p. 362.
216. *Confederate Veteran*, Vol. 16, 1908, p. 17. (The title of this entry is mine. L.S.)c
217. *Confederate Veteran*, Vol. 17, 1909, p. 52. (The title of this entry is mine. L.S.)
218. *Confederate Veteran*, Vol. 17, 1909, pp. 76-77.
219. *Confederate Veteran*, Vol. 19, 1911, p. 138. (The title of this entry is mine. L.S.)

220. *Confederate Veteran*, Vol. 19, 1911, p. 531.
221. See Battine, p. 77.
222. *Confederate Veteran*, Vol. 19, 1911, pp. 575-576.
223. *Confederate Veteran*, Vol. 20, 1912, p. 58. (The title of this entry is mine. L.S.)
224. *Confederate Veteran*, Vol. 20, 1912, p. 280. (The title of this entry is mine. L.S.)
225. *Confederate Veteran*, Vol. 21, 1913, p. 41. (The title of this entry is mine. L.S.)
226. *Confederate Veteran*, Vol. 22, 1914, p. 352.
227. *Confederate Veteran*, Vol. 22, 1914, pp. 357-358. (The title of this entry is mine. L.S.)
228. *Confederate Veteran*, Vol. 23, 1915, p. 69.
229. *Confederate Veteran*, Vol. 23, 1915, pp. 171-172. (The title of this entry is mine. L.S.)
230. *Confederate Veteran*, Vol. 23, 1915, pp. 174-175. (The title of this entry is mine. L.S.)
231. Brock, pp. 274-275. (The title of this entry is mine. L.S.)
232. *Confederate Veteran*, Vol. 23, 1915, pp. 456-457.
233. *Confederate Veteran*, Vol. 26, 1918, p. 19.
234. Lee (Fitzhugh), *General Lee*, pp. 152-153. (The title of this entry is mine. L.S.)
235. F. Lee, pp. 35-36. (The title of this entry is mine. L.S.)
236. *Confederate Veteran*, Vol. 26, 1918, p. 23. (The title of this entry is mine. L.S.)
237. *Confederate Veteran*, Vol. 26, 1918, p. 142. (The title of this entry is mine. L.S.)
238. *Confederate Veteran*, Vol. 26, 1918, p. 189.
239. *Confederate Veteran*, Vol. 26, 1918, p. 474. (The title of this entry is mine. L.S.)
240. Trent, pp. 68-69. (The title of this entry is mine. L.S.)
241. Gilman, pp. 115-116. (The title of this entry is mine. L.S.)
242. *Confederate Veteran*, Vol. 26, 1918, p. 510.
243. *Confederate Veteran*, Vol. 27, 1919, p. 11.
244. *Confederate Veteran*, Vol. 27, 1919, p. 52.
245. *Confederate Veteran*, Vol. 27, 1919, p. 225. (The title of this entry is mine. L.S.)
246. *Confederate Veteran*, Vol. 27, 1919, p. 264.
247. *Confederate Veteran*, Vol. 27, 1919, p. 265.
248. R. E. Lee (Jr.), p. 96. (The title of this entry is mine. L.S.)
249. See article by Col. W. Gordon McCabe in the London *Saturday Review* of March 5, 1910. [McKim's note.]
250. For detailed discussions on the topics of slavery, its history, and the South, see my books *Everything You Were Taught About American Slavery is Wrong, Ask a Southerner!* and *Slavery 101: Amazing Facts You Never Knew About America's "Peculiar Institution."*
251. *Confederate Veteran*, Vol. 27, 1919, pp. 286-287. (The title of this entry is mine. L.S.)
252. *Confederate Veteran*, Vol. 27, 1919, p. 293. (The title of this entry is mine. L.S.)
253. *Confederate Veteran*, Vol. 27, 1919, pp. 330-331.
254. *Confederate Veteran*, Vol. 27, 1919, pp. 414-415. (The title of this entry is mine. L.S.)
255. *Confederate Veteran*, Vol. 28, 1920, p. 28. (The title of this entry is mine. L.S.)
256. *Confederate Veteran*, Vol. 28, 1920, p. 30. (The title of this entry is mine. L.S.)
257. *Confederate Veteran*, Vol. 28, 1920, p. 54. (The title of this entry is mine. L.S.)
258. McKim, p. 144. (The title of this entry is mine. L.S.)
259. *Confederate Veteran*, Vol. 28, 1920, p. 65. Also see Warner, *Generals in Blue*, s.v. "Joseph Jackson Bartlett." (The title of this entry is mine. L.S.)
260. *Confederate Veteran*, Vol. 29, 1921, pp. 213-214.
261. *Confederate Veteran*, Vol. 30, 1922, p. 18. (The title of this entry is mine. L.S.)
262. *Confederate Veteran*, Vol. 30, 1922, p. 223. (The title of this entry is mine. L.S.)
263. *Confederate Veteran*, Vol. 30, 1922, p. 331. (The title of this entry is mine. L.S.)
264. *Confederate Veteran*, Vol. 30, 1922, p. 445. (The title of this entry is mine. L.S.)
265. *Confederate Veteran*, Vol. 31, 1923, p. 17. (The title of this entry is mine. L.S.)
266. *Confederate Veteran*, Vol. 31, 1923, pp. 55-56.
267. *Confederate Veteran*, Vol. 31, 1923, p. 244. (The title of this entry is mine. L.S.)
268. *Confederate Veteran*, Vol. 31, 1923, p. 269. (The title of this entry is mine. L.S.)
269. *Confederate Veteran*, Vol. 32, 1924, p. 47.

270. *Confederate Veteran*, Vol. 32, 1924, p. 63. (The title of this entry is mine. L.S.)
271. *Confederate Veteran*, Vol. 32, 1924, pp. 260-263. (The title of this entry is mine. L.S.)
272. *Confederate Veteran*, Vol. 33, 1925, p. 178. (The title of this entry is mine. L.S.)
273. *Confederate Veteran*, Vol. 33, 1925, p. 329. (The title of this entry is mine. L.S.)
274. *Confederate Veteran*, Vol. 34, 1926, p. 124. (The title of this entry is mine. L.S.)
275. *Confederate Veteran*, Vol. 34, 1926, p. 221. (The title of this entry is mine. L.S.)
276. *Confederate Veteran*, Vol. 34, 1926, pp. 260, 261. (The title of this entry is mine. L.S.)
277. *Confederate Veteran*, Vol. 34, 1926, p. 334. (The title of this entry is mine. L.S.)
278. *Confederate Veteran*, Vol. 34, 1926, p. 461. (The title of this entry is mine. L.S.)
279. *Confederate Veteran*, Vol. 35, 1927, p. 113. (The title of this entry is mine. L.S.)
280. *Confederate Veteran*, Vol. 35, 1927, p. 261. (The title of this entry is mine. L.S.)
281. *Confederate Veteran*, Vol. 35, 1927, p. 376. (The title of this entry is mine. L.S.)
282. *Confederate Veteran*, Vol. 35, 1927, p. 255.
283. *Confederate Veteran*, Vol. 35, 1927, pp. 258-259. (The title of this entry is mine. L.S.)
284. *Confederate Veteran*, Vol. 37, 1929, p. 198. (The title of this entry is mine. L.S.)
285. *Confederate Veteran*, Vol. 38, 1930, p. 451. (The title of this entry is mine. L.S.)
286. *Confederate Veteran*, Vol. 39, 1931, p. 100. (The title of this entry is mine. L.S.)
287. *Confederate Veteran*, Vol. 39, 1931, p. 103. (The title of this entry is mine. L.S.)
288. *Confederate Veteran*, Vol. 40, 1932, pp. 217-218. (The title of this entry is mine. L.S.)
289. McDonald, p. 84. (The title of this entry is mine. L.S.)
290. Cooke, pp. 51-52. (The title of this entry is mine. L.S.)
291. Borcke, pp. 14-16. (The title of this entry is mine. L.S.)
292. Henderson, Vol. 2, pp. 347-349. Note: This entry is a quote from Confederate Major Heros von Borcke. (The title of this entry is mine. L.S.)
293. Avary, pp. 229-243. (The title of this entry is mine. L.S.)
294. *Confederate Veteran*, Vol. 40, 1932, p. 303. (The title of this entry is mine. L.S.)
295. *Confederate Veteran*, Vol. 40, 1932, p. 442. (The title of this entry is mine. L.S.)
296. Jones, *Christ in the Camp*, pp. 102-104. (The title of this entry is mine. L.S.)
297. Williamson, p. 192. (The title of this entry is mine. L.S.)
298. Williamson, p. 192. (The title of this entry is mine. L.S.)
299. Williamson, p. 193. (The title of this entry is mine. L.S.)
300. Williamson, p. 194. (The title of this entry is mine. L.S.)
301. Williamson, pp. 195-198. (The title of this entry is mine. L.S.)
302. Hopkins, pp. 156-160. (The title of this entry is mine. L.S.)
303. Neese, p. 282. (The title of this entry is mine. L.S.)
304. Battine, pp. 77-78. (The title of this entry is mine. L.S.)
305. Gold, pp. 285-286. (The title of this entry is mine. L.S.)
306. Mosby, p. vi.
307. Garnett, p. 16 (a). (The title of this entry is mine. L.S.)
308. La Bree, p. 56. (The title of this appendix is mine. L.S.)
309. For more on the topic of Southern secession see my book, *All We Ask Is To Be Let Alone: The Southern Secession Fact Book*.
310. For more on the topic of the C.S. Constitution see my books, *The Constitution of the Confederate States of America Explained: A Clause-by-Clause Study of the South's Magna Carta*, and *America's Three Constitutions: Complete Texts of the Articles of Confederation, Constitution of the United States of America, and Constitution of the Confederate States of America*.
311. For more on the topic of the true causes behind the War Between the States see my books, *Lincoln's War: The Real Cause, the Real Winner, the Real Loser*, and *Everything You Were Taught About the Civil War is Wrong, Ask a Southerner!*
312. For more on the topic of Tennessee and Lincoln's War see my book, *The McGavocks of Carnton Plantation: A Southern History - Celebrating One of Dixie's Most Noble Confederate Families and Their Tennessee Home*.
313. For more on the topic of the Battle of Fort Donelson (and associated conflicts) see my book, *A Rebel Born: A Defense of Nathan Bedford Forrest - Confederate General, American Legend*.

314. For more on the topic of the Battle of Chancellorsville, as well as the wounding and death of Stonewall Jackson, see my books, *The Quotable Stonewall Jackson: Selections From the Writings and Speeches of the South's Most Famous General*, and *The Old Rebel: Robert E. Lee As He Was Seen By His Contemporaries*.

315. For more on the topic of the Battle of Chickamauga (and associated conflicts) see my book, *A Rebel Born: A Defense of Nathan Bedford Forrest - Confederate General, American Legend*.

316. For more on the topic of the Battle of Okolona (and associated conflicts) see my book, *A Rebel Born: A Defense of Nathan Bedford Forrest - Confederate General, American Legend*.

317. For more on the topic of Sherman's March to the Sea, as well as the overall devastation inflicted upon the South by the U.S.A., see my book, *The Unholy Crusade: Lincoln's Legacy of Destruction in the American South*.

318. For more on this specific conflict see my book, *The Battle of Spring Hill: Recollections of Confederate and Union Soldiers*.

319. For more on this specific conflict see my books, *The Battle of Franklin: Recollections of Confederate and Union Soldiers*, and *Encyclopedia of the Battle of Franklin*.

320. For more on this specific conflict see my book, *The Battle of Nashville: Recollections of Confederate and Union Soldiers*.

321. For more on this specific topic see my book, *The Hampton Roads Conference: The Southern View*.

322. *Confederate Veteran*, Vol. 24, 1916, pp. 444-445. Note: Some of the dates and names in this list do not agree with modern scholarship. However, I have left the original text unedited for historical value. L.S.

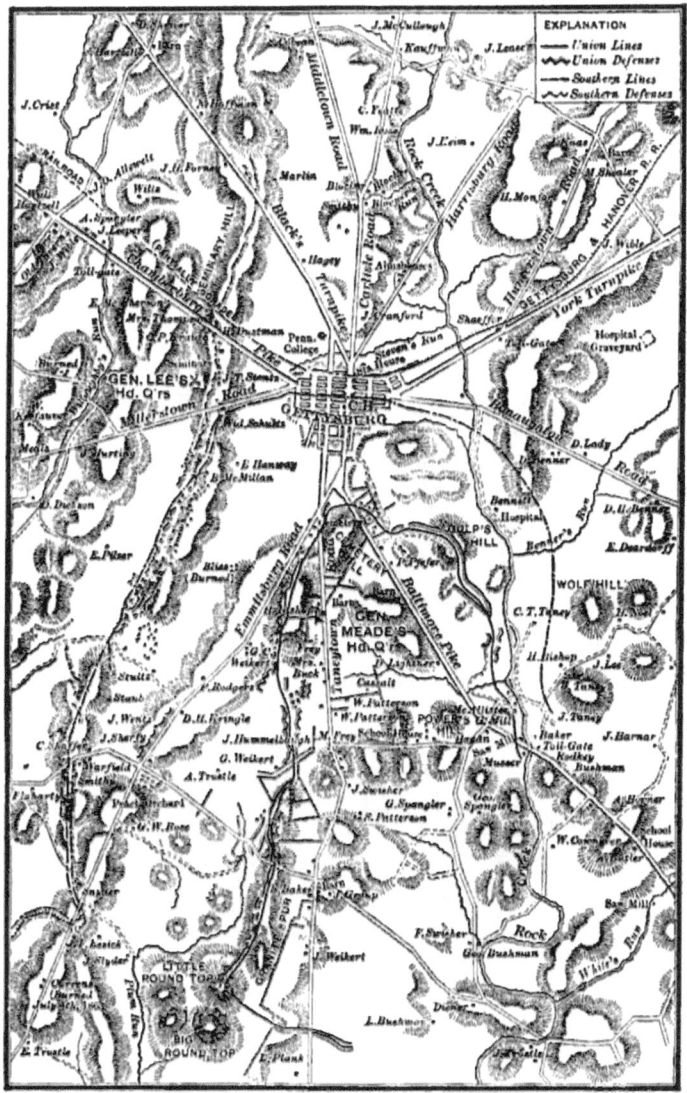

The Battlefield of Gettysburg, PA., July 1, 2, and 3, 1863.

This Victorian print is entitled "The Conflagration of Richmond." In April 1865 parts of the city were set ablaze by Confederate soldiers in order to prevent things like military supplies and commercial goods from falling into the hands of invading Yankee forces.

BIBLIOGRAPHY

And Suggested Reading

Adam, Graeme Mercer. *The Life of General Robert E. Lee*. New York: A. L. Burt Co., 1905.
Alexander, Edward Porter. *Military Memoirs of a Confederate*. New York: Charles Scribner's Sons, 1907.
Anderson, Mabel Washbourne. *Life of General Stand Watie: The Only Indian Brigadier General of the Confederate Army and the Last General to Surrender*. Pryor, OK: self-published, 1915.
Armstrong, J. M. *The Biographical Encyclopedia of Kentucky of the Dead and Living Men of the Nineteenth Century*. Cincinnati, OH: J. M. Armstrong and Co., 1878.
Ashe, Samuel A'Court. *History of North Carolina*. 2 vols. Greensboro, NC: Charles L. Van Noppen, 1908.
Avary, Myrta Lockett. *A Virginia Girl in the Civil War, 1861-1865: Being a Record of the Actual Experiences of the Wife of a Confederate Officer*. New York: D. Appleton and Co., 1903.
Battine, Cecil. *The Crisis of the Confederacy: A History of Gettysburg and the Wilderness*. London, UK: Longmans, Green, and Co., 1905.
Benson, Al, Jr., and Walter Donald Kennedy. *Lincoln's Marxists*. Gretna, LA: Pelican, 2011.
Bond, P. S. (ed.). *Military Science and Tactics: A Text and Reference for the Reserve Officers' Training Corps*. Washington, D.C.: P. S. Bond Publishing Co., 1938.
Borcke, Heros von. *Memoirs of the Confederate War for Independence*. 2 vols. Edinburgh, Scotland: William Blackwood and Sons, 1866.
Boyd, James P. *Parties, Problems, and Leaders of 1896: An Impartial Presentation of Living National Questions*. Chicago, IL: Publishers'

Union, 1896.
Bradford, Gamaliel. *Confederate Portraits*. Boston, MA: Houghton Mifflin Co., 1913.
Brock, Robert Alonzo (ed.). *Gen. Robert Edward Lee: Soldier, Citizen, and Christian Patriot*. Richmond, VA: Royal Publishing Co., 1897.
———. *Southern Historical Society Papers*. 52 vols. Richmond, VA: Southern Historical Society, 1876-1943.
Browder, Earl. *Lincoln and the Communists*. New York, NY: Workers Library Publishers, Inc., 1936.
Bryan, William Jennings. *The First Battle: A Story of the Campaign of 1896*. Chicago, IL: W. B. Conkey Co., 1896.
Burns, James MacGregor. *The Vineyard of Liberty*. New York, NY: Alfred A. Knopf, 1982.
Carpenter, Stephen D. *Logic of History - Five Hundred Political Texts: Being Concentrated Extracts of Abolitionism; Also Results of Slavery Agitation and Emancipation; Together With Sundry Chapters on Despotism, Usurpations and Frauds*. Madison, WI: self-published, 1864.
Christian, George Llewellyn. *Abraham Lincoln: An Address Delivered Before R. E. Lee Camp, No. 1 Confederate Veterans at Richmond, VA, October 29, 1909*. Richmond, VA: L. H. Jenkins, 1909.
———. *A Capitol Disaster: A Chapter of Reconstruction in Virginia*. Richmond, VA: self-published, 1915.
———. *Confederate Memories and Experiences*. Richmond, VA: self-published, 1915.
Commons, John R., David J. Saposs, Helen L. Sumner, E. B. Mittelman, H. E. Hoagland, John B. Andrews, Selig Perlman. *History of Labour in the United States*. New York: Macmillan Co., 1918.
Confederate Veteran (Sumner Archibald Cunningham, ed., 1893-1913; Edith Drake Pope, ed., 1914-1932). 40 vols (original forty year run). Nashville, TN: Confederate Veteran, 1893-1932.
Cooke, John Esten. *Commercial Enfranchisement of the Confederate States of America*. Richmond, VA: West and Johnston, 1862.
———. *Stonewall Jackson: A Military Biography*. New York: D. Appleton and Co., 1866.
———. *Surry of Eagle's-nest; or, the Memoirs of a Staff-Officer Serving in Virginia*. New York: F. J. Huntington and Co., 1866.
———. *Mohun; or, The Last Days of Lee and His Paladins: Final Memoirs of a Staff Officer Serving in Virginia*. New York: F. J. Huntington and Co., 1869.

———. *Hammer and Rapier*. New York: Carleton, 1870.
———. *Virginia: A History of the People*. Boston, MA: Houghton, Mifflin and Co., 1883.
Curry, Jabez Lamar Monroe. *The Southern States of the American Union Considered in Their Relations to the Constitution of the United States and to the Resulting Union*. New York: G. P. Putnam's Sons, 1894.
Dabney, Robert Lewis. *Life and Campaigns of Lieut.-Gen. Thomas J. Jackson*. New York: Blelock and Co., 1866.
Dean, Henry Clay. *Crimes of the Civil War, and Curse of the Funding System*. Baltimore, MD: self-published, 1869.
Dodd, Bella. *School of Darkness*. New York, NY: P. J. Kennedy and Sons, 1954.
Early, Jubal Anderson. *A Memoir of the Last Year of the War for Independence, in the Confederate States of America*. Lynchburg, VA: Charles W. Button, 1867.
Edmonds, George. *Facts and Falsehoods Concerning the War on the South, 1861-1865*. Memphis, TN: self-published, 1904.
Evans, Clement Anselm (ed.). *Confederate Military History*. 12 vols. Atlanta, GA: Confederate Publishing Co., 1899.
Ewing, E. W. R. *Northern Rebellion, Southern Secession*. Philadelphia, PA: The John C. Winston Co., 1904.
Fitzhugh, George. *Cannibals All! Or, Slaves Without Masters*. Richmond, VA: A. Morris, 1857.
Franklin, John Hope. *Reconstruction After the Civil War*. Chicago, IL: University of Chicago Press, 1961.
Gardiner, C. *Acts of the Republican Party as Seen by History*. Washington, D.C.: self-published, 1906.
Garnett, Theodore Stanford. *J. E. B. Stuart (Major-General) Commander of the Cavalry Corps, Army of Northern Virginia, C.S.A.* New York: Neale Publishing Co., 1907.
Gilman, Bradley. *Robert E. Lee*. New York: Macmillan Co., 1915.
Gold, Thomas Daniel. *History of Clarke County Virginia, and Its Connection With the War Between the States*. Berryville, VA: self-published, 1914.
Hasselberg, P. D. (ed.). *Parliamentary Debates: First Session, Fortieth Parliament, 1982, House of Representatives* (Vol. 445). Wellington, New Zealand: Government Printer, 1982.
Henderson, George Francis Robert. *Stonewall Jackson and the American Civil War*. 2 vols. London, UK: Longmans, Green, and Co., 1898.
Hopkins, Luther W. *From Bull Run to Appomattox: A Boy's View*. Baltimore, MD: Fleet-McGinley Co., 1908.

Johnson, Robert Underwood, and Clarence Clough Buel (eds.). *Battles and Leaders of the Civil War.* 4 vols. New York, NY: The Century Co., 1884-1888.
Johnstone, Huger William. *Truth of War Conspiracy, 1861.* Idylwild, GA: H. W. Johnstone, 1921.
Jones, John William. *Christ in the Camp: or Religion in Lee's Army.* Richmond, VA: B. F. Johnson and Co., 1887.
——. *The Davis Memorial Volume; Or Our Dead President, Jefferson Davis and the World's Tribute to His Memory.* Richmond, VA: B. F. Johnson, 1889.
——. *Life and Letters of Robert Edward Lee: Soldier and Man.* New York: Neale Publishing Co., 1906.
Kamman, William F. *Socialism in German American Literature.* Philadelphia, PA: Americana Germanica Press, 1917.
La Bree, Ben. *The Confederate Soldier in the Civil War, 1861-1865.* Louisville, KY: The Prentice Press, 1897.
Lane, Charles Arthur. *Illustrated Notes on English Church History.* 2 vols. London, UK: Society for Promoting Christian Knowledge, 1906.
Lee, Fitzhugh. *Chancellorsville: Address of Gen. Fitzhugh Lee Before the Virginia Division, of the Army of Northern Virginia* (Oct. 29, 1879). Richmond, VA: Virginia Division, A.N.V., 1879.
——. *General Lee.* New York: D. Appleton and Co., 1894.
Lee, Robert Edward, Jr. *Recollections and Letters of General Robert E. Lee.* New York: Doubleday, Page and Co., 1904.
Lenin, Vladimir. *"Left Wing" Communism: An Infantile Disorder.* Detroit, MI: The Marxian Educational Society, 1921.
Livermore, Thomas L. *Numbers and Losses in the Civil War in America, 1861-65.* 1900. Carlisle, PA: John Kallmann, 1996 ed.
Magliocca, Gerard N. *The Tragedy of William Jennings Bryan: Constitutional Law and the Politics of Backlash.* New Haven, CT: Yale University Press, 2011.
Marx, Karl, and Frederick Engels. *Manifesto of the Communist Party.* Chicago, IL: Charles H. Kerr and Co., 1906.
Maurice, Frederick. *Robert E. Lee the Soldier.* Boston, MA: Houghton Mifflin Co., 1925.
——. (ed.) *An Aide-de-camp of Lee: Being the Papers of Colonel Charles Marshall.* Boston, MA: Little, Brown, and Co., 1927.
McCarty, Burke (ed.). *Little Sermons in Socialism by Abraham Lincoln.* Chicago, IL: The Chicago Daily Socialist, 1910.
McClellan, Henry Brainerd. *The Life and Campaigns of Major-General J.E.B. Stuart, Commander of the Cavalry of the Army of Northern Virginia.* Boston, MA: Houghton, Mifflin and Co., 1885.

McDonald, William Naylor. *A History of the Laurel Brigade: Originally the Ashby Cavalry of the Army of Northern Virginia and Chew's Battery*. Baltimore, MD: Mrs. Kate S. McDonald, 1907.

McKim, Randolph Harrison. *The Soul of Lee: By One of His Soldiers*. New York: Longmans, Green and Co., 1918.

McPherson, James M. *Abraham Lincoln and the Second American Revolution*. New York, NY: Oxford University Press, 1991.

Meriwether, Elizabeth Avery (pseudonym, "George Edmonds"). *Facts and Falsehoods Concerning the War on the South, 1861-1865*. Memphis, TN: A. R. Taylor and Co., 1904.

Messer-Kruse, Timothy. *The Yankee International: Marxism and the American Reform Tradition, 1848-1876*. Chapel Hill. NC: University of North Carolina Press, 1998.

Miller, Francis Trevelyan, and Robert S. Lanier (eds.). *The Photographic History of the Civil War*. 10 vols. New York, NY: The Review of Reviews Co., 1911.

Minutes of the Eighth Annual Meeting and Reunion of the United Confederate Veterans, Atlanta, GA, July 20-23, 1898. New Orleans, LA: United Confederate Veterans, 1907.

Minutes of the Ninth Annual Meeting and Reunion of the United Confederate Veterans, Charleston, SC, May 10-13, 1899. New Orleans, LA: United Confederate Veterans, 1907.

Minutes of the Twelfth Annual Meeting and Reunion of the United Confederate Veterans, Dallas, TX, April 22-25, 1902. New Orleans, LA: United Confederate Veterans, 1907.

Mosby, John Singleton. *Stuart's Cavalry in the Gettysburg Campaign*. New York: Moffat, Yard and Co., 1908.

Muzzey, David Saville. *The United States of America: Vol. 1, To the Civil War*. Boston, MA: Ginn and Co., 1922.

——. *The American Adventure: Vol. 2, From the Civil War*. 1924. New York, NY: Harper and Brothers, 1927 ed.

Neese, George Michael. *Three Years in the Confederate Horse Artillery*. New York: Neale Publishing Co., 1911.

Nichols, John. *The "S" Word: A Short History of an American Tradition . . . Socialism*. London, UK: Verso, 2011.

Nicolay, John G., and John Hay (eds.). *Abraham Lincoln: A History*. 10 vols. New York, NY: The Century Co., 1890.

——. *Complete Works of Abraham Lincoln*. 12 vols. 1894. New York, NY: Francis D. Tandy Co., 1905 ed.

——. *Abraham Lincoln: Complete Works*. 12 vols. 1894. New York, NY: The Century Co., 1907 ed.

ORA (full title: *The War of the Rebellion: A Compilation of the Official Records of the Union and Confederate Armies*). 128 vols.

Washington, DC: Government Printing Office, 1880.
ORN (full title: *Official Records of the Union and Confederate Navies in the War of the Rebellion*). 30 vols. Washington, DC: Government Printing Office, 1894.
Pollard, Edward Alfred. *The Lost Cause*. New York, NY: E. B. Treat and Co., 1867.
——. *Lee and His Lieutenants: Comprising the Early Life, Public Services, and Campaigns of General Robert E. Lee*. New York, NY: E. B. Treat and Co., 1867.
Powers, William Dudley. *Uncle Isaac; Or, Old Days in the South. A Remembrance of the South*. Richmond, VA: B. F. Johnson Co., 1899.
Randall, James Garfield. *Constitutional Problems Under Lincoln*. New York: D. Appleton and Co., 1926.
Rawle, William. *A View of the Constitution of the United States of America*. Philadelphia, PA: self-published, 1825.
Richardson, John Anderson. *Richardson's Defense of the South*. Atlanta, GA: A. B. Caldwell, 1914.
Rodenbough, Theophilus Francis (ed.). *The Photographic History of the Civil War in Ten Volumes*. Springfield, MA: Patriot Publishing Co., 1911.
Rogers, William P. *The Three Secession Movements in the United States: Samuel J. Tilden, the Democratic Candidate for Presidency; the Advisor, Aider and Abettor of the Great Secession Movement of 1860; and One of the Authors of the Infamous Resolution of 1864; His Claims as a Statesman and Reformer Considered*. Boston, MA: John Wilson and Son, 1876.
Ross, Earle Dudley. *The Liberal Republican Movement*. New York: Henry Holt and Co., 1919.
Rove, Karl. *The Triumph of William McKinley: Why the Election of 1896 Still Matters*. New York, NY: Simon and Schuster, 2015.
Rutherford, Mildred Lewis. *Truths of History: A Fair, Unbiased, Impartial, Unprejudiced and Conscientious Study of History*. Athens, GA: n.p., 1920.
Scharf, John Thomas. *History of the Confederate States Navy From its Organization to the Surrender of its Last Vessel*. New York: Rogers and Sherwood, 1887.
Schlüter, Herman. *Lincoln, Labor and Slavery: A Chapter From the Social History of America*. New York: Socialist Literature Co., 1913.
Seabrook, Lochlainn. *Carnton Plantation Ghost Stories: True Tales of the Unexplained from Tennessee's Most Haunted Civil War House!* 2005. Franklin, TN, 2016 ed.

———. *Nathan Bedford Forrest: Southern Hero, American Patriot*. 2007. Franklin, TN, 2010 ed.
———. *Abraham Lincoln: The Southern View*. 2007. Franklin, TN: Sea Raven Press, 2013 ed.
———. *The McGavocks of Carnton Plantation: A Southern History - Celebrating One of Dixie's Most Noble Confederate Families and Their Tennessee Home*. 2008. Franklin, TN, 2011 ed.
———. *A Rebel Born: A Defense of Nathan Bedford Forrest*. 2010. Franklin, TN: Sea Raven Press, 2011 ed.
———. *Everything You Were Taught About the Civil War is Wrong, Ask a Southerner!* 2010. Franklin, TN: Sea Raven Press, 2024 ed.
———. *The Quotable Jefferson Davis: Selections From the Writings and Speeches of the Confederacy's First President*. Franklin, TN: Sea Raven Press, 2011.
———. *The Quotable Robert E. Lee: Selections From the Writings and Speeches of the South's Most Beloved Civil War General*. Franklin, TN: Sea Raven Press, 2011 Sesquicentennial Civil War Edition.
———. *Lincolnology: The Real Abraham Lincoln Revealed In His Own Words*. Franklin, TN: Sea Raven Press, 2011.
———. *The Unquotable Abraham Lincoln: The President's Quotes They Don't Want You To Know!* Franklin, TN: Sea Raven Press, 2011.
———. *Honest Jeff and Dishonest Abe: A Southern Children's Guide to the Civil War*. Franklin, TN: Sea Raven Press, 2012.
———. *Encyclopedia of the Battle of Franklin - A Comprehensive Guide to the Conflict that Changed the Civil War*. Franklin, TN: Sea Raven Press, 2012.
———. *The Quotable Nathan Bedford Forrest: Selections From the Writings and Speeches of the Confederacy's Most Brilliant Cavalryman*. Spring Hill, TN: Sea Raven Press, 2012.
———. *Forrest! 99 Reasons to Love Nathan Bedford Forrest*. Spring Hill, TN: Sea Raven Press, 2012.
———. *Give 'Em Hell Boys! The Complete Military Correspondence of Nathan Bedford Forrest*. Spring Hill, TN: Sea Raven Press, 2012.
———. *The Constitution of the Confederate States of America Explained: A Clause-by-Clause Study of the South's Magna Carta*. Spring Hill, TN: Sea Raven Press, 2012 Sesquicentennial Civil War Edition.
———. *The Great Impersonator: 99 Reasons to Dislike Abraham Lincoln*. Spring Hill, TN: Sea Raven Press, 2012.
———. *The Old Rebel: Robert E. Lee As He Was Seen By His Contemporaries*. Spring Hill, TN: Sea Raven Press, 2012 Sesquicentennial Civil War Edition.
———. *The Quotable Stonewall Jackson: Selections From the Writings and Speeches of the South's Most Famous General*. Spring Hill, TN: Sea

Raven Press, 2012 Sesquicentennial Civil War Edition.

———. *Saddle, Sword, and Gun: A Biography of Nathan Bedford Forrest for Teens*. Spring Hill, TN: Sea Raven Press, 2013.

———. *The Alexander H. Stephens Reader: Excerpts From the Works of a Confederate Founding Father*. Spring Hill, TN: Sea Raven Press, 2013.

———. *The Quotable Alexander H. Stephens: Selections From the Writings and Speeches of the Confederacy's First Vice President*. Spring Hill, TN: Sea Raven Press, 2013 Sesquicentennial Civil War Edition.

———. *Give This Book to a Yankee! A Southern Guide to the Civil War for Northerners*. Spring Hill, TN: Sea Raven Press, 2014.

———. *The Articles of Confederation Explained: A Clause-by-Clause Study of America's First Constitution*. Spring Hill, TN: Sea Raven Press, 2014.

———. *Confederate Blood and Treasure: An Interview With Lochlainn Seabrook*. Spring Hill, TN: Sea Raven Press, 2015.

———. *Nathan Bedford Forrest and the Battle of Fort Pillow: Yankee Myth, Confederate Fact*. Spring Hill, TN: Sea Raven Press, 2015.

———. *Everything You Were Taught About American Slavery War is Wrong, Ask a Southerner!* Spring Hill, TN: Sea Raven Press, 2015.

———. *Confederacy 101: Amazing Facts You Never Knew About America's Oldest Political Tradition*. Spring Hill, TN: Sea Raven Press, 2015.

———. *The Great Yankee Coverup: What the North Doesn't Want You to Know About Lincoln's War!* Spring Hill, TN: Sea Raven Press, 2015.

———. *Slavery 101: Amazing Facts You Never Knew About America's "Peculiar Institution."* Spring Hill, TN: Sea Raven Press, 2015.

———. *Confederate Flag Facts: What Every American Should Know About Dixie's Southern Cross*. Spring Hill, TN: Sea Raven Press, 2016.

———. *Nathan Bedford Forrest and the Ku Klux Klan: Yankee Myth, Confederate Fact*. Spring Hill, TN: Sea Raven Press, 2016.

———. *Seabrook's Bible Dictionary of Traditional and Mystical Christian Doctrines*. Spring Hill, TN: Sea Raven Press, 2016.

———. *Everything You Were Taught About African-Americans and the Civil War is Wrong, Ask a Southerner!* Spring Hill, TN: Sea Raven Press, 2016.

———. *Nathan Bedford Forrest and African-Americans: Yankee Myth, Confederate Fact*. Spring Hill, TN: Sea Raven Press, 2016.

———. *Women in Gray: A Tribute to the Ladies Who Supported the Southern Confederacy*. Spring Hill, TN: Sea Raven Press, 2016.

———. *Lincoln's War: The Real Cause, the Real Winner, the Real Loser*. Spring Hill, TN: Sea Raven Press, 2016.

——. *The Unholy Crusade: Lincoln's Legacy of Destruction in the American South*. Spring Hill, TN: Sea Raven Press, 2017.

——. *Abraham Lincoln Was a Liberal, Jefferson Davis Was a Conservative: The Missing Key to Understanding the American Civil War*. Spring Hill, TN: Sea Raven Press, 2017.

——. *All We Ask is to be Let Alone: The Southern Secession Fact Book*. Spring Hill, TN: Sea Raven Press, 2017.

——. *The Ultimate Civil War Quiz Book: How Much Do You Really Know About America's Most Misunderstood Conflict?* Spring Hill, TN: Sea Raven Press, 2017.

——. *Rise Up and Call Them Blessed: Victorian Tributes to the Confederate Soldier, 1861-1901*. Spring Hill, TN: Sea Raven Press, 2017.

——. *Victorian Confederate Poetry: The Southern Cause in Verse, 1861-1901*. Spring Hill, TN: Sea Raven Press, 2018.

——. *Confederate Monuments: Why Every American Should Honor Confederate Soldiers and Their Memorials*. Spring Hill, TN: Sea Raven Press, 2018.

——. *The God of War: Nathan Bedford Forrest as He Was Seen by His Contemporaries*. Spring Hill, TN: Sea Raven Press, 2018.

——. *The Battle of Spring Hill: Recollections of Confederate and Union Soldiers*. Spring Hill, TN: Sea Raven Press, 2018.

——. *I Rode With Forrest! Confederate Soldiers Who Served With the World's Greatest Cavalry Leader*. Spring Hill, TN: Sea Raven Press, 2018.

——. *The Battle of Nashville: Recollections of Confederate and Union Soldiers*. Spring Hill, TN: Sea Raven Press, 2018.

——. *The Battle of Franklin: Recollections of Confederate and Union Soldiers*. Spring Hill, TN: Sea Raven Press, 2018.

——. *A Rebel Born: The Screenplay* (for the film). Written 2011. Franklin, TN: Sea Raven Press, 2020.

——. (ed.) *A Short History of the Confederate States of America* (Jefferson Davis, Belford Company, NY, 1890). A Sea Raven Press Reprint. Spring Hill, TN: Sea Raven Press, 2020.

——. (ed.) *Prison Life of Jefferson Davis: Embracing Details and Incidents in his Captivity, With Conversations on Topics of Public Interest* (John J. Craven, Sampson, Low, Son, and Marston, London, UK, 1866). A Sea Raven Press Reprint. Spring Hill, TN: Sea Raven Press, 2020.

——. *What the Confederate Flag Means to Me: Americans Speak Out in Defense of Southern Honor, Heritage, and History*. Spring Hill, TN: Sea Raven Press, 2021.

——. *Heroes of the Southern Confederacy: The Illustrated Book of Confederate Officials, Soldiers, and Civilians*. Spring Hill, TN: Sea

Raven Press, 2021.

———. *Support Your Local Confederate: Wit and Humor in the Southern Confederacy*. Spring Hill, TN: Sea Raven Press, 2021.

———. *America's Three Constitutions: Complete Texts of the Articles of Confederation, Constitution of the United States of America, and Constitution of the Confederate States of America*. Spring Hill, TN: Sea Raven Press, 2021.

———. *Vintage Southern Cookbook: 2,000 Delicious Dishes From Dixie*. Spring Hill, TN: Sea Raven Press, 2021.

———. *The Bittersweet Bond: Race Relations in the Old South as Described by White and Black Southerners*. Spring Hill, TN: Sea Raven Press, 2022.

———. (ed.) *The Rise and Fall of the Confederate Government* (Jefferson Davis, D. Appleton, New York, 1881). 2 vols. A Sea Raven Press Facsimile Reprint. Spring Hill, TN: Sea Raven Press, 2022.

———. *I, Confederate: Why Dixie Seceded and Fought in the Words of Southern Soldiers*. Spring Hill, TN: Sea Raven Press, 2023.

———. *Twelve Years in Hell: Victorian Southerners Expose the Myth of Reconstruction, 1865-1877*. Cody, WY: Sea Raven Press, 2023.

———. *Seabrook's Complete Battle Book: The War Between the States, 1861-1865*. Cody, WY: Sea Raven Press, 2023.

———. *The Hampton Roads Conference: The Southern View*. Cody, WY: Sea Raven Press, 2024.

Steel, Samuel Augustus. *The South Was Right*. Columbia, SC: R. L. Bryan Co., 1914.

Steele, Matthew Forney. *American Campaigns*. 2 vols. Washington, D.C.: Byron S. Adams, 1909.

Stephens, Alexander Hamilton. *Speech of Mr. Stephens, of Georgia, on the War and Taxation*. Washington, D.C.: J & G. Gideon, 1848.

———. *A Constitutional View of the Late War Between the States: Its Causes, Character, Conduct and Results*. 2 vols. Philadelphia, PA: National Publishing, Co., 1870.

———. *Recollections of Alexander H. Stephens: His Diary Kept When a Prisoner at Fort Warren, Boston Harbour, 1865*. New York, NY: Doubleday, Page, and Co., 1910.

Taylor, Walter Herron. *General Lee: His Campaigns in Virginia, 1861-1865*. Norfolk, VA: self-published, 1906.

Thompson, Holland. *The New South: A Chronicle of Social and Industrial Evolution*. New Haven, CT: Yale University Press, 1920.

Trent, William Peterfield. *Robert E. Lee*. London, UK: Kegan Paul, Trench, Trübner and Co., 1899.

Walsh, John Henry. *The Horse: In the Stables and the Field—His Varieties, Management in Health and Disease, Anatomy, Physiology, etc.* 2 vols. London, UK: George Routledge and Sons, 1907.

Warner, Ezra J. *Generals in Gray: Lives of the Confederate Commanders.* 1959. Baton Rouge, LA: Louisiana State University Press, 1989 ed.

———. *Generals in Blue: Lives of the Union Commanders.* 1964. Baton Rouge, LA: Louisiana State University Press, 2006 ed.

Williamson, Mary Lynn. *The Life of Major Gen. J.E.B. Stuart.* Richmond, VA: B. F. Johnson Publishing Company, 1914.

Woods, Thomas E., Jr. *The Politically Incorrect Guide to American History.* Washington, D.C.: Regnery, 2004.

Young, Bennett Henderson. *Confederate Wizards of the Saddle: Being Reminiscences and Observations of One Who Rode With Morgan.* Boston, MA: Chapple Publishing Co., 1914.

Virginia Female Institute,

STAUNTON, VA.

MRS. GEN. J. E. B. STUART, Principal.

54th Session Opens September 16, 1897.

Located in the mountain region of Virginia, with its health-giving climate. High standard. Unsurpassed advantages in all departments. Home comforts. Terms reasonable.

Apply for Catalogue to the Principal.

1897 magazine ad for the Virginia Female Institute at Staunton, operated by Gen. Stuart's widow, Flora (Cooke) Stuart.

Confederate Gen. Thomas J. Jackson standing like a "stonewall" at the Battle of First Manassas.

INDEX

INCLUDES TOPICS, PEOPLE, KEYWORDS, KEY PHRASES, & SPELLING VARIATIONS

A
A. P. Hill Camp, 172
abolitionism, 302
abolitionist, 15
abolitionists, 15, 51
account, 42, 63, 68, 73, 78, 101, 128-131, 136, 142, 170, 171, 173, 183, 209, 216, 221, 233, 256
action, 25, 35, 52, 64, 70, 103, 115, 129, 131, 134, 136, 141, 155, 173, 184, 205, 221, 235, 284, 285
Adams, Richard H. T., 203
Adams, Samuel B., 255
adventure, 72
affair, 86, 88, 199, 220
Alabama, 283, 284, 286, 287, 290
Alabama (vessel), 290
Alder, Frank, 188
Alderson, J. Coleman, 151
Aldie, VA, 245
Alexander, Edward P., 69, 203, 235, 236, 246
Alexander's Artillery, 128
Alleghenies, 87
Allen, David H., 117
Allen, John, 118
alternative health, 335
America, 2, 3, 6, 8, 12, 14, 16, 17, 43, 52, 64, 67, 205, 287, 302-307, 309, 310
American Campaigns (Steele), 207
American liberty, 107
American Revolution, 46
American Revolutionary War, 13
American slavery, 2, 209, 308, 337
Americanism, 12, 206, 219, 227, 271
Americanism, defined, 16
Americans, 2, 15, 17, 18, 308, 309
Anderson, George T., 66, 195
Anderson, Joseph R., 179
Anderson, Richard H., 203, 204
Anglo-Saxon race, 254
animal, 74, 91, 173
animals, 226
Antarctica, 335
Appalachia, 335

apparitions, 85
Appomattox Court House, 57, 290
Appomattox, VA, 49, 83, 170, 196
Aquia Creek, 165
Arkansas, 115, 287
Arlington Heights, 89
armies, 23, 58, 84, 91, 101, 142, 157, 158, 174, 186, 209, 228, 231, 305
armory, 51
army, 8, 15, 21, 23, 24, 31, 33, 35, 36, 39, 46, 53-55, 57, 59, 61, 63, 66-71, 86, 87, 89, 92, 96-99, 115, 122, 124-128, 131-134, 139, 141-145, 150, 153, 157, 161, 164, 165, 171, 176, 179, 180, 182, 187, 188, 194, 197-199, 201, 203, 205-207, 209, 210, 214-216, 218-223, 225-227, 229, 231-233, 236, 243-247, 249, 250, 254, 255, 260, 264, 266, 268, 271, 272, 274-280, 283, 290, 301, 303-305
army of France, 145
Army of Northern Virginia, 21, 126, 131, 134, 139, 141-143, 150, 153, 187, 205, 209, 220, 222, 231, 249, 268, 271, 279, 290, 303-305
Army of Tennessee, 8
Army of the Potomac, U.S., 139, 165
Army of Virginia, 215
Arnold, Mrs. Eugenia H., 217
Articles of Confederation, 2, 16, 287, 308, 310
artillerymen, 223, 226, 240
Ashby, Turner, 107, 115, 142, 187, 244, 266
Ashby's Gap, 129
Ashland, VA, 165
asleep, 61, 178
astronomy, 335
Athens, GA, 187
Atkins, Chet, 335
Atlanta, GA, 201, 213
Atlee, VA, 177
attack, 51, 52, 59, 61, 64, 94, 95, 100, 101, 133, 183, 189, 212,

215, 226, 232, 235, 236, 239, 246, 256, 268, 283, 289
Augusta County, VA, 31
aunt, 247, 250, 261, 264, 266
Austin, AR, 190
Avary, Myrta L., 260, 262, 263, 266, 267
Averell, William W., 211, 212
Averett, Thomas H., 40
Ayers, Mr., 45

B
B. F. Johnson Co., 135
Babcock, Orville E., 77
Bacchus, 79
Bach, Johann S., 77
Bachelder, John B., 242
bacon, 236
Bacon, Elizabeth (Custer), 236
Baker, Lieut.-Col., 285
Baldwin, Col., 81
Ball, Dabney, 249
Baltimore and Ohio Railroad, 250
Baltimore Light Artillery, 171
Baltimore riot, 287
Baltimore, MD, 102, 129, 173, 175, 205, 224, 247, 250
banjo, 129, 246
Barboursville, WV, 134
Barnwell, Robert W., 247
Bartlett, Joseph J., 76, 218
Bartow, Francis S., 116
Battine, Cecil, 179, 278
battle, 2, 9, 14, 21, 25, 33, 35, 37, 47, 51, 52, 54, 55, 57, 58, 61, 62, 66, 70, 71, 73, 74, 85, 87-90, 93, 95-99, 102, 103, 107-110, 114, 117-119, 121, 125, 127-132, 139, 144, 152-159, 162, 169-171, 175-193, 195, 197-202, 204, 208, 209, 211, 212, 215, 218-221, 227, 229-233, 236, 237, 239, 243, 244, 246-248, 250, 251, 255, 258, 259, 264, 266, 268, 269, 272, 274-277, 279, 283, 286, 288-290, 302, 307-310, 312
Battle near Winchester, 289
Battle of Antietam, 250
Battle of Atlanta, 290
Battle of Baker's Creek, 289
Battle of Baton Rouge, 288
Battle of Beaver Dam Creek, 107
Battle of Bentonville, 290
Battle of Berryville, 159
Battle of Big Bethel, 287

Battle of Big Blue River, 290
Battle of Booneville, 288
Battle of Brandy Station, 129, 156, 157
Battle of Bristoe Station, 268, 289
Battle of Brook Church, 132
Battle of Bull Run, 251
Battle of Cape Hatteras, 288
Battle of Carnifix Ferry, 287
Battle of Carthage, 288
Battle of Cedar Run, 288
Battle of Chancellorsville, 21, 52, 70, 81, 95, 128, 133, 179, 181, 191, 198, 200, 215, 229, 246, 277, 280, 289
Battle of Charleston, 289
Battle of Chickamauga, 289
Battle of Cold Harbor, 215, 289
Battle of Cool Spring, 158
Battle of Corinth, 288
Battle of Cross Keys, 288
Battle of Cumberland Gap, 289
Battle of Dranesville, 88, 283-287
Battle of Drury's Bluff, 289
Battle of Elkhorn Tavern, 289
Battle of First Manassas, 117, 287
Battle of Fisher's Hill, 289
Battle of Fishing Creek, 288
Battle of Five Forks, 290
Battle of Fort Donelson, 288
Battle of Fort Sumter, First, 14
Battle of Fort Wagner, 289
Battle of Franklin (II), 290
Battle of Frazier's Farm, 288
Battle of Fredericksburg, 52-54, 60, 73, 93, 288
Battle of Front Royal, 288
Battle of Gaines's Mill, 288
Battle of Germanna Ford, 289
Battle of Gettysburg, 99, 135, 139, 146, 157, 195, 197, 201, 208, 216, 220, 221, 232, 289
Battle of Guilford Court House, 35
Battle of Hagerstown, 130
Battle of Hampton Roads, 289
Battle of Hastings, 179
Battle of Helena, 289
Battle of Island No. 10, 288
Battle of Jonesboro, 290
Battle of Kelly's Ford, 211
Battle of Kernstown, 288
Battle of Leesburg, 287
Battle of Malvern Hill, 288
Battle of Mansfield, 290
Battle of Mechanicsville, 107, 288
Battle of Missionary Ridge, 289
Battle of Monocacy, 289

Battle of Morris Island, 289
Battle of Murfreesboro, 288
Battle of Nashville, 290
Battle of New Hope, 290
Battle of New Market, 289
Battle of Newbern, 288
Battle of Oak Hill, 288
Battle of Ocean Pond, 290
Battle of Okolona, 290
Battle of Perryville, 288
Battle of Pleasant Hill, 290
Battle of Port Republic, 288
Battle of Port Royal, 288
Battle of Prairie Grove, 289
Battle of Reams's Station, 289
Battle of Rich Mountain, 287
Battle of Richmond (KY), 288
Battle of Savage Station, 288
Battle of Second Manassas, 53, 244, 288
Battle of Seven Pines, 209, 288
Battle of Sharpsburg, 53, 288
Battle of Shiloh, 288
Battle of Spotsylvania Court House, 274
Battle of Spring Hill, 290
Battle of the Shallow Ford, 37
Battle of the Wilderness, 116, 176, 184, 215, 274
Battle of Trevilian Station, 222
Battle of Vicksburg, 289
Battle of Williamsburg, 288
Battle of Winchester, 289
Battle of Yellow Tavern, 21, 48, 49, 54, 56, 102, 129, 132, 165, 170, 171, 174, 177, 186, 196, 205, 227, 250, 269, 274, 275, 279, 289
Battles of Spotsylvania Court House, 289
Battles of the Wilderness, 289
Bayard, Chevalier, 23
bayonet, 203
Beale, H. D., 250
Beale, Richard L. T., 54, 123, 141, 153
beard, 51, 60, 61, 71, 72, 74, 79, 85, 150, 179, 187
Beaufort, SC, 139
Beauregard, Pierre G. T., 26, 87, 116, 243, 251, 289
bedside, 80, 102, 103, 178, 179, 269
Bee, Barnard E., 116
bell, 71, 138, 186
bells, 209
Benning, Anna C., 144
Berryville, VA, 245

Beverly's Ford, 98, 188, 190
Bible, 3, 80, 202, 291, 308, 335
big government, 14
big house, 186
Billmyer, M. J., 173
biography, 2, 3, 302, 308, 335
bird, 25, 61
bird dogs, 25, 61
birds, 3
Birmingham, AL, 164
birth, 39, 42, 133, 137, 243, 268
bivouacs, 26
black Confederate, 8, 135
black Confederates, 135
Black Horse Cavalry, 76, 169
Black Horse Company, 211
Blackhall, Scotland, 43
Blaudell, Miss Estelle, 25
Bledsoe, Mrs. Sidney, 119
blockade, 172, 267, 287
blockade proclamation, 287
blood, 2, 24, 58, 61, 62, 64, 70, 77, 82, 102, 137, 138, 167, 169, 196, 204, 215, 229, 241, 265, 286, 308
Blue Ridge, 37, 87, 92, 197, 233, 245
Blue Ridge Mountains, 39
boar, 100
boat, 44, 194, 250
Bocock, Thomas S., 51
bodies, 47, 94, 206, 224, 232
body, 3, 36, 37, 47, 51, 63, 67, 72, 87, 91, 94, 97, 102, 112, 125, 130, 154, 155, 167, 173, 182, 185, 204, 208, 235, 240, 272-274, 283, 336
Bolling, Edith, 335
Bolling, Mary T., 163
Bond, Frank A., 131
bondage, 152, 208
Bonnie Blue Flag, 59, 62
Bonnie Blue Flag (song), 59
Boone, Pat, 335
boots, 59, 74, 85, 154, 184, 267
boots and saddles, 154
Borcke, Heros von, 64, 96, 259
Boston, MA, 83
Bottom's Bridge, 132
Botts, John M., 211, 265, 266
Bower, Charles, 138
Bower, the, 129
Bowles, James W., 149
boy, 33, 34, 42-45, 48, 49, 61, 66, 74, 161, 200, 202, 211
Boykin Rangers, 89
boys, 2, 26, 34, 40, 44, 66, 133, 147, 169, 173, 175, 178, 186, 192,

194, 195, 263, 307
Bradford, Gamaliel, 83
Bradford, Mr., 261, 264, 266
Bradwell, I. G., 219, 220, 222, 246
Bragg, Braxton, 101, 116, 177, 214
Brandy Station, VA, 97, 98, 118, 153, 218
Brantley, AL, 219, 220, 222, 246
breakfast, 141, 188, 248, 249
Breathed, James, 133, 134, 170, 241
Breckinridge, John C., 116
Brewer, Charles, 177, 269
bridges, 89
bridles, 276
Bristoe Station, 156
Bristoe, VA, 245
Britain, 13
British Army, 243
British Empire, 13
British military tanks, 27
Brock, Robert A., 198
Brook Church, 132
Brook turnpike, 124, 277
brother, 32, 39, 45, 125, 130, 177, 188, 236, 255, 269
brothers, 305
Brown, John, 21, 46, 51, 52, 63, 86, 202, 206
Bruce, Robert, 147, 173
Bruce, Robert the, 24, 179, 277
Brunson, J. W., 204
Buchanan, Franklin, 255
Buchanan, Patrick J., 335
Buckingham, Mr., 45
Buckland Races, 101
Bucktail rifles, 88
Bucktown Races, 268
Buell, Don C., 214
Buford, John, 187-190, 231
buglers, 124, 240
Bull Run, 193
Bull Run Mountains, 245
Bull Run, VA, 100
Butler, Benjamin F., 289
Butler, M. C., 136
Butler, Matthew C., 153
Butler, Otelia, 162

C
C.S.A., 8, 13, 46, 49, 64, 80, 82, 111, 113, 114, 116, 118, 121, 126, 131, 134, 144, 152, 154, 156, 166, 167, 170, 172, 180, 186, 191, 193, 195, 196, 199, 202, 203, 206, 211, 219, 220, 226, 235, 241, 244, 246, 255, 264, 303

C.S.M.A., 164
Cabell, J. Gratton, 118
cadets, 34, 114, 274
Caesar, 145
caissons, 284
Calhoun, John C., 37
Campbell Co., VA, 36
Campbell, Joseph, 335
Campbell, William, 126
Campbell, William J., 141, 142
camps, 26, 57, 133, 153, 201, 209, 218, 228, 260
capital, 49, 54, 99, 101, 114, 142, 150, 178, 254, 274
capitalism, 16, 17
Carlisle, PA, 197, 220, 225, 231
Carnton Plantation, 3, 287, 306, 307
cars, 97
Carson, Martha, 335
Carter, T. H., 203
Cash, Johnny, 335
Cashtown, PA, 231
castle, 56
Castleman's Ferry, 158
cat, 114
Catlett's Station, 91, 99, 220, 245, 255
cats, 3
Cauthorn, R. S., 123
cavalry, 2, 6, 8, 21, 23-27, 35, 40, 42, 51-57, 59, 60, 64, 67, 69, 71, 74, 77, 79, 80, 85-87, 89-91, 93, 97-102, 111-114, 116-120, 123, 126-129, 131-136, 139, 141, 143, 144, 147, 149-151, 153-158, 160, 165-167, 169, 171-177, 181, 184-193, 197, 201, 202, 204, 206-209, 211, 212, 214, 216-227, 231-237, 240, 242-247, 249, 254, 255, 257-259, 261-264, 266-279, 283, 285, 286, 290, 303-305, 309
Cavalry and Horse Artillery, Stuart's, 135
cavalrymen, 25, 26, 49, 83, 91, 129, 145, 148, 153, 201
Cedar Creek, 255
Cemetery Hill, 234
Cemetery Ridge, 150, 151
Centerville, VA, 193
central government, 12
centralists, 11
centralization, 17
Centreville, VA, 89, 285
chair, 55, 144, 261
Chambersburg, PA, 92, 128, 197, 231

Chambliss, John R., Jr., 233
champagne, 72
Chancellor, M. S., 122
Chancellor, Melzil, 120
Chancellor, Mrs. Sue, 218
Chancellor, Thomas, 119
Chancellorsville Court House, 200
Chancellorsville, VA, 90, 120, 191, 192, 203, 218
chapel, 305
Chaplains' Association, 268
character, 12, 18, 39-42, 55, 66, 70, 76, 81, 86, 102, 103, 113, 115, 143-145, 180, 207, 217, 272, 310
Charles City road, 89
Charles I, King, 43
Charles II, King, 37, 43
Charleston, WV, 151
charm, 49
Chase, Salmon P., 217
Chattanooga, TN, 118, 214
Chesapeake and Ohio Canal, 194
Chesapeake Bay, 272
Chester, James, 238, 240
Chevalier of the Southern Cause, 187
Chew, Roger P., 189, 196
Chew's Battery, 189
Chicago, IL, 229
Chickahominy River, 54, 55, 71, 75, 89, 90, 108, 132, 149, 214, 253, 273, 277
chickens, 194
child, 21, 35, 37, 75, 103, 134, 161, 202, 246, 335
children, 3, 35, 38, 45, 49, 56, 78, 80, 107, 129, 143, 227, 247, 272
Children of the Confederacy, 247
Childs, Buck, 130
Childs, Soper, 130
Christ, 3, 23, 268, 270, 304
Christian, 3, 17, 33, 39, 48, 54, 56, 82, 84, 111, 129, 143, 147, 160, 162, 202, 217, 254, 268, 302, 304, 308
Christian faith, 143
Christian ministry, 54
Christian officers, 268
Christian virtues, 33, 160
Christian, Julia J., 162
Christian, V. K., 147
Christianity, 3, 268
Christians, 39, 84
Christmas, 3, 135
church, 31, 33, 39, 80, 82, 102, 119, 124, 125, 132, 138, 156, 163, 179, 188, 209, 270, 273, 285,
304
churches, 45
Cincinnati and Ohio Railroad, 181
citizens, 13, 17, 93, 107, 135, 136, 143, 164, 258, 273, 274, 285
Civil War, 2, 3, 11-16, 23, 117, 286, 287, 301, 303-309, 335, 337
civilization, 204
Clark and Rockingham Companies, 118
Clark Cavalry, 117
Clarke County, VA, 248
clay, 303
cloak, 112, 113, 212
clothes, 61, 64, 74, 141
clothing, 60, 101, 244
Clyde, River, 43
coal, 267
coat, 60, 91, 154, 218, 244, 259, 260
Cobb, Howell, 116
Cobb, Thomas R. R., 116
Cobblers Spring, VA, 45
coffin, 273
collier, 117
Collier, W. A., 117
Colston, Capt., 81
Colston, F. M., 129
Colston, Raleigh E., 192, 193
Comanche Battalion, 189
combat, 58, 98, 99, 136, 258
Combs, Bertram T., 335
communion, 39, 45, 80, 179
communism, 15, 304
communist, 11, 15, 17, 304
communists, 13, 302
Company D, 175, 220, 221
Company E, 181
Company K, 149, 175, 177
Company Q, 208
Compson, H. B., 157
Concord, MA, 204
Confederacy, 2, 3, 17, 24, 25, 44, 48, 57, 61, 69, 116, 118, 126, 134, 142, 150, 152, 159, 179, 187, 196, 199, 208-210, 228, 247, 262, 267, 268, 271, 274, 276, 287, 301, 308-310
Confederate, 2, 3, 6, 8, 11, 12, 14-19, 21, 23-27, 31, 42, 50, 52, 53, 56, 62, 67, 69, 71, 72, 79, 84, 86-90, 95, 97, 98, 101, 103, 104, 107-109, 111, 112, 114-119, 122, 123, 126, 127, 129, 131, 132, 134-136, 138, 139, 141-152, 154, 157-162, 164, 165, 167, 168, 170, 174-176, 180, 181, 183,

185-187, 189, 190, 197, 201-210, 212, 213, 216-223, 225-239, 241-244, 246-251, 253-258, 260, 262, 264-266, 268, 270-274, 276, 277, 279, 280, 286-290, 300-312, 335, 337
Confederate arms, examples, 254
Confederate army, 21, 24, 69, 115, 161, 165, 223, 225, 226, 231, 301
Confederate artillery, 235
Confederate battery, 186, 238
Confederate Capital, 274
Confederate cause, 206
Confederate cavalrymen, 145
Confederate Congress, 273
Confederate flag, 2, 17, 243, 266, 308, 309, 337
Confederate forces, 53, 144, 234
Confederate generals, 14, 145, 168, 251, 264
Confederate government, 3, 15, 273, 287, 310
Confederate Historical Committee, 135
Confederate military, 303
Confederate monument, 50
Confederate navy, 21
Confederate Navy Yard, 21
Confederate pickets, 248
Confederate sailor, 145
Confederate service, 123
Confederate sharpshooters, 238
Confederate Southern Memorial Association, 164
Confederate States, 2, 3, 12, 16, 67, 86, 287, 302, 303, 306, 307, 309, 310
Confederate States of America, 2, 3, 12, 16, 67, 287, 302, 303, 307, 309, 310
Confederate train, 225
Confederate troops, 95, 108, 143, 239, 257
Confederate Veteran Education Committee, 135
Confederate veterans, 14, 15, 18, 26, 158, 164, 213, 230, 302, 305, 335
Confederate Veterans Reunion, 1907, 158
Confederate war, 115, 145, 213, 301
Confederate War Department, 213
Confederate women, 180
Confederate yell, 107
Confederates, 14, 88, 94, 135, 142, 155, 163, 166, 174, 198, 224,
231, 232, 236-238, 240, 274
confederation, 2, 16, 287, 308, 310
Congress, 6, 32, 37, 43, 51, 273, 287
consciousness, 3, 272
conservatism, 12, 16
Conservatives, 11, 12
consolidation, 12
Constitution, 2, 6, 14, 16-18, 27, 42, 86, 152, 246, 255, 282, 287, 303, 306-308, 310, 335
Constitution of the Confederate States, 2, 16, 287, 307, 310
Constitutional Convention, 37
Constitutional Conventions, 37
constitutional law, 304
constitutionalism, 16
Continental army, 31
conventions, 6
Conway, William B., 213
Cook, John E., 112
Cooke, Flora, 21, 46, 56, 58, 162, 227
Cooke, John E., 48, 52, 56, 70, 74, 78, 79, 134, 172, 183, 187, 195, 258, 261, 263
Cooke, John R., 46
Cooke, Philip St. George, 46, 56, 227
cooking, 249
Corinth, MS, 214
corn, 192, 245-247, 265, 266
corpse, 94
corpses, 110
Couch, Darius N., 203
couriers, Confederate, 242
cows, 194
Cox, Thelmar W., 62
Coxe, John, 187
Craige, Kerr, 132
Crawford, Cindy, 335
creeds, 335
Creek, 165, 197, 255, 257, 288, 289
Cress's Ridge, 237
cries, 76, 109, 145, 240
Crossland, Maj., 286
Crowell, TX, 216
Cruise, Tom, 335
Crutchfield, Stapleton, 124
Culpeper Court House, 97, 98, 128, 153, 181, 211, 212
Culpeper, VA, 248, 260, 266
Culp's Hill, 151
Cumberland County, VA, 36
Curtis, J. S., 140, 141, 143
Custer, George A., 133, 171, 174, 183, 187, 197, 235-238, 240
Custer, Thomas W., 236
Cutts, A. S., 283, 285

Cutt's Battery, 284, 286
Cyrus, Miley, 335

D
Dabney, Robert L., 96
Dan River, 37, 43
dancing on Sundays, 129
Dandridge girls, 129
Dandridge, Alexander S., 129
Dangerfield, F. A., 116
Davenant, Captain, 257
Davis, 26
Davis, Benjamin F., 188
Davis, Jefferson, 11, 12, 15, 67, 70, 102, 127, 139, 143, 160, 161, 168, 178, 207, 208, 214, 247, 255, 269, 273, 287
Davis, Jefferson H., 161
Davis, Varina A. "Winnie", 134
Davis, Varina H., 208
death, 3, 21, 26, 27, 33, 38, 46, 52-55, 57, 67-69, 71, 73, 76, 80, 83, 96, 101-103, 109-111, 114, 115, 122, 124, 128, 131, 134, 137, 141, 151, 165, 172, 174, 178, 179, 181, 186, 213, 227, 228, 241, 243, 253, 255, 268-272, 276, 280, 289
death-bed, 103
Debs, Eugene V., 11
debunk, 2
Declaration of Independence, 13, 16
Dee, River, 43
Deep Bottom, 198
Deering, John R., 117
Delaplane, VA, 220
Delaware, 224
Dement, T. J., 118
Democrat Party, right-wing, 17
Democratic Party, 11, 12, 17
demonstration, 142, 225
Depression, 136
Der Au, Miss Margaret L. von, 187
Desha, officer, 286
despair, 78, 167
despotism, 302
development, 68
Devil, 47, 57, 61, 87
dimensions, 94
dinner, 77, 96, 97, 100, 131, 155, 162, 259-261, 264, 265
Dinwiddie, Robert, 43
disaster, 72, 88, 302
disease, 118, 311
disloyalty, 49
disorder, 76, 88, 91, 123, 134, 185, 216, 284, 304

ditch, 75, 275
Dixie, 3, 25, 26, 59, 110, 139, 243, 310
Dixie (song), 243
doctor, 270
doctors, 122
dog, 96
dogs, 25, 44, 55
Doon, River, 43
door, 32, 38, 46, 63, 193, 203
Dorsey, Frank, 148, 174
Dorsey, Gustavus W., 147, 149, 170, 172, 173, 175, 177
Dover, PA, 207, 225
Dowdall house, 122
Dowdall Tavern, 120
Dranesville, VA, 283, 285
dread, 243
dream, 266
dreams, 39, 187, 198
dress, 156, 250
drinking, 87
Drury's Bluff, 102
DuBose, John W., 213
Dulaney, Richard H., 153, 154
Dumas, Alexandre, 75
Duvall, Robert, 335
dying, 50, 80, 94, 110, 111, 129, 143, 183, 202, 205, 209, 217, 244, 247

E
eagle, 137
Earl of Oxford, 335
Early, Jubal A., 116, 127, 197, 226
earth, 46, 89, 103, 110, 179, 184, 273
Easley, Ned, 119
education, 17, 18, 31, 36, 135
educational institutions, 122
educators, 335
Eighteenth Virginia, 285
Eighth Pennsylvania Cavalry, 120
election of 1896, 12
electricity, 260
Eleventh Virginia, 283, 286
Eleventh Virginia Cavalry, 156
Eleventh Virginia Regiment, 189
Eleventh Virginia Volunteers, 286
Eliason, Dr., 196, 259
Elijah, 195
Elkins, WV, 217
Ellis, Couriers, 177
Ely's Ford, 202
Elzy, Arnold, 116
Emmitsburg, MD, 92
Emory and Henry College, 33, 39, 40, 46, 51

empire, 13, 111, 116
employment, 52
Enfield guns, 186
enfranchisement, 302
engagement, 54, 174, 187, 189, 221, 224, 226, 238, 242, 245, 267, 284, 286
engineers, 186
England, 145, 243
English, 11, 13, 15, 96, 243, 288, 304
Englishman, 243
Enobarbus, 78
entertainment, 335
Episcopal church, 33, 39, 80
equality, 16
equestrian statue, Stuart's, 48, 135, 180
Essex Light Dragoons, 122, 123
European royalty, 335
evil, 17
Ewell, Richard S., 108, 112, 116, 197, 220, 231, 233, 235, 241, 251
experience, 94, 184, 221
experiences, 14, 243, 301, 302
eye, 48, 65, 79, 95, 96, 103, 113, 115, 117, 128, 137, 166, 167, 183, 203, 216, 230, 249, 267, 273
eyes, 44, 54, 56-58, 62, 71, 74, 75, 85, 86, 94, 96, 103, 107, 112, 115, 133, 151, 153, 155, 163, 179, 181, 186, 187, 201, 212, 219, 222, 240, 244, 253, 258, 259, 261, 265, 270, 271
Eyster, E. G., 242

F
Faded Old Letters (song), 59
Fair Oaks, VA, 215
Fairfax Court House, 140, 193
Fairfax Station, 193
farmer, 144
farmers, 149, 275
farms, 277
father, 2, 21, 32, 34-37, 41, 42, 44, 103, 219, 227, 246, 250, 308, 335
Fauquier Black Horse Company, 211
Fauquier County, VA, 220
Federal cavalry, 54, 211, 233
Federal Regular Artillery, 251
Federals, 88, 121, 124, 134, 155, 166, 183, 185, 186, 188, 189, 192, 212, 225, 226, 242, 250, 273, 274, 287
Feilden, H. W., 243
Ferry, Noah H., 239

fever, 103
field, 25, 35, 47, 48, 61, 73, 75, 81, 91, 93-95, 118, 120, 122, 124, 125, 131, 137, 139, 150, 155, 156, 166, 167, 170, 175, 177, 181-183, 185, 186, 193, 209, 218, 221, 226, 229-231, 235, 237, 238, 241, 242, 246, 259, 264, 265, 267, 269, 275, 276, 278, 284-286
Field, Charles W., 118, 186
Field's Brigade, 120
Fifth Michigan, 239
Fifth United States Regulars, 124
Fifty-fifth Virginia, 120
Fight at Berry's Ferry, 159
Fight at Buck Marsh, 159
Fight at Col. Morgan's Lane, 159
Fight at Gold's Farm, 159
Fight at Mt. Airy, 159
Fight at the Double Tollgate, 159
fire, 42, 52, 57, 58, 74, 97, 100, 101, 130, 137, 141, 163, 166, 185, 186, 189, 192, 198, 199, 201-203, 213, 237, 239, 240, 249, 256, 257, 259, 273, 278, 284-286
First Delaware Cavalry, 224
First Federal Army Corps, 231
First Kentucky, 284
First Kentucky Volunteers, 286
First Maryland, 240
First Maryland Cavalry, 174, 220
First Michigan, 240
First New Jersey, 238, 239
First North Carolina, 239
First North Carolina Cavalry, 235
First Regiment, 183
First Regiment of South Carolina Volunteers, 198
First Regiment Virginia Cavalry, 117
First Virginia Cavalry, 89, 149, 172, 173, 175, 177, 181, 197, 234
First Virginia Regiment, 150, 212
Fleetwood Hill, VA, 189, 211
Fleming, W. L., 247
floating, 56, 91, 97, 150, 155
Florence, SC, 247
Florida, 21, 287, 290
Florida (vessel), 290
Flournoy, Cabell E., 118
Floyd, John B., 144
Fontaine, John B., 177
Foote, Shelby, 335
foppery, 27
foreigners, 18
forest, 56, 87, 91, 181, 200, 279

Forney, J. H., 283-285
Forrest, Nathan B., 14, 26, 111, 115, 117, 119, 134, 142, 144, 148, 168, 204, 206, 214, 217
Fort Fisher, 290
Fort Harrison, fall of, 289
Fort Leavenworth, 39, 51, 227
Fort McHenry, 173
Fort Riley, 227
Fort Sanders, 77
Fort Sumter, 14, 224, 243, 287, 289
Fort Warren, 310
Fortress Monroe, 290
Founders, 31
Founding Fathers, 12, 17
Fourth Regiment, 181
Fourth Regiment of Virginia Cavalry, 211
Fourth Virginia Cavalry, 89, 135, 174, 220, 224
France, 24, 145
Fred (Stuart's bugler), 178
Frederick the Great, 202
Frederick, MD, 92
Fredericksburg, VA, 98, 112, 123, 155, 191, 198, 211, 212, 218
freedom, 33, 113, 152, 209
Fremantle, Arthur L., 68
Frémont, John C., 11
French, Jared, 213, 277
Froissart, Jean, 73
frontier Indians, 51
Fryingpan Church, 285
Fulton, J. H., 145
funeral, 102, 179, 228, 272, 273
funeral procession, 273

G
Gaines' Cross Roads, 143
Galahad, Sir, 24, 44
gallows, 38
Garland, S., 283, 284, 286
Garnett, Richard B., 135
Garnett, Theodore S., 48, 67, 158, 180, 280
gaslighting, 18
gastronomy, 335
Gayheart, Rebecca, 335
Geary, John W., 258
genealogy, 335
generals, Confederate, 168
George III, King, 13
Georgetown, MD, 141, 142
Georgia, 116, 285, 287, 290, 310
Gettysburg campaign, 207
Gettysburg, PA, 92, 128, 131, 193, 226, 237

ghost, 3, 187, 306
Gibson, Bruce, 275
Gibson, Pierre, 224
Gilkeson, H. S., 147
Gilman, Bradley, 206
girl, 32, 74, 79, 80, 112, 161, 163, 227, 249, 260, 301
girls, 78-80, 129, 164, 180, 258
Glencoe, Scotland, 43
gloom, 109, 115, 139, 176, 215, 272
God, 2, 3, 35, 47, 49, 50, 54, 56, 58, 67, 70, 79, 81, 93, 94, 102, 107, 110, 137, 143, 145, 179, 191, 202, 207, 208, 217, 244, 253, 269-271, 309
God of battles, the, 207
gold, 2, 5, 25, 47, 52, 74, 79, 85, 159, 218, 228, 259, 267, 279, 303, 335
Gold, Thomas D., 159, 279
golden spurs, 25, 52, 74, 85, 102
Goochland County, VA, 37
Goolrick, John T., 207
Goose Creek, 257
Gordon, James B., 26, 101, 112, 131, 132, 141, 150, 177, 178
Gordon, John B., 14, 18, 128, 206, 207
Gordon, John W., 158
Gordon, Maj., 286
Gordonsville, VA, 164
government, 3, 12-17, 60, 123, 143, 208, 209, 273, 287, 303, 306, 310
Gracey, Frank P., 115
Graham, John, 73
grain, 194, 234, 243
Grand Review, 153, 201, 265, 266
grandfather, 31, 32, 38, 51, 161
grandmother, 162
granite, 158
Grant, Ulysses S., 53, 132, 174, 176, 185, 194, 197, 209, 214, 222, 272, 274, 290
Grant's army, 274
grass, 58, 246
grave, 94, 102, 103, 110, 111, 138, 164, 229, 243, 273, 275
graves, 31, 158, 174, 180, 335
Graves, Robert, 335
Great Britain, 13
Green, Thomas, 26, 119
Greg, Percy, 179
Gregg, David M., 187, 189, 190, 236-238, 242
Gregg, J. Irvine, 143
Grey, Dan, 260, 262, 267

Griffin, Charles, 76
Griffith, Andy, 335
Groveland, CA, 187
Grumble Jones, 67
guerrillas, 47
Guilford Court House, 35, 51
gun, 2, 3, 32, 38, 101, 114, 133, 155, 177, 185, 189, 204, 214, 256, 308, 335
guns, 47, 49, 52, 58, 59, 62, 81, 93, 94, 97, 100, 101, 107, 114, 115, 133, 153, 156, 157, 166, 167, 170, 177, 179, 186, 189, 190, 199, 201, 207, 234, 238, 257, 267, 271

H
Haden, B. J., 183
Hagerstown, MD, 92, 131
Hairston, George, 38
Hamilton's Crossing, 201
Hammond, Capt., 172
Hammond, Wesley, 183
Hampton Roads Conference, 2, 290, 310
Hampton Roads, VA, 44
Hampton, Wade, 26, 47, 49, 97, 98, 119, 136, 139, 142, 153, 162, 169, 187, 188, 193-195, 204, 206, 222, 225, 232-235, 240, 264, 272, 278
Hampton's Brigade, 188, 226
Hancock, VA, 92
handkerchief, 196
Hanover County, VA, 122
Hanover Court House, 90, 124, 132
Hanover Junction, 274, 275
Hanover road, 238
Hanover, PA, 197, 224
happiness, 3, 113
harbour, 310
Hardee, William J., 116
Hardesty, Joseph R., 117
Harding, William G., 335
Harman, Asher W., 189
harmony, 128
Harpers Ferry, 46, 47, 51, 52, 86, 117, 287, 288
Harris, N. W., 172
Harrison, Julian, 118
Harrison's Landing, 132
Harry of Navarre, 203, 268
Hart, James H., 241
Hart's Ford, 255
Harvey, Dr., 131
Haskell, Alex C., 204
Hastings, UK, 243

hat, 52, 56, 57, 60, 64, 74, 79, 85, 91, 113, 149, 155, 156, 164, 180, 202, 212, 218, 242, 243, 267, 276
hate, 217
haunt, 243
haunted, 3, 187, 306
Hawkes, Bishop, 39
hay, 12, 247, 283, 305
Hayes, Joel A., Jr., 161
Hayes, Lucy W., 161
Hayes, Margaret H. D., 161
Hayes, William H. D., 161
Hazel Grove road, 122
health, 3, 85, 134, 311, 335
heaven, 54, 152, 179
hell, 2, 11, 71, 307, 310
Henderson, George F. R., 260
Henderson, Lizzie G., 164
Henry County, VA, 38
Henry IV, King, of France, 24
Henry of Navarre, 95
Herman, M. C., 196
heroism, 23, 26, 187, 207, 235, 254
Hicks's Hill, 123
Hill, Ambrose P., 26, 95, 107, 108, 116, 119, 121, 141, 145, 162, 167, 172, 174, 197, 203, 209, 231, 251
Hill, Benjamin J., 116
Hill, Daniel H., 108, 116, 141, 145, 174, 207
Hill, Mrs. A. P., 162
hills, 45, 107, 116, 129, 141, 145, 151, 174, 228
Hindman, Thomas C., 116
history, 2, 3, 6, 12, 14, 15, 17-19, 25, 31, 37, 43, 46, 48, 58, 117, 132, 134, 152, 154, 165, 180, 183, 198, 207-209, 214-216, 220, 226, 228, 232, 263, 265, 267, 271, 272, 287, 301-307, 309, 311, 335
Hoar, George F., 204
Hollywood Cemetery, 102, 158, 179, 180, 227, 274, 276
holy communion, 45
Homer, 73
Hood, J. M., 198, 201
Hood, John B., 116, 145, 186
Hooker, Joseph, 98, 108, 128, 198, 200, 203, 215
Hopkins, Luther W., 276
Horace, 73, 79
Horatius, 46
horse, 34, 45, 48, 54, 66, 72, 76, 79, 81, 89, 91, 93, 97, 98, 101, 102,

109, 112, 114, 117, 119-121, 125, 128, 133-135, 141, 144, 147, 149-151, 155, 164, 166, 169-173, 175, 177, 180, 183, 187, 188, 192-196, 204, 207, 211-213, 218, 231, 240, 242, 245, 247-249, 258, 262, 267, 276, 277, 285, 305, 311
horse artillery, 188, 207
horsemanship, 35
horses, 35, 44, 59, 60, 66, 67, 72, 74, 76, 78, 93, 101, 102, 112, 120, 126, 128, 133, 153, 172, 181, 188, 189, 194, 197, 200, 208, 213, 217, 221, 222, 225, 226, 233, 235, 240-242, 246, 249, 256, 259, 266, 267, 274, 285
hospital, 122, 174, 178, 242, 250
house, 3, 11, 32, 35, 38, 46, 51, 53, 57, 60, 87, 90, 94, 97, 98, 100, 107, 119-122, 124, 129, 132, 134, 140, 154, 155, 176, 177, 181, 185, 186, 191-193, 195, 196, 198, 200, 204, 211-213, 218, 238-240, 242, 243, 248, 269, 274, 277, 278, 284, 285, 289, 290, 303, 306
House of Representatives, 303
houses, 43, 90, 94, 97, 143
Houston, Sam, 37
howitzer, brass, 186
Hughes, Hannah, 37
human nature, 160
humor, 3, 37, 54, 55, 71, 79, 81, 263, 310, 335
hunt, 26, 38, 85, 117, 162, 232, 233
hunter, 32, 159, 200, 289
Hunter, Alexander, 159
Hunter, Jimmie, 200
Hunterstown, PA, 226
hunting, 65, 96
husband, 38, 54, 102, 103, 163, 227, 251

I
ignorance, 18, 336
ill, 75, 103, 229
Illinois, 31, 36
illness, 35, 243
immorality, 42
immortal, 23, 25, 56, 110, 144, 145, 169, 180, 215, 273
immortality, 23, 50, 134, 176, 270
independent thinking, 16
Indian country, 127
Indian raids, 34
Indian skirmish, 57

Indian warfare, 46, 64
Indiana, 114
Indians, 21, 51, 64
Indians, fight against, 21
individualism, 16
industry, 13, 14
infant, 38
insurance companies, 149
intelligence, 23, 36, 55, 68, 103, 283
investment, 260
Ireland, 3, 31, 35-37, 43
Irish, 58, 94, 116, 117
Irish blood, 58
Irish brigade, 94
iron, 51, 166, 167, 183, 249
Isaac, Uncle (black Confederate), 135
Ivanhoe, 73

J
J. E. B. Stuart Camp, 158
Jackson, Mrs. Mary A., 162
Jackson, Mrs. Stonewall, 162
Jackson, Stonewall, 21, 24, 26, 27, 54-58, 61, 68-70, 73, 74, 76, 83, 88, 90, 93, 95, 96, 107, 108, 111, 114, 117, 119-122, 128, 132, 134, 139, 141, 145, 148, 152, 164, 165, 174, 179, 180, 191, 192, 198, 199, 203-206, 208, 215, 217, 229, 244, 246, 251, 254, 255, 259, 260, 266, 275, 278-280
Jackson, TN, 111
Jackson's Brigade, 251
Jackson's Corps, 52, 69, 198, 203, 246
James City, VA, 126
James River, 44, 59, 272
James River Road, 132
Jeff Davis Legion, 89, 235, 239
Jefferson Barracks, 250
Jefferson Davis Historical Gold Medal, 2, 5, 335
Jefferson Davis Monument Association, 160
Jefferson Hotel, 160
Jefferson, Thomas, 11
Jenkins, Albert G., 231, 233, 234, 241
Jenkins's Brigade, 234
Jenkin's cavalry brigade, 231
Jesus, 3, 217, 246
jewels, 110
Jine the Cavalry (song), 55, 59
Johnson, J. J., 121
Johnston, Albert S., 26, 83, 111, 134, 139, 145, 152, 174, 204, 206, 251, 255

Johnston, Joseph E., 14, 26, 52, 64, 87-89, 111, 127, 134, 139, 141, 144, 145, 174, 204, 206, 209, 214, 255, 287, 290
Jones, Hilary P., 203
Jones, John, 304
Jones, John W., 109, 143, 270
Jones, William E., 27, 117, 144, 153, 154, 187-189, 191
Judaism, 84
Judd, Ashley, 335
Judd, Naomi, 335
Judd, Wynonna, 335

K
Kane, Col., 285
Kansas, 21, 46, 51, 64
Kelly's Ford, 98, 189, 211
Kennedy, B. F., 147
Kentucky, 16, 18, 37, 114, 115, 117, 283, 284, 286, 301, 335
Kentucky and Virginia Resolutions, 16
Keough, Riley, 335
Kerr, W. S., 147
Kiles, Mrs., 192
Kilpatrick, Hugh J., 100, 225, 235, 236, 268
Kilpatrick's Division, 225, 235
kindness, 208
Kinney, Ernest L., 239, 240
knight of the golden spurs, 25
Knoxville, TN, 77
Ku Klux Klan, 2, 308
Kyle, David J., 122

L
La Calprenède, 75
labor, 72, 123, 209, 306
Lacy Mill, 120
lake, 145
Lamar, Lucius Q. C., 116
lamp, 34
Lane's Brigade, 201
Langhorne, Maj., 286
Latane, Henry W., 122
Latane, John, 125
Latane, Susan A., 122
Latane, William, 122-125
laughter, 48, 56, 58, 62, 71, 72, 75, 76, 78, 80, 85, 96, 97, 103, 113, 165, 181
Laurel Hill, 32, 38
law, 3, 6, 21, 31, 36, 41, 107, 177, 227, 269, 288, 304
Law of Attraction, 3
lawyers, 148, 216
Le Mat revolvers, 25

Lechlider, Mr. (Confederate orderly), 131
Lee Camp Hall, 145
Lee, Fitzhugh, 26, 34, 40, 63, 67, 72, 74, 90, 97, 100, 101, 112, 118, 127, 136, 144, 145, 149, 153, 155, 169, 170, 175, 177, 187-189, 191-195, 197, 202, 203, 209, 211, 212, 217, 222, 226, 233-235, 239, 240, 253, 269, 271, 274, 278
Lee, George W. C., 33
Lee, Mary, 162
Lee, Mary A., 102
Lee, Miss Mary C., 243
Lee, Mrs. William H F., 163
Lee, Richard H., 107
Lee, Robert E., 21, 24-26, 33, 49, 51-53, 55, 57, 61, 63, 67-70, 73, 74, 79, 81, 86, 88, 89, 91, 93, 95, 97-99, 107, 108, 111, 112, 123, 128, 132, 134, 139-141, 143, 145, 150-153, 157, 162, 164, 165, 168, 174, 176, 180, 181, 188, 191, 193, 197-199, 201-209, 214, 216, 218, 221, 222, 226, 228, 231, 233, 243, 245, 246, 249, 254, 255, 266, 271, 272, 274, 276, 278, 280, 290
Lee, Robert E., Jr., 152, 163, 243
Lee, Stephen D., 158
Lee, William F., 247, 250
Lee, William H. F., 97, 98, 112, 119, 123, 153, 163, 187, 188, 222, 233, 234, 239, 278
Lees, the, 145
Leesburg, VA, 92, 283
Lee's army, 201, 274
Left-wing, 12, 14, 16, 17
lemons, 108
Letcher, Bethenia, 32, 38
Letcher, Giles, 37
Letcher, John, 37
Letcher, Robert P., 37
Letcher, Stephen, 37
Letcher, William, 32, 37, 38
Lewis, Richard, 220
Lexington, VA, 31, 144
Liberal party, 16, 17
liberalization, 17
liberals, 11-14
libertarian, 11
libertinism, 80
liberty, 7, 16, 31, 32, 43, 107, 110, 136, 152, 204, 208, 237, 302
Liberty Hall, 31

liberty, love of, 16
library, 6, 302
light, 18, 44, 57, 59, 87, 91, 94, 98, 101, 103, 113, 118, 122, 123, 127, 160, 165, 171, 192, 193, 204, 211, 218, 265, 267
Lincoln, Abraham, 11, 13-15, 17, 18, 58, 61, 123, 255, 287
Lincoln's War, 2, 3, 11, 13, 16, 18, 287, 308, 337
Lincoln's War (Seabrook), 16
liquor, 202
Litchfield, Connally T., 175
Little Rock, AR, 180
Little Round Top, 151
Little Sorrel (Jackson's horse), 108
Little's Run, 238
Lively (Kilpatrick's horse), 101
Lomax, Elizabeth W., 167
Lomax, Lunsford L., 118, 136, 149, 153, 156, 167, 170, 171, 175, 177, 181, 189
Londonderry, Ireland, 31, 35
Lone Star State, 141
Longstreet, James, 8, 14, 69, 71, 107, 128, 145, 150, 151, 164, 195, 197, 205, 231, 251
Longstreet's Corps, 128
Lord, 57, 80, 263
Los Angeles, CA, 197
Lost Cause, 306
Lott's house, 238
Louis XIV, King, 260
Louisiana, 247, 287, 311
Louisiana State University, 247, 311
Louisville, KY, 149
love, 2, 3, 16, 25, 27, 33, 35, 39, 45, 47, 49, 54, 58, 62, 67, 74, 75, 78, 80, 81, 83, 97, 102, 161, 163, 170, 177, 178, 180, 181, 187, 219, 220, 227, 253, 261, 263, 279, 307
Loveless, Patty, 335
Lowe, Private, 220
Lower Chickahominy River, 126
Loyalists, 32
Luray Valley, 244
Luray, VA, 230
Lyne, Mrs. William, 255

M
macadamized road, 277
Macaulay, Thomas B., 46
machine shops, 92, 214
Macon Telegraph, 290
magic, 25, 59
Magna Carta, 2, 287, 307

Magruder, John B., 116
Mahone, Mrs. William, 162
Mahone, William, 162
malice, 18
Manassas, VA, 47, 87, 90, 100, 114, 245
manhood, 23, 39, 44, 153, 202
Mann, Anna B., 268
mansion, 32, 44, 248
Manson, H. W., 112
marble, 64
markers, 158
Marmaduke, John S., 26, 116, 119
marriage, 3, 38, 209
Martin, Lieut.-Col., 284
Marvin, Lee, 335
Marx, Karl, 15
Marxism, 305
Mary, 35, 162, 163, 181, 208, 243, 274, 311
Maryland, 92, 126, 131, 139, 148, 149, 167, 170, 174, 175, 177, 183, 194, 195, 220, 223, 240, 247, 248, 267, 288, 289
Maryland (Stuart's horse), 25, 247
Maryland campaign, 131
Maryland cavalry, 167
Mason, George, 117
Mason, James, 288
Massachusetts, 204
Massaponnax Creek, 52
Maurice, Fredrick, 165
McCabe, W. Gordon, 243
McCarthy, Mayo, 158
McClellan, George B., 25, 55, 59, 71, 72, 89, 92, 122, 123, 126, 132, 164, 202, 205, 206, 209, 214-216, 252, 254, 255
McClellan, Henry B., 42, 48, 66, 136, 171, 177, 195, 196, 246, 250, 269
McClellan's army, 210
McClure, Alexander K., 128
McCormick, Cyrus, 254
McCulloch, Ben, 26
McDonald, William N., 256
McDowell, Irvin, 132
McDowell, Samuel, 35
McGavocks, 3, 287, 307
McGowan, Samuel, 199
McGowan's Brigade, 204
McGraw, Tim, 335
McGregor, William, 114
McIntosh, John B., 238, 240
McKim, Randolph H., 152, 209, 218
McLane, Lieut., 124
McNeilly, James H., 204

Meade, George G., 141, 142
meadows, 44
Meagher, Thomas F., 94
Mechanicsville, VA, 177
medicine, 122
Melrose, Andrew, 40
memorial, 158, 164, 273, 304
Memorial Day, 158
memories, 15, 18, 44, 57, 142, 145, 174, 176, 187, 266, 277, 302
memory, 7, 37, 39, 82, 115, 116, 122, 126, 138, 149, 150, 158, 161, 169, 174, 176, 243, 244, 271, 280, 304
Memphis, fall of, 288
men, 5, 24-26, 42-44, 47-49, 54-62, 64-67, 69, 71-75, 86, 88, 89, 92, 94-96, 98, 101, 102, 107-110, 112, 114, 115, 118, 119, 121, 123-131, 133, 134, 136, 138-144, 147-150, 152-155, 157, 164-167, 170-173, 175-180, 183-185, 187-190, 192-198, 200, 202-204, 206, 208, 209, 213, 215-222, 225, 226, 234, 237, 240, 241, 245, 246, 251, 253-255, 269, 271, 272, 274, 275, 277, 279, 285, 286, 301
Mercer Calvary, 124
meritocracism, 16
Merritt, Wesley, 171, 187
Methodist church, 33, 39, 80
Mexico, 86
Michigan, 237-240
Middleburg, PA, 207
Middleburg, VA, 258
military, 2, 9, 14, 18, 23-27, 32-35, 40, 42, 47-49, 52, 57, 58, 60, 63, 69, 86, 103, 105, 117, 127, 133, 142, 151, 159, 174, 179, 187, 201, 202, 204, 207, 211, 214, 236, 243, 255, 257, 271-273, 276, 278, 300-303, 307, 335
military escort, 273
Military Memoirs of a Confederate (Alexander), 236
military science, 142
military stores, 276
Miller, William E., 237, 239, 240
mills, 183, 224
Milroy, Robert H., 129, 258
Mineral, VA, 244
Minié ball, 101
Minor, Benjamin B., 33, 34
miracle, 94, 131

misery, 101
Missionary Ridge, 289
Mississippi, 214, 287-290
Missouri, 32, 36, 51, 115
mists, 181
Mitchell, S. W., 125
Mobile, AL, 114
Moffett, George H., 157
monarchy, 13
Monday, 145, 201
money, 80, 209
Montgomery, AL, 114, 227, 242, 246
moon, 3, 184
morality, 16
morals, 42, 54, 80
Morgan, John H., 26, 115-117, 119, 134, 139, 142, 144, 148, 194, 206, 217, 264
Morgan, Kitty, 162
Morgan, William A., 212, 213
Morrison, Mary A., 162
Morse, Miss, 264
Morton, A. S., 111
Morton, Mrs. Annie B., 139
Mosby, John S., 47, 67, 72, 91, 279, 335
Mosby's Confederacy, 91, 159
Moses, 107
Moss Neck, 96
mother, 3, 32, 33, 39, 44, 45, 49, 54, 63, 80, 111, 145, 163, 202, 211, 217, 229, 250, 335
Mount Ivory, VA, 45
mountain, 88, 92, 111, 120, 121, 133, 171, 178, 181, 182, 233, 287
mountains, 32, 39, 44, 47, 49, 144, 231, 244, 245, 335, 336
Mounted Rifles, 51
Mt. Carmel Fight, 159
mules, 61, 65, 76, 142, 194, 226, 253
Munford, Thomas T., 118, 136, 153, 170, 174
Murat, Joachim, 79, 133, 202, 228
Murry, John W., 224
music, 24-26, 49, 72, 77, 129, 165, 180, 190, 212, 246, 335
musicians, 335
Mussolini, Benito, 12
My Wife's in Castle Thunder (song), 56
Myosotis, 43

N
Napoleon gun, 114
Napoleon III, 53, 73, 74, 145, 204
national government, 17
National Peace Conference, 287

nationalism, 12
nature, 3, 33, 39, 63, 115, 127, 160, 184, 335
navies, 306
navy, 21, 254, 287, 306
Neese, George M., 277
negro, 59, 192, 256, 260
negro servants, 59
negroes, 209, 265
Nelson, Hugh M., 118
nephew, 67
New Jersey, 237-239, 241
New Jersey Cavalry, 237
New Mexico, 86
New Orleans, fall of, 288
New South, 310
New Testament, 3
New World, 37
New York, 14, 150, 156, 157, 190, 227, 301-306, 310
New York City, NY, 227
Newby's Cross Roads, 143
Newhall, Frederick C., 240
news, 58, 151, 159
newspaper, 73, 99
newspapers, 58, 63
Ney, Michel, 24
Nichols, the Tory, 38
niece, 264
night, 48, 54, 61, 64, 72, 75, 76, 78, 81, 89-91, 102, 103, 109, 113, 125, 126, 129, 133, 134, 136, 141, 170, 176, 177, 184, 189, 191-194, 196-199, 201, 203, 218, 221, 222, 224-226, 232-234, 244, 246, 256, 274
nightfall, 116, 177
nightmare, 58
Ninth Georgia, 285
Ninth Virginia Cavalry, 89, 123, 139
Ninth Virginia Regiment, 141
Norfolk Navy Yard, 287
North, 2, 3, 18, 32, 37, 38, 46, 52, 58, 62, 83, 93, 99, 108, 131, 149, 154, 177, 178, 181, 184, 192, 201, 202, 206, 214, 216, 224, 235, 239, 244, 255, 276, 280, 283, 286, 287, 301, 305, 308, 335
North Carolina, 32, 37, 38, 131, 177, 178, 202, 235, 239, 283, 286, 287, 301, 305, 335
North Carolina Cavalry, 286
Northern abolitionists, 15
Northern historians, 53
Northerners, 2, 308
Northernization, 17

Northwest, 171, 231, 238, 277
nullification, 37, 43
nullification crisis, 37

O
O'Mera, Jim, 116
Oak Shade, VA, 188
Obenderfer, Buddy, 221
occupation, 287, 290
ocean, 279, 290
Odenheimer, Mrs. Cordelia P., 126
officers, 8, 54, 56, 63-67, 69, 78, 87, 90, 94, 96, 97, 101, 102, 112, 117, 118, 120, 121, 123, 124, 127, 131, 134, 142, 144, 153, 159, 170, 179, 180, 186, 190, 204, 205, 207, 212, 235, 264, 268, 271, 273, 285, 286
Official Records, 305, 306
Ohio, 181, 194, 250
oil, 213, 277
Old Church, 124
Old Mountain road, 121
Old Osawatomie Brown, 46
Old Salem Church, 119
Old South, 2, 3, 16, 204, 310
Oliver, J. D., 149
Oliver, J. R., 175
Oliver, William A., 123, 124
onomastics, 335
opossum, 85
optimism, 72
Orange and Alexandria Railroad, 91, 193, 245
Orange County, VA, 119
Orange Court House, 90, 191, 198, 204, 248
Orange, VA, 255
Ord, Edward O. C., 88
Oregon, 157
Osawatomie Brown, 46, 64
ostrich feather, 56, 276
ostrich plume, 74
outlaws, 51
O'Mera, Jim, 116

P
Pacific coast, 157
pain, 149
painter, 42, 45
Painter, Mr., 45
palaces, 43
Palmer, W. Ben, 136, 147
Pamunkey River, 89
Pannill, David, 32, 38
Pannill, Elizabeth L., 32, 37, 38, 43, 51

Pappenheim, Graf G. H. von, 228
parade, 74, 158
paranormal, 335
Parkersburg, WV, 157
Parton, Dolly, 335
party, 11-13, 15-17, 51, 59, 65, 71, 73, 76, 113, 140, 143, 218, 220, 238, 240, 241, 303, 304
Pate, Henry C., 275
Patrick County, VA, 31, 32, 35-38, 51, 86, 202, 279
Patrick, VA, 43
patriotism, 16, 31, 114, 142
patriots, 18, 107, 255
Patterson, Francis E., 87
Paxton, Elisha F., 67
Payne, Elizabeth W., 167
Payne, William H., 118, 136
peace, 31, 64, 65, 88, 114, 129, 138, 148, 169, 198, 217, 274, 287
Peake, John W., 246
Pearl of the Gray, 137
Pegram, William M., 205
Pelham, John, 47, 114, 133, 211, 213
Pendleton, Lieut., 248
Pendleton, William N., 116, 207
Peninsular raid, 71
Pennington, Alexander C. M., Jr., 238, 240
Pennsylvania, 31, 35, 43, 59, 92, 93, 97, 120, 128, 131, 153, 183, 188, 223, 227, 237, 239, 242, 266, 289
Pennsylvania campaign, 97, 131, 227, 237
Pennsylvania, Confederate invasion of, 153
Pensacola, FL, 21
Perkins, Capt., 87
Perkins, Elizabeth, 37
Perkins, Nicholas, 37
Peterkin, Joshua, 179, 270, 273
Petersburg, VA, 83, 172, 260, 261
Peticolas, Arthur L., 229
Philadelphia Times, 167
Philadelphia, PA, 122
Phillips, Capt., 94
Pickett, George E., 116, 135
Pickett's charge, 135
Pike, Albert, 116
pillow, 2, 308
Pitts, Fred L., 149, 150, 173, 175
Pittsylvania County, VA, 37, 38
Pitzer, Capt., 283
Plane, Mrs. C. Helen, 116
plantation, 3, 39, 59, 198, 265, 287, 306, 307

plantations, 47
plantations, Southern, 47
planters, 148, 149, 216
Plasterco, VA, 50
Pleasanton, Alfred, 154, 155, 157, 187-189, 203, 236
plunder, 255, 256
Po River, 186
Poe, Orlando M., 76, 77
political parties, 11, 12
political party, 15
politically incorrect, 311
politics, 304, 335
Pollard, Edward A., 103
Pope, John, 61, 91, 92, 156, 164, 244, 245, 255
popular sovereignty, 17
Port Republic, 244
Porter, Fitz J., 108, 132
Portland, OR, 157
Potomac River, 87, 88, 92, 93, 99, 141, 151, 194, 197, 223, 224
powers, 113, 135, 158, 306
Powers, Dudley, 158
Powers, William D., 135
Powhatan Troop, 135
prayer, 84, 165, 179, 227, 244, 270
preachers, 54
presentism, 17
preservationist, 335
Presley, Elvis, 335
Presley, Lisa M., 335
Preston, John S., 168
Price, Sterling, 26, 116
pride, 34, 60, 66, 74, 97, 113, 117, 137, 138, 155, 210, 218, 229, 272
Prince of Wales, 114
prisoners, 76, 87, 89, 99, 126, 132, 140, 141, 185, 194, 195, 198, 225, 235, 242, 256, 276, 285
procession, 89, 273, 336
prophecy, 270
prostitution, 3
Providence, 41, 73, 276
provisions, 274
Prussian cavalry, 69
Purifoy, John, 227, 242, 246
purity, 24, 115
Purnell, W. S., 173

Q
queen of May, 79
Quixote, Don, 73

R
R. E. Lee Camp, 213, 243

Raccoon Ford, 67, 112
railroad bridge, 255
Ramseur, Stephen D., 265
Randol, Alanson M., 238
Randolph, George W., 179
Randolph, Mrs. N. V., 150
Rapidan River, 53, 67, 90, 119, 133, 134, 201
Rapidan Station, 248
Rapidan Valley, 248
Rappahannock Ford, 154
Rappahannock River, 53, 54, 56, 153, 154, 164, 188, 198, 201, 211, 213, 216, 233, 244, 255
Ravensdale, Cassidy, 6
Rebel Yell, 163, 184, 199, 200, 213, 266
rebellion, 123, 303, 305, 306
rebels, 58, 91, 107, 145, 157, 194, 255, 266
reconnoissance, 89, 93, 215, 246
Reconstruction, 2, 11, 302, 303, 310
Rector's Crossroads, 224
Reever house, 239
refreshments, 258
religion, 31, 39, 42, 80, 81, 84, 304, 335
religiosity, 82
Renfroe, John D., 115
Republican Party, 11-13, 16, 17, 303
republicanism, defined, 16
restricted government, 16
reunion, 15, 18, 118, 158, 160, 163, 242, 305
revenge, 164
Revere, Paul, 159
revolution, 15, 17, 31, 32, 46, 305
Revolutionary War, 13, 31, 32, 35, 37, 51, 335
revolvers, 153
Rich Mountain, 88
Richardson, John, 306
Richmond City Council, 279
Richmond lines, 89
Richmond Medical College, 122
Richmond Reunion, UCV, 160
Richmond Times, 145
Richmond, VA, 33, 36, 37, 49, 53, 58, 61, 79, 89, 91, 97, 101, 102, 110, 118, 124, 126, 131, 132, 134, 135, 138, 143, 145, 150, 158, 160, 163-165, 176, 177, 179, 185, 187, 199, 205, 209, 213, 214, 222, 227, 243, 250, 254, 267, 269, 270, 272-274, 276, 277
river, 37, 38, 43, 44, 53, 54, 59, 79, 89, 93, 98, 99, 111, 119, 125, 132, 149-151, 154, 155, 157, 164, 186, 188, 189, 192, 194, 195, 198, 200, 201, 206, 211, 213, 223, 224, 233, 244, 253, 290
Roanoke Island, 288
Robbins, Lieut., 75
Roberts, W. P., 136
Robertson, Beverly H., 82, 187, 189, 223, 231, 244
Robertson, Mrs. W. B., 50
Robinson, Beverly, 118
Robinson, Leigh, 210
Rock of Ages (song), 179
Rockville, MD, 141, 142, 194, 197, 223
Rocky Mountains, 335, 336
Rodenbough, Theophilus F., 83, 128
Rodes, Robert E., 95, 100, 150, 192, 203
Rogers, James, 240
Roland, 179
Roller, Dr., 147
Roman army, 145
romance, 72
room, 33, 34, 113, 160
rooms, 160
Ross, E. B., 115
Rosser, Thomas L., 153, 256
Rucker, Edmund W., 335
ruins, 32, 162
Rummel farm, 238
Rummel, Mr., 241
Rummel's lane, 241
Rupert, Prince, 24, 79, 111, 202, 268

S
S.C.V., 147
Sabbath, 81, 200
saber, 207
sabers, 153
saddles, 153, 276
sailor, 145
Salem Depot, 222
Saturday, 76, 81, 129, 209
Sayers, Robert, Jr., 145
Scheibert, J., 65, 68, 69
Schmidt, Karl von, 69
school, 31, 33, 36, 39, 40, 45, 49, 161, 183, 227, 303
Schuyler, Leonora S. G. R., 228
science, 142, 301, 335
scientific method, 17
Scotch descent, 31
Scotch-Presbyterian, 35
Scotland, 31, 43, 44, 301

Scott, George C., 335
Scott, W. N., 147
Scott, Walter, 73, 75
SCV, 5
sea, 3, 5, 6, 15, 181, 290, 307-310, 336, 337
Sea Raven Press, 3, 5, 6, 15, 307-310, 336, 337
Seabrook, Lochlainn, 2, 3, 27, 306, 335, 337
seceded states, 287
secession, 2, 13, 208, 246, 247, 255, 287, 303, 306, 309, 337
Second Corps, 179
Second Regiment, 181
Second South Carolina, 184
Second United States Dragoons, 56
Second Virginia Cavalry, 174
Secrest, Lieut.-Col., 283, 286
Seddon, James A., 66
Sedgwick, John, 52, 64, 205, 278
Seidlitz, Anton F. von, 202
self-government, 209
Selvage, Edwin, 220
Seneca Creek, 197
Seneca Falls, NY, 223
servant, 23, 134, 220, 260
servants, 59, 96, 218
Seven Days' Battle, 131
Seventh Michigan, 239
Seventh Michigan Cavalry, 237
Seventh Virginia Cavalry, 154, 255
Sévigné, Madame de, 75
Shakespeare, William, 75
Sharpsburg, MD, 131
sharpshooters, 82, 93, 130, 186, 189, 211, 212, 225, 233, 234, 238, 284
Shelby, Joseph O., 26, 115, 119
Shenandoah, 109
Shenandoah Valley, 57, 132
Shephard (soldier, CSA), 248
Shepherdstown, VA, 250
Shepherdstown, WV, 173, 247, 250
Sheridan, Philip H., 53, 101, 109, 132, 165, 171, 174, 176, 177, 181, 187, 222, 254, 269, 270, 274
Sherman, TX, 143
Sherman, William T., 148, 174, 216, 217
Sherman's march to the sea, 290
Shields, James, 244
ship, 59
ships, 44
shops, 92, 128, 214
Shreveport, LA, 62

sighs, 73
Simms, W. M., 122
Simonson, Maj., 127
Simpson, W. F. Lee, 251
sing, 270
singing, 34, 45, 55, 71, 72, 79, 96, 109, 158, 179, 180, 246, 263
sister, 45, 46, 49, 162, 218, 250
sisters, 44, 45, 218, 335
Sixteenth North Carolina Infantry, 202
Sixth Michigan Cavalry, 238
Sixth New York Battery, 190
Sixth South Carolina, 283, 284, 286
Sixth South Carolina Volunteers, 286
Sixth Virginia Cavalry, 188, 246
Skaggs, Ricky, 335
skirmish, 57, 165, 177, 189, 192, 199, 237
Skylark (Stuart's horse), 91
Slaughter Mountains, 244
slave, 152, 208, 209
slave power, 208
slavery, 2, 15, 152, 208, 209, 302, 306, 308, 337
slavery and Stuart, 208
slaves, 152, 208, 209, 303
sleep, 34, 58, 64, 72, 78, 88, 91, 109, 164, 184, 225, 246, 249, 270, 272
sleeping, 90, 111, 229
Slidell, John, 288
Smith, Channing M., 220
Smith, Edmund K., 116, 207
Smith, Gustavus W., 116
Smith, W., 207
Smith, W. N., 207
Smythe, Gerald, 243
socialism, 12, 15, 304, 305
socialist, 11, 15-17, 52, 304, 306
socialists, 13, 51
soldiers, 2, 3, 27, 33, 48, 52, 57, 58, 64, 65, 72-74, 82, 87, 94, 100, 107, 135, 136, 143, 145, 152, 157, 160, 161, 192, 194, 198, 200, 201, 208, 209, 216, 238, 249, 258, 260, 263, 271-273, 276, 290, 300, 305, 309, 310, 335
Sons of Confederate Veterans, 15, 230, 335
soul, 3, 42, 47, 50, 102, 111, 128, 137, 163, 165, 205, 263, 305
souls, 57, 103, 179
sounds, 46, 89, 109, 111, 129, 286
South, 2, 3, 5, 13, 14, 16-18, 24, 28, 39, 46, 47, 52, 83, 95, 97, 111, 114, 121, 122, 135, 142, 148,

152-154, 170, 184, 196, 198, 204, 206-209, 215, 216, 222, 228, 238, 243, 248, 255, 277, 279, 283, 284, 286-290, 303, 305, 306, 309, 310, 335
South Carolina, 170, 184, 198, 283, 284, 286, 287
Southern armies, 152, 209
Southern cause, 3, 16, 23, 27, 159, 187, 254, 271, 278, 309
Southern Confederacy, 2, 3, 17, 25, 48, 152, 209, 210, 274, 308-310
Southern Cross, 152
Southern Historical Society Papers, 172
Southern states, 145, 208, 303
Southern Troopers Song, 27
Southerners, 2, 3, 11, 13, 14, 16, 23, 44, 73, 287, 310
Southland, 125, 153, 228, 229, 253
Spangler house, 240
Spangler's house, 238
Spartans, 145
Spencer, C. R., Jr., 207
spies, 69, 159
Spirit, 3, 25, 26, 39, 45, 46, 48, 64, 68, 70, 72-74, 102, 103, 125, 128, 145, 176, 204, 219, 220, 222, 233, 243, 246, 272, 336
spirits, 23, 34, 45, 54, 80, 96, 117, 122, 128, 180, 215, 263
Spotsylvania Court House, 53, 132, 176, 181, 185, 195, 196, 274
Spotsylvania, VA, 116, 124, 186
spurs, Stuart's, 250
squirrel, 117
St. James Church, 179, 188, 273
St. Louis, MO, 39, 250
St. Paul, MN, 111
Stallsmith farm, 237
Standard Encyclopedia, 274
Stars and Bars, 47, 139
starvation, 94
states' rights, 11, 12, 16
Staunton, VA, 36, 196, 227
Steele, Matthew F., 132, 207
Stephens, Alexander H., 11, 14, 287, 335
Stevensburg, VA, 211
Stiles, John C., 208
Stoneman, George, 92
Stonewall Brigade, 145
Strahan, Charles, 244
Strickler, H. M., 230
Stuart Horse Artillery, 81, 89, 133
Stuart monument, 158, 159
Stuart, Alec, 45

Stuart, Alexander, 31, 35, 51
Stuart, Alexander H. H., 35
Stuart, Archibald, 31, 32, 35, 36, 38, 41, 43, 51, 63
Stuart, Elizabeth, 54
Stuart, Flora, 54, 80, 100, 102, 227, 270, 271, 312
Stuart, Flora (daughter), 21
Stuart, James E. B., 8, 23-27, 31-34, 36, 37, 39-41, 45, 47, 49, 51-53, 55, 56, 58-60, 62-64, 66, 68-71, 73-80, 85-88, 90-97, 99-101, 103, 104, 107-119, 122, 125, 127, 129, 131, 133-136, 138, 139, 141-145, 147, 148, 150-160, 164-166, 168-171, 173-177, 179-188, 190-201, 203-207, 209, 212, 214, 217-222, 225-229, 231, 233-237, 242-256, 259, 261-263, 266, 268, 270-272, 274-283, 286, 312
Stuart, James E. B., II, 21, 227, 253
Stuart, Mrs. J. E. B., 44, 160, 162, 172
Stuart, Philip St. George Cooke, 21
Stuart, Virginia P., 21
Stuart's Horse Artillery, 277
Stuart's Cavalry, 131, 132, 181, 185, 187, 227
Stuart's cavalry corps, 221
Stuart's Confederate Cavalry, 207
Stuart's Equestrian Monument, 279
Stuart's Horse Artillery, 114
Stuart's lightning horse-hitcher, 34
Stubbs, William, 11
students, 39, 40
Sturgis, H. H., 201
suffering, 134, 149, 152, 193, 209
sugar, 202
Sumner, Edwin, 51
Sumter Flying Artillery, 283
sun, 47, 89, 97, 109, 110, 133, 138, 154, 181, 203, 211, 215, 222, 240, 248, 250, 254, 259
Sunday, 45, 81, 126, 129, 199, 246
Sunshine Sisters, the, 335
supper, 131, 184, 218
supply trains, 99
Surrey of Eagle's Nest (Cooke), 195
Sweeney, Joe, 52, 55, 56, 58, 77, 86, 129, 263
Sweet Evelina (song), 55, 59, 263
Sydnor, T. W., 135

T
Taliaferro mansion, 248

Talladega, AL, 114
Talley, James, 120
Tattnall, Josiah, 255
Taylor, Charles E., 268
Taylor, Clifford M., 139
Taylor, Richard, 14
Taylor, Thomas H., 283, 284, 286
Taylor, Walter H., 114, 220
Taylor, William, 117
telegram, 103
telegraph, 61, 147, 159, 172, 177, 223, 277, 290
Telegraph Road, 277
telegraph station, 61
Tennessee, 3, 8, 115, 214, 287, 307, 335
Tenth Alabama, 284
Tenth Alabama Regiment, 286
Tenth Alabama Volunteers, 286
Terrail, Pierre, 23
terror, 26, 38, 71, 75, 119, 220, 243, 256, 258
Texas, 37, 46, 51, 112, 114, 140, 287
The Bittersweet Bond (Seabrook), 16
The Bugles Sang Truce (song), 56
The Campaigns of Stuart's Cavalry (McClellan), 171
The Crisis, 179, 240, 301
The Crisis of the Confederacy (Battine), 179
The Dew Is on the Blossom (song), 56
the East, 194, 233, 244, 250
The Farmer, 144
the Left, 17, 18, 53, 114, 116, 120, 122, 124, 130, 141, 147, 171, 172, 175, 177, 181, 184-186, 192, 233, 234, 236, 238, 240, 246, 283, 284, 286
the North, 2, 46, 58, 93, 99, 108, 149, 154, 177, 178, 181, 201, 214, 216, 255, 276, 308
The Rise and Fall of the Confederate Government (Davis), 15
The Sentinel, 221
The South, 13, 14, 18, 24, 28, 39, 46, 47, 95, 97, 111, 121, 122, 135, 142, 148, 152-154, 204, 206-209, 215, 216, 222, 228, 243, 255, 290, 303, 305, 306, 310
The Vineyard Fight, 159
the West, 21, 88, 244
Third Pennsylvania, 239
Third Pennsylvania Cavalry, 237, 242
Third Regiment, 181, 185, 186
Third Virginia Cavalry, 174, 255
Thirteenth Amendment, 209

Thirty-Fifth Battalion of Virginia Cavalry, 189
Thirty-third Virginia, 251
Thirty-third Virginia Infantry, 247
Thomas, George H., 174
Thompson, John R., 125
Thoroughfare Gap, 245
those people (Yankees), 151
Throckmorton, J. A., 118
Thursday, 124, 234
timber, 124, 192, 194, 240
Timrod, Henry, 46
Tinkling Spring Church, 31
Tinsley, Alexander L., Jr., 247, 251
Tinsley, Alexander, Sr., 250
tobacco, 54
Todd Tavern road, 195
tools, 144
Tories, 32, 37, 38
traditionalism, 12, 16
traitors, 107, 255
Traveler (Lee's horse), 150, 151
travels, 183
tree, 43, 49, 89, 121, 185, 196, 199, 200
trees, 32, 111, 199, 272
Treichel, Charles, 240
Trent (vessel), 288
Trent Affair, 288
Trent, William P., 205
Trenton, NJ, 138
Trimble, Isaac R., 66, 82, 203
Troop K, 172, 173
trousers, 218
truth, 13, 17-19, 49, 107, 111, 152, 166, 185, 304, 336
Tuesday, 201
Tunbridge Wells, UK, 243
Turkey, 260
Turner, Mrs. H. S., 158
Twelve Years in Hell (Seabrook), 11
Twenty-second Virginia Battalion, 120

U
U.C.V., 18, 164
U.D.C., 19, 25, 26, 126, 150, 162, 164, 244
U.S.A., 13, 14, 16, 92, 98, 123, 132, 148, 165, 211, 227, 251, 290
uncle, 8, 45, 135, 306
Uncle Isaac; or Old Days in the South (Powers), 135
Union, 2, 6, 11, 12, 15, 21, 25-27, 48, 57, 58, 61, 71, 73, 128, 132, 142-144, 174, 182, 183, 198, 205, 209, 216, 217, 221, 224, 227, 236, 247, 255, 290, 302,

303, 305, 306, 309, 311
Union army, 61, 132, 144, 198, 205, 255
Union forces, 227
Union generals, 58, 142
Union Mills, MD, 224
Union Mills, VA, 183
Union pickets, 221
United Confederate Veterans, 14, 15, 18, 158, 164, 305
United Daughters of the Confederacy, 116, 126, 268
United States, 2, 6, 12, 16, 32, 33, 36, 39, 40, 43, 46, 51, 56, 60, 63, 76, 93, 124, 127, 152, 163, 198, 202, 218, 246, 250, 278, 287, 302, 303, 305, 306, 310
United States Army, 36, 246, 278
United States Ford, 198, 218
United States government, 60
United States Marines, 51
United States Military Academy, 33, 40, 202
United States of America, 2, 6, 16, 43, 287, 305, 306, 310
University of Virginia, 122
Upperville, VA, 259
Utah, 285

V
Valentine, Edward V., 104, 281
Vallentine, Mrs. Mark, 180
Valley of Virginia, 113
Van Dorn, Earl, 116
Van Wert house, 121
Vaughan, B. B., 172
Venable, Charles S., 177
Verdiersville tavern, 155
Verdiersville, VA, 60, 90, 91, 112, 113
Versailles, France, 260
Veteran Cavalry Association, 136, 150, 158
Victorian Southern women, 24
Victorians, 23
violence, 75, 231
Virginia, 8, 16, 21, 27, 31, 35-37, 40, 43, 44, 46, 51, 56, 57, 60, 61, 73, 82, 85-89, 91, 99, 101, 111, 113-118, 120, 122-126, 129, 131, 134, 135, 139, 141-144, 147, 149, 150, 153, 154, 156, 158-160, 162, 163, 169, 172-175, 177, 181, 183, 187-189, 197, 205, 209, 211, 212, 215, 217, 220, 222, 224, 227, 229, 231, 234, 235, 239,

240, 243, 246, 247, 249, 251, 255, 260, 265, 268, 271, 272, 279, 281, 283-290, 301-305, 310, 312, 335
Virginia Female Institute, 312
Virginia Military Institute, 211
Virginians, 150
vision, 49, 187
voice, 5, 34, 40, 46, 49, 55, 56, 60, 65, 72, 87, 89, 102, 127, 131, 133, 137, 151, 155, 179, 180, 203, 209, 212, 216
voices, 23, 133

W
wages, 209
Wagner, Captain, 240
Wales, 37, 114
Waller, R. Page, 227
Waller, Thomas, 123
Waller, Virginia S., 160
war, 2, 3, 6, 8, 9, 11-18, 21, 23-27, 31, 32, 35-37, 39, 47, 51, 56, 58, 60, 64-66, 70, 71, 74, 77, 79, 85-89, 93, 94, 96-99, 103, 113, 115-119, 124, 134, 143-145, 148, 149, 152, 159, 169, 170, 173, 178-180, 187, 189, 197, 204, 207-209, 211, 213, 214, 216, 218, 227, 243, 245, 249, 250, 264, 271, 276-278, 282, 286, 287, 301, 303-310, 335, 337
War Between the States, 2, 15, 51, 211, 213, 214, 227, 243, 250, 287, 303, 310
War Department, 173, 180, 214
War for Southern Independence, 11, 14
War for the Constitution, 6, 14, 27, 86, 282, 335
War of 1812, 32, 36
Ware, Jaquelin S., 217
Waring, William L., 123
Warren, Gouverneur K., 185
Washington, 6, 12, 13, 31, 36, 38, 51, 59, 77, 92, 99, 125, 129, 141, 158, 162, 163, 175, 194, 197, 208, 223, 264, 287, 301, 303, 306, 310, 311
Washington and Baltimore Railroad, 99
Washington and Lee University, 31, 36
Washington City, 51
Washington College, 31, 36
Washington County, VA, 175

Washington, D.C., 6, 59, 92, 99, 141, 158, 197, 208, 223, 264, 301, 303, 310, 311
Washington, George, 13
water, 134, 141, 161, 192, 193, 223
Waterloo Bridge, 255
Waters, Tom, 175
Watson, Thomas J., 150
wealth, 3
Weekly Sun, 250
Weller, Ben, 150, 191-193, 195, 197
Wellington, Arthur, 145
Welsh, 37
Welsh extraction, 37
Welsh families, 37
West Point, 24, 33-35, 40, 42, 46, 51, 57, 63, 86, 114, 202, 274
West Pointers, 205
West Tennessee, 214
West Virginia, 134, 335
Western states, 86
wheat, 116, 266
Wheatley, Charles, 147, 149, 173, 177
Wheeler, Joseph, 26, 119, 142, 166, 204, 206, 214
Whig party, 12
Whigs, 37, 38
whirlwind, 156, 257
White House, 11, 132
White House, VA, 132
white labor, 209
White, Elijah V., 189, 195
Whiteville, NC, 207
White's Ford, 93
Whitsett, W. H., 213
Wickham, William C., 170, 175, 181, 194
Wickham's Brigade, 211
wife, 31-33, 35, 38, 39, 43, 45, 54, 56, 58, 80, 100, 102, 129, 130, 160, 163, 167, 179, 208, 227, 236, 250, 261, 263, 264, 270, 301, 335
Wilcox, Cadmus M., 116
Wiles, J. R., 111
Wilkins, Charles, 288
Wilkinson, Myrtle H., 244
Williams, Camille, 111
Williamsburg, VA, 33
Williamson, Mary L., 35, 274
Williamsport, VA, 92
Willich, August von, 15
Wilson, Woodrow, 335
Wiltshire (soldier, CSA), 248
Winchester, VA, 87
window, 58, 61, 91, 267

windows, 180
wine, 44, 45, 72, 80
wisdom, 35, 42
Wise, Henry A., 37, 116
Withers, Jones M., 116
Witherspoon, J. G., 216
Witherspoon, Reese, 335
witness, 12, 95, 115, 160, 201, 203, 240, 286
witnesses, 286
Wolf's Hill, 238
Womack, Lee Ann, 335
womanhood, 32, 44
women, 2, 3, 24, 25, 43, 49, 52, 58, 78, 79, 109, 113, 126, 129, 143, 150, 159, 180, 228, 243, 268, 308
women, Southern, as spies, 159
woods, 11, 75, 88, 89, 91, 93, 101, 107, 112, 113, 119, 120, 122, 124, 149, 175, 184-186, 201, 233, 237, 240, 241, 256, 260, 268, 279, 311
Woodward, Maj., 284, 286
wounding, 81, 119, 170-172, 174, 181, 199, 289
wounds, 110, 118, 187, 201, 205
Wright, William, 149
writing, 3, 15, 45, 48, 58, 66, 70, 73, 76, 160, 335
Wyoming, 5, 6, 27
Wytheville, VA, 33, 39

Y
Yadkin River, 37
Yankee Cause, 94
Yankee myth, 2, 308
Yankees, 103, 119, 131, 149, 151, 199-201, 213, 217, 244, 262
Yellow Tavern Road, 175
Yellow Tavern, VA, 129, 132, 165, 181, 242, 277
York Pike, 237
York, PA, 197, 225
Young, Bennett H., 17, 119, 142, 206
Young, Pres, 153
Young, S. W., 188
Young, T. J., 190

MEET THE AUTHOR-EDITOR

NEO-VICTORIAN SCHOLAR LOCHLAINN SEABROOK, a descendant of the families of Alexander Hamilton Stephens, John Singleton Mosby, Edmund Winchester Rucker, and William Giles Harding, is a 7th generation Kentuckian and one of the most prolific and widely read writers in the world today. Known by literary critics as the "new Shelby Foote," the "American Robert Graves," and the "Southern Joseph Campbell," and by his fans as the "Voice of the Traditional South," he is a recipient of the United Daughters of the Confederacy's prestigious Jefferson Davis Historical Gold Medal, and is considered the foremost Southern interpreter of American Civil War history—or what he refers to as the War for the Constitution (1861-1865). A lifelong nonfiction writer, the Sons of Confederate Veterans member has authored and edited books ranging in topics from history, politics, science, comparative religion, spirituality, astronomy, entertainment, military, biography, mysticism, and Bible studies, to nature, music, humor, gastronomy, etymology, onomastics, mysteries, alternative health, comparative mythology, genealogy, Christian history, and the paranormal; books that his readers describe as "game changers," "transformative," and "life altering."

One of the world's most popular living historians, he is a 17th generation Southerner of Appalachian heritage who descends from dozens of patriotic Revolutionary War soldiers and Confederate soldiers from Kentucky, Tennessee, North Carolina, and Virginia. Also a history, wildlife, and nature preservationist, the well-respected polymath began life as a child prodigy, later maturing into an archetypal Renaissance Man. Besides being an accomplished and esteemed author, historian, biographer, creative, and Bible authority, the influential litterateur is also a Kentucky Colonel, eagle scout, entrepreneur, screenwriter, nature, wildlife, and landscape photographer and videographer, artist, graphic designer, content creator, genealogist, former history museum docent, and a former ranch hand, zookeeper, and wrangler. A songwriter (of some 3,000 songs in a dozen genres), he is also a film composer, multi-instrument musician, vocalist, session player, and music producer who has worked and performed with some of Nashville's top musicians and singers.

Currently Seabrook is the multi-genre author and editor of nearly 100 adult and children's books (totaling some 30,000 pages and 15,000,000 words) that have earned him accolades from around the globe. His works, which have sold on every continent except Antarctica, have introduced hundreds of thousands of vital facts that have been left out of our mainstream books. He has been endorsed internationally by leading experts, museum curators, award-winning historians, bestselling authors, celebrities, filmmakers, noted scientists, well regarded educators, TV show hosts and producers, renowned military artists, venerable heritage organizations, and distinguished academicians of all races, creeds, and colors.

Of northern, western, and central European ancestry, he is the 6th great-grandson of the Earl of Oxford and a descendant of European royalty through his Kentucky father and West Virginia mother. His modern day cousins include: Johnny Cash, Elvis Presley, Lisa Marie Presley, Billy Ray and Miley Cyrus, Patty Loveless, Tim McGraw, Lee Ann Womack, Dolly Parton, Pat Boone, Naomi, Wynonna, and Ashley Judd, Ricky Skaggs, the Sunshine Sisters, Martha Carson, Chet Atkins, Patrick J. Buchanan, Cindy Crawford, Bertram Thomas Combs (Kentucky's 50th governor), Edith Bolling (second wife of President Woodrow Wilson), Andy Griffith, Riley Keough, George C. Scott, Robert Duvall, Reese Witherspoon, Lee Marvin, Rebecca Gayheart, and Tom Cruise.

A constitutionalist, avid outdoorsman, and gun rights advocate, Seabrook is the author of the international blockbuster, *Everything You Were Taught About the Civil War is Wrong, Ask a Southerner!* He lives with his wife and family in the magnificent Rocky Mountains, heart of the American West, where you will find him hiking, filming, and writing.

For more information on author Mr. Seabrook visit
LOCHLAINNSEABROOK.COM

Keep Your Body, Mind, & Spirit Vibrating at Their Highest Level

YOU CAN DO SO BY READING THE BOOKS OF

SEA RAVEN PRESS

There is nothing that will so perfectly keep your body, mind, and spirit in a healthy condition as to think wisely and positively. Hence you should not only read this book, but also the other books that we offer. They will quicken your physical, mental, and spiritual vibrations, enabling you to maintain a position in society as a healthy erudite person.

KEEP YOURSELF WELL-INFORMED!

The well-informed person is always at the head of the procession, while the ignorant, the lazy, and the unthoughtful hang onto the rear. If you are a Spiritual man or woman, do yourself a great favor: read Sea Raven Press books and stay well posted on the Truth. It is almost criminal for one to remain in ignorance while the opportunity to gain knowledge is open to all at a nominal price.

We invite you to visit our Webstore for a wide selection of wholesome, family-friendly, well-researched, educational books for all ages. You will be glad you did!

Artisan-Crafted Books & Merch From the Rocky Mountains!

SeaRavenPress.com

LochlainnSeabrook.com
TheBestCivilWarBookEver.com
AmbianceGoneWild.com
Pond5.com/artist/LochlainnSeabrook

LOCHLAINN SEABROOK ~ 337

If you enjoyed this book you will be interested in Colonel Seabrook's popular related titles:

☛ Abraham Lincoln Was a Liberal, Jefferson Davis Was a Conservative
☛ Everything You Were Taught About the Civil War is Wrong, Ask a Southerner!
☛ All We Ask is to be Let Alone: The Southern Secession Fact Book
☛ Everything You Were Taught About American Slavery is Wrong, Ask a Southerner!
☛ Confederate Flag Facts: What Every American Should Know About Dixie's Southern Cross
☛ Lincoln's War: The Real Cause, the Real Winner, the Real Loser

Available from Sea Raven Press and wherever fine books are sold

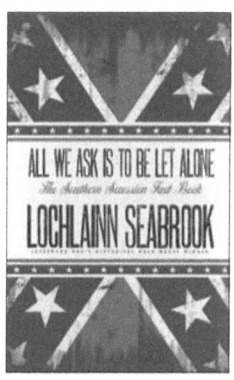

ALL OF OUR BOOK COVERS ARE AVAILABLE AS 11" X 17" COLOR POSTERS, SUITABLE FOR FRAMING

SeaRavenPress.com

www.ingramcontent.com/pod-product-compliance
Lightning Source LLC
Chambersburg PA
CBHW020349170426
43200CB00005B/108